a startling chess opening repertoire

by Chris Baker

EVERYMAN CHESS

Published by Everyman Publishers, London

First published in 1998 by Cadogan Books plc, (now Everyman Publishers plc)
Gloucester Mansions, 140A Shaftesbury Avenue, London, WC2H 8HD

British Library Cataloguing in Publication Data
A CIP catalogue record for this book is available from the British Library.

ISBN 1-85744-553-8

Distributed in North America by The Globe Pequot Press, 6 Business Park Road,
P.O. Box 833, Old Saybrook, Connecticut 06475-0833.
Telephone 1-800 243 0495 (toll free)

All other sales enquiries should be directed to Everyman Chess
Gloucester Mansions, 140A Shaftesbury Avenue, London WC2H 8HD
tel: 0171 539 7600   fax: 0171 379 4060   email: dan@everyman.uk.com
website: http://www.everyman.uk.com

CADOGAN CHESS SERIES

Chief Advisor: Garry Kasparov
Series Editor: Murray Chandler

To my friend Peter Carpenter and mentor Roy Woodcock

Edited by Graham Burgess and typeset by Petra Nunn for
Gambit Publications Ltd.

Printed in Great Britain by Redwood Books, Trowbridge, Wilts.

Contents

Symbols

+	check
++	double check
#	checkmate
x	capture
!!	brilliant move
!	good move
!?	interesting move
?!	dubious move
?	bad move
??	blunder
Ch	championship
Cht	team championship
Wch	world championship
Echt	European Team Championship
Wcht	World Team Championship
Ct	candidates event
IZ	interzonal event
Z	zonal event
OL	olympiad
ECC	European Clubs Cup
jr	junior event
wom	women's event
mem	memorial event
rpd	rapidplay game
corr	correspondence game
qual	qualifying event
1-0	the game ends in a win for White
½-½	the game ends in a draw
0-1	the game ends in a win for Black
(n)	nth match game
(D)	see next diagram

Introduction

This book is designed to offer a complete opening repertoire for White. The repertoire is based on logical systems that pose Black immediate and unusual problems – Black cannot just 'go through the motions' of straightforward development and achieve a sensible position. He will need to be extremely well prepared and constantly 'on his toes' to avoid an accident.

A great deal of thought has been given to creating a coherent repertoire. Lines have been selected against each of Black's defences that fit well together – for example, given that against the Pirc I am recommending 4 f4 (the Austrian Attack), after the moves 1 e4 d6 2 d4 ♘f6 3 ♘c3 c6 it would therefore be inconsistent to offer anything but 4 f4 as after 4 ♘f3 Black could transpose to a Classical Pirc with 4...g6, and so side-step our repertoire. Also transpositions from the Caro-Kann set-ups with an early ...g6 into lines of the Modern have been taken into consideration, as have variations in the Sicilian where Black can play several natural moves in different orders. In particular I have tried to give White a consistent approach against the Sicilian to help you develop a general feel of what you should be aiming for.

One of the beauties of this book though in my mind is that players who normally open with **1 e4** can choose to adopt a system recommended as a second line or as a **surprise weapon** against a particular opponent. Good examples of this would be the Koltanowski Variation in the Max Lange Attack, with which I have enjoyed immense practical success; or the system recommended against the Latvian Gambit (with is based on some ideas put forward by Dr John Nunn). The advantage of this approach is that it gives you more flexibility, for example by using a more aggressive system against a particular opponent or strength of opponent and not getting 'tagged' as someone that always plays a particular line. Having a predictable repertoire can be a severe drawback as it allows opponents more leeway – if they wish to surprise you with an opening they would not normally play, they need only prepare against the line you play. Now they would have to think twice. To a point then any one chapter can be used in isolation as a system against a particular defence as, apart from the Modern/Pirc, they are 'mutually exclusive' as opposed to irrevocably entwined.

Those of you who are looking for a full repertoire as White can enjoy the book as a whole. One advantage of the majority of variations given against the most popular defences is that, while not considered 'offbeat', they are not thought of as main-line. This gives the benefit of catching your opponent 'off guard'. The analysis presented in this book is quite comprehensive, thus leaving you well prepared. In particular I chose systems against the Sicilian which avoided open main lines as these require immense preparation and are already well dealt with in other publications that specialize on just the Sicilian Defence.

Another point about this book is the combination of the accepted (for example the lines given to play against the Caro-Kann) with new ideas, e.g. against the Pirc and French in particular. I would also like to think of this book as complete as it offers guidance on how to deal with some of the more unusual systems Black can play against 1 e4, for example the Elephant Gambit, the St George and Owen's Defence.

Whereas systems recommended are in the main potentially very aggressive this has not been done at the cost of basic soundness and so readers should not expect to play one of the systems and find his opponent 'wheeling out' a refutation. In some parts though there is still a lot of scope for original analysis (e.g. in the section on the French Defence) so giving you a sound base for you to work from without feeling stifled by variations that have been analysed to death.

For those of you who cannot face 'memorizing' even a book of this length for your total repertoire I would suggest playing through the main lines to get a general idea of what is happening. Alternatively, you may wish to adopt the systems one by one, adding them to your existing repertoire. In this way you would build up your new repertoire over a period of time. Then when complete this gives you the advantage of taking just this book with you to tournaments as it would provide the one source of reference you need. I would even take it a stage further and suggest that if you come across a game between strong players in one of the variations insert it at the relevant point as a way of continually updating the work.

Whichever way you choose to use this book, though, I can guarantee that with some of these systems you will catch out even some of the better, more experienced, players that you may currently hold in high regard, taking points from them that you might not generally expect to do. Moreover you should have some fun while you are doing it, knowing that they have to be constantly alert to avoid a crushing and painful defeat. So, for now, 'happy hunting' and let the 'bad guys' beware!

Chris Baker,
Bath, July 1998

1 Max Lange Attack

This opening is named after the German analyst Max Lange, who developed its ideas in the mid-nineteenth century. The Max Lange leads immediately to sharp tactical play. With open lines, diagonals and commonly castling on opposite sides, both players have to be constantly aware of weaknesses in both their opponent's and their own position. A single slip can easily prove fatal. In this kind of variation the better prepared player usually wins – and quickly! Some of the tactics available at times come like a bolt of lightning out of the blue and players of all standards will enjoy being able to play some of the 'flashy' moves available.

After **1 e4 e5 2 ♘f3 ♘c6 3 ♗c4** this chapter will split into three parts depending on Black's response. Part 1 looks at the Max Lange Attack itself (**3...♘f6 4 d4 exd4 5 0-0 ♗c5**), in Part 2 we investigate the Anti-Max Lange (**3...♘f6 4 d4 exd4 5 0-0 ♘xe4**) and Part 3 considers the Koltanowski Variation (**3...♗c5 4 0-0 ♘f6 5 d4!?**).

Part 1: The Max Lange

1 e4 e5 2 ♘f3 ♘c6 3 ♗c4 ♘f6 4 d4 exd4 5 0-0 ♗c5 6 e5 *(D)*

Here Black has two possibilities, the second of which is played far more frequently and has the better reputation:

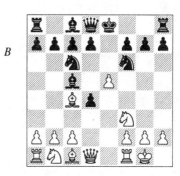

B

| A: **6...♘g4** | 7 |
| B: **6...d5!** | 8 |

Inferior is 6...♘e4, when 7 ♗d5! f5 8 exf6 ♘xf6 9 ♗g5 ♗e7 10 ♗xf6! ♗xf6 11 ♖e1+ ♘e7 12 ♘e5 ♗xe5 13 ♕h5+ g6 14 ♕xe5 ♖f8 15 ♘d2 c6 16 ♘c4! d6 17 ♘xd6+ ♔d7 18 ♗e6+ ♔c7 19 ♘xc8+ with mate next move is an old game of Morphy's.

A)

6...♘g4

Black attempts to put pressure on White's pawn on e5.

7 ♗f4!

Others fail to impress:

a) 7 h3?! ♘gxe5 8 ♘xe5 ♘xe5 9 ♖e1 d6 10 f4 d3+ 11 ♔h2 ♕h4 12 fxe5 dxc2 13 exd6+ ♗e6 14 ♖xe6+ fxe6 15 d7+ ♔e7 16 ♕xc2 ♗d6+ and Black is winning (Steinitz).

b) 7 ♗xf7+? ♔xf7 8 ♘g5+ ♔g8 9 ♕xg4 d5! is better for Black.

c) 7 ♗g5 ♗e7 is fine for Black.

d) 7 c3!? d5! (7...dxc3? 8 ♕d5! ♕e7 9 ♗g5 with advantage) 8 exd6 ♕xd6 9 ♖e1+ ♗e6 10 ♗xe6 fxe6 11 b4 ♗b6 12 ♕b3 0-0-0 13 ♖xe6 ♕d7 14 h3 h5! and Black's position is very strong, Estrin-Smyslov, Moscow Ch 1946.

e) 7 ♖e1 d3! 8 ♗xf7+ ♔f8! 9 ♕xd3 ♗xf2+ 10 ♔f1 ♗xe1 11 ♗g5 ♘xh2+ 12 ♔e2 ♘xf3 13 ♗xd8 ♘fxe5 14 ♕e3 ♘xf7 15 ♗xc7 ♗h4 16 ♘c3 b6 is good for Black because his rook and minor pieces outweigh White's queen, Saligo-Perfilev, USSR corr. 1959-60.

After 7 ♗f4! Black can try:

A1: 7...0-0   8
A2: 7...d6   8

A1)

7...0-0 8 h3 ♘h6 9 ♗xh6! gxh6 10 c3 d5 11 ♗b3! dxc3

11...♗f5 may be best, though White is on top after 12 ♘xd4!.

12 ♘xc3 d4 13 ♘d5!

Now Nugteren-Messer, corr. 1996 continued 13...♕h8 (13...♗e7 14 ♕d3! and Black cannot stop ♗c2 coming) 14 ♕d3 ♖g8 15 ♘f6 ♖g7 16 ♘h5 ♖g5 17 ♘xg5 ♕xg5 18 ♖ac1 ♕xh5 19 ♖xc5 ♗f5 20 ♕b5 ♖g8 21 e6 ♕xh3 22 ♗d5 fxe6 23 ♗xc6 bxc6 24 ♕xc6 ♕d3 25 ♕xc7 ♕e4 26 f3 ♕e3+ 27 ♖f2 d3 28 ♕e5+ ♕xe5 29 ♖xe5 ♖d8 30 ♖d2 h5 31 ♖a5 ♖d7 32 ♔f2 ♔g7 33 ♔e3 ♔f6 34 g4 1-0.

A2)

7...d6 8 exd6 ♗xd6 9 ♖e1+ ♔f8 10 ♗xd6+ ♕xd6 11 c3! ♕c5

11...♗f5 12 cxd4 ♖d8 13 ♗b5! g6 (not 13...♘xd4?? 14 ♘xd4 ♕xd4 15 ♕xd4 ♖xd4 16 ♖e8#) 14 ♗xc6 ♕xc6

15 ♘c3 ♘f6 16 ♖c1, when White is better, Rossolimo-O'Kelly de Galway, Trenčianske 1949.

12 ♘xd4! ♕xc4 13 ♘xc6

Black has problems.

B)

6...d5! (D)

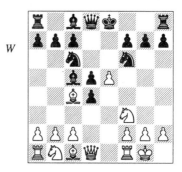

7 exf6 dxc4 8 ♖e1+

8 fxg7 ♖g8 9 ♖e1+ (or 9 ♗g5 ♗e7 10 ♗xe7 ♔xe7! 11 ♘bd2 ♖xg7 12 ♘xc4 ♗e6 13 ♖e1 and Black is better, Foltis-Stulik, Czechoslovakia 1940) 9...♗e6 10 ♘g5 ♕d5 11 ♕g4 0-0-0 12 ♘xe6 fxe6 13 ♖xe6 ♖xg7 14 ♖g6+ ♖gd7 and Black has the upper hand.

Now Black can run the gauntlet with 8...♔f8 or play the natural 8...♗e6.

B1: 8...♔f8   8
B2: 8...♗e6   9

B1)

8...♔f8 (D)
9 ♗g5! gxf6

9...♕d7 10 ♗h6!! gxh6 11 ♕d2 wins outright and 9...♕d6 10 ♘bd2 ♗f5 11 ♘xc4 is good for White.

10 ♗h6+ ♔g8 11 ♘c3

11 ♘xd4?! ♗xd4 12 c3 ♗e5! 13 ♕xd8+ ♘xd8 14 f4 ♘c6 15 fxe5 fxe5

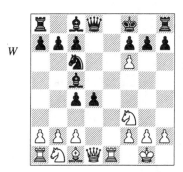

W

16 ♖e3 f5 17 ♘a3 ♗e6 18 ♖g3+ ♔f7
19 ♖g7+ ♔f6 20 ♖xc7 ♔g6 and Black
is winning.

Black now should choose between:

B11: 11...♗f5 9
B12: 11...♗f8 9

11...♗g4? 12 ♘e4 b6 13 c3 ♘e5? 14
♘xe5!! ♗xd1 15 ♘d7! ♗e7 16 ♘exf6+
♗xf6 17 ♖e8+! ♕xe8 18 ♘xf6# (1-0)
Kazić-Vuković, Yugoslavia 1940 shows
what can happen in the Max Lange if
Black plays what looks like a sensible
move but it doesn't quite work!

B11)

11...♗f5

12 ♘e4 ♗f8

Sensibly trying to exchange off the
dark-squared bishops to give his king
a little more breathing space.

13 ♕d2!

Now:

a) 13...♗g7 14 ♘g3! ♗xh6 15
♕xh6 ♗xc2? loses to 16 ♘h5.

b) 13...♗xh6 14 ♕xh6 ♗xe4 15
♖xe4 f5 16 ♖f4 ♕d5 17 ♘h4 ♘e7 18
♘xf5!.

c) 13...♗g6 14 ♗xf8 ♔xf8 15
♕h6+ ♔g8 16 ♘h4 gives White excellent attacking chances.

d) 13...♘e5 14 ♘xd4! ♗xe4 15
♖xe4 ♕d5 16 ♖ae1 ♖e8 17 ♗xf8
♖xf8? 18 ♖xe5! fxe5 19 ♕g5# (1-0)
Rautenburg-Nurnberg, Germany 1949.

B12)

11...♗f8

It's far more logical to exchange off
the dark-squared bishops straight away
than interpose the moves 11...♗f5 and
12 ♘e4, as this only enhances White's
attacking possibilities.

12 ♗xf8

12 ♘xd4? ♘xd4! 13 ♕xd4 ♕xd4
14 ♖e8 ♕d6 15 ♘e4 ♗f5! 16 ♘xd6
♖xe8 is winning for Black.

12...♔xf8 13 ♘e4 f5 14 ♘g3 *(D)*

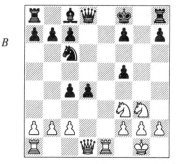

B

The position at the end of this line is
hard to evaluate. Black is two pawns
up but has his kingside pawn-structure
shattered. With White's lead in development his attacking chances should
not be underestimated.

B2)

8...♗e6 *(D)*

This is Black's most logical choice.
He blocks the check while developing
his light-squared bishop to a sensible
square and gets one move closer to

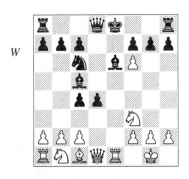

W

queenside castling (a common feature of the Max Lange). However, it is also a target for attack because of the pin down the e-file. This, combined with the tenderness of Black's kingside, not only at g7 but surprisingly enough at f7, means that Black must tread carefully to avoid falling for one of the many tactical tricks White has at his disposal.

9 ♘g5

Best, as after 9 fxg7 ♖g8, 10 ♗g5 ♗e7! 11 ♗xe7 ♕xe7 12 ♘xd4 0-0-0 13 c3 ♖xg7 is fine for Black, Bernstein-Wade, Amsterdam 1961, while 10 ♘g5 ♕d5 gives Black more flexibility than the main line.

9...♕d5

Necessary in view of the following lines:

a) 9...♕xf6?? 10 ♘xe6 fxe6 11 ♕h5+ ♕g6 12 ♕xc5 1-0 Heider-Platz, Cologne 1920.

b) 9...♕d6? 10 ♘xe6 fxe6 11 fxg7 ♖g8 12 ♕h5+ ♔d7 13 ♘d2! ♕e7 14 ♘e4 ♗b4 15 ♗g5 is very strong for White as in Yuchtman-Kim, Tashkent 1950.

c) 9...♗b6?! 10 ♘xe6 fxe6 11 ♕g4! is unpleasant to meet.

d) 9...0-0? 10 fxg7 ♖e8 (10...♔xg7 11 ♖xe6! h6 12 ♖xh6! ♔xh6 13

♘xf7++ wins) 11 ♕h5 ♔xg7 12 ♕xh7+ ♔f8 13 ♖xe6 wins.

e) 9...g6!? narrowly fails to 10 ♕f3! ♕d7 (10...♗d7 11 ♘xf7! ♗xf7 12 ♕g4+ ♔d6 13 ♗f4+ winning; 10...0-0 11 ♖xe6! fxe6 12 f7+ ♔h8 13 ♘xe6 ♕e7 14 ♗g5! ♕xf7 15 ♘xc5 is just good for White, Felić-Veksei, corr. 1920) 11 ♖xe6+ fxe6 12 f7+ ♔e7 13 ♘e4 ♕d5 14 ♗g5+ ♔f8 15 ♕f6 and Black can throw in the towel.

10 ♘c3

Gaining a tempo on the black queen while developing a piece and at the same time exploiting the pin on the e-file (10...dxc3?? 11 ♕xd5)

10...♕f5 11 ♘ce4 *(D)*

Better than either 11 g4 or 11 ♘xe6 immediately as White would still have to deal with the knight hanging on c3 thereby giving Black more flexibility.

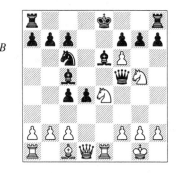

B

After 11 ♘ce4 Black has six replies worth consideration, of which the second half make up the bulk of analysis.

B21)
11...0-0?

Black castles 'into it'.

12 fxg7 ♖fe8

12...♔xg7 13 ♘xc5 ♕xc5 14 ♖xe6! h6 15 ♖xh6! winning.

13 g4! ♕e5 14 ♘xh7!

Black can pack up his bags and go home!

B22)
11...gxf6? 12 g4!

This wins material by force.

12...♕e5

12...♕xg4+ 13 ♕xg4 ♗xg4 14 ♘xf6++.

13 ♘f3 ♗xg4

What else?

14 ♘xc5

Black can save himself from further embarrassment by resigning.

B23)
11...♗b4?! *(D)*

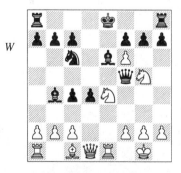

While the idea of Black getting his dark-squared bishop out of the way is commendable, it happens to fall short of the mark.

12 c3 dxc3 13 bxc3 ♗a5 14 g4 ♕g6 15 ♘xe6 fxe6 16 f7+! ♔xf7 17
♘g5+ ♔g8 18 ♖xe6 ♕d3 19 ♕e1 ♖f8??

19...♕d7! might leave the position murky but I would rather be White than Black.

20 ♖xc6!

White wins.

Up to move twenty we had been following a blindfold simultaneous game(!) of Koltanowski which concluded 20 ♖e8? ♕d7 21 ♖xf8+ ♔xf8 22 ♗a3+ ♘e7 23 ♖d1! ♕xg4+ 24 ♔f1!! ♕xg5 25 ♖d5! ♕h4 26 ♖h5! ♕f6 27 ♖f5! and Black resigned. A game that really impressed me – in particular the move 24 ♔f1!! as 24 ♔h1? would have meant that 25 ♖d5? could have been met by 25...♕xd5+!. However, 20 ♖xc6! seems to win outright and after 26 ♖h5! in the game quoted Black could have made sure White didn't have it all his own way with 26...♗xc3! 27 ♕e6 ♕f6 28 ♖f5 ♔e8! 29 ♖xf6 ♗xf6 when White has to take the draw to avoid being worse with 30 ♗xe7 ♗xe7 31 ♕c8+ ♗d8 32 ♕e6+, etc. However, the game shows the way Black can go 'down the tubes' when he is constantly under pressure to find all of the right moves just to survive!

B24)
11...♗b6!? *(D)*

Again Black tries to keep his dark-squared bishop. However, by accurate play White can still demonstrate a strong initiative.

12 fxg7

12 ♘g3 was also thought to be promising, e.g. 12...♕g6 13 ♘xe6 fxe6 14 ♖xe6+ ♔d7 15 ♘h5! ♖he8 16 ♘f4 ♕f7 17 ♕f3 with attacking chances,

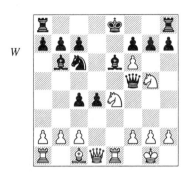

W

Chigorin-Charousek, Budapest 1896 although after 17...♖xe6! 18 ♕d5+ ♔c8 19 ♘xe6 d3! it's not clear White is any better at all.

12...♖g8 13 g4!

Forcing Black to pick a square for his queen before exchanging on e6.

13...♕g6 14 ♘xe6 fxe6 15 ♗g5!

The main aim of this move is to prevent Black from castling. Last century G.Abels analysed this position in depth, concluding that White has a distinct edge due to his attack, and practice seems to concur with this.

15...♖xg7

15...h6 is met by 16 ♕f3! hxg5 17 ♘f6+ ♔f7 18 ♖xe6! ♖xg7 (18...♔xe6 19 ♖e1+ ♘e5 20 ♕d5+ mating) 19 ♖ae1 winning.

16 ♕f3!

Better than 16 ♘f6+, when Black wriggles out.

16...♖f7

Alternatives have been tried:

a) 16...h6? 17 ♘f6+ ♔d8 18 ♖xe6 ♘e7 19 ♗xh6! ♕xh6 20 ♕d5+! and White mates, Holzhausen-Zoge, Leipzig 1899.

b) 16...e5? 17 ♘f6+ ♔f7 18 h4! with a very powerful attack, Chigorin-Teichmann, London 1899.

c) 16...♔d7!? (the main alternative to the text-move) 17 ♘f6+ ♔c8 18 ♖xe6! ♕xg5 19 h4! (19 ♖xc6? ♔b8!) was analysed in detail by Sämisch:

c1) 19...♕xh4? 20 ♖e8+ mating.

c2) 19...♕g6 20 h5 ♕g5 (20...♕xc2 21 ♕d5!) 21 ♖ae1 ♘d8 22 ♖6e5 ♕h4 23 ♖e8 c6 24 ♕f5+ ♔b8 25 h6! ♕xh6 26 ♕e5+ ♔c8 27 ♕e6+ winning.

c3) 19...♕a5 20 ♖e8+ ♘d8 21 ♘d5 c6 (21...♖d7 22 ♕f5 ♕xd5 23 ♖xd8+ mates) 22 ♕f5+ ♖d7 23 ♘e7+ ♔c7 24 ♕f4+ ♖d6 25 ♘f5 winning.

c4) 19...♕b5 20 a4 ♕c5 21 ♖ae1 ♘d8 22 ♖e8 c6 23 ♖1e5 ♕d6 24 ♕f5+ ♔b8 25 ♖5e6 ♕b4 26 ♕f4+ ♔c8 27 ♘e4 ♗c7 (27...a6 28 ♘d6+ ♔b8 29 ♘f7+ ♔a7 30 ♘xd8 wins) 28 ♕f5 ♔b8 29 ♖xd8+! ♗xd8 30 ♕e5+ ♖c7 31 ♖e8 a5 32 ♖xd8+ ♔a7 33 ♕xd4+ b6 34 ♖xa8+ ♔xa8 35 ♕d8+ ♔b7 36 ♘d6+ ♔a6 37 ♕a8+ mating.

17 ♘f6+ ♖xf6 18 ♗xf6 ♔d7 19 g5 ♖e8 20 ♕e2 ♘b4 21 ♖ed1!

White is well on top, Chigorin/Bartolich-Shabsky/Tereshchenko, consultation game 1900.

B25)

11...♗f8 *(D)*

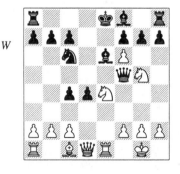

W

Once more Black tries to retain his dark-squared bishop and at the same time guards g7. The drawback is that with his king still in the centre Black leaves himself open to a typical Max Lange tactical counter. The move 11...♗f8 is a recommendation of Rubinstein and while play is complex, it takes a brave man to play this line as Black unless he is extremely well prepared to face the consequences.

Now after...

12 ♘xf7! ♚xf7 13 ♘g5+

...Black has to make the choice between:

B251)

13...♚g6?!

After this White has two good choices. In the past 14 fxg7 has been advocated but recent examples seem to indicate that White has been doing well with...

14 ♘xe6

...and judging from the positions he has got I have no reason not to go along with this.

14...gxf6

Black can also try 14...♖e8!?, in which case 15 g4! ♕xf6 16 f4 ♗d6 (16...h6 17 f5+ ♚f7 18 g5 ♕e7 19 g6+ ♚g8 20 ♗f4 ♘d8 21 ♘xf8! and then 21...♕xf8 22 ♕xd4 or 21...♕xe1+ 22 ♕xe1 ♖xe1+ 23 ♖xe1 ♚xf8 24 ♗xc7 ♘c6 25 ♗d6+ wins) 17 f5+ ♚f7 18 ♗g5 is good enough.

15 g4!

Better than 15 ♗d2 immediately, as in the game Hartl-Kovacova, Slovakian Ch 1994.

15...♕a5 16 ♗d2 c3

16...♗b4 17 ♗xb4 ♕xb4 18 c3 dxc3 19 ♕d7 ♘e7 20 ♘f4+ ♚f7 21 ♕e6+ wins.

16...♕b6 17 ♕f3 ♗e7 18 ♕f5+ ♚f7 19 ♕h5+ ♚g8 20 ♕h6 ♗f8 21 ♕xf6 ♘e7 22 ♗h6 ♗xh6 23 ♕xh6 1-0 Koltanowski-NN, Scotland blindfold simul 1937.

17 bxc3 dxc3 18 ♗f4 ♗d6 19 ♕d3+ ♚f7

Now, rather than 20 ♕c4 ♚g6 21 h4 h5 22 g5 ♘e5 23 ♗xe5 ♗xe5 24 ♖ad1 ♗d6 25 ♖d5 ♕b4 26 ♕d3+ ♚f7 27 ♖d4 ♕a5 28 ♘f4 ♖ag8 29 ♕c4+ ♚f8 30 ♖xd6 ♖xg5+ 31 hxg5 ♕xg5+ 32 ♚f1 b5 33 ♖d8+ ♚g7 34 ♕xc7+ 1-0 Immer-Rothacher, Baden 1993, 20 ♘xc7! is an even stronger continuation for White.

B252)

13...♚g8 *(D)*

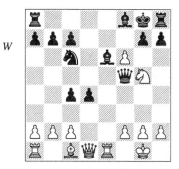

This is the critical follow-up to 11...♗f8. It seems far more sensible for Black to tuck his king away than to come forward to g6! Both sides need to play carefully now, as analysis shows:

14 g4!

14 ♘xe6? ♖e8! 15 fxg7 ♗xg7 16 ♘xc7 ♖xe1+ 17 ♕xe1 ♗e5 18 ♘d5 ♔f7 is good for Black.

14...♕g6!

14...♕xg4+?? 15 ♕xg4 ♗xg4 16 f7#.

14...♕d5 15 ♘xe6 ♘e5? 16 f7+ ♔xf7 17 ♘g5+ ♔g8 18 ♖xe5! ♕xe5 19 ♕f3! 1-0 Denker-Avram, New York 1940.

14...♕xf6? 15 ♖xe6 ♕d8 16 ♕f3 ♕d7 17 ♖e7!! winning, Sämisch-Reiman, Bremen 1927.

15 fxg7

15 ♖xe6!? is less clear and although the resulting positions are a total mess, with correct play Black should hang on.

15...♗d5!?

15...♗xg7?! 16 ♖xe6 ♗f6 17 ♘e4 ♖f8 18 ♕f3 ♔g7 19 ♗g5 and Black is in severe difficulties.

16 gxh8♕+ ♔xh8 17 ♗f4!

Black gets too much play after 17 f3? ♗c5 18 ♘e4 ♖f8 19 g5 ♘e5 20 ♘f6 ♘xf3+ 0-1 Kintzel-Steiner, Austria 1967.

17...♗c5

17...♗d6 18 ♗xd6 cxd6 19 f4 ♖f8 20 ♖f1 h6 21 ♘h3 ♗e6 22 f5 ♗xf5 23 ♘f4 ♕g7 24 h3 d3 25 c3 ♘e5 26 ♔h2 ♗xg4 27 hxg4 ♘xg4+ 28 ♔h3! (better than 28 ♔h1) 28...♘e3 29 ♘g6+ ♕xg6 30 ♖xf8+ ♔g7 31 ♕f3 winning – analysis by Koltanowski.

18 ♗e5+ ♔g8

18...♘xe5? 19 ♖xe5.

19 ♘h3 d3 20 cxd3 cxd3 21 ♘f4 ♕f7 22 ♕xd3 ♖d8

White has a won ending after 22...♘xe5? 23 ♕xd5 ♕xd5 24 ♘xd5 ♘f3+ 25 ♔g2 ♘xe1+ 26 ♖xe1.

23 ♕f5!

White's position is very strong, e.g. 23...♕xf5 24 gxf5 ♗f3 25 ♗c3 ♖f8 26 ♘e6 ♖xf5 27 ♘xc5 ♖xc5 28 ♖e3.

B26)

11...0-0-0! *(D)*

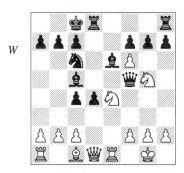

Best by test! Black immediately gets his king into safety and as far away as possible from the pin lurking down the e-file.

12 g4!

12 fxg7? ♖hg8 13 g4 ♕e5! (making use of White's move-order) 14 ♘g3 ♕xg7 15 ♖xe6 fxe6 16 ♘xe6 ♕e5 17 ♘xd8 ♖xd8 and Black is clearly better.

12 ♘xe6!? fxe6 13 fxg7 ♖hg8 14 ♗h6 ♗b6 15 ♕f3! is unclear, as in Cohn-Przynski, Guatemala 1937 although Black may well equalize after 15...♕xf3.

12...♕e5

12...♕xg4+?? loses to 13 ♕xg4 ♗xg4 14 ♘xc5.

12...♕d5 13 ♘xe6 fxe6 14 fxg7 ♖hg8 15 ♘f6 ♕d6 16 ♘xg8 ♖xg8 17 ♗h6 d3 18 ♕f3 ♘d4 19 ♕f7 is strong for White, Radulov-Anastasopulov, Sofia 1967.

13 ♘xe6

Or:

a) 13 ♘f3?! ♕d5 14 fxg7 ♗xg4 15 gxh8♕ ♖xh8 16 h3 ♗h5 17 ♗f4 (17 ♘f6!? ♕xf3 18 ♘xh5 ♕xh3 19 ♘g3 h5 20 ♕f3 ♖g8 21 ♕xf7 ♖xg3+! with a perpetual) 17...♖g8+ 18 ♗g3 (18 ♔f1!? is not clear but is asking for trouble) 18...♘e5 19 ♘xe5 ♗xd1 20 ♘f6 ♖xg3+ 21 fxg3 d3+ 22 ♔h2 d2 23 ♖e4 ♕d8 24 ♖xd1 ♕xf6 25 ♖xd2 ♕f1 26 ♖g2 b5 27 b3 f6 28 ♘c6 c3 29 a4 bxa4 30 ♖xa4 ♔d7 31 ♘a5 h5 32 ♖f4 ♕d1 33 ♘c4 ♗d4 34 h4 c5 35 ♖f5 ♔e6 36 ♖f4 f5 37 ♔h3 ♗g1 38 ♘a5 ♕g4+ 0-1 Schoch-P.Littlewood, Winterthur 1986.

b) 13 f4?! d3+ 14 ♔g2 ♕d5 15 fxg7 ♖hg8 16 cxd3 (16 f5? ♗xf5! 17 gxf5 ♖xg7 18 f6 ♖g6 19 ♕g4+ ♔b8 20 ♖f1 ♘e5 and Black is winning, Bogdan-D.Dimitrache, Romanian Ch 1992) 16...cxd3 17 ♗d2 ♖xg7 and Black is better placed.

c) 13 fxg7 ♖hg8 14 ♘xe6 will transpose to the main line while attempts to improve for White with 14 ♘xc5 ♕xc5 15 ♘e4 lead to nothing special, e.g. 15...♕e5 16 ♗h6 ♗d5 17 ♘g3 ♕f6 18 g5 ♕f4 19 ♘h5 ♕f5 20 ♘g3 ♕f4 and the game Smolnikov-Trofimokh, corr. 1958-9 was drawn by repetition.

13...fxe6 14 fxg7

14 ♗g5!? h6! 15 fxg7 hxg5 16 gxh8♕ ♖xh8 17 ♘g3 ♕d6! gives Black good compensation – analysis by Estrin.

14...♖hg8 15 ♗h6! *(D)*

Best as 15 f4? d3+ 16 ♔f1 ♕d5 is good for Black.

15...d3!

15...♗b4? 16 f4 ♕a5 17 ♘f6 ♗xe1 18 ♕xe1 ♕xe1+ 19 ♖xe1 d3 20 c3 (even better is 20 cxd3 cxd3 21 f5! with

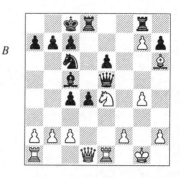

a won endgame) 20...♘e7 21 ♔f2 ♖d6 22 ♘xg8 ♘xg8 23 ♗g5 and White is well on top, Carlier-Rate, Torcy 1991.

16 c3

The critical position is now reached. At this point Black has tried the following four different plans:

B261: 16...♗b6?! 15
B262: 16...♗d6!? 15
B263: 16...♗e7 16
B264: 16...d2! 16

B261)

16...♗b6?!

Black tries to preserve his dark-squared bishop while keeping it on the a7-g1 diagonal. However, although this stops the advance of White's f-pawn, f2 itself is not under pressure and Black's f6-square is ripe for occupation by White's knight. Prokopchuk-Abashev, Russia 1993 continued 17 ♕f3! ♕d5 18 ♕g2 ♘e5 19 ♘f6 ♘f3+ 20 ♔f1 ♘xe1 21 ♕xd5 exd5 22 ♖xe1 d2 23 ♖d1 d4 24 ♘xg8 ♖xg8 25 ♖xd2 d3 26 ♖d1 ♗c5 27 ♖e1 ♔d7 28 ♖e4 b5 29 ♖f4 ♔e8 30 ♖f5 1-0.

B262)

16...♗d6!? 17 f4! ♕d5 18 ♕f3 ♗e7 19 g5

19 ♔g2!?.
19...♕f5 20 ♘g3 ♕f7 21 ♕g4
Now 21...d2! 22 ♖e4 yields approximate equality. Instead 21...♖de8?! 22 ♖e4! b5 23 a4! a6 24 axb5 axb5 25 ♔g2! ♘d8 26 ♕f3 ♕g6 27 ♖d4! c6 28 ♖xd8+ ♔xd8 29 ♕xc6 1-0 was Marshall-Tarrasch, Hamburg 1910.

B263)
16...♗e7 17 f4!
17 ♕f3 was played with success in the game Marshall-Capablanca, New York 1910 but the text-move seems even better.
17...♕d5 18 ♕d2
Blockading Black's d-pawn before developing his own kingside pawn majority.
18...♖d7
18...♘b8?! 19 ♖e3 ♘d7 20 g5 is strong for White.
19 ♖e3 ♘d8
Planning to hit the h6-bishop with ...♘f7.
20 b3! ♘f7 21 bxc4 ♕a5
21...♕xc4 22 g5!.
22 ♖h3 ♘xh6 23 ♖xh6 ♖xg7 24 h3!
White is a little better.

B264)
16...d2! *(D)*
This advance is double-edged. Black hopes that the future vulnerability of the pawn on d2 will be outweighed by the fact that it ties up the white pieces, and so diverts White's attention from his own kingside play.
17 ♖e2
17 ♘xd2? loses to 17...♗xf2+! 18 ♔xf2 ♕xh2+, while the alternative 17

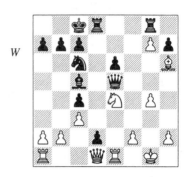

♗xd2 relinquishes the pawn on g7, which is just too high a price to pay.
17...♖d3
Almost invariably played because after 17...♗b6?! White can unpin his f-pawn with 18 ♔g2! with advantage, e.g. 18...♖d3 19 f3 ♘d8 20 ♖xd2.
18 ♕f1!
Clearing d1 for his rook while bringing the queen around to a useful post on the kingside.
18 ♘g5?? loses to 18...♕f4!, as in Poignant-Rate, Torcy 1991.
18 ♘xc5 is the main alternative to 18 ♕f1, and leads to an approximately equal position after 18...♕xc5 19 ♖xd2 ♘e5 20 ♖xd3 cxd3. This position has occurred several times with mixed results. White's extra pawn is counterbalanced by his kingside weaknesses. If White can avoid any nasty accidents then his endgame prospects are good.
18...♕d5
Instead:
a) 18...♗b6!? 19 ♖d1 ♖xg7!? (the original idea behind 18...♗b6 was for Black to play the manoeuvre ...♘d8-f7 with the idea of embarrassing the white h6-bishop, but after 19...♘d8, 20 ♘g3! is good for White, e.g. 20...♕f6 21 g5 ♕f4 22 ♕h3! when the

pressure on Black's pawns on d2 and e6 combined with threats of 23 g6! give White the advantage; or 20...♕d5 21 ♖exd2 ♘f7 22 ♖xd3 cxd3 23 ♖xd3 when Black's trump card, his pawn on d2, has fallen) 20 ♗xg7 ♕xg7 21 ♕g2 ♘e5 22 ♖exd2 a5 23 ♖xd3 cxd3 24 ♕g3? ♕g6 25 ♕f4? ♘xg4 26 ♕f8+ ♔d7 27 ♖xd3+ ♔c6 28 ♖d6+ cxd6 29 ♕xd6+ ♔b5 30 ♕d3+ ♔c6 31 ♕d6+ ½-½ Pieri-Yilmaz, Forli 1991. White could have maintained a distinct advantage by playing the calm 24 h3! or 25 h3!.

b) 18...♗e7!? 19 ♖d1! (19 ♘g3? ♕d5 20 ♖d1 ♘e5! is good for Black as White's knight is misplaced on g3 in this position) 19...♕d5 will transpose back to the main line.

19 ♖d1 ♘e5 20 ♘f6

20 ♕g2!? was considered good, the analysis continuing 20...♘f3+ 21 ♔f1 ♘h4 22 ♕g1 ♘f3 23 ♕g3 ♘d4?!. However, 23...♗d6! may well be an important improvement, after which it seems that Black is better.

20...♕f3 21 ♘xg8 ♕xg4+ 22 ♔h1 ♕f3+

With a perpetual.

In conclusion the Max Lange Attack is extremely dangerous for Black to meet unless he is very well prepared. Although dating back to the eighteenth century new ideas for both sides are always being found. For example, the very last line quoted was thought to be good for White until I came across 23...♗d6!. There is still a lot of scope for players to experiment and in my experience the better prepared player will usually prevail.

Part 2: The Anti-Max Lange

1 e4 e5 2 ♘f3 ♘c6 3 ♗c4 ♘f6 4 d4 exd4 5 0-0 ♘xe4 *(D)*

Instead of developing his dark-squared bishop (by 5...♗c5), Black grabs a second central pawn! Often White regains the pawns and maintains a slight initiative due to his superior development.

6 ♖e1

This is best, since 6 ♘c3?!, while tricky, is basically unsound in view of 6...♘xc3! (6...dxc3 7 ♗xf7+!? ♔xf7 8 ♕d5+ ♔e8 9 ♖e1 ♗e7 10 ♖xe4 is messier) 7 bxc3 d5 8 ♗b5 ♗e7 9 ♘xd4 ♗d7 10 ♘e2 a6 11 ♗a4 ♘a5, when Black is strongly placed.

6 ♗d5? is also bad, as after 6...♘f6 7 ♗xc6 dxc6 8 ♘xd4 ♗e7 Black is already clearly better due to his bishop-pair and extra pawn, Wiersma-Euwe, Amsterdam 1921.

6...d5

6...f5? 7 ♘xd4 ♗c5? fails to 8 ♖xe4+ fxe4 9 ♕h5+ followed by 10 ♕xc5.

6...♗e7?! 7 ♖xe4 d5 8 ♖xe7+ ♘xe7 9 ♗f1 c5 10 b4! and White is better.

7 ♗xd5!

7 ♘c3!? holds no fear for Black if he is properly prepared while 7 ♘xd4? ♘xd4 8 ♕xd4 ♗e6 is just good for Black.

7...♕xd5 8 ♘c3 (D)

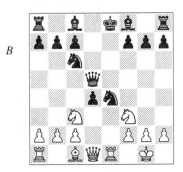

Now it is for Black to decide where he wants to put his queen for the ensuing middlegame. He has tried no fewer than five different squares, of which the last two seem both the most common and sensible:

A: 8...♕c4?   18
B: 8...♕f5!?   18
C: 8...♕d8   18
D: 8...♕h5   18
E: 8...♕a5   19

A)

8...♕c4? 9 ♘d2!

Stronger than the direct 9 ♖xe4+.

9...♕a6 10 ♘d5! ♕a5 11 c4 ♗e6

11...dxc3? 12 ♘c4!.

12 ♘b3 ♕a4 13 ♘xc7+ ♔d8 14 ♘xe6+ fxe6 15 ♖xe4

White is well placed.

B)

8...♕f5!? 9 ♘xe4 ♗e7 10 ♘xd4 ♘xd4 11 ♕xd4 0-0

11...♗d7? 12 ♗h6! ♖g8 13 ♗d2 with advantage.

12 ♘g3 ♕f6

With approximate equality.

C)

8...♕d8 9 ♖xe4+ ♗e7

9...♗e6 10 ♘xd4 ♘xd4 11 ♖xd4 ♕c8 12 ♗g5 ♗d6 13 ♘e4 0-0? 14 ♘f6+! was good for White in Tringov-Rossetto, Amsterdam 1964.

10 ♘xd4 f5

10...0-0?! 11 ♗f4 and White has an edge due to his centralized pieces while Black still has to complete his development, Neimann-Letreguilly, French Cht 1989.

11 ♖f4 0-0

11...♗g5 12 ♕e2+! is good.

12 ♘xc6 ♕xd1+ 13 ♘xd1 bxc6 14 ♖c4

White should enjoy a long-term edge in the ending in view of Black's pawn-structure.

D)

8...♕h5 (D)

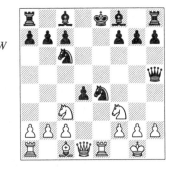

9 ♘xe4 ♗e6

9...♗e7?! 10 ♗g5! ♗e6 (but not 10...f5? 11 ♘g3 ♕f7 12 ♘e5 ♘xe5 13

罝xe5 奧e6 14 奧xe7 含xe7 15 豐e2
罝he8 16 罝e1 含d7 17 豐b5+ 含c8 18
句xf5 1-0 Beltran-Mitjavila, Sitges
1995) 11 奧xe7 句xe7 12 句xd4 and
White has a pleasant edge, Chigorin-
Janowski, Paris 1900.

10 奧g5!

Now Black has tried the following:
D1: 10...h6!? 19
D2: 10...奧d6!? 19
D3: 10...奧b4 19

10...奧e7 transposes to the above
note to Black's 9th move.

D1)

10...h6!? 11 奧f6 豐g6!

11...豐a5? 12 句xd4 gxf6 13 句xf6+
含e7 14 b4!! 句xb4 15 句xe6! 含xf6 16
豐d4+ winning for White, Rossolimo-
Prins, Bilbao 1951.

12 句h4 豐h7 13 豐h5 含d7

13...奧b4!? 14 c3 dxc3 15 bxc3
奧a3 16 句f5! and in practice White
should do well in the unclear complications.

14 罝ad1!

White has an edge.

D2)

10...奧d6!? 11 c4!? 0-0

11...dxc3? 12 句xd6+ cxd6 13 豐xd6
gives White a strong attack.

12 c5 奧e5!

12...奧e7?! 13 奧xe7 句xe7 14 句xd4
豐xd1 15 罝axd1 奧xa2 16 句c3! and
White is on top.

**13 句xe5 豐xd1 14 罝axd1 句xe5 15
罝xd4 f6**

15...奧xa2 16 句c3 句c6 17 罝d7
罝fe8 18 罝xe8+ 罝xe8 19 f3 奧c4 20
罝xc7 and White has a pleasant edge.

16 奧f4 奧xa2 17 句c3 奧f7 18 奧xe5
fxe5

18...罝ae8 19 罝d7! is good.

19 罝xe5?!

With equality, Sveshnikov-Bezgo-
dov, St Petersburg 1994.

However, 19 罝d7! would have kept
an edge.

D3)

**10...奧b4 11 句xd4 豐xd1 12 罝exd1
句xd4 13 罝xd4 奧e7 14 罝e1**

Better than 14 奧xe7?!.

14...罝d8 15 罝a4

White is a little better, Plijter-Taze-
laar, corr. 1994.

E)

8...豐a5 *(D)*

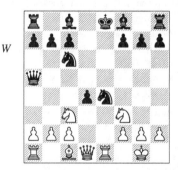

9 句xe4

9 罝xe4+ is less reliable, for example 9...奧e6 10 句xd4 0-0-0 11 奧e3
句xd4! 12 罝xd4 奧b4 13 豐f3 奧xc3 14
bxc3 豐xc3 and White does not have
enough for the pawn, Krastev-S.Ser-
giew, corr. 1991.

9...奧e6

9...奧e7!? 10 奧g5! f6 (10...0-0? 11
奧xe7 句xe7 12 句xd4 and White has
the edge) 11 句xf6+!? gxf6 12 奧xf6

♖f8 13 ♗xe7 ♘xe7 14 ♕xd4 ♕b6 15 ♕e5 ♕f6 16 ♕xc7 with a difficult position to assess although White may do well practically, Gayson-Howell, British Ch (Plymouth) 1989.

10 ♗d2

At this point Black has four different moves:

E1: 10...♕b6!? 20
E2: 10...♕f5 20
E3: 10...♕d5 20
E4: 10...♗b4 21

E1)

10...♕b6!?

Unusual but not as bad as its reputation.

11 ♗g5 h6 12 ♗h4 ♗e7

12...g5?! 13 ♘f6+ ♔d8 14 ♗g3 with good attacking prospects for White, A.Geller-Neishtadt, USSR 1956.

13 ♗xe7 ♔xe7 14 b4! ♖ad8 15 ♘c5 ♖he8 16 ♘xe6 fxe6 17 ♕d3! ♘xb4 18 ♕g6

White has decent attacking chances against Black's exposed king in compensation for the two pawns, Donev-Radulov, Bulgarian Ch 1991.

E2)

10...♕f5 (D)

11 ♗g5 h6

11...♗d6!? 12 ♘xd4 ♘xd4 13 ♕xd4 0-0 14 ♘xd6 ♕xg5 15 ♖e5! and White is a little better.

12 ♗h4 ♗c5

Or:

a) 12...♕h5!? 13 ♗f6 ♕g6 14 ♘h4 ♕h7 transposes into Line D1 with an extra move played by both sides, White having played ♗c1-d2-g5 and Black having played ...♕d5-f5-h5.

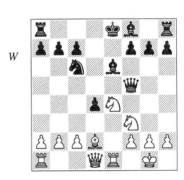

b) 12...g5? 13 ♘xd4 ♘xd4 14 ♕xd4 and White is winning, Estrin-Ryskin, USSR 1963.

c) 12...♕d5 13 ♗f6 ♕d7? and Black has tied himself up nicely, Pieri-Brancaleoni, Forli 1992.

d) 12...♗b4?! 13 ♘xd4!? ♘xd4 14 ♕xd4 ♗xe1 15 ♕xg7 and after the incorrect 15...♔d7? 16 ♖xe1 White had excellent compensation for the exchange in the game Zelčić-Villeneuve, Torcy 1991. However, the superior 15...♗xf2+! gives Black better chances of holding.

13 b4 ♗b6

13...♗xb4 14 ♘xd4!? ♘xd4 15 ♕xd4 ♗xe1 16 ♕xg7 and now 16...♔d7? gives White very good compensation for the material deficit. Note the similarity to the position given in the note to 12...♗b4?! and so 16...♗xf2+! is the critical test.

14 a4 a6 15 b5 axb5 16 axb5 ♖xa1 17 ♕xa1

White is a little better, Helvensteijn-Jonkman, Holland 1996.

E3)

10...♕d5 (D)

11 ♗g5 ♗e7

Or:

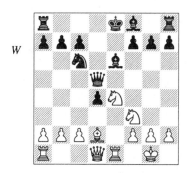

W

a) 11...h6? 12 ♗f6! ♕a5 (12...♔d7?! 13 ♘xd4! is good) 13 ♘xd4! gxf6 14 ♘xe6 fxe6 15 ♘xf6+ ♔f7 16 ♕d7+ ♗e7 17 ♕xe6+ ♔g7 18 ♘d5! and White is much better.

b) 11...♔d7?! 12 c3 ♖e8 13 ♘xd4 ♘xd4 14 cxd4 ♔c8 15 ♕a4! and White is well placed for a queenside attack, Bauer-Paulsen, Bundesliga 1986/7.

c) 11...♗d6 12 ♗f6 0-0 13 ♗xd4! (an important improvement on 13 ♘xd4, which is normally played in this position) 13...♘xd4 14 ♕xd4 ♕xd4 15 ♘xd4 and White is better as Black will lose the bishop-pair and end up with an inferior pawn-structure, Voller-Voracek, Czech Ch 1994.

d) 11...d3!? 12 ♖e3 h6 13 ♗h4 ♗c5 14 c4 ♕f5 15 ♘xc5 ♕xc5 16 ♕xd3 0-0 17 b3 a5 18 ♖ae1 and White has an edge due to the fact that his dark-squared bishop covers d8 making life a little awkward for Black, Schlingensiepen-Mainka, Bundesliga 1995/6.

12 ♗xe7 ♔xe7 13 c4! dxc3 14 ♕c2 ♖he8 15 ♘eg5 cxb2 16 ♖ad1 ♕b5 17 ♕xh7

White has a strong attack, e.g. 17...♖g8 18 ♘xe6 fxe6 19 ♕g6 ♘d8 20 ♘g5 ♕c4 21 ♖xe6+ ♕xe6 22

♘xe6 ♘xe6 23 ♖e1 ♖ae8 24 ♕xe6+ 1-0 Levi-Sarapu, Australia 1990.

E4)
10...♗b4 *(D)*

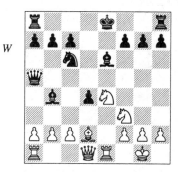

W

This very logical developing move offers to relieve the tension with exchanges.

11 ♘xd4! ♘xd4

11...♗xd2?! 12 ♘xc6 ♕b6 13 ♕xd2 ♕xc6 14 ♘g5 ♖d8 15 ♕b4! is pleasant for White, Pieri-Wagman, Forli 1991.

11...0-0-0? 12 ♘xc6 bxc6 13 ♗xb4! ♕xb4 14 ♕e2 and White has the edge, Ng-Schepel, Manila OL 1992.

12 c3

Black has now tried the following:

E41:	12...♘e2+?	21
E42:	12...0-0-0!?	22
E43:	12...0-0	22
E44:	12...♗e7	22

E41)
12...♘e2+? 13 ♕xe2 ♗e7 14 c4 ♕f5 15 ♗c3 0-0 16 ♘g3 ♕g5 17 ♘h5! g6

Now instead of 18 ♘g3 with a slight advantage, Sveshnikov-Makarychev, Russia 1975, 18 ♘g7!! is very strong, e.g. 18...♗h3 19 f4! ♕c5+ 20 ♔h1 ♕c6 21 ♕e4 and White is clearly better.

E42)

12...0-0-0!?

There is little practical experience of this move but after 13 cxb4 White's attacking chances on the queenside are better than Black's on the other wing.

E43)

12...0-0 13 cxb4 ♕d5

13...♕f5!? 14 ♖c1 ♗xa2 (14...♖ad8? 15 ♖c5 ♖d5 16 ♘g3 wins a piece, Fudurer-Daja, Yugoslavia 1949) 15 ♖xc7 (15 ♖c5! ♕d7 16 ♗c3 ♖ad8 17 ♖g5 f6 18 ♖g4 ♘c2! and Black is fine) leads to sharp play.

14 ♖c1 b6!

To stop ♖c5. After 14...♖ad8? 15 ♖c5 ♕xa2 16 ♗c3 ♘f5 (Black has to be very wary of White playing ♘f6+!) 17 ♕g4 ♘d4 18 ♘f6+ ♔h8 19 ♕h4 White is winning, Vitolinš-Koriakin, USSR 1966.

15 ♖xc7 ♖ad8

Now 16 ♗c3?! ♘b5! is approximately equal, Marić-Gligorić, Yugoslav Ch 1957. However, 16 ♖xa7 gives White a definite plus.

E44)

12...♗e7

Black aims to keep the bishop-pair but at the cost of leaving his king in the centre a move too long to achieve his aim.

13 cxd4 ♕d5

13...♕f5?! 14 ♗b4 ♗xb4 15 ♕a4+ ♗d7 16 ♘c5+? led to a draw in

Marić-Ivkov, Yugoslavia 1958 but 16 ♘d6+!! ♔f8 17 ♕xb4 cxd6 18 ♕xd6+ ♔g8 19 ♖e5! ♕g4 20 h3 is winning.

14 ♖c1

14 ♗b4 ♗xb4 15 ♕a4+ ♕c6 16 ♕xb4 0-0-0 17 ♘c5 ♗d5 18 ♖ac1 ♕g6 (18...♗xg2? 19 ♘e6! and Black does not get enough for the queen after 19...fxe6 20 ♖xc6 ♗xc6) 19 g3 ♕g4! and both sides have attacking chances.

14...c6 15 ♗g5! ♗b4 16 ♖e3 h6 17 ♗f6 ♗f8 18 ♘c3

White has the better game.

Part 3: The Koltanowski Variation

1 e4 e5 2 ♘f3 ♘c6 3 ♗c4 ♗c5 4 0-0 ♘f6 5 d4!? *(D)*

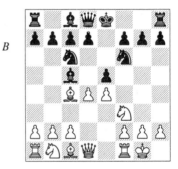

This line is named after Grandmaster George Koltanowski who both played and developed the system over three decades in the mid-twentieth century. It offers dynamic play in return for a pawn, yet is almost neglected by theory. Therefore, a well-prepared player with the white pieces can easily obtain a very strong initiative or even a totally winning position should his opponent fall for one of the numerous tactical shots available. If nothing else, it stops even strong players 'reeling off' long lines of theory and gets them to think for themselves from a very early stage.

From the diagram Black has three possibilities, firstly to play **5...exd4**, when **6 e5** transposes to the Max Lange Attack (which is probably the last thing Black had in mind when he played 3...♗c5), secondly to play **5...♘xd4?!** or finally **5...♗xd4**. As the Max Lange Attack is covered in Part 1 of this chapter we will concentrate here on the other two options available, namely:

A: 5...♘xd4?! 23
B: 5...♗xd4 23

A)

5...♘xd4?! 6 ♘xe5 ♘e6

6...0-0? 7 ♗e3 ♘e6 (7...♕e7? 8 ♗xd4 ♗xd4 9 ♕xd4 c5 10 ♕c3 ♘xe4 11 ♕e3 ♕xe5 12 ♘c3 1-0 Estrin-Klaman, Leningrad 1957) 8 ♗xe6 ♗xe3 9 ♗xf7+ ♔h8 10 ♗b3 ♗b6 11 ♘f7+ ♖xf7 12 ♗xf7 and White is winning, Lakos-Bogar, Hungary 1994.

7 ♗xe6 fxe6

7...dxe6?? loses to 8 ♕xd8+ ♔xd8 9 ♘xf7+.

8 ♘d3

Black has problems equalizing, e.g. 8...♗b6 9 e5 ♘d5? 10 c4! ♘e7 11 c5 winning a piece; 8...♗e7 9 e5 ♘d5 10 ♕f3! is awkward for Black; or 8...♕e7 9 ♗g5! e5 10 ♗xf6 gxf6 11 ♕h5+ with a pleasant edge.

B)

5...♗xd4 (D)

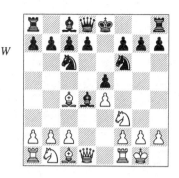

This is the best move for Black to play after 5 d4!? if he wishes to avoid the Max Lange Attack.

6 ♘xd4 ♘xd4

6...exd4? 7 e5 is very strong for White.

7 f4

I have chosen to recommend this move as I believe this to be more direct and testing than the alternative 7 ♗g5.

7...d6

This is Black's best move. Instead:

a) 7...♘c6? gives Black a very poor game after the tactical shot 8 ♗xf7+!:

a1) 8...♔e7 9 fxe5 ♘xe5 10 ♗b3 h6 11 ♘c3 c6 12 ♗f4 d6 13 ♕e1 ♗g4 14 h3 ♗e6 15 ♗xe5 dxe5 16 ♕g3 ♕d4+ 17 ♔h1 g5 18 ♖ad1 ♕b4 19 ♘d5+ cxd5 20 exd5 ♕d6 21 dxe6 ♕c5 22 ♕f3 1-0 Denny-Haces, Thessaloniki OL 1988.

a2) 8...♔xf7 9 fxe5 ♘xe5 10 ♕d5+ ♔f8 11 ♕xe5 d6 12 ♕g3 ♔f7 13 ♘c3 is strong for White.

b) If 7...♕e7?! then 8 fxe5 ♕xe5 9 ♗f4 ♕c5 (what else?) 10 ♗xf7+ ♔xf7 11 ♗e3 ♕xc2 12 ♕xd4 d6 13 ♘c3 ♕xb2 14 ♖xf6+ gxf6 15 ♖f1 1-0 Koltanowski-Donnelly, San Francisco simul 1947.

8 c3!? (D)

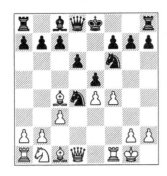

This is the critical position after 6...♘xd4. In this position Black has four choices which we will examine in turn:

B1: 8...♘e6 24
B2: 8...♗e6 24
B3: 8...♗g4 25
B4: 8...♘c6 25

B1)

8...♘e6

Black's plan is to redevelop the knight via e6 to the c5-square hoping to put pressure on White's pawn on e4.

9 f5 ♘c5 10 ♘d2 0-0

10...♘cxe4? 11 ♘xe4 ♘xe4 12 ♕g4 and White penetrates on the kingside.

11 ♕f3 a5

The idea behind 11...a5 is to stop White gaining space on the queenside. If Black fails to do this, for example 11...c6 intending action in the centre, White gets the upper hand with 12 b4! ♘a4 13 ♗b3 ♘b6 14 ♖e1 ♖e8 15 ♘f1 d5 16 ♘g3 dxe4 17 ♘xe4 ♘xe4 18 ♖xe4. With his extra space, bishop-pair and well-placed rook on e4 White has good kingside chances and good compensation for the pawn, Koltanowski-Barringtor, Cleveland simul 1968.

12 ♖f2!

A subtle move leaving the f1-square available for White's knight to transfer it over to the kingside via f1-g3-h5 from where it will inflict maximum pressure.

12...♗d7 13 b4!

Combining queenside expansion with dislodging the black knight from c5 and at least temporarily pushing it out of play.

13...axb4 14 cxb4 ♘a4 15 ♘f1 ♗c6 16 ♗g5 b5 17 ♗b3 ♗b7 18 ♖d1 ♕e7 19 ♘g3 ♘b6 20 ♘h5

White's pressure compensates for the pawn.

B2)

8...♗e6 (D)

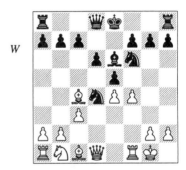

Developing a piece while offering to exchange White's strong light-squared bishop. While this move looks clever, White will avoid the exchange and later gain back a tempo with f4-f5.

9 ♗d3 ♘c6 10 f5 ♗d7 11 ♗g5!

An annoying pin typical of this line and one which is hard to break.

11...♕e7 12 ♕f3!

Not only guarding e4 but more to the point making it difficult for Black to play ...h6 and ...g5 due to fxg6 (*en passant*) with threats down the f-file.

12...0-0-0

Black hopes to find refuge on the queenside rather than castle 'into it'.

13 b4

Once again with the bishop-pair, more space, a bind and better attacking chances White's position is preferable.

B3)

8...♗g4 9 ♕d2! *(D)*

9...♗e6!?

Losing a tempo on 8...♗e6 but hoping that White's queen is worse on d2 than d1. Alternatively:

a) 9...♘xe4? 10 ♕e3 ♘c2 11 ♕xe4 ♘xa1 12 ♗xf7+ ♔xf7 13 fxe5+ and White wins.

b) 9...♘c6 10 f5! is good: 10...h5 (10...♘xe4 11 ♕d5 ♘g5 12 ♗xg5 ♕xg5 13 ♕xf7+ ♔d8 14 ♘a3 is good for White) 11 h3 ♘xe4 12 ♕d5 ♘g5 13 hxg4 hxg4 14 f6 ♘e6 15 fxg7 ♖g8 16 ♖xf7 ♔xf7 17 ♕xe6+ ♔xg7 18 ♕h6# (1-0) Younglove-Steininger, Missouri 1980.

10 ♗d3 ♘c6 11 f5 ♗d7 12 ♕g5 ♕e7 13 b4 0-0-0 14 b5 ♘b8

Now after 15 a4?!, Baker-Spanton, Hastings Challengers 1997/8, Black should be no worse, but 15 ♗e3! gives White good attacking chances.

B4)

8...♘c6 *(D)*

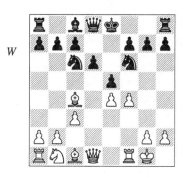

9 f5!

Almost automatic in this variation. White cramps Black's position and stops ...♗e6.

9...♘e7!

Better than:

a) 9...d5?! 10 exd5 ♘e7 (10...♘a5? 11 ♕a4+ c6 12 dxc6 ♘xc6 13 ♗e3! is very strong for White) 11 ♕e2 e4 12 ♗g5 ♗xf5 13 ♘d2 ♕d6 14 ♗xf6 ♕xf6 (14...gxf6? 15 ♘xe4) and White is better.

b) 9...♘xe4?! 10 ♕g4! d5 (10...♘f6 11 ♕xg7 ♖f8 12 ♗h6 and Black is struggling) 11 ♕xg7 ♕f6 12 ♗h6!! dxc4 (12...♕xg7 13 ♗xg7 ♖g8 14 ♗xd5 ♘xc3 15 ♗xc6+ is excellent for White) 13 ♕xf6 ♘xf6 14 ♗g7 ♖g8 15 ♗xf6 ♘e7 16 ♗xe7 ♔xe7 17 ♘a3 and White is doing well.

c) 9...0-0 10 ♗g5 ♘a5 11 ♗d3 d5 12 ♗xf6 gxf6 (12...♕xf6 13 exd5) 13 ♘d2 c6?! 14 b4! ♘c4 15 ♘xc4 dxc4

16 ♕g4+ ♔h8 17 ♗xc4 and White is well on top.

10 ♕f3!? h6 11 g4 c6 12 ♗b3 ♕c7 13 ♘d2

The position is unbalanced but as usual White has compensation for the pawn.

To summarize, it is a brave man who will enter into the black side of the Max Lange Attack unless he is extremely well prepared, although variation B264 in Part 1 may equalize. If Black plays the Anti-Max Lange as in Part 2 he needs to be very careful not to drift into an inferior middle-game/endgame and with little material available the Koltanowski variation offers interesting play, leaves room for original analysis and may well catch even very strong players unaware.

2 Petroff Defence

1 e4 e5 2 ♘f3 ♘f6 *(D)*

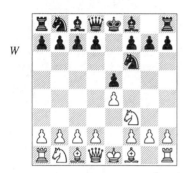

This is the basic position of the Petroff. Its reputation is one of solidity and it is played regularly at the highest levels as a genuine equalizing defence. It is not so popular at club/tournament level mainly because it offers little in the way of quick winning chances for Black. Local leagues tend to have fairly short time-controls, while in tournaments there is the pressure of trying to win on a regular basis, even as Black. Because of these factors it has psychologically the reverse effect of being solid and leaves Black feeling frustrated at not seeming to have many chances of his own. The main idea of the Petroff is to exchange off a pair of central pawns and the struggle then features minor-piece play and a battle for control of the open e-file. Black hopes that the advantage of White's first move will be dissipated over a period of time. It is only then that Black will look at exploiting White's position if he has played some inaccurate moves or forms a bad plan.

When looking for a line then to '**startle**' my opponent I realized that this would be a difficult choice. A player who normally plays the Scotch Four Knights may look at playing 3 ♘c3 hoping for 3...♘c6 in reply and only needing to prepare against 3...♗b4 as an independent line. However, this would not be consistent with playing the Max Lange, so maybe we should consider one of the main lines which may well offer an edge if prepared thoroughly. The problem with this is the amount of preparation needed just to face the occasional player who plays the Petroff. Taking these things into consideration, I have decided to give you analysis of an unusual and aggressive line. You may feel that it should be regarded more as a 'one-off' weapon to catch somebody by surprise than as a regular choice, but bear in mind that the strong Latvian master Vitolinš has played the line repeatedly and with success for many years.

3 ♘xe5 d6

Alternatives for Black at this point are unusual:

a) 3...♘xe4?! is a strange-looking move against which White just needs to play calmly to achieve an advantage. 4 ♕e2 ♕e7 (4...♘f6?? 5 ♘c6+ wins the queen; 4...d5? 5 d3 ♕e7 6 dxe4 ♕xe5 7 exd5 and White is a pawn up for nothing) 5 ♕xe4 d6 6 d4 and now:

a1) 6...f6 7 f4 ♘d7 (7...fxe5 8 fxe5 dxe5 9 dxe5 and Black will not recover the pawn easily) 8 ♘c3 dxe5 9 ♘d5 ♕d6 10 fxe5 fxe5 11 dxe5 ♕c6? (11...♘xe5? 12 ♗f4 wins a piece) 12 ♗b5 ♕c5 13 ♗e3 and the queen falls, 1-0 Wills-Sparks, USA 1942.

a2) 6...dxe5 7 dxe5 ♘c6 8 ♗b5 ♗d7 9 ♘c3 0-0-0 10 ♗f4 and Black has insufficient play for the pawn, Yudasin-Montecatine, Dos Hermanas 1992.

b) 3...♕e7 4 d4 d6 5 ♘f3 and now:

b1) 5...♗g4?! 6 ♗d3 ♘c6 (the main trouble with 6...♘xe4 – or 5...♘xe4 for that matter – is that the black queen on e7 is then misplaced as it blocks Black's dark-squared bishop and is a target for attack on the e-file; whereas it may not be fatal to move the queen again at some stage it is the kind of loss of time that as Black means that you are likely to drift into an inferior position without any chances other than 'hanging on in there') 7 c3 d5? (after 7...♘xe4 the comment in the previous note becomes relevant again, e.g. 8 0-0 d5 9 ♖e1 0-0-0 10 b4 and Black's position is already uncomfortable, especially since if White were to move his queen then ...♗xf3 may not be an option as gxf3 will win a piece due to the pin down the e-file) 8 e5 g6 9 0-0 ♘d7 10 h3 ♗xf3 11 ♕xf3, and White is a pawn up with the bishop-pair and in a better position, Haack-Bicker, Bargteheide 1989.

b2) 5...♕xe4+ 6 ♗e2 ♗f5 7 ♘a3 and then:

b21) 7...♕e6?! 8 0-0 ♗e7 9 ♖e1 ♕d7 (already Black has moved his queen four times in the first nine moves and yet on d7 it is still not a good piece) 10 d5 and White has an edge due to his extra space and the option of using the d4-square for a knight where it will become a dominant piece, Sucher-Maux, Schaan 1996.

b22) 7...♘c6 8 0-0 ♗g4?! 9 h3 ♗h5 (9...♗xf3? 10 ♗xf3 ♕xd4?? 11 ♗xc6+ wins the queen) 10 ♗g5 0-0-0 11 ♖e1 and White has an edge, e.g. 11...♖e8 (11...♗xf3 12 ♗xf3?! ♕xd4 13 ♗xc6 ♕xd1 14 ♗xb7+ ♔b8 15 ♖axd1 ♔xb7 16 ♘c4 and Black has problems completing his development satisfactorily) 12 ♗xf6 gxf6 13 d5 ♘d8 (13...♗xf3 14 ♗xf3 ♕xe1+ 15 ♕xe1 ♖xe1+ 16 ♖xe1 ♘e5 17 ♗e4 and Black's pawn-structure leaves him battling for equality) 14 ♕d2! and White has a pleasant position.

4 ♘xf7!? (D)

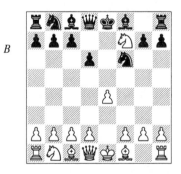

What's all this then?! White hopes that two pawns (not only two pawns but a preponderance of pawns in the centre) a lead in development and space together with the placement of Black's king will compensate for the piece.

4...♔xf7 5 d4!

This is the starting point for this variation and the time for Black to decide on a plan and set-up. The fact that Black has tried eleven different moves in this position either shows that people are not certain of how to deal with this sacrifice or are not properly prepared to meet it. Let's look at Black's options:

A:	5...♘xe4?	29
B:	5...♕d7?!	29
C:	5...♕e7	30
D:	5...♕e8	31
E:	5...♘bd7	32
F:	5...♗g4	33
G:	5...♗e6	33
H:	5...♗e7	34
I:	5...c6	36
J:	5...c5!?	37
K:	5...g6	39

A)

5...♘xe4? *(D)*

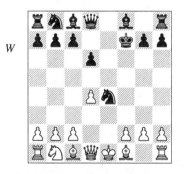

W

The direct approach, but not a particularly good one, otherwise the whole line would probably be short-lived.

6 ♕h5+ ♔e7

6...♔g8?? 7 ♕d5+ 1-0 Hess-Born, Kirchheim 1990.

6...g6? 7 ♕d5+ followed by ♕xe4 leaves White a sound pawn ahead.

7 ♕e2 ♔f7

7...d5?? 8 ♗g5+ 1-0 Lazarev-Kundyshev, Moscow 1982.

8 ♕xe4 ♕e7?! 9 ♗c4+ ♗e6?

After 9...♔e8 Black is just in a poor position a pawn down.

10 ♕f5+

1-0 Soderström-Tzannetakis, corr. 1981. 10 ♗g5! would have much the same effect.

B)

5...♕d7?! 6 ♗c4+ ♔e7

6...d5!? 7 exd5 and White has full material compensation for the piece, for example 7...♗d6 8 0-0 ♕g4!? 9 ♕xg4 ♗xg4 10 h3 ♗f5 11 ♗b3 and White's queenside pawns will start to roll.

7 ♘c3 h6 8 h3 ♕c6 9 ♕d3 ♕e8 10 e5 ♘h7

10...dxe5 11 dxe5 ♘fd7 12 f4 and White has compensation based on the openness of the black king, for example 12...♘b6 13 ♗b3 ♕d7 14 ♕g3 ♘c6 15 ♗e3 ♘d4 16 ♖d1 c5 17 ♘e2 and White is doing fine.

10...♘fd7 11 ♘d5+ ♔d8 12 ♘f4 ♘b6 13 ♘g6 ♘xc4 14 ♘xh8 and White has regained full material equality, e.g. 14...♗e6 15 ♘g6 ♘b6 16 ♗f4.

11 0-0 ♔d8

11...dxe5 12 ♖e1 ♕d7 13 ♖xe5+ ♔d8 14 ♗e6 ♕c6 15 d5 ♕a6 (15...♕e8 16 ♗xc8 ♕xe5 17 ♗xb7 and Black lacks the necessary killer blow, e.g. 17...♗d6 18 g3 ♘g5 19 ♗xg5+ hxg5 20 ♗xa8 ♖xh3 21 ♕e4 and Black's attack is mainly visual) 16 ♕g6 and

White has good compensation, for example 16...♘d7 (16...♗d6?! 17 ♖e1 and Black's g-pawn is under pressure) 17 ♖e2 ♘hf6 18 ♗f4 ♕b6 (18...♘c5? 19 ♗xc8 ♖xc8 20 ♖ae1 is strong for White) 19 ♖ae1 ♕xb2 20 ♗g8!! and Black has big problems.

12 ♖e1 ♘d7

12...dxe5? loses to 13 dxe5+ ♕d7 14 ♖d1! ♕xd3 15 ♖xd3+ ♔e8 16 ♘d5.

13 ♗f4 dxe5 14 dxe5

Black is helpless to stop e5-e6, and so resigned in Duebon-Steinmann, Bad Dürkheim 1993.

C)

5...♕e7 6 ♘c3 *(D)*

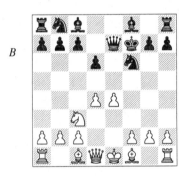

Now Black has tried:
C1: 6...c6 30
C2: 6...♗e6 31

6...g6 will be covered in Line K.

C1)

6...c6 7 ♗d3 g6

Or:

a) 7...♗g4?! 8 f3 ♗e6 9 0-0 ♘bd7 10 f4 ♗g4 11 ♕e1 gives White good practical chances due to his central pawn-mass, e.g. 11...d5 12 e5 ♖e8?! 13 ♕g3 ♕b4! 14 a3! ♕b6 15 ♗e3 and White is doing well as 15...♕xb2 loses to 16 ♘a4.

b) 7...d5 8 e5 ♗g4 9 f3 ♗h5 10 0-0 ♘fd7 11 ♘e4! ♗g8 (11...dxe4 12 fxe4+ ♔g6 13 g4 and again White is doing well, for example 13...♕h4 14 gxh5+ ♕xh5 15 ♗c4!!) 12 ♘d6 ♕d8 (12...♗g6 13 f4 ♗xd3 14 ♕xd3 and Black has to deal with f4-f5-f6) 13 ♘f5 with adequate compensation.

c) 7...♘xe4?! 8 ♘xe4 d5 9 ♗g5 ♕e8 (9...♕e6?! 10 ♕e2! is better for White, e.g. 10...h6 11 ♗e3 ♘d7 12 0-0-0 ♗e7 13 ♘g3 and White's superior development and safer king gives him the edge) 10 ♕f3+ ♔g8 11 0-0-0 dxe4 12 ♗c4+ ♗e6 13 ♕xe4 and White wins.

8 0-0 ♗g7 9 f4 ♘g4

After 9...♗g4!? 10 ♕e1 ♖e8 11 ♕h4 ♗e6 12 f5 gxf5 13 exf5 ♗d7 14 ♗g5 d5 15 ♖ae1 ♕d6 16 ♘e2! ♔g8 17 c4 White still has good compensation.

10 e5 ♕h4

Or 10...♔g8 11 ♘e4 dxe5 12 fxe5 ♗e6 (12...♗f5? loses to 13 ♗c4+ ♗e6 14 ♕xg4 ♗xc4 15 ♕c8+ ♗f8 16 ♗g5) 13 h3 ♘h6 14 ♘f6+ ♗xf6 15 exf6 ♕f8 16 ♕e2! ♗f7 (16...♗d5?! 17 ♗xh6 ♕xh6 18 ♕e7 ♕f8 19 ♕xb7 and White wins) 17 ♕e3 ♘f5 18 ♖xf5! gxf5 19 ♕g5+ ♗g6 20 ♗c4+ ♕f7 21 ♕h6! with mate next move.

11 h3 ♘h6 12 ♘e4 ♖d8

12...d5 13 g3 ♕d8 (13...♕xh3?? 14 ♘g5+) 14 ♘d6+ ♔g8 15 g4 and White has good compensation, e.g. 15...♘d7 16 g5 ♘f7 17 ♘xf7 ♔xf7 18 f5 gxf5 19 ♗xf5 ♔e7 20 g6 ♔e8 21

gxh7 ♕h4 22 ♗g6+ ♔d8 23 ♕g4
♕xg4+ 24 hxg4 and White is doing
well.

13 f5! ♘xf5 14 ♗g5 ♕h5 15 ♗e2!

1-0 Erlbeck-Saring, Bavaria 1995.
It's goodbye queen!

C2)
6...♗e6 7 ♗g5!? (D)

White wishes to provoke weaknesses.

7...h6

7...♘bd7 8 f4 h6 9 ♗h4 c5 (9...♘b6
10 e5 dxe5 11 fxe5 ♗g4 12 ♗e2 ♗xe2
13 ♘xe2 ♕b4+ 14 c3 ♕xb2 15 exf6
and White is better) 10 e5 ♗g4 11
♗e2 dxe5 12 dxe5 ♗xe2 13 ♕xe2 (13
♘xe2 ♖d8! is unclear) 13...g5 14 ♗g3
gives White good chances, for example 14...gxf4 (14...♖e8 15 0-0-0 ♘b6
16 ♕f3 ♘fd7 17 ♖he1) 15 ♗xf4 ♘h7
16 ♘d5! and Black has problems.

8 ♗h4 g5 9 ♗g3 ♗g4

9...♗g7 10 ♗e2 ♖f8 11 0-0 ♔g8 12
f4 gxf4 13 ♗xf4 and White has reasonable compensation.

10 ♗e2 ♗xe2 11 ♕xe2 ♘c6

11...♗g7 12 e5! dxe5 (if Black
moves the knight from f6 then ♕f3+
and ♕xb7 is strong, and 12...♖e8 13

0-0! dxe5 14 dxe5 ♕b4 15 ♕f3 g4 16
♕f5 leaves White doing well) 13 dxe5
♖e8 14 0-0-0 ♘h7 15 ♕f3+ ♔g8 16
♕xb7 is very good for White.

**12 0-0-0 h5 13 h4 g4 14 ♖he1
♗h6+ 15 ♔b1 ♖ad8**

15...♖he8 16 ♕b5! and White is
fine, e.g. 16...♘d8 (16...♖ab8 17 e5
dxe5 18 dxe5 ♘g8 19 e6+ ♔g7 20
♖d7! ♕xd7 21 ♗e5+ and White wins)
17 e5 ♔f8 18 f3 c6 19 ♕f1! dxe5 20
dxe5 ♘d5 21 fxg4+ and White is
well-placed.

16 e5 dxe5 17 dxe5 ♖xd1+

17...♖he8 18 ♖xd8 ♕xd8 19 ♖d1
♘d7 20 ♕e4! and White is doing well.

18 ♖xd1 ♘d7 19 ♘d5! ♕c5

19...♕e6 20 ♘xc7 wins.

20 e6+

1-0 Cabejsek-Stmad, corr. 1991.

D)
5...♕e8 6 ♘c3 g6 (D)

6...♘xe4?! 7 ♕h5+ g6 8 ♕d5+ and
White emerges a good pawn up,
Ballon-Andrae, 1990.

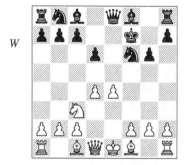

7 ♕f3 ♔g7

7...♗f5 8 ♗c4+ ♔g7 9 0-0 ♗xe4
(9...♘xe4 10 ♖e1! and Black is in
deep trouble, e.g. 10...♘c6 11 ♘xe4

♘xd4 12 ♕e3 winning; 9...♗g4 10 ♗h6+! ♔xh6 11 ♕xf6 ♗g7 12 ♕f4+ ♔h5 13 h3 and White wins) 10 ♗h6+! ♔xh6 11 ♕xf6 and Black is helpless to the oncoming threats of ♕xh8 and ♕f4+ picking up a piece.

8 ♗c4 ♗e6

8...♗f5? transposes to the previous note.

9 ♗h6+! ♔g8

9...♔f7 10 ♘d5! ♕d8 (10...♗xd5 11 ♗xd5+ ♔e7 12 ♗g5 ♗g7 13 e5 is very strong for White) 11 ♗g5 ♘bd7 (11...♗g7 12 e5 dxe5 13 dxe5 ♖e8 14 0-0-0 wins for White) 12 ♘xf6 ♘xf6 13 ♗xe6+ ♔xe6 14 ♕b3+ ♔d7 15 ♕h3+ and Black cannot parry the threats.

10 ♗xe6+ ♕xe6 11 ♗xf8 h5?!

11...♔xf8!? 12 ♘d5 ♕xe4+ 13 ♕xe4 ♘xe4 14 ♘xc7 ♘a6 15 ♘xa8 ♔f7 16 f3 ♘f6 17 ♘b6 axb6 18 ♔d2 leads to a difficult position to judge although with ♖+2♙ vs 2♘ and Black's pawn-structure a little ropy White should be better.

12 0-0-0 ♘bd7

12...♘a6?! is no improvement, e.g. 13 e5 dxe5 14 ♗e7!! ♕xe7 15 ♕xb7 ♔g7 16 ♕xa6 and Black is in trouble.

Up to now we have been following Claus-Wilkie, Aguadilla 1989 when White played 13 ♕g3?! (but still went on to win!). However, there is a better way to continue:

13 e5 ♘g4!

13...dxe5?! 14 ♗a3 e4 15 ♕g3 is very good for White.

14 ♗e7!! ♕xe7 15 h3 ♘h6

15...♕g5+?! just improves White's king: 16 ♔b1 ♘h6 17 ♕xb7 ♕d8 18 ♘d5 ♖b8 19 ♕c6 and White has

enormous compensation for the sacrificed piece.

16 ♕xb7 ♖f8 17 ♕xc7

White starts mopping up the black pawns.

17...dxe5 18 ♕xa7 ♖xf2 19 dxe5 ♖f7 20 ♖he1

Black has little chance of survival.

E)

5...♘bd7 6 e5! *(D)*

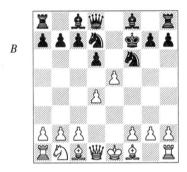

6...dxe5

6...♕e7 7 ♗c4+ and now:

a) 7...d5 8 ♗d3! is awkward for Black to meet, for example 8...♘e4 9 ♕f3+ ♔e8 (9...♔g8 10 ♘d2 ♕f7 11 ♘xe4 dxe4 12 ♗xe4 ♕xf3 13 ♗xf3 and White has full compensation for the piece) 10 0-0 ♕h4 11 c4 c6 12 cxd5 cxd5 13 g3 ♕h3 14 ♗xe4 dxe4 15 ♕xe4 ♘b6 16 ♘c3 ♗e7 17 d5 and White has good compensation for the piece.

b) 7...♔e8 8 f4 ♘b6 9 ♗e2 ♘e4 10 0-0 ♗f5 11 c4 with good play for White.

7 dxe5 ♕e7 8 ♗c4+ ♔e8 9 f4 ♘b6

9...♘e4 10 ♗d5 ♘dc5 (10...♘df6?! 11 exf6 ♘xf6+ 12 ♔f1 ♗g4 13 ♗f3 ♖d8 14 ♕e2 ♗xf3 15 ♕xf3 and Black has insufficient play for the pawn; 10...♕h4+!? 11 g3 ♘xg3 12 hxg3 ♕xg3+ 13 ♔f1 ♗c5 14 ♕f3 ♕xf3+ 15 ♗xf3 ♖f8 16 ♔g2 h6 17 ♘c3 and White has the slightly better of it) 11 ♕f3 ♘f6! 12 ♗c6+! ♘fd7 13 ♗b5 c6 14 ♗e2 leads to a messy position in which my gut feeling tells me Black should have the edge but with practical chances for both sides, for example 14...♘b6 15 b4 ♘ca4 16 a3 ♗f5 (16...♗e6 17 ♘d2 ♕d7 18 ♘e4 ♗c4 19 ♗e3 ♗xe2 20 ♕xe2 ♖d8 21 0-0 ♕e6 22 ♖ad1 ♖xd1 23 ♖xd1 and the position remains unclear) 17 c4 ♕d7 18 ♘d2 ♖d8 19 c5 ♘d5 20 g4 ♗c2 21 ♖a2 ♗g6 22 f5 ♘ac3 23 ♖c2 ♘xe2 24 ♔xe2 ♗f7 25 ♘e4 with unclear play and chances for both sides.

10 ♗e2 ♘e4 11 ♗f3 ♗f5 12 ♕e2 ♘c5

12...♕b4+? 13 c3 ♕c4 14 g4 and White is back on top.

13 ♘c3

With an unclear position, e.g. 13...♖d8 14 0-0 c6 15 ♗e3 ♘ba4! 16 ♘xa4 ♘xa4 17 ♗xa7 ♘xb2 18 ♗b6 ♖d7 19 ♖fe1 and the position remains murky to say the least.

F)
5...♗g4 6 f3 ♗h5

Even 6...♗c8?! has been played before, in which case White should play 7 ♗d3 and in effect be a tempo ahead of 6...♗e6 lines which are discussed in the next section.

Black's threat after the text-move is ...♘xe4!.

7 ♘c3 c6 8 h4! ♗g6

8...h6 9 g4 ♗g6 10 ♗e3 ♗e7 11 ♕d2 d5 12 h5 ♗h7 13 e5 ♘fd7 14

0-0-0 and with f4-f5 looming White has plenty of play.

9 ♗g5 ♕e8

9...♗e7 10 ♕d2 ♖e8 11 0-0-0 ♔g8 12 g4 d5 13 e5 ♘fd7 14 f4 and White has good compensation, e.g. 14...h6 15 ♗xe7 ♕xe7 16 f5 ♗h7 17 ♗d3 and White's play on the kingside is obviously while Black still has to form an active plan.

10 ♕d2 d5 11 0-0-0

White has a lot of play for the piece.

G)
5...♗e6 6 ♗d3 *(D)*

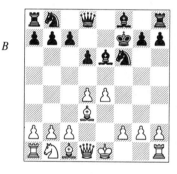

6...g6

6...♗e7 7 0-0 g6!? (again forward planning to meet f4-f5 and make space for the king) 8 c4! (a different plan from White altogether now: gaining territory in the centre and restricting Black's space) 8...♔g7 (8...c5 9 d5 ♗c8 10 f4 ♘bd7 11 ♘c3 and it is difficult to see how Black will prevent an eventual e4-e5) 9 ♘c3 ♘a6 10 a3 c6 11 h3 ♘c7 (11...♕b6 12 ♗e3 hardly helps Black's cause as 12...♕xb2?? 13 ♘a4 traps the queen) 12 d5 ♗f7 13 ♗e3 h6 (13...♖f8 seems more consistent) 14 f4 c5?! 15 e5 ♘g8 16 ♘e4

(White's play for the piece becomes more and more obvious) 16...♗xd5 17 cxd5 ♘xd5 18 ♗d2 (18 ♗c1! may be more accurate in view of the next note) 18...dxe5 (18...♕b6! gives Black some chances) 19 fxe5 ♕d7 20 ♗c4 1-0 Shirazi-Lane, Los Angeles 1983. Black's position falls apart.

7 0-0 ♔g7?!

Black is trying to get his king out of the line of fire.

8 f4 ♘bd7

8...c6 9 f5 gxf5 10 exf5 ♗f7 (10...♗d5?! 11 c4 ♗e4? 12 ♗xe4 ♘xe4 13 ♕g4+ is obviously good for White) 11 ♕e1! with good counterplay, e.g. 11...♖g8 12 ♕h4 ♔h8 13 ♗g5 ♗e7 14 ♘c3 ♘bd7 15 ♖ae1 and all White's pieces are ready for action.

9 ♘d2 ♗e7

9...c6 10 c3! maintains the tension.

10 ♘f3 ♖f8

10...♗g4!? 11 h3 ♗xf3 12 ♕xf3 c6 13 e5 ♘d5 14 e6 ♘7f6 15 c3 ♖f8 16 f5 and White still has a lot of compensation.

11 f5! gxf5 12 ♘g5 ♗g8

12...♗f7 13 ♖xf5 ♕e8 14 ♕f3 is stronger for White than in the game.

13 ♖xf5 h6?!

This creates another target.

14 ♘h3 ♗e6

Or 14...♗h7 15 ♘f4! ♗xf5 16 exf5 ♕c8 17 ♕e1! and White has very good attacking chances for the material invested.

15 ♗xh6+! ♔h8

15...♔xh6 16 ♕d2+ ♔g7 17 ♕g5+ ♔h8 (17...♔f7?? 18 ♕h5+ and mate next move) 18 ♕h6+ ♘h7 19 ♕xe6 gives White excellent compensation for the piece.

16 ♗xf8

White is well on top, with ♖+2♙ vs ♗+♘ together with Black's exposed kingside, Nagrocka-R.Khadilkar, Naleczow 1982.

H)

5...♗e7 6 ♘c3 *(D)*

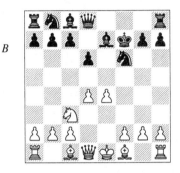

Now:

H1:	**6...c6**	34
H2:	**6...♖e8**	35

6...g6 transposes to 5...g6 6 ♘c3 ♗e7, considered in Line K.

H1)

6...c6 7 ♗c4+ ♔f8

Probably best. Others:

a) 7...♗e6?! 8 ♗xe6+ ♔xe6 9 f4 with an unprepossessing choice for Black:

a1) 9...d5 10 e5 ♘e4 11 ♕g4+ ♔f7 12 ♕f5+ ♔e8 (12...♔g8 allows White at least a draw with ♕e6+) 13 ♘xe4 dxe4 14 c3! ♘a6 15 ♕xe4 and White has full compensation for the piece.

a2) 9...♖f8 10 ♕d3 ♕a5 11 ♗d2 ♕h5 12 0-0 ♔f7 13 e5 ♘fd7 14 ♕c4+ ♔e8 (14...d5 15 ♘xd5 cxd5 16 ♕xd5+ ♔e8 17 ♕xb7 ♘b6 18 a4 ♕f7 19 a5

♕d5 20 ♕xd5 ♘xd5 21 c4 with an obscure position) 15 ♖ae1 with strong pressure.

a3) 9...♘bd7 10 0-0 ♖e8 11 e5 dxe5 12 fxe5 ♘d5?? (12...♘xe5 13 ♖e1! is enough to keep White on top) 13 ♕g4# (1-0) Hoffer-Evans, corr. 1987.

b) 7...d5?! 8 exd5 cxd5 9 ♘xd5 ♘xd5 (9...♗e6 10 ♘e3 ♗xc4 11 ♘xc4 ♘c6 12 c3 ♖e8 13 0-0 with approximate equality) 10 ♕h5+ ♔f8 11 ♗xd5 ♕e8 12 ♕f3+ ♗f6+ 13 ♗e3 and White has full compensation for the piece, Markus-Klugert, corr. 1989.

c) 7...♔e8?! 8 0-0 b5 9 ♗d3 b4 10 e5!? dxe5 11 dxe5 ♘g4 (11...bxc3 12 exf6 ♗xf6 13 ♖e1+ ♔f8 14 bxc3! with good play, for example 14...♕a5 15 ♕e2 ♗d7 16 ♖b1 and Black is awfully tied up) 12 ♘e4 ♘xe5 13 ♕h5+ ♘f7 (13...♘g6 14 ♘g5! and Black has problems) 14 ♖e1 and now:

c1) 14...♔f8 15 ♗c4 g6? (15...♕e8 16 ♕f3! ♗f6 17 ♗d2 and Black is in deep trouble) 16 ♗h6+ ♔g8 17 ♘g5 1-0 Klock-Klafki, Trier 1992.

c2) 14...♕d5 15 ♘g5 g6 16 ♕e2 ♕c5 (16...♕d6 17 ♘xf7 ♔xf7 18 ♗c4+ ♔e8 19 ♗g5 wins) 17 ♘xf7 ♔xf7 18 ♗c4+ ♔e8 19 ♗h6 and Black's task is not a happy one.

8 ♕f3 ♘bd7

8...♗g4 9 ♕f4 d5 (9...♕e8 10 ♗e3! and Black has nothing better than 10...d5 11 e5 and White will regain the piece, for example 11...♗d6 12 ♗e2 ♗xe2 13 ♘xe2 ♗c7 14 ♕f3) 10 e5 ♕e8 11 ♗e2! and White wins the piece back.

9 ♗b3 ♘b6

9...♕a5!? 10 0-0 ♕h5 11 ♕g3 ♕g4 12 ♕d3 ♘b6 13 f3 ♕h4 14 a4 a5 15

♗e3 and White still has reasonable compensation for the piece.

10 e5 ♗g4 11 ♕f4

White is better.

H2)

6...♖e8 7 ♗c4+ ♔f8 (D)

7...d5?! 8 ♘xd5 ♗e6 9 0-0 and now:

a) 9...♘xd5? loses to 10 exd5 ♗xd5 11 ♕h5+.

b) 9...c6 10 ♘xf6 ♗xf6 (10...♗xc4 11 ♘xe8 ♗xf1 12 ♕h5+ ♔g8 13 ♘xg7 and White emerges on top) 11 ♗xe6+ ♖xe6 12 e5 ♗e7 13 c4 gives White excellent compensation for the piece.

c) 9...♗xd5 10 exd5 ♗d6 11 ♗b3 ♔g8 12 c4 and White has full compensation.

d) 9...♘bd7 10 ♘xf6 ♘xf6 (or 10...♗xc4 11 ♘xe8 ♗xf1 12 ♕h5+ ♔g8 13 ♕d5+ ♔h8 14 ♘xg7 ♗xg2 15 ♔xg2 ♔xg7 16 ♕xb7 and White is doing fine) 11 d5 ♗g4 12 d6+ and White recovers the piece with advantage, Ristić-Ballandras, Avoine 1991.

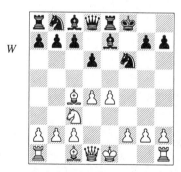

8 ♕f3 ♘c6 9 ♗e3 ♘a5

9...♕d7?! 10 h3 ♘a5 11 ♗d3 ♘c6 12 g4 h6 13 0-0-0 and White's activity, extra space and kingside play gives him good chances, 'Cyberpunk' – 'Megabute', USA 1993.

10 ♗d3 ♔g8 11 e5! dxe5 12 dxe5 ♘g4 13 0-0-0 ♘xe5??

13...♖f8?! 14 ♕e4 ♗f5 15 ♕a4 is good for White, while 13...♘xe3!? 14 ♗xh7+ ♔xh7 15 ♖xd8 ♖xd8 16 ♕xe3 should lead to some interesting play with ♕+3 vs ♖+2♗.

14 ♗xh7+ ♔xh7 15 ♕h5+ ♔g8 16 ♖xd8 ♖xd8 17 ♕xe5

White is winning, M.Albert-Köhler, Rheinland-Pfalz U-20 1991.

I)

5...c6 6 ♗d3 *(D)*

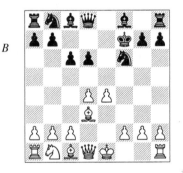

Now that White's light-squared bishop is unlikely to go quickly to the a2-g8 diagonal it is logical to develop it to this square so that White can castle quickly.

6...♗e7

6...g6 7 ♘c3 transposes to Line K1.

6...♕a5+ does not truly activate Black's queen and so constitutes a waste of time. 7 c3 ♗e6 8 0-0 ♕h5 9 ♗e2 and now:

a) 9...♕g6 10 ♘d2! ♔g8 (but not 10...♘xe4?? 11 ♗h5) 11 f4 ♘xe4 12 ♗d3 d5 (12...♘f2 13 f5!! ♕xg2+ 14 ♔xg2 ♘xd1 15 ♖xd1 ♗f7 16 ♘f3 with approximate equality) 13 f5 ♗xf5 14 ♕f3 ♘d6 15 ♗xf5 ♘xf5 16 ♕xf5 ♕xf5 17 ♖xf5 ♘d7 18 ♘b3 with equality.

b) 9...♕a5 10 ♘d2 with active compensation (and an improvement on 10 f4?! Midjord-I.Jones, Manila OL 1992), for example 10...♗e7 11 f4 g6 (11...♖f8 12 e5 ♘d5 13 f5 ♗c8 14 ♘b3 ♕c7 15 c4 ♘b6 16 ♗f4 and White has good chances) 12 f5 gxf5 13 exf5 ♗c8 14 ♗h5+! and now:

b1) 14...♔f8 15 ♘c4 ♕c7 16 ♗h6+ ♔g8 17 ♕f3 ♗f8 18 ♕g3+ ♗g7 19 ♖ae1! ♘xh5 20 ♖e8+ ♔f7 21 ♕xd6! ♕xd6 22 ♘xd6+ ♔f6 23 ♗xg7+ (23 ♘e4+ ♔f7 24 ♘d6+ with a draw by perpetual) 23...♔xg7 24 ♖xh8 ♔xh8 25 ♘xc8 ♘d7 26 ♘d6 ♖f8 27 ♖e1 gives White an edge.

b2) 14...♔g7 15 ♕e1! ♕c7 16 ♕g3+ ♔f8 17 ♕h3 with an unclear position where White has good practical chances.

7 0-0 g6

Or:

a) 7...♕a5 8 c3 (8 f4?! ♗g4 forces off the queens) 8...♖d8 9 f4 ♕h5 10 ♕e1! ♔g8 11 f5 and White's positional compensation offers good practical chances, for example 11...♖e8 12 ♗f4 d5 13 e5 and now Black has a choice of three lines:

a1) 13...♘g4 14 h3 ♘h6 15 f6 ♗xf6 (15...gxf6 loses to 16 ♗xh6 ♕xh6 17 exf6) 16 ♗e2! ♕g6 17 exf6 ♗xh3 18 ♖f2 with an unclear position.

a2) 13...♘e4 14 f6! gxf6 (14...♗f8 15 fxg7 ♗xg7 16 ♗xe4 dxe4 17 ♘d2 ♗f5 18 ♘xe4 ♗xe4 19 ♕xe4 with balanced chances) 15 exf6 ♗xf6 16

♗xe4 dxe4 17 ♗xb8 is good for White due to ♕g3+ as a follow-up.

a3) 13...♗f8 14 ♗e2 ♘g4 15 h3 ♗xf5 16 ♕g3 and White is well placed.

b) 7...♘a6!? 8 ♘c3 ♗e6 9 f4 ♕c7 10 e5 ♕b6?! 11 ♗xa6! (instead of 11 ♔h1?!, Vitoliňš-Aleksandrov, Riga rpd 1990) 11...♕xa6 12 exf6 ♗xf6 13 ♘e4 and White is doing well.

8 c4! ♗g7 9 ♘c3 ♘bd7 10 ♗e3

Black is struggling for activity and desperately needs a break in the centre.

10...♘f8

After 10...♖f8 or 10...♖e8 then 11 f4 just builds up the pressure.

11 h3 d5 12 e5 ♘e8 13 cxd5 cxd5 14 f4 ♗b4 15 f5 ♗xc3 16 bxc3 gxf5

16...♗xf5 is no better in view of 17 ♗xf5 gxf5 18 ♕h5.

17 ♕h5 ♔g8

17...♘g6 18 ♗h6+ ♔g8 19 ♗xf5 ♗xf5 (19...♘g7 20 ♗xg6! hxg6 21 ♕xg6 is strong for White) 20 ♕xf5 ♕e7 21 ♗g5! ♕c7 22 ♕e6+ ♔g7 23 ♖f5 gives Black big problems.

18 ♗xf5

White has a massive position, Vito-liňš-Butnorius, Vilnius 1985.

J)

5...c5!? 6 dxc5 (D)

Now Black can choose from:

Others:

a) 6...♕a5+ 7 ♘c3 ♕xc5 8 ♗e3 ♕c7 (8...♕a5 9 ♗c4+ ♗e6 10 ♗xe6+ ♔xe6 11 0-0 ♘c6 12 f4 with equal

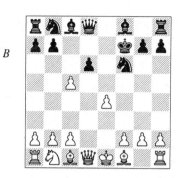

chances, Bielak-Borys, corr. 1990; 8...♕b4?! 9 a3! and Black has nothing better than to move the queen again because after 9...♕xb2?? 10 ♗d4 ♘c6 {10...♗e6 11 ♘b5 traps the queen} 11 ♖a2 ♗g4 12 f3 the black queen is still trapped) 9 ♗e2 ♗e7 10 0-0 ♖e8 11 ♘b5! ♕c6 12 ♘xa7 ♕xe4 13 ♗f3 and White has good positional compensation for the small material deficit, Bezgodov-Vasiliev, Ufa 1993.

b) 6...♗e6? 7 e5! ♘g4 8 ♕f3+ ♔g8 9 exd6 ♘c6 10 ♘c3? (10 ♕xg4! wins) 10...♖c8 11 ♕xg4 (White doesn't miss a second chance) 1-0 Messinger-Rack, Berlin 1989.

J1)

6...♕e8

Putting pressure on White's e-pawn as well as unpinning his own d-pawn.

7 ♘c3

7 ♗c4+? ♗e6 is fine for Black.

7...d5

7...♘xe4?? loses to 8 ♕d5+, while after 7...dxc5, 8 ♗g5!? is awkward for Black to meet.

8 ♗g5 ♘bd7

8...dxe4? 9 ♗xf6! gxf6 (9...♔xf6? 10 ♘d5+ ♔g6 11 ♘c7 is very strong for White) 10 ♕h5+ ♔e7 11 ♘d5+

&d8 12 ♕xe8+ ♔xe8 13 ♘c7+ and
White wins.

9 ♗b5 ♕e6

After 9...dxe4, 10 ♗xf6 with the
idea of playing ♘d5-c7 is excellent
for White.

10 0-0 ♗xc5?!

Better is 10...dxe4 11 ♕e2, with an
unclear position.

**11 exd5 ♕f5 12 ♕d2 ♘e5 13 ♖ae1
a6**

13...♖d8? loses to 14 ♗xf6 ♕xf6
15 ♘e4.

14 ♗e2 ♖d8 15 ♔h1 ♗b4

15...♗xf2? 16 ♖xf2 ♕xf2 17 ♗h5+
wins the black queen, while 15...♔g8
16 f4 gives White excellent attacking
chances.

**16 f4 ♘g6 17 ♗d3 ♕d7 18 f5 ♘f8
19 d6! ♔g8**

White wins after either 19...♕xd6
20 ♗c4+ or 19...♗xd6?? 20 ♗c4+.

**20 ♗c4+ ♔h8 21 ♗xf6 gxf6 22
♕d5 ♕g7 23 ♖e7 ♕g4**

23...♕xe7?? 24 ♕g8#.

24 h3 ♖xd6 25 ♕f7 ♗e6 26 ♕xf6+

1-0 Savko-Meijers, Latvian Ch
1994.

(Notes based on those by Blatny.)

J2)

6...d5!?

Black is happy to give up another
pawn if he can blast away White's centre and gain the initiative. However, in
doing so Black treads a thin line.

7 e5 ♕e8

7...♘e4 8 ♕f3+ ♔e8 (8...♔g8??
loses to 9 ♕xe4) 9 ♗d3 ♕c7 10 0-0
♕xe5 11 ♖e1 ♗e7 12 ♗xe4 dxe4 13
♖xe4 ♕xc5 14 ♘c3 and the position
remains a real mess.

**8 f4 ♗g4 9 ♗e2 ♗xe2 10 ♕xe2
♗xc5!?**

After 10...♘e4 11 ♗e3 ♘a6 12 ♘d2
♘xd2 13 ♕xd2 ♖d8 14 0-0-0 ♗xc5
15 ♗d4 ♖f8 16 f5 ♖g8?!, instead of 17
♖he1?! ♕a4!, Savko-Bauer, Denmark
1993, White can play 17 e6+!:

a) 17...♔f8 18 f6! is very strong for
White, e.g. 18...♕xe6 19 fxg7+ ♔f7
20 ♖hf1+ ♔g6 21 ♖de1 or 18...gxf6
19 ♕h6+ ♔e7 20 ♕xf6+ ♔d6 21 e7+,
winning for White in both cases.

b) 17...♔e7 18 ♕g5+ ♔d6 19
♗xg7 and Black is in trouble.

11 exf6 ♕c6 12 ♔d1! g6

Black has some compensation for
the pawns, Vitolinš-Khalifman, Bor-
zhomi 1984.

J3)

6...♘c6 7 ♗c4+ d5

After 7...♗e6 8 ♗xe6+ ♔xe6 9
cxd6 ♗xd6 10 0-0 ♕c7 11 f4 the position is unclear, Wach-Vanka, Prague
1989. White has regained material
parity but Black has his pieces actively
placed. However, Black's king in the
centre is not a help!

8 ♗xd5+ ♗e6

After 8...♘xd5? 9 exd5, not only
has White got four pawns for the piece
but Black has poor development, no
centre, and his king in the open –
White is well placed.

9 ♗xe6+ ♔xe6 10 ♕e2

Now Black cannot conveniently recover the pawn on c5 by 10...♗xc5
due to 11 ♕c4+.

10...♕a5+ 11 ♘c3 ♗xc5 12 0-0

White has an edge as the black king
cannot easily find a safe haven.

12...♔f7 13 ♕c4+ ♔g6 14 ♘d5

The complications are in White's favour, Vitolinš-Raetsky, USSR Cht 1988.

K)

5...g6 *(D)*

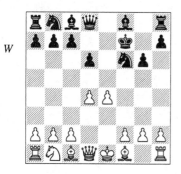

W

This is the most flexible move as it opens up a natural developing square for Black's dark-squared bishop or else a bolt-hole for his king. On top of that it provides extra cover for the f5-square, hopefully to discourage White from playing f2-f4-f5. However, if White can get in that plan successfully then it does tend to blast away Black's kingside cover.

6 ♘c3

Now:

K1:	**6...c6**	39
K2:	**6...♗e6**	40
K3:	**6...♗e7**	41
K4:	**6...♔g7**	41
K5:	**6...♗g7**	42

6...♕e8 transposes back to variation D.

K1)

6...c6 7 ♗d3

Now:

K11:	**7...♗e6**	39
K12:	**7...♗g7**	40

Or 7...♗g4 8 f3 ♗e6 9 ♗e3 ♗g7 10 ♕d2 with a tense position in which White's play will be based on getting his kingside/central pawns moving, i.e. with g4, h4 and h5 or g4, h3 and f4.

K11)

7...♗e6 8 ♗g5 *(D)*

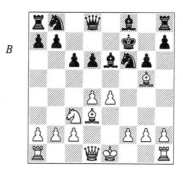

B

8...h6

Or 8...♕b6 9 e5:

a) 9...♕xb2 10 ♘a4 ♕a3 11 ♕f3 and Black is in trouble.

b) 9...♘g4 10 h3 ♘h6 (10...♕xb2 11 ♘a4 ♕a3 12 ♕f3+ ♔g8 13 ♗f5!! ♕xf3 14 ♗xe6+ ♔f7 15 ♗xf7+ ♔xf7 16 hxg4 and White is on top) 11 ♕f3+ ♘f5 12 g4 ♕xb2 13 ♔d2! and White is doing well.

c) 9...dxe5 10 ♕f3 and White is fine.

9 ♗h4 g5 10 ♗g3 ♗g7

10...♕b6 11 ♘a4 ♕a5+ (11...♕xd4?? 12 c3 traps the queen!) 12 c3 b5 13 e5 dxe5 (13...♕xa4 14 ♗c2 ♕a5 15 exf6 is unclear) 14 dxe5 ♘fd7 15 ♕f3+ and now:

a) 15...♔g8 16 ♕h5 ♗f7 17 ♗g6 ♗d5 18 ♗f5 ♖h7 (18...♗f7 19 ♗e6!! ♗xe6 20 ♕g6+ ♗g7 21 ♕xe6+ with a draw by perpetual as 21...♔f8 22 ♕d6+ ♔e8?? 23 ♕g6+ ♔d8 24 ♕xg7 ♖e8 25 0-0-0 ♕xa4 26 e6 ♖xe6 27 ♗xb8 wins) 19 ♗xh7+ ♔xh7 20 e6 ♗xe6 (20...♕xa4 21 ♕f7+ ♔h8 22 ♗e5+ ♘xe5 23 ♕xf8+ ♔h7 24 ♕f5+ is unclear) 21 ♕e8 ♗d5 22 ♗xb8 is also unclear.

b) 15...♔e8 leads to very unclear positions, e.g. 16 ♗g6+ ♔d8 17 0-0-0 ♔c8 18 ♖xd7!! ♗xd7 19 ♕f6 ♖g8 20 e6 and White is on top.

11 f4 gxf4 12 ♗xf4 ♕b6 13 ♗xd6 ♕xb2 14 ♘e2

White has play, with the b- and f-file on which to operate, as well as e4-e5 looming.

K12)

7...♗g7 8 0-0 ♖f8 *(D)*

8...♖e8 is no better, e.g. 9 h3 ♔g8 10 ♗e3 ♘bd7 11 f4 ♘d5!? 12 ♘xd5 cxd5 13 e5 ♘f8 14 ♕f3 ♗e6 15 g4 dxe5 16 dxe5 ♘d7 17 ♗d4 ♖f8 18 ♕g3 ♕c7 19 ♖ae1 ♘c5 20 f5 ♘xd3 21 ♕xd3 gxf5 22 gxf5 ♗f7 and White is doing fine, Rob-Torsten, Edmonton 1992.

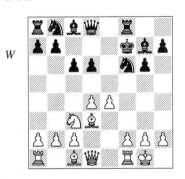

9 ♗g5! h6 10 ♗c4+ ♔e8

10...♗e6 11 ♗xe6+ ♔xe6 12 ♗h4 permits White the usual compensation for the piece.

11 ♗h4 ♕b6 12 ♗b3 ♘h5 13 e5 dxe5 14 dxe5 ♖f4

14...♘f4 15 ♘e4·g5 (15...♗xe5 16 ♖e1! leaves Black with problems) 16 ♘d6+ ♔e7 17 ♘xc8+ ♖xc8 18 ♕g4 and White is doing well.

15 ♗f6 ♖d4

15...♗xf6 16 exf6 ♖xf6 17 ♖e1+ ♔f8 18 ♘e4 is good for White.

15...♘xf6 16 exf6 ♖xf6 (after 16...♗xf6, 17 ♕d6 is strong) 17 ♖e1+ ♔f8 18 ♕e2 is also very good for White.

16 ♕c1

The position remains unclear but with good practical chances for White, for example 16...♘xf6 17 exf6 ♗xf6 18 ♖e1+ ♔d8 19 ♕xh6 and White's counterplay is obvious since Black's queenside remains undeveloped and his king is open.

K2)

6...♗e6 7 ♗d3 ♗g7 8 0-0 ♖f8 9 ♗g5! *(D)*

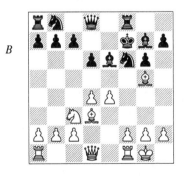

9...♕e8

9...h6 10 &h4 &bd7 11 f4 &g4 (11...c6? 12 f5 gxf5 13 d5 is fine for White) 12 &c4+ &e8 (12...d5 13 &xd5!! &xd1 14 &xf6+ &e7 15 &d5+ &e8 16 &xd8 and White will come out of the complications on top, e.g. 16...&xd4+ 17 &h1 &xc2 18 &xc7) 13 &e1 and with e4-e5 coming White is doing fine.

10 f4 &g8 11 f5 gxf5 12 exf5 &f7 13 &d2

In Stamnov-Morgado, Thessaloniki open 1988 White played 13 &f3?! and eventually lost. However, the text-move leads to interesting play.

13...&c6

After 13...c6 14 &ae1 &d8 15 &e4 Black must be careful, e.g. 15...d5 16 &c5 &b6 17 c3 and the white knight is heading for e6.

14 &h6 &xh6 15 &xh6 &bd7 16 &f4 &b6

16...&ae8? 17 &b5! &b6 18 &xd7 is good for White.

17 b3 &ae8 18 &af1

White still has a lot of play for the piece with two pawns, active pieces and a kingside initiative.

K3)

6...&e7 7 f4 d5 8 e5 &e4 9 &xe4 dxe4 10 &c4+ &g7 11 0-0 &f8 12 d5 *(D)*

It is awkward for Black to untangle.

12...&c5+

12...&d7 13 &e3 &b6 (13...&c5?! 14 &xc5 &xc5 15 &d4 b6 16 b4 and the e-pawn falls as well) 14 &b3 and now:

a) 14...h5 15 &d4 &f5 16 c4 &d7 17 e6+ &f6 (17...&f6 18 &d2 &b6 19 c5 &c8 20 &ad1 and White has

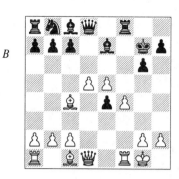

B

obvious counterplay) 18 &c3 b6 19 &ad1 and White has quite a bind.

b) 14...&f5 15 g4! &c8 16 c4 and the pawns are marching on.

13 &h1 &f5

13...h5 14 &e2 &f5 15 &e3 &d7 16 &xc5 &xc5 17 &e3 b6 18 b4 &b7 (18...&d7 19 &b3 a5 20 a3 is no better) 19 &ad1 a5 20 a3 and Black is still struggling for space and freedom to operate.

14 g4 &c8 15 f5 &h4

15...gxf5 16 gxf5 &h8 (16...&xf5? 17 &xf5 &xf5 18 &g4+ is good for White) 17 &h5 and Black must be very careful, e.g. 17...&e8 18 &xe8 &xe8 19 e6 e3 20 f6 and the pawns are not going to be stopped easily or only at too high a price.

16 f6+ &h8 17 &f4 e3 18 b4! g5

18...&xb4 19 &b2 g5 20 e6 and Black is in big trouble.

19 &b2 gxf4 20 e6 &xf6 21 bxc5

With an obscure position in which Black may well be in trouble.

K4)

6...&g7 7 f4 &e8 *(D)*

Or 7...d5 8 e5 &e4 9 &xe4 dxe4 10 &c4 with possibilities similar to Line K3.

7...♗g4 8 ♗e2 ♗xe2 9 ♕xe2 does little to improve Black's chances.

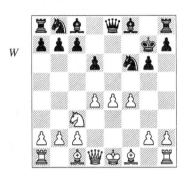

8 e5 dxe5

8...♗f5 9 ♗d3 ♗xd3 10 ♕xd3 ♘fd7 11 0-0 ♘a6 (11...c6 12 ♕h3 ♗e7 13 e6 ♘f6 14 f5 is awkward for Black) 12 ♕h3! dxe5 13 fxe5 h6 14 ♘d5 c6 15 e6! cxd5 16 ♖f7+ and now:

a) 16...♕xf7 17 exf7 ♖d8 (Black has problems after 17...♘f6 18 ♕b3! b6 19 ♗f4 ♔xf7 20 ♗e5) 18 ♗f4 and White has a lot of pressure, for example 18...♔xf7 19 ♖e1 ♔g7 20 ♕h4! ♖c8 21 ♖e7+! winning.

b) 16...♔g8 17 ♖xd7 ♖h7 18 ♖xh7 ♔xh7 19 ♗g5 is unclear, e.g. 19...♗g7 20 ♖f1 ♗xd4+ 21 ♔h1 h5 22 ♖f7+ ♔g8 23 ♗f6 ♗xf6 24 ♕d3!! ♕xf7 25 exf7+ ♔g7 26 ♕b5! ♖f8 (26...♘c7 27 ♕d7 ♖f8 28 ♕xc7 ♖xf7 29 ♕c5 with advantage to White) 27 ♕xb7 ♘c5 28 ♕xd5 ♘a4 is unclear.

9 fxe5 ♗b4 10 a3 ♗xc3+ 11 bxc3 ♘c6 12 ♗e2 ♘xe5!?

12...♘d5 (12...♘e4 13 ♗f3 ♘xc3 14 ♕d2 comes to the same thing) 13 ♗f3 ♘xc3 14 ♕d2 ♘b5! (14...♘xe5 15 ♕h6+ ♔g8 16 dxe5 ♕xe5+ 17 ♗e3 and White has excellent play for the pawn) 15 c3 ♘xe5 16 ♕h6+ ♔g8

17 dxe5 ♕xe5+ 18 ♕e3 ♕xe3+ 19 ♗xe3 gives White good compensation for the pawn.

13 dxe5 ♕xe5 14 0-0 ♗f5

14...♕xc3 15 ♖f3! ♕c6 (15...♕c5+ 16 ♗e3 ♕e7 17 ♕d4 and White has excellent play for the pawn as 17...♗g4 18 ♖xf6 ♕xf6 19 ♗h6+ ♔xh6 20 ♕xf6 ♗xe2 21 ♕f4+ (from now on Black's moves are forced if he doesn't wish to lose the loose bishop on e2) 21...g5 22 ♕f6+ ♔h5 23 ♕f7+ ♔g4 24 h3+ ♔h4 25 ♔h2 g4 26 g3+ ♔g5 27 h4+ ♔h6 28 ♕f6+ ♔h5 29 ♕g5#) 16 ♗b2 (White has excellent play) 16...♗f5 (16...♖f8? loses to 17 ♖xf6 ♖xf6 18 ♕d8 ♕d6 19 ♕xd6 cxd6 20 ♖f1 ♗f5 21 g4) 17 ♕d4 ♖hf8 18 ♗d3 and White is better.

15 ♕d2!

I believe this to be an improvement on 15 ♗f4?!, which has always been played in the past.

15...♕c5+

Black should go in for 15...h6!? 16 ♖b1, with equal chances.

16 ♔h1 ♘e4 17 ♕h6+ ♔f7

17...♔g8 18 ♖xf5!! gxf5 (18...♕xf5 loses to 19 ♗c4+) 19 ♕e6+ ♔g7 20 ♗h6#.

18 ♗e3 ♕xc3

18...♕c6 19 ♗d4 and Black has all sorts of problems.

19 g4

This is very good for White.

K5)

6...♗g7 7 ♗c4+ ♗e6 *(D)*

7...d5?! 8 ♘xd5 ♗e6 9 ♗g5 ♖e8 (9...c6 10 ♗xf6 ♗xf6 11 ♘xf6 and now 11...♕xf6 12 ♕d3 is approximately equal, while 11...♗xc4 12 ♘g4 ♕a5+

13 ♕d2 ♕xd2+ 14 ♔xd2 gives equal chances) 10 0-0 h6 11 ♗xf6 ♗xf6 12 ♘xf6 ♕xf6 13 e5 ♕f4 14 g3 ♕f5 15 ♗xe6+ ♖xe6 16 f4 with an unbalanced position where if White manages to keep control he may be a little better, Skotorenko-Sivets, Petroff mem corr. 1987.

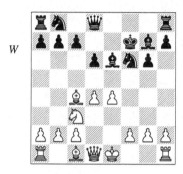

8 ♗xe6+ ♔xe6 9 f4 ♔f7
9...♖e8 10 e5 ♔f7 transposes.
10 e5 ♖e8
10...♘c6 11 0-0 dxe5?! 12 fxe5 ♕xd4+ (12...♘xd4 13 ♗g5! ♘f5 14 exf6 and Black has problems) 13

♕xd4 ♘xd4 14 exf6 ♗f8 and White has the edge, Saksis-Viksna, Latvian corr. Ch 1990.
10...♘e8?! 11 ♕f3 c6 12 0-0 is unclear.
11 0-0 ♘c6
11...♘fd7 12 ♕f3 and here White has good practical chances, for example:
a) 12...c6? 13 ♘e4 ♗f8 14 ♕b3+ is strong for White.
b) 12...♘c6? 13 ♕d5+ ♔f8 14 f5 and Black has problems.
c) 12...♔g8!? 13 ♕xb7 ♘b6 14 ♘d5! ♘a6! 15 c4 ♕c8 16 ♕c6 with approximately equal chances.
12 exf6 ♕xf6
12...♗xf6 13 ♘e2 ♕e7 14 ♖f2 and White remains a pawn ahead and must just untangle, e.g. 14...d5 (14...♔g7 15 d5!♘a5) 15 c3 followed by f4-f5 is better for White.
13 ♘b5! ♖e7 14 c3 a6 15 ♕b3+ ♔f8 16 f5!
White is on top, O'Neill-Solomon, Australia 1985.

3 Philidor Defence

1 e4 e5 2 ♘f3 d6

Although one of the long-standing defences to 1 e4, the Philidor tends to go in and out of fashion. One minute it is regarded as too passive (except for 3 d4 f5?! which is regarded as too risky!) the next a very solid approach to the opening, the next not offering Black any real winning chances except against inept play by White. Whatever your point of view it is a hard nut to crack and what's more there are several ways in which Black may employ it.

The normal and main move for White is...

3 d4 *(D)*

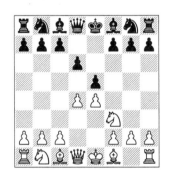

Against this we will consider the following:

A)
3...f5?!

I have not had this move played against me personally, though at one time Jonathan Mestel used to dabble with it, and it is best to be prepared just in case.

4 ♗c4! *(D)*

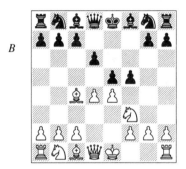

With the following variations:

a) 4...♗e7 5 dxe5 fxe4 (5...dxe5 6 ♕xd8+ ♗xd8 7 ♘xe5 ♘f6 8 ♘f7 ♖f8 9 e5 ♘e4 10 ♘xd8 ♔xd8 11 f3 and White is a pawn up with the two bishops) 6 ♕d5 exf3 7 ♕f7+ ♔d7 8 ♕xg7 fxg2 9 ♖g1 ♘h6 10 ♗xh6 and White is well placed.

b) 4...exd4 5 ♘g5 ♘h6 (after 5...♕e7, 6 0-0! is simple but good; 6...♘f6 7 exf5 gives Black problems) 6 ♘xh7 and now:

b1) 6...♖xh7 7 ♕h5+ ♔d7 8 ♕g6 ♖h8 (8...♕e8 9 ♕xh7 ♕xe4+ 10 ♗e2 ♕xg2 11 ♖f1 and White is a little better) 9 ♗xh6 and Black is in trouble as 9...♖xh6 or 9...gxh6 is met by 10 ♕xf5+ mating.

b2) 6...♕e7 7 ♗g5 ♕xe4+ (7...♕e5 8 ♕h5+ ♔d7 9 ♗xh6 ♖xh7 10 ♕f7+ ♗e7 11 ♗g5 and White has the edge especially as 11...♕xe4+? 12 ♔d2! asks for trouble down the e-file) 8 ♔d2! and Black has problems. Possibly the best try is 8...d5 9 ♖e1 ♗b4+ 10 c3 dxc4 11 ♕h5+ ♘f7 12 cxb4 but Black obviously doesn't get enough.

b3) 6...♘g4! 7 ♘g5 and now:

b31) 7...♕e7 8 ♗f7+ ♔d8 (8...♔d7 9 ♗e6+ ♔d8 10 exf5 is very strong for White) 9 ♗b3 ♖h5 (9...♖xh2 10 ♖xh2 ♘xh2 11 ♕h5 ♘g4 12 ♘f7+ ♔e8 13 ♘xd6+ ♔d8 14 ♘f7+ ♔e8 15 ♘d2! ♘f6 16 ♕g6 fxe4 17 ♘g5+ ♔d8 18 ♘dxe4 and White has the edge) 10 h3 ♘f6 11 0-0 fxe4 12 ♕xd4 ♘c6 13 ♕a4 ♗d7 14 ♘c3 is unclear but probably favours White.

b32) 7...♘xh2 8 ♗f7+ ♔e7 9 ♗h5 g6 10 ♗xg6 ♘f3+ 11 ♔e2 and Black has big problems.

c) 4...♘c6 5 ♘g5 ♘h6 6 d5 ♘b8 7 ♘c3 f4 8 h4 ♗g4 9 f3 ♗d7 10 g3! fxg3 11 f4 and White will eventually recover the pawn with a terrific bind.

d) 4...♘f6 5 ♘g5 ♕e7 (5...d5 6 dxe5 dxc4 {6...♘xe4 7 ♕xd5!} 7 ♕xd8+ ♔xd8 8 exf6 leaves White on top) 6 ♗f7+ ♔d8 7 ♗b3 exd4 8 0-0 and White once again is well placed.

e) 4...fxe4 5 ♘xe5! d5 (5...dxe5 6 ♕h5+ ♔d7 7 ♕f5+ ♔c6 8 ♕xe4+ with two pawns and strong attacking chances for the piece) 6 ♕h5+ g6 7 ♘xg6 ♘f6 8 ♕e5+ ♗e7 9 ♗b5+ (or 9 ♘xh8 dxc4 10 ♘c3 ♘c6 11 ♕g5 ♗e6 12 0-0 ♕d7 13 d5 is also very strong) 9...c6 10 ♘xe7 ♕xe7 11 ♗e2 ♖g8 12

g3 is better for White as he is a sound pawn ahead.

f) 4...c6 5 exf5 e4 (5...d5 6 ♘xe5! dxc4 7 ♕h5+ g6 8 fxg6 ♘f6 9 g7+ ♘xh5 10 gxh8♕ ♕xd4 11 0-0 and White is winning) 6 ♘g5 ♘f6 7 ♘f7 wins.

B)

3...♗g4?

One of the original and not so good ideas behind the Philidor.

4 dxe5 ♗xf3

4...♘d7!? 5 exd6 ♗xd6 6 ♘c3 ♕e7 (6...♘gf6 7 h3 ♗h5 8 ♗d3 and Black has no real compensation for the pawn) 7 h3 ♗h5 8 ♗d3 c6 9 g4 ♗g6 10 ♗g5 f6 11 ♗d2 ♗f7 12 ♕e2 0-0-0 13 0-0-0 and Black has little to show for the pawn, Shabalov-Laub, Bern 1992.

5 ♕xf3 dxe5 6 ♗c4 *(D)*

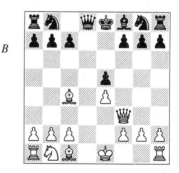

B

6...♘f6?

Alternatives:

a) 6...f6? 7 ♕b3 ♕d4?? 8 ♗f7+ ♔e7 9 ♕e6+ ♔d8 10 ♕e8# (1-0) Rotman-Bornarel, Bern 1992.

b) 6...♕f6 7 ♕b3 ♗c5 8 0-0 ♗b6 (8...b6 9 ♗e3 ♘d7 10 ♘c3 c6 11 ♖ad1 ♘e7 12 ♖xd7! ♔xd7 13 ♗xc5 g6

{13...bxc5 14 ♕b7+ wins} 14 ♗xf7 ♔c7 15 ♗e3 ♖af8 16 ♗e6 1-0 Sulliman-Bernschutz, Dubai OL 1986) 9 a4 a5 10 ♘c3 ♘e7 11 ♗e3 ♘d7 12 ♖ad1 and with the two bishops and superior development White has very good prospects of an attack.

c) After 6...♕d7!? Black still has little to show for the fact that White has two bishops in an open position, and in the long term White's light-squared bishop on the a2-g8 diagonal is always going to prove to be a real monster. 7 0-0 c6 8 ♖d1 ♕c7 9 a4 ♘f6 10 ♘d2! (much better than the obvious c3-square; this knight has a real future) 10...♗e7 11 ♘f1 ♘bd7 12 ♘g3 0-0 13 ♘f5 ♘c5 14 ♗h6! ♘e8 15 ♕g4 ♗f6 16 ♗e3 ♘e6 17 ♘h6+ ♔h8 18 ♘xf7+ and White is obviously doing very well, Apicella-Assaf, Moscow OL 1994.

7 ♕b3 ♕e7

7...♕d7 8 ♕xb7 ♕c6?? 9 ♗b5 wins the black queen.

8 ♗xf7+! ♔d8

8...♕xf7 9 ♕xb7 wins.

9 ♕xb7 ♕b4+ 10 ♕xb4 ♗xb4+ 11 c3

White is already two pawns to the good.

11...♗c5 12 ♗g5 ♘bd7 13 ♘d2 ♖f8 14 ♗e6 h6 15 ♗xd7 hxg5 16 ♗c6 ♖b8 17 ♘f3 ♖xb2? 18 0-0-0+

1-0 Tenk-Egert, Brno 1930.

C)

3...♘d7 4 ♗c4 *(D)*

The main two moves for Black now are:

C1: **4...♗e7**   47
C2: **4...c6**   47

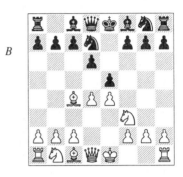

B

Others that have been tried are:

a) 4...h6? gives White a choice between 5 0-0!, heading for a main line where Black's ...h6 should be out of place as it not only loses time but weakens the g6-square, or speculating with 5 dxe5 dxe5 6 ♗xf7+!? ♔xf7 7 ♘xe5+ ♔f6 8 ♕d4 c5 9 ♘xd7++ ♔e7 10 ♕xc5+ ♔xd7 11 ♕b5+ ♔e7 12 ♘c3 ♕d7 13 ♘d5+ ♔f7 14 ♕b3 ♔g6 15 ♗f4 ♘f6 16 ♘c7 ♖b8 17 f3 ♘h5 18 ♗e5 ♕e7 19 ♕c3 ♕b4 20 ♘d5 ♕xc3+ ½-½ F.Meyer-C.Herbrechtsmeier, 2nd Bundesliga 1991/2.

b) 4...♕e7?! misplaces the queen since ...g6 and ...♗g7 is not going to offer Black an easy road to equality. After 5 ♘c3 c6 6 a4 a5 7 0-0 g6 8 ♘g5 ♘h6 9 f4 ♘b6 10 ♗b3 f6 11 ♘f3 White has a nice edge, Kopp-J.Fischer, 2nd Bundesliga 1991/2.

c) 4...♘b6?! 5 ♗b3 exd4 6 ♕xd4 ♗e6 7 ♗xe6 fxe6 8 0-0 (Black's main problem is not so much his lack of development or king safety as the long-term problem of his dark-squared bishop) 8...e5 9 ♕d3 h6 (after 9...♕d7 10 ♘c3 ♘f6 11 a4 a5 12 ♗e3 c5? 13 ♘d2 ♖c8 14 ♘c4 ♘xc4 15 ♕xc4 Black has more holes than a PGA Tour, Schlechter-Mortimer, Paris 1900) 10

Ꮚc3 c6 11 a4 a5 12 ♗e3 ♗e7 13 ♖fd1 ♕c7 14 ♖a3! (the kind of move that's hard to see – a bit of lateral rook development) 14...♖d8 15 ♖b3 Ꮚd7 16 ♕c4 ♖c8 17 ♕e6 Ꮚf8 18 ♕g4 g6 19 ♗b6 Ꮚf6 (19...♕d7? 20 Ꮚxe5) 20 ♗xc7 Ꮚxg4 21 ♗xd6 ♗xd6 22 ♖xd6 and White has a technically won position, Vujanović-Spajić, Yugoslav Cht 1994.

d) 4...exd4!? 5 Ꮚxd4 Ꮚgf6 6 0-0 g6 (6...Ꮚxe4? 7 ♖e1 Ꮚdf6 8 ♗b5+! ♗d7 {8...c6 9 Ꮚxc6!} 9 ♗xd7+ ♕xd7 {9...♔xd7 10 ♖xe4 Ꮚxe4 11 ♕g4+ is good for White} 10 f3 wins a piece) 7 ♖e1 ♗g7 8 Ꮚc3 0-0 with approximate equality, Golubev-Yanvariov, Moscow 1995.

e) 4...Ꮚgf6? 5 dxe5 Ꮚxe5 (5...dxe5 6 Ꮚg5!) 6 Ꮚxe5 dxe5 7 ♗xf7+ ♔xf7 8 ♕xd8 ♗b4+ 9 ♕d2 ♗xd2+ 10 Ꮚxd2 and White is a sound pawn ahead.

C1)

4...♗e7? *(D)*

It is surprising how many people fall for the same old trap!

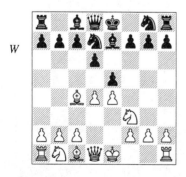

5 dxe5

Now Black must decide which way to recapture!

5...Ꮚxe5

5...dxe5? 6 ♕d5 ♗b4+ (6...Ꮚh6?? 7 ♗xh6 wins a piece for nothing) 7 c3 ♕e7 8 cxb4 Ꮚb6 9 ♕d3 ♕xb4+ 10 Ꮚbd2 1-0 Rantanen-Tuomala, Kuopio 1992.

6 Ꮚxe5 dxe5 7 ♕h5 g6 8 ♕xe5 Ꮚf6

8...f6?! 9 ♕c3 leaves Black a pawn down in a miserable position.

9 ♗h6 ♕d6

9...♖g8?! is not really any better, e.g. 10 ♕b5+ ♕d7 (10...c6? 11 ♕b3 or 10...Ꮚd7? 11 ♕d5 ♗b4+ 12 c3 ♕f6 13 cxb4 and in either case White is winning) 11 ♕xd7+ and White is a pawn up for nothing.

10 ♕xd6 cxd6 11 Ꮚc3

White is just a pawn up in a good position.

C2)

4...c6 5 0-0 ♗e7

5...h6? 6 dxe5 dxe5 (6...Ꮚxe5? 7 Ꮚxe5 dxe5 8 ♗xf7+ and White is well on top) 7 ♗xf7+! ♔xf7 8 Ꮚxe5+ ♔f6 (8...♔e6 9 Ꮚg6 ♖h7 10 e5! ♔f7 11 ♕d3 ♔e8 {11...♗c5 12 Ꮚf4! and Black has no defence} 12 Ꮚf4 wins as well) 9 ♕d4 ♔e6 (notice how after 9...c5 Black is a tempo down on the note given to 4...h6? – then 10 Ꮚxd7+ ♔e7 11 ♕xc5+ wins) 10 Ꮚg6 ♖h7 11 ♕c4+ ♔f6 (11...♔d6 12 ♗f4+ and Black falls apart) 12 e5+ ♔xg6 (12...Ꮚxe5? 13 ♕h4+ wins the queen) 13 ♕e4+ ♔f7 14 e6+ ♔f6 (14...♔e7? 15 exd7+ and Black has gone) 15 exd7 ♗xd7 16 ♕xh7 and Black is quite lost.

6 dxe5 dxe5

6...Ꮚxe5? 7 Ꮚxe5 dxe5 8 ♕h5! wins a pawn.

7 ♘g5! *(D)*

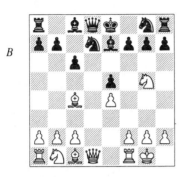

Now Black has played:

C21: 7...♘h6   48

C22: 7...♗xg5   48

C21)

7...♘h6 8 ♘e6! fxe6 9 ♗xh6

With the following possibilities for Black:

a) 9...0-0 10 ♕g4 ♗f6 11 ♗xe6+ ♔h8 12 ♗e3 ♕e7 and Black has little to show for the pawn, Akopian-Radulov, Cannes 1993.

b) 9...♘b6 10 ♕h5+ and now:

b1) 10...g6 11 ♕e2 and then:

b11) 11...♕d4!? 12 ♗b3 ♕xb2 13 ♘d2 and White's piece activity more than compensates for Black's extra e-pawn, e.g. 13...♗f8 14 ♗e3 ♗g7?! (14...♗e7 15 ♕g4 0-0 16 ♗xe6+ ♔h8 17 ♗xc8 ♖axc8 18 ♕e6 ♖ce8 19 ♕b3! and White has an edge; 14...♕c3 15 ♕g4 ♗e7 16 a4! is better for White) 15 ♗xb6 axb6 16 ♘c4 ♕d4 17 ♖ad1 ♕c5 18 ♘d6+ ♔e7 19 ♕g4 is very strong for White.

b12) 11...♘xc4 12 ♕xc4 ♕c7 13 ♘d2 ♗d7 14 ♘f3 ♗f6 15 ♖ad1 and White has a nice comfortable position with very good prospects of converting

it long term for the full point, Zhu-rakhov-E.Rotshtein, Ukraine 1966.

b2) 10...♔f8? 11 f4!! ♗c5+ (or 11...♕d4+ 12 ♔h1 ♕xc4 13 ♘d2) 12 ♔h1 ♔g8 13 f5! gxh6 (13...♘xc4 14 f6 gxf6 15 ♕g4+ ♔f7 16 ♕g7+ ♔e8 17 ♕xh8+ ♔d7 18 ♕xh7+ ♕e7 19 ♕g6 is very strong for White) 14 fxe6 ♕e7 15 ♖f7 ♕g5 16 ♖f8+ 1-0 Van der Wiel-Van Baarle, Amsterdam 1983.

c) 9...♗f6 10 ♕h5+ ♔e7 (10...g6 11 ♕g4 is pleasant for White) 11 ♗e3 ♕e8 12 ♕h3 ♘f8 13 ♗c5+ ♔f7 and now, rather than 14 f4?!, which was unclear in Wittmann-Granda, Thessaloniki OL 1988, it was time for White to be calm – the simple 14 ♘c3 leaves White with all the chances.

C22)

7...♗xg5 8 ♕h5 *(D)*

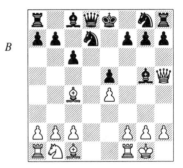

Black has now tried:

a) 8...g6 9 ♕xg5 ♕xg5 10 ♗xg5 ♘c5 11 ♘d2 ♘e6 12 ♗e3 ♘f6 13 ♘f3 and then:

a1) 13...♘g4?! 14 ♗d2 ♘d4 15 ♗c3! ♘xc2 16 ♖ac1 ♘d4 17 ♘xd4 exd4 18 ♗xd4 f6 19 ♗b3 ♔e7 20 ♖fd1 ♘e5 (20...♗e6 21 ♗c5+! ♔f7 22 ♖d7+ wins) 21 ♗xe5 fxe5 22 ♖c5 and White wins an important pawn, Krakops-Jirovsky, Zagan jr Wch 1997.

a2) 13...♘xe4 14 ♘xe5 ♘d6 15 ♗d3 gives White an advantage due to his bishop-pair, extra space and better development, Vasiukov-Murshed, Qatar 1993.

b) 8...♕e7 9 ♕xg5! ♕xg5 10 ♗xg5 ♘gf6 11 f3 and here:

b1) 11...♘c5 12 ♘d2! (it has much more of a future here than on c3) 12...♘fd7 13 b4 ♘a4 14 ♗b3 ♘ab6 15 c4 f6 16 ♗e3 ♘f8 17 c5 ♘bd7 18 ♘c4 and White, with the two bishops, an outpost on d6, more space and completed development, has every chance scoring the full point, Dreev-Korhonen, Kiljava jr Wch 1984.

b2) 11...b5! 12 ♗e2 ♘b6 13 ♘d2 ♗e6 and now, instead of 14 b3?!, Topalov-Franco, Pamplona 1994/5, 14 c4! still leaves White some advantage, e.g. 14...♘xc4 15 ♗xc4 bxc4 16 ♖fc1 ♖b8 17 ♘xc4 ♗xc4 18 ♖xc4 ♖xb2 19 ♖xc6 and Black still has work to do to equalize.

c) 8...♕f6 9 ♗xg5 ♕g6 10 ♕xg6 (10 ♕h4!? is also possible) 10...hxg6 11 ♘d2 ♘gf6 12 f3 ♘c5 13 ♗e3 ♘e6 14 ♗b3 ♔e7 15 ♘c4 ♘d7 16 ♖ad1 b6 17 ♖f2 ♖d8 18 ♖fd2 and White has a definite edge, Wittmann-Barua, Frunze 1983.

Overall 3...♘d7 leaves Black hard-pressed to gain anything more than a grim fight for survival.

D)

3...exd4 4 ♘xd4 *(D)*

Black now normally plays either:

D1: 4...g6   50
D2: 4...♘f6   53

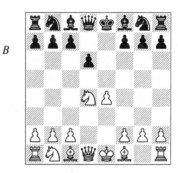

B

Others:

a) 4...c5?! 5 ♗b5+ and now:

a1) 5...♘d7 6 ♘f5! a6 7 ♗xd7+ ♕xd7 8 ♘e3 ♘f6 9 ♘c3 and White's control of d5 together with Black's backward d-pawn gives him a positional plus especially since 9...g6 10 ♘ed5 ♘xd5 (10...♕d8 11 ♗g5 ♗g7 12 ♕f3 winning a piece) 11 ♘xd5 ♕d8 12 ♕f3 ♗g7 13 ♗g5 ♕xg5 (13...♕a5+ 14 c3 leaves White with a pleasant position) 14 ♘c7+ ♔e7 15 ♘xa8 ♗xb2 16 ♖b1 ♗e6 17 0-0 ♕e5 18 c3! gives Black insufficient play for the exchange.

a2) 5...♗d7 6 ♗xd7+ ♘xd7 (or 6...♕xd7 7 ♘f3 ♘f6 8 ♘c3 and White has a positional plus) 7 ♘f3 ♘gf6 8 ♘c3 a6 9 ♗f4 ♘b6 (9...♕b6 10 ♖b1! is fine for White) 10 0-0 ♗e7 11 ♕d3 ♘h5 12 ♗e3 0-0 13 ♖ad1 c4 14 ♕d4 and White is doing well, Gallinnis-Frese, corr. 1982.

b) 4...♘d7 5 ♘c3 ♘gf6?! 6 ♗e2 ♘c5 7 0-0! ♗e7 (7...♘cxe4? 8 ♘xe4 ♘xe4 9 ♗b5+ ♗d7 {9...c6 10 ♘xc6!} 10 ♗xd7+ ♕xd7 {10...♔xd7? 11 ♕g4+} 11 ♖e1 d5 12 f3 winning a piece) 8 f3 and Black is solid but passive.

c) 4...♘c6 5 ♘c3 and then:

c1) 5...♘xd4 6 ♕xd4 c6? 7 ♗f4 ♕b6 8 0-0-0 ♗e6 9 ♕xb6 axb6 10 ♗xd6 ♘f6 (10...♗xa2 11 ♗xf8 ♔xf8 12 b3 and the bishop on a2 is dead) 11 ♗xf8 ♖xf8 12 ♗e2 (White is a good pawn up for nothing) 12...♔e7 13 f4 b5 14 a3 g6 15 ♗f3 ♗g4? 16 e5 1-0 Ag.Fernandez-Navarro, Spain 1992.

c2) 5...g6 6 ♘d5! ♗d7 (6...♗g7? 7 ♘b5 and Black is in trouble) 7 h4 ♗g7 8 ♘b5 ♖c8 9 ♗g5 ♘ce7 (9...f6 10 ♗f4 a6?! 11 ♘bxc7+ ♖xc7 12 ♘xc7+ ♕xc7 13 ♕xd6 and with ♖+2 vs 2♘ White is doing fine; 9...♘ge7 10 ♘xa7!) 10 ♕f3 ♗xb5 11 ♗xb5+ c6 12 ♘xe7 ♘xe7 13 ♗c4 0-0 14 c3 and with the two bishops White has the edge, Vaïsser-Foisor, Bern 1992.

d) 4...d5?! 5 exd5 ♕xd5 6 ♗e3 ♘f6 7 ♘c3 ♗b4 8 ♘db5 0-0 (8...♕c6 9 ♕d4 ♗xc3+ 10 ♕xc3 ♕xc3+ 11 bxc3! ♘a6 12 ♘xa7 ♗f5 13 ♗d3 with advantage to White) 9 ♘xc7 ♕a5 10 ♘xa8 ♗g4 (10...♗xc3+ 11 bxc3 ♕xc3+ 12 ♗d2 ♖e8+ 13 ♗e2 ♕e5 14 0-0 ♕xe2 15 ♘c7 and White is a clear exchange up; 10...♕d5 11 ♗d2 and Black has nothing) 11 ♗e2 ♖d8 12 0-0!? ♖xd1 13 ♖axd1 ♘c6 14 ♗xg4 ♘xg4 15 ♖d5 ♕a6 16 ♘c7 ♕c4 17 ♘7b5 ♘f6 (17...♘xh2? 18 ♖fd1 a6 19 ♖1d4! ♘xd4 20 ♖xd4 ♕c6 21 ♖d8+ ♗f8 22 ♘d5 winning) 18 ♖d3 ♗xc3 (18...a6 19 ♘a7!) 19 ♘xc3 and with 2♖+♙ vs ♕ White is doing very well, Kapengut-G.Kuzmin, USSR 1972.

e) 4...♗e7 5 ♘c3 ♘f6 transposes to 4...♘f6 5 ♘c3 ♗e7, which is discussed shortly in D2.

D1)
4...g6 5 ♘c3 ♗g7 6 ♗e3 *(D)*

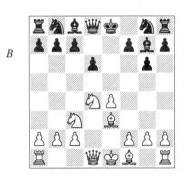

6...♘f6
Alternatives:

a) 6...♘c6 7 ♕d2 and now 7...♘f6 will transpose to the main line, while 7...♘ge7?! reaches line 'b'.

b) 6...♘e7?! (the knight simply is not as useful on this square as on f6) 7 ♕d2 ♘bc6 8 0-0-0 0-0 9 h4! ♘xd4 10 ♗xd4 ♗xd4 11 ♕xd4 ♘c6 12 ♕d2 h5 13 ♗e2 ♘e5 14 ♖df1! (a good preparatory move) 14...♗e6 15 f4 ♘c4 (15...♘g4 16 f5! and things start to get a little embarrassing for Black) 16 ♕d3 c6 17 b3 ♘b6 18 f5 ♗c8 19 g4! (this is almost like an attack against the Dragon with Black getting virtually no counterplay!) 19...hxg4 20 ♗xg4 ♘d7 21 ♕g3 ♘e5 22 ♗e2 ♔h7 23 f6 ♖g8 24 ♕g5 ♕a5 25 ♘b5!! ♗g4 (25...♕xa2 26 h5 ♕a1+ 27 ♔d2 ♕a5+ 28 c3 ♕a2+ 29 ♔e3 and Black has run out of checks) 26 h5 1-0 Ivkov-Fallon, Moscow OL 1956. A beautifully controlled attacking game by White.

7 ♕d2 0-0
7...♘c6 8 f3 0-0 9 0-0-0 transposes back to the main line.

7...d5!? 8 exd5 ♘xd5 9 ♘db5 ♘xc3 (9...♘xe3 10 ♕xe3+ ♗e6 11 ♖d1 ♘d7 12 ♗c4 and White is better; 9...c6 10 0-0-0 a6 { 10...♗e6 11 ♘xd5

♗xd5 12 ♗c5 is good for White} 11 ♗d4 0-0 {11...♗xd4 12 ♕xd4 0-0 13 ♘xd5 and White is better} 12 ♗xg7 ♔xg7 13 ♘a3 ♕f6 14 ♘xd5 cxd5 15 ♕xd5 ♕xf2 16 ♗c4 with advantage to White) 10 ♕xd8+ ♔xd8 11 ♘xc3 and White has a small edge.

8 0-0-0

And now this variation splits:

8...a6 9 f3 b5 10 ♗g5 ♕e8?! (after 10...♖e8 play transposes back to main lines) 11 ♗h6! b4 12 ♗xg7 ♔xg7 (12...bxc3 13 ♕h6 is too much for Black to handle) 13 ♘d5 ♘xd5 14 exd5 and White is well placed.

D11)

8...♖e8 9 f3 *(D)*

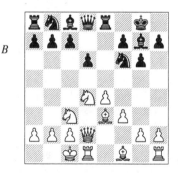

9...♘c6

9...d5?! 10 ♘b3 c6 11 ♗h6 ♗h8 12 exd5 cxd5 (12...♘xd5 13 ♘xd5 cxd5 14 ♕xd5 and White is a good pawn up, for example 14...♕f6 15 ♕d4! ♕c6 16 ♕f4) 13 ♘xd5 ♘c6 14 ♘c3 ♕b6 15 ♗c4 ♘e5 16 ♗b5 ♗d7 17 ♗xd7 ♘fxd7 18 ♖he1 (White is a good pawn ahead with d5 begging for his

knight) 18...♘f8 19 ♘d5 ♕a6 20 ♔b1 ♖ac8 (20...♘c4 21 ♕b4!) 21 ♕b4 ♕c6 22 ♕xf8+! ♖xf8 23 ♘e7# (1-0) Van Mil-Reinderman, Wijk aan Zee 1993.

9...a6?! 10 g4 b5 11 ♗g5 ♗b7 12 h4 ♘bd7 13 h5 c5 14 ♘b3 and White has the better attacking prospects, Jokšić-Lehmann, Plovdiv 1975.

10 h4 ♘e5

10...♘xd4 11 ♗xd4 ♗e6 12 h5 c6 (12...♘xh5 13 ♗xg7 ♘xg7 {13...♔xg7 14 g4 ♘f6 15 ♕h6+ ♔g8 16 e5! and White's attack crashes through} 14 ♕h6 is obviously good for White) 13 hxg6 fxg6. Now instead of 14 ♕g5?!, Radulov-Uusi, USSR 1970, 14 g4! seems better as with moves like ♕d2-h2 White's attacking chances look the stronger.

11 ♗h6 ♗h8 12 h5!

A typical pawn sac *à la* Dragon!

12...♘xh5

12...gxh5 13 g4 hxg4 14 f4 ♘ed7 (14...♘f3 15 ♘xf3 gxf3 16 ♖g1+ wins) 15 f5 ♘xe4 16 ♕f4 is strong for White.

12...a6 (Black tries to avoid being tempted to take on h5 hoping this will keep him more solid) 13 ♗g5 b5 14 ♕e1! (coming round to h4 with the idea of then forcing open the h-file) 14...♕d7 15 ♕h4 and Black has nothing better to do than open up the h-file for White, Bryson-I.Robertson, Scottish Ch (Aviemore) 1997.

13 g4 ♘g3 14 ♖h3 ♘xf1 15 ♖xf1

Now Black needs to be active or White will come on down the h-file.

15...c5 16 ♘f5! ♘c4

Now and for the remainder of the game it is too dangerous for Black to take, e.g. 16...gxf5 17 gxf5 ♗f6 18 ♘d5 ♔h8 19 ♖fh1 ♖g8 20 ♗f8!! and White's attack comes crashing through with, for example, 20...♗h4 (20...♖xf8 21 ♖xh7+ ♔g8 22 ♖h8+ ♗xh8 23 ♕h6 and mate cannot be avoided) 21 ♗e7 ♖g1+ 22 ♖xg1 ♗xe7 23 ♘xe7 ♕xe7 24 ♖xh7+! and mates.

17 ♕d3 ♗e6 18 ♗f4 ♕b6 19 b3 ♘e5 20 ♕d2 ♗xf5 21 gxf5 ♕b4 22 ♖xh7!! ♔xh7 23 ♖h1+ ♔g8 24 ♖xh8+!!

1-0 Emms-Summerscale, London 1997. Just so as you know, White mates by force: 24...♔xh8 (24...♔g7 25 f6+! ♔xf6 26 ♕xd6+ ♔g7 27 ♗h6+ ♔xh8 28 ♕f6+) 25 ♗xe5+ ♔g8 26 ♕h6 f6 27 ♕xg6+ ♔f8 28 ♕xf6+.

D12)

8...♘c6 9 f3 ♘xd4

9...♖e8 transposes to Line D11.

10 ♗xd4 ♗e6 11 g4 *(D)*

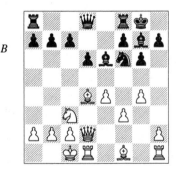

The difference between this and the last variation is that now (at least temporarily) White's dark-squared bishop is on the a1-h8 diagonal, and therefore this thrust (rather than 11 h4) is more logical. In fact the threats are so apparent that Black feels obliged to kick the bishop off the long diagonal immediately.

11...c5 12 ♗e3 ♕a5 13 ♗h6 ♗xh6

Alternatives:

a) 13...♖fd8!? (as opposed to a queenside thrust Black aims for a central break while 'unpinning' his dark-squared bishop) 14 ♗xg7 ♔xg7 15 h4 and now:

a1) 15...♗xa2? 16 h5 ♗e6 17 hxg6 ♕a1+ 18 ♘b1 ♗a2 19 ♕h6+ ♔h8 (19...♔g8 20 gxh7+ ♘xh7 21 ♕xh7+ ♔f8 22 ♔d2! {calm as you like!} 22...♕xb2 23 ♕h8+ and White wins) 20 g7+ ♔g8 21 ♕xf6 d5 (21...♕xb1+ 22 ♔d2 and Black's queen is trapped) 22 ♕h6 ♕xb1+ 23 ♔d2 dxe4+ 24 ♔e3!.

a2) 15...h5 16 gxh5 ♘xh5 17 ♖g1 b5 18 ♕g5 b4 19 ♘b1 and White has the better prospects, Yurtaev-Gulko, Frunze 1985.

b) 13...b5!? 14 ♗xg7 ♔xg7 15 g5 ♘h5 16 ♕xd6! b4 (16...♖ad8 17 ♕e5+ ♔g8 18 ♖xd8 ♖xd8 19 ♗xb5! is strong for White) 17 ♘d5 and now:

b1) 17...♕xa2? 18 ♕e5+ f6 19 ♕xe6 ♕a1+ 20 ♔d2 ♕xb2 21 ♕e7+ ♔h8 (21...♖f7? 22 ♕xc5) 22 ♕xc5! ♖ac8 23 ♕xb4 ♕xc2+ 24 ♔e1 and where is Black's attack?

b2) 17...♗xd5 18 ♕xd5 ♕c7 (after 18...♖ad8 19 ♕e5+ ♔g8 20 ♗c4 Black has no real compensation for the pawn) 19 ♕d6! and White is a pawn up in a better position.

14 ♕xh6 b5

14...♗xa2? 15 h4 ♗e6 16 h5 c4 17 hxg6 fxg6 18 g5 ♘h5 19 ♖xh5 1-0 Bauer-Kuhn, corr. 1990.

15 ♗xb5 ♖ab8 16 ♕f4 ♘e8 17 ♗xe8 ♖fxe8 18 ♖xd6 ♗xa2

18...罝xb2!? 19 當xb2 罝b8+ (after 19...豐b4+ 20 當c1 豐xc3 21 罝hd1 豐a3+ 22 當d2 豐b4+ 23 當e2 White's king escapes) 20 當c1 豐xc3 21 罝hd1 豐a3+ 22 當d2 and Black's compensation is mainly optical.

19 豐f6 魚e6 20 罝hd1 豐a1+ 21 當d2 豐a5

21...豐xb2? 22 罝b1 豐a3 23 罝xb8 罝xb8 24 罝xe6 fxe6 25 豐xe6+ and White will pick up the black rook.

22 當e3! c4

22...罝xb2? 23 罝xe6! wins.

23 h4!?

23 罝b1 is the 'safe' option, when White should have good chances of securing the full point if he is careful.

23...罝xb2 24 當f4!

24 罝xe6? 豐c5+! is strong for Black.

After the text-move the position is still unclear but should favour White. Here is the finish of the game Tseshkovsky-Vorotnikov, Aktiubinsk 1985, so you can draw your own conclusions: 24...罝b6 25 罝d8 罝b8 26 罝xb8 罝xb8 27 h5 gxh5 28 gxh5 罝e8 29 h6 當f8 30 罝g1 豐c7+ 31 e5 1-0.

D2)

4...ᗒf6 5 ᗒc3 魚e7

This line, known as the Antoshin Variation after the player who popularized it, has the reputation of being extremely solid. The only other move that is relevant in this position is 5...g6 but after 6 魚e3 we have transposed back into variations discussed in D1.

6 豐f3!? (D)

This is a new idea which puts a bit of life back into the white side of the Antoshin Variation.

6...0-0

6...ᗒbd7 7 魚e2 ᗒe5 8 豐g3 0-0 9 h4!? 罝e8 (9...c6 10 f4 ᗒeg4 11 f5 豐b6 12 ᗒb3 ᗒe5 13 魚e3 豐c7 14 0-0-0 and White has a nice position; 9...c5 10 ᗒb3 豐b6 11 f4 ᗒc6 12 魚e3 ᗒd4 13 魚d3 is fine for White) 10 魚h6 ᗒeg4 11 魚xg4 ᗒxg4 12 魚g5 魚xg5 13 hxg5 豐xg5 14 f4 and White has good play for the pawn, Van der Wiel-Bosboom, Leeuwarden 1994.

7 ᗒf5 魚xf5

7...ᗒc6 8 ᗒxe7+ 豐xe7 9 魚g5 ᗒe5 10 豐f4 ᗒed7 11 0-0-0 h6! 12 魚xf6 (12 魚h4 g5 13 魚xg5 hxg5 14 豐xg5+ and White has nothing more than a perpetual) 12...ᗒxf6 (12...豐xf6 13 豐xf6 ᗒxf6 14 f3 with a balanced position) 13 f3 魚e6 14 g4 and White has good kingside attacking chances.

8 豐xf5 ᗒc6 9 魚e3 ᗒe5

Other tries are:

a) 9...豐c8 10 豐xc8 罝axc8 11 魚e2 a6 12 g4 h6 13 h4 and White has a pleasant position, Ziatdinov-Hofman, Groningen 1994.

b) 9...g6 10 豐h3 ᗒe5 11 魚e2 b5 12 0-0-0 b4 13 ᗒd5 ᗒxd5 (13...ᗒxe4 14 f4 ᗒc6 15 魚f3 f5 16 g4 and White is much better) 14 exd5 罝b8 15 f4 ᗒd7 16 g4 and White has the better attacking chances, Nijboer-Bosboom, Leeuwarden 1994.

10 ≗e2 c6 11 ≗d4 g6 12 ♕h3 ♕a5 13 f4 ♘ed7 14 0-0 ♖fe8 15 ♖ae1 ♕b4 16 ≗xf6 ♘xf6 17 e5! dxe5 18 fxe5 ♕d4+ 19 ♔h1 ♕xe5 20 ≗c4

With excellent play for the pawn, e.g. 20...♕h5 (20...♕d6 21 ≗xf7+ ♔xf7 22 ♕xh7+ ♔f8 23 ♘e4 winning) 21 ♕xh5 gxh5 22 ♖xe7 ♖xe7 23 ♖xf6 with a long technical struggle ahead but all the fun is White's, Gross-Ramik, Olomouc 1995.

E)

3...♘f6 4 dxe5

This variation offers White an edge without risk, and is the reason why a lot of Philidor players opt for other ways of transposing to their favourite solid set-ups.

4...♘xe4 5 ♕d5 ♘c5 6 ≗g5 *(D)*

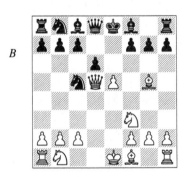

Now Black has a choice (for the first time!):

One side-line worth noting: 6...f6?! 7 exf6 gxf6 8 ≗e3 ≗e6 9 ♕h5+ ≗f7 10 ♕h4 ♘bd7 11 ♘c3 c6 12 0-0-0 and

White has an edge due to his safer king and Black's disrupted pawn-structure, Maroczy-Bogoljubow, Bled 1931.

E1)

6...≗e7 7 exd6 ♕xd6 8 ♘c3 *(D)*

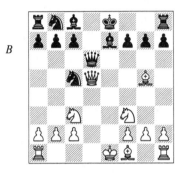

8...c6

Other moves have been tried:

a) 8...♕xd5?! (if only it were that simple!) 9 ♘xd5 ≗d6 10 0-0-0 ♘e6 11 ≗e3 ♘c6 12 ≗b5 ≗d7 and White has an edge in view of his more active pieces and extra space, for example 13 ♘g5 a6 14 ≗a4 h6 15 ♘e4 ≗e7 16 ♘xe7 ♔xe7, Alvarez-Toledano, Oropesa del Mar 1996.

b) 8...h6 9 ≗e3 ♕xd5 (9...c6 10 ♕xd6 ≗xd6 11 0-0-0 ≗e7 12 ≗c4 ♘ba6 13 ♖he1 ≗e6 14 ≗xe6 ♘xe6 15 ♘d4! {heading for f5 given half a chance!} 15...♘xd4 16 ≗xd4 f6 and White has a slight plus, due to his extra space and completed development of his pieces on natural squares, Prié-Shaw, Moscow OL 1994) 10 ♘xd5 ♘e6 11 ♘xe7 ♔xe7 and White's advantage lies in his better development and the bishop-pair, Korneev-Hoffman, Linares 1997.

c) 8...a6?! 9 0-0-0 ♗e6 10 ♗xe7 ♕xe7 (10...♗xd5? 11 ♗xd6 ♗xf3 12 ♗xc5 ♗xd1 13 ♔xd1 and White has two pieces for a rook) 11 ♕e5 f6 (11...0-0? 12 ♘d5 and Black has problems) 12 ♕h5+ ♗f7 (12...♕f7?? 13 ♕xc5) 13 ♕h4 and Black has an up-hill battle, Keitlinghaus-Gretarsson, Reykjavik 1997.

d) 8...♗e6 9 ♕xd6 ♗xd6 10 ♘b5 ♘c6 (10...0-0 11 ♘xd6 cxd6 and White has the edge on account of the bishop-pair and Black's disrupted pawns, Augustyniak-Bukowska, Polish Cht 1990) 11 ♘xd6+ cxd6 12 0-0-0 0-0 13 ♗b5 ♖fc8 and now 14 ♖he1 leaves White with an edge for the same reasons and is an improvement on 14 ♘d4?! ♘xd4 15 ♖xd4 ♗xa2!, O'Hanlon-Charlesworth, Nottingham 1946.

e) 8...♘e6 9 ♗xe7 ♕xe7 10 0-0-0 c6 (10...♘c6, although a natural developing move, leaves Black cramped, viz. 11 ♕e4 ♕b4 12 ♗c4 0-0 13 ♘d5 ♕c5 14 ♕h4 ♖d8 15 ♖he1 b5 16 ♗b3 ♗b7 17 ♖xe6! a5 18 ♘g5 h6 19 ♖xh6 with a winning attack, Ionov-Yandemirov, Russian Ch 1994; 10...0-0 11 ♕e4 ♕f6 12 ♘d5 ♕h6+ 13 ♔b1 ♘d7 14 ♘e7+ ♔h8 15 ♕f5 and White has a nice position) 11 ♕e4 0-0 12 ♗d3 f5 13 ♕e3 ♘a6 14 ♖he1 ♘ac5 15 ♗c4 f4 16 ♕e5 and White is much better due to his pressure down the e-file and a2-g8 diagonal.

9 ♕xd6 ♗xd6 10 0-0-0 ♗c7 11 ♗e3 ♘e6 12 ♘e4

We can see how White has gradually built up pressure over the last few moves.

12...0-0 13 ♘d6 ♗xd6 14 ♖xd6

Now White has the bishop-pair and superior control of the d-file.

14...♘d7 15 ♗c4 ♘f6 16 ♘e5 ♘e4

16...♘c7?! 17 ♘xf7! with the following possibilities:

a) 17...♖xf7 18 ♖d8+ ♘ce8 (after 18...♘fe8 19 ♗f4 ♗e6 20 ♖xa8 ♖xf4 21 ♖xe8+ ♘xe8 22 ♗xe6+ ♔h8 23 f3 White is a good pawn ahead) 19 ♗d4! ♔f8 20 ♗c5+ ♔g8 21 ♖e1 and White wins.

b) 17...♘cd5 18 ♘g5 ♔h8 19 ♗d4 ♗f5 20 ♗xf6 gxf6 21 ♘e6 ♘b6 22 ♘xf8 ♘xc4 23 ♖xf6 1-0 Howell-Shaw, Oakham 1994.

17 ♖dd1 b5 18 ♗b3 ♘4c5 19 ♗xe6 ♘xe6 20 ♘xc6

White is a good pawn ahead, Korneev-Bukacek, Austria 1992.

E2)
6...♕d7

Black tries to 'mix it' due to his lack of success at trying to equalize with 6...♗e7.

7 exd6 ♗xd6 8 ♘c3 *(D)*

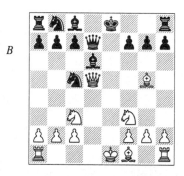

B

8...♕e6+

After 8...0-0 9 0-0-0 Black can try:
a) 9...♘c6 10 ♘b5 ♕g4 (10...♕e6 11 ♘xd6 cxd6 12 ♗c4 ♘b4 13 ♕xd6!

wins a pawn in view of 13...♕xc4 14 ♕xf8+ ♔xf8 15 ♖d8#) 11 ♘xd6 cxd6 12 h3 ♕f5 13 ♗c4 ♘b4 14 ♕xf5 ♗xf5 15 ♘d4 with an edge to White.

b) 9...a6 10 ♗e3 ♕c6 11 ♕h5 ♘bd7 (11...b6 12 ♗c4 ♕d7 13 ♘g5 ♕f5 14 b4! ♘cd7 15 ♗d3 ♘f6 16 ♗xf5 ♘xh5 17 ♗xh7+ ♔h8 18 ♗e4 ♖a7 19 ♗xb6 and White is well on top) 12 ♗d4 ♗f4+ 13 ♔b1 ♕h6 14 ♕xh6 ♗xh6 15 ♘d5 ♘e6 16 ♘e7+ ♔h8 17 ♘xc8 ♖axc8 18 ♗xg7+ with advantage to White.

c) 9...♕c6 10 ♘b5 ♘e4 11 ♘xd6 cxd6 12 ♗h4 ♗e6 13 ♕xc6 bxc6 14 ♘d4 ♖e8 15 ♘xe6 ♖xe6 16 ♗d3 d5 17 ♖he1 ♘c5 18 ♗f5 ♖xe1 19 ♖xe1 and White's bishop-pair, better pawn-structure and lead in development give him a clear advantage, Maliutin-Valdes, Candas 1992.

9 ♗e3 ♕xd5

9...c6 10 ♕d4 0-0 11 ♗c4 ♕g6 12 0-0-0 ♗e7 (12...♖d8? 13 ♕xc5! ♗xc5

14 ♖xd8+ ♗f8 15 ♘e5 wins) 13 ♘e5 ♕f6 14 ♘xf7! ♕xd4 15 ♗xd4 (White is very strongly placed) 15...♘e6 (after 15...♖xf7 16 ♗xc5 ♗xc5 17 ♖d8+ ♗f8 18 ♖xc8 White will win at least the exchange and Black cannot develop his queenside) 16 ♘e5 and Black is up against it, Rublevsky-Zarubin, Voronezh 1991.

10 ♘xd5 ♘e6 11 0-0-0 ♘c6 12 ♘d2! ♗d7 13 ♘e4 ♗e7 14 ♗e2

With the idea of ♖he1 and f4.

14...0-0-0

14...f5?! 15 ♗h5+ g6 16 ♘ef6+ and Black is in trouble.

15 ♗xa7! f5

15...b6?? 16 ♗a6#.

16 ♘xe7+ ♘xe7 17 ♘c3 ♘f4

17...♘c6 18 ♗e3 f4 19 ♗d2 and White has consolidated his extra pawn.

18 ♗d4 ♘xe2+ 19 ♘xe2 ♖hg8 20 ♘f4

White is a pawn up for nothing, Chandler-Gulko, Reykjavik 1991.

4 Latvian Gambit

1 e4 e5 2 ♘f3 f5!?

The main idea of the Latvian is for Black to come out of his corner fighting! White, as usual against an opening with such aggressive intentions, has to be well versed in the tactical possibilities but can expect to come out with an advantage if he is. I recommend...

3 ♘xe5 *(D)*

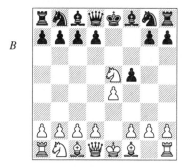

B

Black should choose between:

A: 3...♘c6   58
B: 3...♕f6   60

Others:

a) 3...fxe4? 4 ♕h5+ g6 5 ♘xg6 ♘f6 6 ♕e5+ and now:

a1) 6...♗e7 7 ♘xe7!? (although 7 ♘xh8 is probably correct I see no point analysing anything at all complex when simple moves just leave me two pawns ahead with a better position) 7...♕xe7 8 ♕xc7 ♘c6 9 ♘c3 ♘d4 (9...♘b4 10 ♘b5 ♘fd5 11 ♕c4 and Black has nothing) 10 ♘b5! ♘d5 11 ♕c4 and Black has no compensation.

a2) 6...♔f7 7 ♘xh8+ ♔g7 8 ♘c3 ♘c6 (8...d5? 9 ♕g5+ ♔xh8 10 ♘xd5! ♗g7 11 ♘xf6 ♗xf6 12 ♕f4 and Black has nothing to show for the material invested) 9 ♘f7! and here:

a21) 9...♘xe5 10 ♘xd8 ♗e7 11 d4 exd3 (11...♘g6 12 ♗g5 ♗xd8 13 ♘xe4 wins) 12 ♗f4 d6 (12...♘g6 13 ♗xc7 ♘e8 14 ♘d5 is winning for White) 13 ♗xe5 dxe5 14 ♗xd3 ♗xd8 15 0-0 and White is the exchange and a pawn up.

a22) 9...♔xf7 10 ♗c4+ ♔g7 11 ♕g5+ ♔h8 12 ♘xe4! ♗g7 13 ♘xf6 ♗xf6 14 ♕h5 ♕e7+ (14...♘d4 15 0-0 ♘xc2?? 16 ♗d3 wins further material) 15 ♕e2 and Black has no real compensation.

b) 3...d6 4 ♕h5+ g6 5 ♘xg6 ♘f6 6 ♕h4 hxg6 (6...♘c6?! 7 ♘xh8 ♘d4!? 8 ♘a3 fxe4 9 d3 ♗g7 10 ♗g5 and Black's position is falling apart, e.g. 10...♘f5 11 ♗xf6 ♗xf6 12 ♕h5+) 7 ♕xh8 ♕e7 8 ♗b5+! (the object of this move is to make the c6-square unavailable for the black knight) 8...c6 (8...♘c6? 9 d3 fxe4 10 0-0 and Black is badly placed) 9 ♗e2 fxe4 (9...♘xe4 10 d3 ♘f6 11 ♗g5 ♘bd7 12 ♘c3 d5 13 0-0! ♔f7 {13...d4? 14 ♖ae1 dxc3 15 ♗f3 wins} 14 ♖ae1 ♗g7 15 ♕h4 and Black has nothing) 10 0-0 ♗f5 (10...d5 11 d3 ♗f5 12 ♘c3 ♘bd7 13 dxe4 ♘xe4 14 ♘xe4 ♗xe4 15 ♗d3

0-0-0 16 ♗h6! and Black has little to show in compensation) 11 d3 ♘bd7 (11...d5 transposes to the previous note) 12 ♘c3 0-0-0 13 ♗h6 and again Black has little to show.

c) 3...♕e7 4 ♕h5+ g6 5 ♘xg6 ♕xe4+ 6 ♗e2 ♘f6 7 ♕h3 hxg6 8 ♕xh8 ♕xg2 (8...♘d5 9 ♕d1! is strong for White) 9 ♖f1 ♔f7 10 ♕h4 ♘c6 11 c3 ♗d6 12 d4 ♘d8 (12...♕xh2?! 13 ♗c4+ ♔g7 14 ♗h6+ ♔h7 15 ♕xf6 ♔xh6 16 ♘d2 and Black is in deep trouble; 12...♘e7 13 ♗c4+ ♘ed5 14 ♗g5 ♘h5 15 ♘d2 and again Black has little to show for the material) 13 ♗g5 ♗e7 14 ♘d2 ♕c6 (14...♘e6? 15 ♘f3 wins) 15 ♘f3 ♕b6 (15...d6? 16 ♖g1 ♘e6 17 ♗xf6 ♗xf6 18 ♕h7+ and Black is lost) 16 ♘e5+ ♔e6 17 0-0-0 d5 18 ♘xg6 ♘f7 19 ♘xe7 and Black can resign, Hegedus-Kurucsai, corr. 1984.

d) 3...♘f6 4 exf5 and now:

d1) 4...♘c6 5 ♘xc6 dxc6 6 ♕f3 ♗d6 7 ♗c4 g6 8 ♕e3+ ♕e7 (8...♗e7!? 9 ♗e6! and Black has dubious compensation) 9 ♕xe7+ ♔xe7 10 fxg6 hxg6 (White just needs to be careful now to complete his development safely – the extra material will then tell) 11 d3 ♗g4!? (11...♖xh2? 12 ♖xh2 ♗xh2 13 g3 and Black has problems) 12 h3 b5 13 ♗b3 ♖ae8 14 0-0! and Black doesn't have enough for the pawns.

d2) 4...♕e7 5 ♕e2 d6 6 ♘c4 ♗xf5 7 ♕xe7+ ♗xe7 8 ♘e3 and although Black is solid he is a pawn down for not a lot in a queenless middlegame.

A)

3...♘c6 4 d4! *(D)*

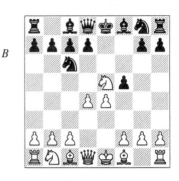

Now:

A1: 4...♘xe5   58
A2: 4...♕h4!?   59

Others:

a) 4...♘f6?! 5 ♘xc6, followed by e5, leaves White a pawn up with a good position.

b) 4...fxe4?! 5 ♘xc6 followed by ♕h5+ is strong as Black cannot play 6...g6 as 7 ♕e5+ picks up the h8-rook.

A1)

4...♘xe5 5 dxe5 ♕e7

5...fxe4 6 ♕d4! ♕h4 (6...d5?! 7 exd6 and Black is going to be a pawn down without any real compensation) 7 ♘c3 and White is going to be a good pawn up.

5...d6 6 exf5! ♗xf5 7 ♕f3 ♕c8 8 ♗d3 ♗g4 (8...♗xd3 9 ♕xd3 and Black will remain a pawn down) 9 ♕e4 dxe5 10 ♕xe5+ and White is a pawn up with the better position.

6 ♕d4!

This seems good for White.

6...d6

6...fxe4?! 7 ♘c3 and Black's e-pawn falls without any real compensation.

7 ♗f4! dxe5

7...fxe4?! 8 &b5+ &d7 (8...c6 9 exd6 ♕e6 10 &c4 and Black's position starts to look a little sad) 9 ♘c3! leaves Black in difficulties.

8 ♕xe5 ♘f6 9 ♘c3 ♕xe5

9...♘xe4 10 ♘d5! ♕xe5 11 &xe5 gives Black problems.

10 &xe5 &b4

10...fxe4 11 ♘b5! is strong for White, e.g. 11...&b4+ (11...♘d5 12 0-0-0 a6 13 ♖xd5 axb5 14 &xc7 and Black has problems) 12 c3 &a5 13 &xc7 a6 14 &xa5 axb5 15 &xb5+.

11 exf5 &xf5 12 0-0-0 0-0

12...♘g4?! 13 &g3 and White is well placed.

13 &c4+ ♔h8 14 &xf6! gxf6

14...♖xf6? loses to 15 ♘d5 ♖c6 16 &d3 &xd3 17 ♘xb4!.

15 ♘d5 &d6

15...&a5 16 b4! &b6 17 ♖he1! &xf2 18 ♖f1 c6 19 ♖xf2 cxd5 20 &xd5 with a very strong endgame for White.

16 ♖he1

Black's bishop-pair is not enough to make up for being a pawn down with a worse pawn-structure.

A2)

4...♕h4!? 5 ♘f3! ♕xe4+ 6 &e2
(D)

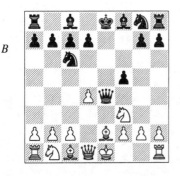

B

Material balance has been restored, but Black's pawn on f5 now looks like a liability rather than any kind of asset. Moreover White will gain a useful developing tempo (or two!) on the black queen sooner or later.

6...&b4+!

The idea of this is to tempt White into playing c2-c3. While this gains yet more time for White, at least it prevents the natural development of his knight to c3.

Other possibilities for Black:

a) 6...♘f6 7 0-0 &e7 8 ♖e1 0-0? 9 &c4+ winning.

b) 6...♘b4 (a direct attempt to exploit Black's temporary activity) 7 0-0! ♕xc2 8 ♕e1 &e7 (8...♕e4 9 ♘c3 ♕e7 10 ♕d1 ♘f6 11 ♖e1 ♘e4 12 a3 ♘c6 13 &d3 winning) 9 ♘c3 ♘f6 10 ♘e5 (with the threat of 11 &d1) 10...f4 11 a3 ♘c6 (11...d6 12 axb4 dxe5 13 dxe5 ♘g4 14 ♘d5 &d8 15 e6 ♘f6 16 ♘xf4 0-0 17 &d3 winning) 12 &d3 ♕b3 13 ♘b5 ♘xe5 14 dxe5 and Black's position is in ruins.

7 c3 &e7 8 0-0 ♘f6 9 c4! d5

9...♘d8 10 ♘c3 ♕c6 11 ♘e5 ♕e6 12 c5 &xc5 13 &c4 d5 14 ♘xd5 ♘xd5 15 dxc5 c6 16 ♖e1 1-0 Elburg-Simmelink, corr. 1998.

9...♘b4?! 10 a3 ♘a6 (10...♘c2?? 11 ♘c3 wins) 11 ♘c3 ♕e6 12 ♖e1 d6 13 c5 ♕f7 14 cxd6 cxd6 (but not 14...&xd6?? 15 &c4+ wins) 15 &b5+ ♔f8 (15...&d7 16 ♘g5 is very strong, e.g. 16...♕g6 17 &xd7+ ♔xd7 18 ♕a4+ ♔d8 19 ♕a5+ ♔d7 20 ♕b5+ ♔d8 21 ♕xb7 and Black's position collapses) 16 ♕e2 h6 17 &c4 ♕e8 (17...d5? 18 ♘e5 ♕e8 19 &b5 wins) 18 ♘h4 ♘e4 19 ♘xe4 &xh4 20 &f4

♕xe4 21 ♗xd6+ ♗e7 22 ♕h5 1-0 Canfell-Van Mil, Holland 1988.

10 ♘c3 ♕e6

10...♕g4?! 11 ♘xd5 ♘xd5 12 cxd5 ♘b4 13 ♘g5 ♕h4 14 g3 ♕h6 15 ♘e6 is sad for Black.

11 ♖e1

Black is in big trouble as 11...0-0 12 cxd5 ♘xd5 13 ♗c4 wins material.

B)

3...♘f6 4 ♗c4 fxe4

4...b5?! 5 ♘e3 fxe4 6 ♕h5+! ♕g6 (6...g6? 7 ♕d5 is strong as the e-pawn falls with check; 6...♔d8? 7 ♗xb5 and Black has nothing to show for the pawn) 7 ♕xg6+ hxg6 8 ♗xb5 c6 9 ♗e2 d5 10 d3! ♘f6 11 dxe4 ♘xe4 (11...d4!? 12 ♘c4 ♘xe4 13 ♘bd2 ♗f5 14 ♘b3 ♗b4+ 15 ♔f1 0-0 16 ♘xd4 and Black has nothing to show for being two pawns down) 12 ♘d2 ♗f5 13 g4! ♘xd2 14 ♗xd2 ♗e6 15 ♗d3 ♔f7 16 h4 and Black's position is grim as 16...d4 17 ♘c4 ♗xg4?? 18 ♘e5+ wins.

5 ♘c3 (D)

Now:

B1: 5...♕g6 61
B2: 5...♕f7 61
Others:

a) 5...c6?! 6 ♘xe4 ♕e6 7 ♕h5+! g6 8 ♕e5 and then:

a1) 8...♕xe5 9 ♘xe5 d5 (9...d6 10 ♘c4! d5 11 ♘ed6+ ♔d7 12 ♘f7 dxc4 13 ♘xh8 b5 14 ♘f7 and the knight escapes) 10 ♘g5 ♘f6 11 d4 and Black has little to show for the pawn.

a2) 8...d5 9 ♘cd6+ ♔d8 (9...♗xd6? 10 ♘xd6+ ♔f8 11 d4! ♕xe5+ 12 dxe5 and Black is a pawn down with the worse position) 10 ♘xb7+ ♔e7 11 ♕xe6+ ♔xe6 12 ♘bc5+ ♔f7 13 ♘g5+ ♔f6 14 d4 ♗xc5 (14...♗f5 15 ♗f4! is strong for White) 15 dxc5 ♘e7 16 ♗d3 and Black has no real compensation for being two pawns down, Klauner-Meyer, corr. Ech 1990.

b) 5...d6 6 d3 exd3 7 ♗xd3 ♕f7 8 0-0 (White is already better due to his large lead in development) 8...♘c6?! 9 ♖e1+ ♗e6 10 ♕g4! ♘d8 11 ♗f5 ♔d7 (11...♘f6 12 ♕h3 ♔d7 13 ♗g5 and White has huge positional pressure) 12 ♗xe6+ ♘xe6 13 ♘e4 and Black has big problems, e.g. 13...♘f6 14 ♘c5+ dxc5 15 ♘e5+ ♔e7 16 ♘xf7 ♘xg4 17 ♘xh8 g6 18 ♗g5+ and the knight escapes.

c) 5...♕e6 6 ♘e3 and here:

c1) 6...♘f6 7 ♗c4 ♕e5 8 d3 ♗b4 9 ♗d2 exd3 10 0-0 ♔d8 (10...♗d6 11 ♘g4! dxc2 {11...♘xg4 12 ♖e1 is obviously strong} 12 ♕xc2 ♕h5 13 ♘xf6+ gxf6 14 ♖ae1+ ♔d8 15 h3 and White has excellent compensation for the pawn; 10...dxc2 11 ♘xc2 ♗e7 12 ♖e1 ♕c5 13 ♕e2 with excellent play for the pawn) 11 ♗xd3 d6 12 ♖e1 ♗xc3 13 ♗xc3 and White is better due to his bishop-pair, lead in development and safer king, Budovskis-Strelis, corr. Behting mem 1974.

c2) 6...c6 7 d3 d5 8 dxe4 dxe4 9 ♗c4 ♕g6 10 ♗xg8 ♖xg8 11 ♕d4 ♗e6 12 ♕xe4 ♕xe4 13 ♘xe4 and White is a good pawn ahead, Krustkalns-Budovskis, corr. Atars mem 1977.

B1)
5...♕g6 6 d3! *(D)*

6...♗b4
6...♘f6 7 dxe4 ♘xe4 (7...♗b4 8 f3 d5!? 9 exd5 0-0 10 ♘e3 ♖e8 11 ♕d2 ♗c5 12 ♘cd1 ♗f5 13 ♗e2 and Black's compensation is inadequate) 8 ♕e2 ♗e7 (8...♗b4 9 ♘d2! and Black has problems) 9 ♘d5 is very strong for White.
7 dxe4 ♕xe4+ 8 ♘e3 ♗xc3+
8...♘f6 9 ♗c4 ♗xc3+ 10 bxc3 transposes to the main line.
9 bxc3 ♘f6
9...♕e5 10 ♕d4 ♕xd4 (10...♘c6 11 ♕xe5+ ♘xe5 12 ♘d5! is very strong) 11 cxd4 and White is better due to the bishop-pair.
10 ♗c4 c6
10...♕e5 11 0-0 ♕xc3 12 ♖e1! and White has excellent compensation for the pawn, e.g. 12...♕xa1? 13 ♘d5+ ♔d8 (13...♔f7 14 ♘xf6+ mating) 14 ♗a3!! ♕xd1 15 ♗e7+ ♔e8 16 ♘xc7#

or 12...♘e4 13 ♘d5! ♕xc4 14 ♕h5+ ♔f8 (14...g6 15 ♕e5+ mates) 15 ♕f5+ ♘f6 16 ♘xf6 with a mating attack.
11 0-0 d5 12 ♘xd5! ♕xc4
12...cxd5?! 13 ♖e1 dxc4 14 ♖xe4+ ♘xe4 15 ♕h5+ winning.
13 ♖e1+ ♔f7 14 ♖e7+ ♔g6
14...♔f8 15 ♘b6!! wins.
15 ♘f4+ ♔f5
15...♔h6 16 ♘h5+ wins.
16 ♕f3 ♘g4 17 ♘d5+ 1-0
Zude-Ruprich, Schwäbisch Gmünd 1994.

B2)
5...♕f7 6 ♘e3 c6
6...♘f6?! 7 ♗c4 ♕g6 8 d3 ♗b4 9 0-0 ♗xc3 10 bxc3 c6 11 dxe4 ♘xe4 12 ♕e1! b5 (12...d5? loses to 13 ♘xd5 cxd5 14 ♗xd5) 13 ♗d3 ♕e6 14 ♗xe4 ♕xe4 15 ♘f5! ♕xe1 16 ♖xe1+ ♔f7 17 ♘d6+ ♔g6 18 f4 ♘a6 19 f5+ ♔f6? (19...♔h5 20 ♖e3! is very strong for White) 20 h4 1-0 (as 20...h6 21 c4 is mating) Budovskis-Gunderam, corr. Behting mem 1970.
7 ♘xe4 d5 8 ♘g5 ♕f6
8...♕f4?! 9 ♘f3 d4 (necessary as otherwise White plays d2-d4 and will then gain a tempo on Black's queen at the right time by moving the knight on e3) 10 ♘c4 ♗e7 11 d3 and White is just a good pawn ahead.
9 ♘f3 *(D)*
Now Black can choose between:
B21: 9...♗e6 61
B22: 9...♗d6 62

B21)
9...♗e6
Preparing to castle queenside.

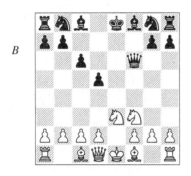

10 d4 ♘d7 11 ♗d3 0-0-0 12 0-0 g5!? 13 c4!

In positions with opposite-side castling, time is of the essence and so, as Nunn pointed out, c2-c4 to develop play in the centre and on the queenside must be correct.

13...dxc4

13...♗d6 14 cxd5 cxd5 15 ♘f5! ♗xf5 (15...♗f4 16 ♗xf4 gxf4 17 ♕c1+ ♔b8 18 ♕xf4+ ♔a8 19 ♕c7 and Black is in real trouble) 16 ♗xg5 ♗xh2+ 17 ♔h1 and Black has serious problems.

13...g4 14 cxd5 cxd5 (14...gxf3 15 dxe6 ♕xe6 16 ♕xf3 and Black has little to show for being two pawns down)

15 ♘e5 and Black is worse, for example 15...♘xe5 16 dxe5 ♕xe5 17 ♘xg4 and Black is not only a pawn down but White has the much stronger attacking chances as well as a lead in development.

14 ♘xc4 h6

14...g4 15 ♘fe5 ♗xc4 16 ♘xd7 ♖xd7 17 ♗xc4 ♖xd4 (17...♕xd4?? 18 ♗e6 wins) 18 ♕b3 ♘h6 19 ♗e3 is very strong for White.

15 ♗e3

White is well placed, not only being a pawn up but with the plan of ♕a4, ♖ac1 and ♘fe5 looming.

B22)

9...♗d6 10 d4 ♘e7 11 c4! 0-0 12 ♕b3 ♔h8!? 13 ♗e2

Black is solid but has negligible compensation for the pawn, for example 13...dxc4 14 ♘xc4 ♗c7 15 0-0 ♘d5 16 ♗g5 ♕g6 17 ♘ce5 ♗xe5 dxe5, and 18...♖xf3?? is not possible because of 19 ♕xf3 and the bishop on g5 is immune because of the back-rank mate.

5 Sicilian Defence

1 e4 c5

The Sicilian is by far the most popular defence to 1 e4 and is the number one choice of many of the world's top players. The reason for this is simple: Black immediately exerts pressure on the centre without taking on the symmetry of 1...e5. Black is able to maintain the tension and play soundly for a win. On top of this Black has a great deal of flexibility in how to arrange his forces and White needs not only to know but also to understand a labyrinth of variations if he is to play an open Sicilian variation (i.e. with 2 ♘f3 and 3 d4). It would take more than the length of this entire book to cover some of the systems Black can play in the Sicilian. Those who play the Open Sicilian as White need to keep abreast of a massive and constantly changing body of theory – this is not for us! Instead I am offering a set of variations which should give White an edge and maintain a certain amount of surprise value, particularly at club level. Although the careful study of this chapter will be required to use these systems, the amount of groundwork needed before they can be used 'over the board' is a fraction of that needed to play open variations without compromising the advantage of the opening move. This chapter is split into four sections depending on how Black meets **2 ♘f3**:

Part 1 covers **2...♘c6 3 ♗b5**
Part 2 **2...d6 3 d4 cxd4 4 ♕xd4**
Part 3 **2...e6 3 ♘c3** and
Part 4 **2...a6, 2...♘f6** and **2...g6**.

Part 1

1 e4 c5 2 ♘f3 ♘c6 3 ♗b5 *(D)*

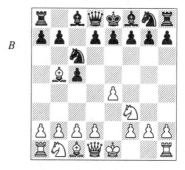

B

White develops a piece and avoids the immediate opening of the position with 3 d4. Meanwhile he maintains the flexibility, depending on how Black reacts, of opening up the position at his convenience. Also White may decide to play a future c2-c3 before playing d2-d4, thus ensuring that he can maintain a pawn on d4. There have been no fewer than ten(!) different replies tried by Black on move three, which tends to show, if nothing else, that there is no clear-cut way that Black should reply to try to obtain equality.

Let's look at Black's options in turn:

The tenth option for Black, 3...d6, is likely to transpose, via 4 d4 cxd4 5 ♛xd4, to Part 2 of this chapter from the move-order 1 e4 c5 2 ♘f3 d6 3 d4 cxd4 4 ♛xd4 ♘c6 5 ♗b5, as after 4 d4 the alternative 4...♗d7 5 c3 ♘f6 6 ♛e2 is unappealing for Black as he must look out for White playing a timely d4-d5 or e4-e5.

A)

3...a6?! *(D)*

This is more popular than you might expect, especially at club level. Black immediately challenges the bishop, but his chances of obtaining equality are not good. While Black obtains the two bishops they are stifled by the blocked nature of the position, and he is hampered by the doubled pawns.

4 ♗xc6

Now Black must decide which way to recapture:

| **A1:** | **4...bxc6** | 64 |
| **A2:** | **4...dxc6** | 67 |

A1)

4...bxc6 5 0-0 *(D)*

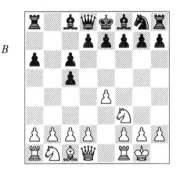

Now:

A11:	**5...♛c7?!**	64
A12:	**5...♘f6?!**	65
A13:	**5...e6**	65
A14:	**5...g6**	65
A15:	**5...d6**	66
A16:	**5...d5**	66

A11)

5...♛c7?!

Not so much a bad move in itself as one that doesn't assist Black in the task at hand. White should continue with 'business as usual' and use the extra move to open the game to his advantage.

6 ♖e1 e5 7 c3 ♘e7 8 d4 cxd4 9 cxd4 ♘g6

After 9...d6 10 dxe5 dxe5 11 ♘bd2 ♘g6 12 ♘c4 ♗e7 13 ♗d2! 0-0 14 ♗a5 ♛b8 15 ♛c2 ♗g4 16 ♖e3! White's pieces are more harmoniously placed while Black's are still searching for good posts. Together with Black's inferior pawn-structure White can enjoy a lasting and pleasant edge.

10 ♘xe5 ♘xe5 11 dxe5 ♕xe5 12 ♘d2! d6 13 ♘c4 ♕e6 14 b3

White has a lovely position with his development near complete while Black has still an uphill task in finishing his development and getting his king into safety. As in a lot of these lines, in trying to maintain the bishop-pair as compensation Black has drifted into an inferior position.

A12)
5...♘f6?!

This just encourages White to press forward before Black is ready with an adequate counter.

6 e5! ♘d5 7 c4 ♘b6 8 d4 cxd4

8...♘xc4 9 ♕c2 ♘b6 10 dxc5 ♘d5 11 ♘c3 ♘xc3 (11...♘b4?! is met by 12 ♕e4 with the idea of a2-a3) 12 ♕xc3 and Black will find it hard to complete his development in satisfactory fashion.

9 ♕xd4

White is already better due to his lead in development and extra space.

A13)
5...e6 6 e5! d5

6...♘e7?! 7 ♘c3 ♘g6 8 ♘e4 d5 9 exd6 ♗xd6 10 ♘xd6+ ♕xd6 11 d3 0-0 12 ♘g5! ♖d8 13 ♕h5 h6 14 ♘e4 ♕e7 15 ♕xc5 ♕xc5 16 ♘xc5 and Black has nothing to show for the pawn deficit, Pritchard-Hoffman, Biel 1980.

6...f6!? 7 d3 fxe5 8 ♘xe5 ♘f6 9 ♖e1 d6 10 ♘c4 (10 ♘xc6? ♕b6 11 ♕f3 ♗b7 12 ♖xe6+ ♔d7 13 ♕f5

♔xc6 and White has insufficient play for the piece) 10...♗e7 11 ♗d2 0-0 12 ♗a5 ♕e8 13 ♘c3 e5 14 f4! ♗g4 15 ♕d2 exf4 16 h3 f3!? (16...♗h5 17 ♕xf4 d5 18 ♕c7! dxc4 19 ♖xe7 ♕g6 20 ♕xc6 cxd3 21 cxd3 favours White) 17 hxg4 ♘xg4 18 gxf3 ♖xf3 19 ♕g2 and Black's attack is repulsed.

7 exd6 ♗xd6 8 ♖e1 ♘f6 9 ♘a3! 0-0 10 ♘c4 ♗e7 11 d3 ♕c7 12 ♗g5 a5 13 a4 ♗a6 14 ♘fe5

White is well placed as Black lacks an active plan and his queenside pawns will prove a long-term liability. On top of this his bishop-pair is no great asset in this type of position.

14...♗xc4 15 ♘xc4 ♖fd8 16 ♗h4 ♘d5 17 ♗g3 ♕b7

White's advantage is obvious, Søbjerg-J.Nielsen, Ålborg 1993.

A14)
5...g6 6 d4 cxd4 7 ♕xd4 *(D)*

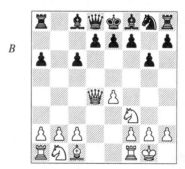

Now Black can choose between:

A141)
7...♘f6!? 8 e5 ♘d5 9 c4 ♘b4 10 e6 f6

10...fxe6?? 11 ♕xh8 ♘c2 12 ♗h6 wins outright.

11 ♕c3! c5 12 ♗e3 ♕b6 13 exd7+ ♗xd7 14 ♘bd2 ♗f5

14...♗g4 15 ♘e4! ♖c8 16 a3 ♗xf3 17 gxf3 ♘c6 18 ♘xf6+! exf6 19 ♕xf6 winning.

15 ♘b3 ♖c8 16 ♘h4 ♗e4 17 ♗xc5! ♖xc5 18 ♕d4 ♗xg2 19 ♖fd1! ♖c6 20 c5 ♕c7 21 ♕xb4 ♗h3 22 ♖d3 ♕c8

22...♗c8 23 ♖ad1 ♗g7 24 ♖d8+ ♕xd8 25 ♖xd8+ ♔xd8 26 ♘d4 ♖c7 27 ♕b6 is better for White due to Black's lack of coordination.

23 ♖ad1 e5

23...♗g7 24 ♘a5 ♖c7 25 ♖d8+ ♕xd8 26 ♖xd8+ ♔xd8 27 ♕b6 and again White is better due to Black's lack of coordination and the strength of the passed c-pawn.

24 ♖d8+ ♕xd8 25 ♖xd8+ ♔xd8 26 ♘a5

Black is worse for all the same reasons.

A142)

7...f6 8 e5! ♗g7 9 ♗f4 fxe5 10 ♗xe5 ♘f6 11 ♕c4!

Making it awkward for Black to castle.

11...♕b6 12 ♘c3 d5

12...♕xb2? grabbing the 'poisoned' pawn deserves the 'full treatment': 13 ♘g5! e6 (13...♖f8 14 ♘e6 wins) 14 ♘xe6 wins.

13 ♘a4! ♕a7 14 ♕d4

White has all the positional pluses, Magem-Remon, Cuba 1991.

A15)

5...d6 6 c3 e5

Alternatives are no better:

a) 6...e6 7 ♖e1 d5 8 d3 ♘f6 9 ♕a4! gives Black problems as 9...♗d7 10 e5 forces the black knight back to g8.

b) 6...♗g4 7 h3 ♗h5 8 d3 e5 9 ♕a4! ♕c7 10 ♘bd2 ♘f6 11 ♖e1 ♗e7 12 ♘h4! is uncomfortable for Black.

7 d4 cxd4 8 cxd4 ♕c7?! 9 ♘a3 ♘e7 10 ♘c4 ♘g6 11 ♗d2! a5 12 ♖c1

Black has problems equalizing.

A16)

5...d5 6 d3 (D)

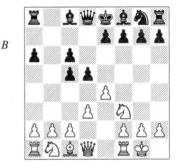

6...♗g4

Or:

a) 6...e6 7 b3 ♘f6 8 ♘bd2 ♗e7 9 ♗b2 0-0 10 ♘e5 ♕c7 11 f4 a5 12 a4 ♖b8 and now not 13 ♕e1?! c4!? 14 dxc4 ♗b4!, when Black has managed to unbalance the position, but rather 13 ♔h1!, keeping everything under control for White, who can anticipate a lasting positional advantage.

b) 6...g6 7 c3 ♗g7 8 ♕a4! ♗d7 9 ♘bd2 ♕b6 10 ♖e1 ♕b5 11 ♕c2 e6 12 c4! ♕b7 13 ♘b3 and White is well on top, Kr.Georgiev-Birinyi, Ano Liosia 1995.

c) The endings after 6...dxe4 7 dxe4 ♕xd1 8 ♖xd1 are uninviting for Black.

7 ♘bd2 e6 8 h3 ♗h5 9 b3 ♗d6 10 ♗b2 d4

10...f6!? 11 ♕e1 ♕d7 12 e5! is better for White.

11 ♘c4

White is already better in view of his outpost on c4 and the weakness of Black's doubled c-pawns, P.Ostojić-P.Bader, Eupen rpd 1994.

A2)

4...dxc6 5 h3 *(D)*

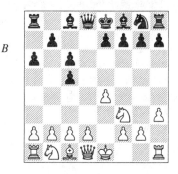

This stops Black developing his light-squared bishop to the natural square of his choice, g4, and leaves Black the long-term problem of what exactly to do with the piece. Now Black can choose between:

A21: 5...♕c7?!   67
A22: 5...♘f6   67
A23: 5...g6   67
A24: 5...e5   68

A21)

5...♕c7?! 6 d3 e5 7 ♘bd2 ♘f6 8 ♘c4 ♘d7 9 a4 b5 10 ♘e3 ♗b7 11 ♗d2 g6 12 0-0 f6 13 ♘h4 ♗e7 14 ♕g4

After a series of quite sensible moves by both players we have reached a position which is nicely better for White,

Leskovar-Alfaro, Mar del Plata 1996. In fact White's plan of development of ♘bd2-c4, ♗d2 and 0-0 is characteristic of this line.

A22)

5...♘f6

There is relatively little experience of this move but it seems that White can obtain a nice position with good prospects by just developing normally.

6 d3 g6 7 ♘c3 ♗g7 8 ♗e3

A common theme in closed Sicilian positions: White develops his dark-squared bishop with tempo.

8...♕a5 9 0-0 ♗e6 10 ♕d2 ♖d8

Now White removes one of Black's main assets, the bishop-pair, by exchanging off his better bishop.

11 ♗h6 0-0 12 ♕g5!

12 ♘d5?! ♕xd2 13 ♘xe7+ ♔h8 14 ♗xg7+ ♔xg7 15 ♘xd2 ♖fe8 wins for Black.

12...♖fe8 13 ♗xg7 ♔xg7 14 a3 ♘d7?! 15 ♘d4 ♘f8 16 b4 f6

Now instead of 17 bxa5, Kulish-Mizhurko, Yalta wom 1996, 17 ♘xe6+ ♘xe6 18 ♕xg6+! hxg6 19 bxa5 leaves White much better, not so much because of the extra pawn but because of his latent pressure down the b-file against the backward pawn at b7.

A23)

5...g6 6 0-0 ♗g7 7 d3

Again White has played the 'normal' set-up of h3, 0-0 and d3 and it is time for Black to form a plan.

7...e5

7...♘f6 is likely to transpose to A22.

8 ♗e3 b6 9 ♕c1 h6

With 9...f5!?, Black logically aims for a quick kingside expansion against which White must play accurately to exploit Black's uncastled king by play down the e-file before Black can consolidate: 10 ♗g5! ♕d6 11 exf5 gxf5 12 ♖e1 ♘e7 13 ♗xe7! ♕xe7 14 ♕e3 e4 15 ♘c3 presents Black with severe problems.

10 ♘bd2 ♗e6

10...f5?! 11 exf5 gxf5 12 ♖e1 ♘e7 13 ♘c4 is good for White.

11 a4!

Preparing to soften up the black queenside.

11...a5 12 b3 ♘e7 13 ♕b2! ♕c7 14 ♘c4 f6 15 ♘fd2 0-0 16 f4 b5 17 fxe5! bxc4

17...fxe5 18 ♖xf8+ ♔xf8 (18...♖xf8 19 axb5 cxb5 20 ♘xa5 ♖a8 21 ♕c3 is strong for White) 19 ♘a3 is good for White.

18 exf6 ♗h8

18...♕g3 19 ♗f4 ♖xf6 (19...♕h4 20 ♗e5!) 20 ♕xf6 ♗xf6 21 ♗xg3 ♗xa1 22 ♖xa1 cxd3 23 ♖c1! is awkward for Black to meet.

19 ♗xh6 ♖f7 20 ♘xc4

White's mass of pawns together with Black's cramped position more than compensates for the piece.

A24)

5...e5 6 0-0 (D)

Now Black has tried:
A241: 6...f6   68
A242: 6...♗d6   68

A241)

6...f6

Now we have a position strongly reminiscent of an Exchange Lopez (1

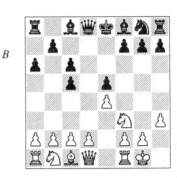

e4 e5 2 ♘f3 ♘c6 3 ♗b5 a6 4 ♗xc6 dxc6 5 0-0 f6) where White's extra move is the useful h2-h3 and Black's is having his c-pawn on c5. Whereas this may be useful in itself in conjunction with having the other c-pawn on c6 instead of c7 this appears to be more of a liability than an asset.

7 d3 ♗e6 8 a4 ♕d7 9 a5!

Exploiting the potentially weak b6-square (again consider this in comparison to the Exchange Lopez line mentioned).

9...0-0-0 10 ♗e3 g5 11 ♘c3 ♔b8 12 ♘a4 c4!? 13 ♗b6 ♖e8

13...g4 14 hxg4 ♖e8 15 dxc4 ♕g7 16 ♕d3! ♗xg4 17 ♖ad1 is strong for White.

14 dxc4 ♕f7 15 b3

White has the better prospects.

A242)

6...♗d6

Again there are great similarities between this and Exchange Lopez positions.

7 d3 ♘f6

7...♘e7 8 ♘bd2 0-0 9 ♘c4 ♘g6 10 a4 b5 11 ♘xd6 ♕xd6 12 ♗e3 ♖d8 13 ♕e2 f6 14 ♘d2 ♗e6 15 b3 ♘f4?! 16 ♕f3 ♖d7 17 axb5 cxb5 18 ♗xf4 exf4

19 e5! ♕d5 20 ♕xf4 and White is better on account of Black's inferior pawn-structure, Shteinberg-Sveshnikov, USSR 1967.

8 a4 b5

8...c4!? 9 ♘a3! cxd3 10 ♕xd3 ♗e6 11 ♘c4 ♗xc4 12 ♕xc4 ♕c7 13 ♗e3 0-0 14 a5 and White has a small but lasting edge.

9 ♗e3 0-0 10 ♘bd2 ♕e7 11 c4!

This leads to the type of blocked position where knights excel.

11...b4 12 ♘b3 ♘e8 13 ♘h2 f6 14 f4 ♘c7 15 f5 g5 16 ♕e2 a5 17 ♕f2

White is very well placed due to the weaknesses at a5 and c5, Jansa-Rehak, Mlada Boleslav 1994.

B)

3...♘d4?! 4 ♘xd4 cxd4 5 0-0 *(D)*

5...e6

Black can instead try:

a) 5...♕b6 6 ♗c4 and Black's queen is not constructively placed.

b) 5...a6 6 ♗c4 *(D)* and here:

b1) 6...♘f6?! 7 e5 d5 8 ♗b3 ♘d7 9 ♖e1 ♘c5 10 d3 ♘xb3 11 axb3 g6 12 ♘d2 ♗g7 13 h3! ♗d7 14 ♘f3 ♕b6 15 ♕d2 ♖c8 16 ♖e2! f6 17 exf6 ♗xf6 18 ♕h6 leaves Black in positional tatters,

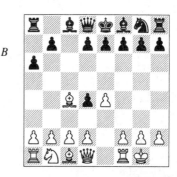

Porubszky-Angyalosine, Hungarian wom Ch 1991.

b2) 6...e6 7 c3 b5 8 ♗b3 ♗c5 9 d3 ♗b7 10 ♘d2 intending ♘f3, when Black has no satisfactory way to maintain his pawn on d4.

c) 5...g6 6 c3 dxc3 (6...♗g7 7 cxd4! ♗xd4 8 ♘c3 e6 9 ♕a4! ♗g7 10 d4 ♘e7 11 ♗f4 0-0 12 ♗d6 ♖e8 13 ♗d3 ♕b6 14 ♘b5! a6 15 e5 ♘d5 16 ♖ac1 ♘f4 17 ♘c7 ♘xd3 18 ♘xa8 ♕a7 19 ♘c7 and White is winning, Mikliaev-Chikhelashvili, USSR Cht 1968) 7 ♘xc3 ♗g7 8 d4 e6 9 ♗f4! (probably stronger than the immediate 9 d5, Kasparov-BCF Girls, London simul 1997) 9...♕b6 10 ♗e3 a6 11 d5 ♕a5 12 ♗e2 and White has a good opening advantage.

d) 5...e5? 6 f4! (we have a position akin to one of the more favourable lines of the King's Gambit) 6...♕b6 7 ♗c4 exf4 (7...d3+ 8 ♔h1 dxc2 9 ♕xc2 exf4 10 ♖xf4 is hardly appealing for Black) 8 ♕h5 d3+ 9 ♔h1 (Black has a miserable position) 9...♕f6 10 ♘c3 g6 11 ♕a5! and Black has very poor prospects of survival.

6 d3 ♗c5

6...♗e7?! 7 ♘d2 a6 8 ♗a4 b5 9 ♗b3 ♗b7 10 ♕g4 ♘f6 11 ♕xg7 ♖g8

12 ♕h6 ♕c7 13 a4! 0-0-0 (13...♖g6 14 ♕h3 b4 15 ♘f3 ♕c5 16 a5 and Black still has to prove any kind of real compensation for the pawn) 14 axb5 axb5 15 ♘f3 ♖g6 16 ♕h3 ♖dg8 17 ♘h4 ♖g4 18 f3! ♖4g7 19 ♗h6 ♘h5 20 ♗xg7 ♘f4 21 ♕g4 ♗f6 22 ♗xf6! ♖xg4 23 fxg4 d5 24 e5 1-0 Dittmar-Peussner, Dortmund 1993.

7 ♕g4 ♕f6 8 f4 ♕g6 9 ♕f3 f5 10 exf5 ♕xf5 11 g4! ♕f7 12 f5 ♘e7 13 fxe6 ♕xe6 14 ♗g5 h6 15 ♗d2

Black has the awful problem of what to do with his king, Bologan-Gillani, Manila OL 1992.

C)

3...♕c7

One of Black's most popular sidelines.

4 0-0 *(D)*

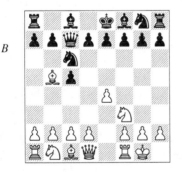

Black has tried:

C1)

4...g6?!

This move doesn't combine well with 3...♕c7.

5 ♖e1 ♗g7 6 c3 d6 7 ♗f1 a6 8 h3 ♘f6 9 d4 cxd4 10 cxd4 ♘d7 11 ♘c3

White has achieved everything he should want: a classical centre, natural development and extra space.

11...0-0 12 ♗e3 b5 13 ♖c1 ♕b7 14 ♘d5

White is well placed, Fierro-Debowska, Erevan wom OL 1996.

C2)

4...e5 5 c3 d6 6 d4 ♗d7 7 d5 ♘ce7 8 ♗xd7+ ♕xd7 9 c4

We have now reached a position similar to a Czech Benoni where Black will find it difficult to get in ...f5 in view of the weakness on e6 now that the light-squared bishops have been exchanged.

9...g6 10 ♘c3 h6 11 ♗e3 ♘f6

Now 11...f5? meets with disaster due to 12 ♗xc5! dxc5 13 ♘xe5 winning.

12 ♖b1 ♘c8 13 b4 b6 14 bxc5 bxc5

In this type of position Black would like to be able to play ...dxc5 and place a knight on d6. However, as Black's e-pawn would be hanging this is not an option.

15 ♖b5

White is well placed in view of his queenside play as Black has failed to create any kingside counter-chances, Kreiman-Beckman, New York 1994.

C3)

4...♘f6 5 ♖e1 e6

Alternatives are:

a) 5...g6 6 ♘c3 ♗g7 gives White a tempo-up version of a normal position

Black gets in a line in the English with colours reversed (1 c4 e5 2 ♘c3 ♘f6 3 ♘f3 ♘c6 4 g3 ♗b4 5 ♗g2 0-0 6 ♕c2 ♖e8) – this is regarded as quite satisfactory for Black. After 7 e5 ♘g4 8 ♗xc6 White can expect to enjoy an edge.

b) 5...a6?! 6 ♗xc6 ♕xc6 7 d4! d5 (7...♘xe4?? is refuted by 8 d5: 8...♕a4 9 b3 ♕b4 10 a3 or 8...♕g6 9 ♘h4!) 8 exd5 ♘xd5 (8...♕xd5 9 ♖e5! is good for White) 9 c4 with an obvious advantage for White.

6 ♘c3 *(D)*

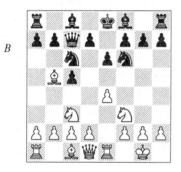

Now there are the following possibilities:

C31)

6...d6

The most common reply to 6 ♘c3 – Black plays a 'normal' Sicilian move.

7 d4 cxd4 8 ♘d5! ♕d8

8...exd5!? 9 exd5+ ♗e7 10 ♘xd4 ♘xd5 11 ♘xc6 bxc6 12 ♕xd5 ♗b7 (12...♗d7 13 ♕g5!) 13 ♗f4! and now:

a) 13...♔d8 14 ♕c4!.

b) 13...0-0 14 ♕e4 ♖fe8 (14...♖ae8? 15 ♗d3 g6 16 ♗h6 f5 17 ♕f4 ♖f7 18 ♗c4) 15 ♗c4 with a pleasant edge.

c) 13...cxb5 14 ♕xd6 ♕d8 15 ♖ad1! ♕xd6 16 ♗xd6 0-0 17 ♖xe7 ♗c6 and Black has an uphill struggle.

9 ♘xd4 ♗d7 10 ♗g5! exd5

Or:

a) 10...♖c8? 11 ♘f5! exf5 12 exf5+ ♘e5 13 ♗xd7+ ♔xd7 (13...♕xd7 14 ♗xf6 ♕xf5 15 ♖xe5+!! dxe5 16 ♘c7+ mates) 14 ♖xe5! dxe5 15 ♘xf6+ ♔c6 16 ♕f3+ wins.

b) 10...♗e7 11 ♘xe7 and now:

b1) 11...♘xd4? 12 ♗xd7+ ♕xd7 13 ♗xf6 gxf6 14 ♘d5 exd5 15 ♕xd4 and Black's position is in tatters, Richter-Groneberg, Berlin 1950.

b2) 11...♕xe7 12 ♗xc6 bxc6 (12...♗xc6 13 e5 dxe5 14 ♘xc6 bxc6 15 ♕f3 0-0 16 ♖xe5 and White has the better chances) 13 ♘f5 exf5 14 exf5 ♗e6 15 ♗xf6 gxf6 16 ♕e2 ♔d7 17 ♖ad1 and Black's king looks a little shaky for the ensuing middlegame.

11 ♗xc6 bxc6 12 exd5+ ♗e7 13 ♗xf6 gxf6 14 dxc6 ♗c8 15 ♕f3! ♖b8 16 ♖e3 ♖xb2

16...0-0 17 ♖ae1 ♖e8 (17...♖xb2 18 h4 ♖e8 19 ♕h5!) 18 ♕h5!.

17 ♖ae1 ♗e6? 18 ♖xe6 fxe6 19 ♕h5+ 1-0

Rozentalis-Slekys, USSR 1978.

C32)

6...♘g4!? 7 ♗xc6 dxc6

7...♕xc6 is met by 8 d4!.

8 e5! ♗d7 9 d3 0-0-0 10 h3 ♘h6 11 ♗g5 ♖e8 12 ♘e4 ♘f5 13 c3 h6 14 ♗f4 ♖d8 15 ♕a4 ♔b8 16 a3 ♗c8 17 ♖ed1

White has a pleasant game.

C33)

6...a6?! 7 ♗xc6 ♕xc6 8 d4 cxd4 9 ♘xd4 ♕c4 10 e5 ♘d5 11 ♘e4 f5?! 12 b3! ♕b4 13 a3 ♕a5 14 ♘xf5! exf5 15 ♘d6+ ♗xd6 16 exd6+ ♔f7 17 ♖e5 ♕c3 18 ♕xd5+ ♔g6 19 h4 h6 20 ♖xf5 ♕xc2 21 ♕f7+ ♔h7 22 ♗xh6!

1-0 Rozentalis-B.Kristensen, Copenhagen 1988.

C34)

6...♗e7 7 ♗xc6! ♕xc6 8 d4 cxd4 9 ♘xd4 ♕c7?!

9...♕c4! is a better try, resembling C33 where Black has the move ...♗f8-e7 rather than ...a7-a6.

10 e5 ♘g8 11 ♘db5 ♕b8 12 ♕g4 g6 13 ♕c4!

Already Black has a dismal position.

13...♗d8 14 ♘e4 a6 15 ♘bd6+ ♔f8 16 a4 ♗c7 17 ♕d4 b6 18 ♖a3!

An excellent way to bring White's last piece into the attack.

18...♗xd6 19 exd6 f6 20 ♘xf6 ♔f7 21 ♖f3

1-0 Kubala-Schroeder, Rimavska Sobota U-14 Ech 1992.

C4)

4...a6 5 ♗xc6 (D)

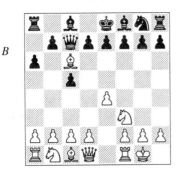

Now Black must choose how to recapture:

C41: 5...dxc6　72
C42: 5...♕xc6　73

5...bxc6? is just a positional mistake, after which we have transposed to Line A11.

C41)

5...dxc6 6 h3 e5 7 d3

Now we have reached a position very similar to that of Line A21 except that White has already castled, giving Black a little more flexibility.

7...f6!?

Again the position takes on an Exchange Lopez character. Others:

a) 7...♘f6 8 ♘bd2 b5 9 ♘b3 ♗e6 (9...c4?! 10 dxc4 ♘xe4 {10...bxc4 11 ♘bd2 c3 12 bxc3} 11 ♖e1 f5 12 ♘bd2 is good for White) 10 ♗e3 ♗xb3 (10...c4?! 11 ♘c5! ♗xc5 12 ♗xc5 cxd3 13 cxd3 ♘d7 14 ♕c2 is awkward for Black to meet) 11 axb3 ♗e7 12 ♘d2 ♗d6 13 ♗g5 ♘d7 14 ♕g4 ♘f8 15 f4 and White has a pleasant advantage, Neumann-Jaeger, Dortmund 1988.

b) 7...♗d6 8 ♗e3 ♘e7 9 ♘bd2 0-0 10 ♘c4 ♗e6 11 ♕e1! f6 (11...♗xc4 12 dxc4 leaves White a little better thanks to his better bishop) 12 ♘xd6 ♕xd6 13 ♕a5 c4 (13...b5? drops a pawn to 14 ♕a3!) 14 ♗c5 ♕d7 15 dxc4 ♖fd8 (15...♗xc4? 16 ♖fd1 ♕e6 17 ♕b4 ♖fe8 18 ♖d6 ♕f7 19 ♖d7 is obviously strong for White) 16 ♗b6 ♖dc8 17 ♖fd1 and White has things well under control, Baklan-A.Kazmin, Yalta 1996.

8 b3 ♗e6 9 a4 ♗d6

9...0-0-0 10 ♘a3 g5 11 ♘d2 h5 12 ♘ac4 g4 13 h4 ♘e7 14 g3 ♘g6 15

&b2 &e7 leads to a tense position in which White's queenside chances are as good as Black's on the kingside, while the positional considerations mean that White's long-term chances must be preferred.

10 ♘a3 ♘e7 11 ♘c4 0-0 12 a5 &xc4 13 bxc4 b5 14 axb6 ♕xb6 15 &d2 a5 16 ♕b1

White is well placed as Black's queenside pawns are weak and White has the better bishop.

C42)
5...♕xc6 6 ♖e1

Left alone White will play c4, b3, &b2, ♘c3 and d4, when on account of his harmonious development and extra space he can enjoy a good position. For this reason Black needs to react quickly in the centre to disrupt this plan and try to achieve equality.

6...d6

6...e6 7 c4 d6 8 ♘c3 e5!? 9 a4 &e7. Now instead of 10 a5?! (Panno-Campos, Mar del Plata 1988) the immediate 10 ♘d5 &d8 11 d3 ♘f6 12 b4! seems to give White a pleasant advantage.

7 h3

A necessary precaution to stop Black activating his light-squared bishop with ...&g4.

7...e5! 8 c4 &e7 9 ♘c3 b6 10 d3 f5?!

This is in my opinion wrong as although it is in principle correct to try to open up a position with the two bishops it leaves far too many weak squares, notably on e4 and d5.

11 exf5 &xf5 12 ♘d5 &e6 13 d4! &xd5

13...cxd4? 14 ♘xd4 exd4 15 ♖xe6 ♕xc4 16 ♖xe7+! ♘xe7 17 ♘xb6 ♕c6 18 ♘xa8 ♕xa8 19 ♕xd4 and White's advantage is obvious.

14 cxd5 ♕xd5 15 dxe5 ♕xd1 16 ♖xd1 ♖d8

On 16...dxe5 17 ♘xe5 White can expect a small advantage due to his lead in development and the potential weakness of Black's queenside pawns.

17 exd6 ♖xd6 18 &f4 ♖e6 19 ♖e1 ♖xe1+ 20 ♖xe1

Black has problems untangling his kingside and completing his development before White can probe his weaknesses, Siklosi-Lenz, Werfen 1989.

C5)
4...e6 5 ♖e1 *(D)*

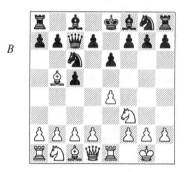

B

Black has now tried:

5...a6 transposes into lines already discussed after 6 &xc6.

5...♘f6 6 ♘c3 transposes into Line C3.

C51)
5...d6 6 c3 a6

6...♗d7 7 d4 ♗e7 8 ♗f4 ♕b6 9 ♘a3 ♘f6 10 d5! ♘e5 11 ♗xd7+ ♘fxd7 (11...♘exd7? 12 dxe6 fxe6 13 ♘c4 winning the d-pawn) 12 ♗xe5 ♘xe5 13 ♘xe5 dxe5 14 ♕a4+ ♔f8 15 ♘c4 and White is doing well, Delanoy-Guglielmi, Robecchetto 1996.

7 ♗f1 g6 8 d4 ♗g7 9 d5! ♘e5 10 ♘xe5 ♗xe5 11 ♘d2 ♗g7 12 a4 ♘e7 13 ♘c4 exd5 14 exd5

We have now reached a Benoni type position in which it is going to be difficult to stop White playing the cramping move a4-a5 as well as putting Black's d-pawn under pressure with ♗f4. White can expect an advantage.

C52)

5...♘ge7!

This natural developing move is best. White needs to be well-versed in the oncoming complications to demonstrate an advantage. Most of the analysis I now give is based on my own work and still leaves scope for alternatives and possible improvements for both sides. However, I believe with careful play White can give his opponent plenty to think about!

6 c3 a6

6...d5 7 exd5 ♘xd5 (7...exd5 8 d4 is a good version of a French Tarrasch position) 8 d4 cxd4 9 ♘xd4 ♗d7 10 ♘xe6 ♗xe6 11 ♕xd5 and White is a pawn up for little compensation.

7 ♗a4 b5 8 ♗c2

Now:

C521: 8...c4!?   74
C522: 8...d5   75

C521)

8...c4!? 9 a4 *(D)*

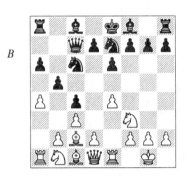

With the following possibilities:

C5211: 9...b4   74
C5212: 9...bxa4   75
C5213: 9...♗b7   75

C5211)

9...b4 10 b3! bxc3

10...d5 11 exd5 exd5 12 h3! (a good move to keep Black's light-squared bishop out of g4) 12...♗b7 13 ♗b2 ♖d8 14 d4 cxd3 (after 14...cxb3 15 ♗xb3 it is difficult to see how Black can best proceed) 15 ♗xd3 bxc3 16 ♘xc3 ♘b4 17 ♖c1 ♘xd3 18 ♕xd3 and Black still has the problem of how to untangle his kingside and get his king into safety.

11 ♘xc3 ♘b4 12 bxc4 ♕xc4

12...♘xc2 13 ♕xc2 ♕xc4 14 ♗a3! (this makes it awkward for Black to maintain the bishop-pair and get castled) 14...d5 15 ♘e5! ♕d4 16 exd5 ♘xd5 17 ♘b5! ♕b6 18 ♘c4 and the black position crumbles.

13 ♗b3 ♕c7

13...♕d3 14 ♗a3 ♘ec6 15 ♘d5! (now Black is in great danger of getting his queen trapped) 15...♘xd5 16 ♗xd5 exd5 17 exd5+ ♔d8 18 dxc6 ♗xa3 19 ♘e5 and everything has gone wrong for Black.

14 d4 ♖b8

14...♘xc3? 15 ♗d2 ♕c7 16 ♗xb4 is good for White.

15 ♕d2 ♘ec6 16 ♗a3

The position is tense but with Black still undeveloped and his king in the centre White's position is preferable.

C5212)

9...bxa4 10 ♖xa4 ♘a5 11 d4 cxd3 12 ♕xd3 ♗b7 13 ♘bd2 d5 14 exd5! ♖d8 15 b4 ♖xd5 16 ♕e2 ♘ac6 17 ♗d3

Black has problems.

C5213)

9...♗b7 10 ♘a3! ♘a7 11 d4 cxd3

11...d5 12 axb5 axb5 13 ♕e2 dxe4 14 ♗xe4 ♘d5 15 ♘e5 ♗d6 and White's powerful centralization guarantees him an edge.

12 ♕xd3 b4 13 ♘c4 d5 14 exd5 ♘xd5 15 ♕d4!

Making use of the control White has on the central dark squares.

15...bxc3 16 bxc3 ♗e7 17 ♖b1 ♗f6? 18 ♖xb7! ♗xd4

After 18...♕xb7 19 ♘d6+ ♔d7 20 ♘xb7 ♗xd4 21 cxd4, with two pieces for the rook White has a significant advantage.

19 ♖xc7 ♗xf2+ 20 ♔xf2 ♘xc7 21 ♘d6+

The strength of the bishop-pair and Black's weakness on the dark squares will tell.

C522)

8...d5 9 d4 cxd4

9...c4 10 b4 a5 11 bxa5 ♖xa5 12 ♗a3 and White can expect a plus.

10 exd5 ♘xd5 11 ♘xd4 ♘xd4

After 11...♗b7?? 12 ♘xe6! fxe6 13 ♕xd5 Black is in deep trouble.

12 ♕xd4 ♗b7

12...♘b4 13 ♗e4 ♘c6 14 ♗f4 is awkward for Black to meet.

13 ♗g5 ♗d6 14 ♕xg7 ♗xh2+ 15 ♔h1 ♖f8 16 ♘d2

White is better mainly due to the fact that the black king is still stuck in the centre.

D)

3...♕b6

A slightly odd-looking move but it is direct and to the point and far more popular than you might expect.

4 ♘c3 *(D)*

B

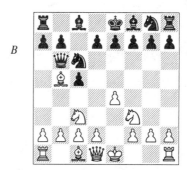

Now we have:

D1:	**4...g6**	75
D2:	**4...a6**	76
D3:	**4...♘d4?!**	76
D4:	**4...e6**	76

D1)

4...g6 5 0-0 ♗g7 6 a4

Black's threat was 6...♗xc3 forcing a favourable exchange of knights after 7 ♗xc6.

6...♘f6 7 e5! ♘g4 8 d4 cxd4 9 ♘d5 ♕d8 10 ♗g5 h6 11 ♗h4 ♘gxe5

11...g5 12 ♗g3 ♘gxe5 13 ♘xe5
♘xe5 14 ♖e1 f6 15 f4 gxf4 16 ♗xf4
and White is doing well.

12 ♘xe5 ♗xe5 13 ♖e1 g5

13...d6? loses to 14 ♗xe7 and
13...f6 14 f4 ♗d6 15 ♘xf6+ ♔f8 16
♘e4! ♗xf4 17 ♖f1 ♕c7 (17...g5 18
♘xg5 hxg5 19 ♗xg5 is very strong) 18
♗xc6 dxc6 19 ♕xd4 ♖h7 20 ♖xf4+
wins for White.

14 ♗xc6 dxc6 15 ♖xe5 cxd5

15...gxh4 16 ♘xe7 ♗e6 17 ♘f5 is
very awkward for Black to meet.

**16 ♕xd4 f6 17 ♖xd5 ♕b6 18
♕xb6 axb6 19 ♗g3**

Despite bishops of opposite col-
our Black has a difficult task ahead,
L.Schneider-Rothen, Eksjö 1981.

D2)

4...a6 5 ♗xc6 ♕xc6

5...dxc6?! 6 h3! ♘f6 7 0-0 ♕c7 8 a4
and White is better for all the same
reasons as in earlier lines where Black
has played an early ...a6 and after
♗xc6 recaptured with a pawn.

6 0-0 e6

6...d6 7 d4 cxd4 8 ♘xd4 ♕c7 9
♗g5! e6 10 ♖e1 ♘f6 11 ♗xf6 gxf6 12
♕h5 ♕c5 13 ♘f5! ♗d7 (13...exf5 14
exf5+ ♗e7 15 ♕e2 ♕e5 16 ♘d5! and
Black is suffering) 14 ♕h4 and Black
has problems, e.g. 14...♗e7 15 ♘xe7
♔xe7 16 e5! ♖hg8 17 ♕xf6+ ♔f8 18
♘e4 ♕c6 19 exd6 ♖e8 20 ♕h6+ ♖g7
21 ♖e3 1-0 Hulak-Simić, Yugoslavia
1976.

7 ♖e1 d6

After 7...♘f6 we transpose to Line
C33.

**8 d4 cxd4 9 ♘d5! e5 10 c3 dxc3 11
♖e3! c2**

11...cxb2 12 ♗xb2 ♗e6 13 ♖c1
♗xd5 14 exd5! (this is stronger than
14 ♖xc6?! ♗xc6, when Black obtains
compensation for the queen) 14...♕b5
15 ♗xe5!! dxe5 16 ♘xe5 ♘e7 (White
wins after 16...♗e7 17 ♕g4 ♕xd5 18
♕xg7) 17 d6 ♖d8 18 d7+ ♖xd7 19
♘xd7 ♕xd7 20 ♖d3 and Black can no
longer defend against the threats.

12 ♕e2

White has plenty of play for the
pawn, Moizhes-Scherbin, Russian Club
Ch 1993.

D3)

**4...♘d4?! 5 ♘xd4! cxd4 6 ♘d5
♕d8**

6...♕c5 7 d3 e6 (7...a6 8 ♗a4 b5 9
♗b3 e6 10 ♘f4 and White has a pleasant position) 8 b4 ♕d6 9 ♗f4 e5 10
♗d2 is slightly better for White.

7 ♕h5! a6??

7...e6?? 8 ♕e5! wins, while after
7...♘f6 8 ♘xf6+ gxf6 9 0-0 White has
a comfortable opening plus.

8 ♕e5 f6 9 ♘c7+ ♔f7 10 ♕d5+

1-0 Smirin-Afek, Israeli Ch 1992.

D4)

4...e6 5 0-0 *(D)*

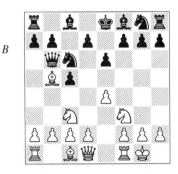

Now Black should choose between:

D41)

5...♘d4 6 ♗c4 ♘e7 7 ♘xd4 cxd4 8 ♘e2 ♘g6

8...d5 9 exd5 ♘xd5 (9...exd5 10 ♗b3 is nice for White) 10 ♗xd5! exd5 11 ♘f4 is awkward for Black to meet.

9 d3 ♗e7 10 c3 dxc3 11 ♘xc3 0-0 12 ♗e3 ♕xb2?!

As usual a dangerous pawn to capture.

13 ♘b5 ♕e5

13...b6?! 14 ♗d4 ♕b4 15 ♖b1 ♕a5 16 ♗c3 ♕a6 17 ♘c7 gives White the advantage, while 13...♗f6 14 ♖b1 ♕e5 15 ♗xa7! is also better for White.

14 f4 ♕b8 15 f5

With good attacking chances for the pawn, Nezhmetdinov-Slutsky, USSR 1965.

D42)

5...♘ge7 6 ♖e1 *(D)*

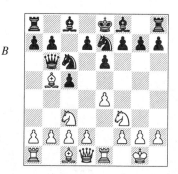

B

Black can try:

Or:

a) 6...♘g6?! 7 ♗xc6 ♕xc6 8 d4, etc.

b) 6...d6!? leads to a strange type of open Sicilian where White can try to make use of his extra tempo after 7 d4 cxd4 8 ♘xd4 ♗d7 (8...a6 9 ♗e3 ♕c7 {9...axb5? 10 ♘dxb5 wins} 10 f4) 9 ♗e3 ♕c7 10 f4 a6 11 ♘f3!.

D421)

6...♘d4 7 a4 a6 8 ♗c4 ♘ec6

8...♘g6 9 d3 ♘xf3+ 10 ♕xf3 ♗d6 11 ♕h5 and White has a nice position, Inkiov-Helmers, Poland 1978.

9 d3 ♘xf3+

After 9...d6 10 ♘xd4 ♘xd4 11 a5 ♕c7 12 ♘e2 ♘xe2+ 13 ♕xe2 ♗e7 14 ♗f4 White is a little better due mainly to his pawn on a5 which is a thorn in Black's side.

10 ♕xf3 ♘d4 11 ♕d1 ♗e7 12 e5! d5 13 exd6 ♕xd6

13...♗xd6 14 ♘d5! ♕d8 15 ♕g4 0-0 16 ♗h6 ♘f5 17 ♗g5! ♕a5 (17...f6 18 ♘xf6+! ♖xf6 19 ♖xe6! ♗xe6 20 ♗xe6+ ♔h8 21 ♗xf5 and White is well on top) 18 ♘f6+ ♔h8 19 ♖e3!! and now:

a) 19...h6 20 ♖h3 ♕b4 21 ♗xh6! ♘xh6 (21...gxh6 22 ♕g5! ♗f4 23 ♕xf4 ♔g7 24 ♖xh6! wins) 22 ♕g5 wins.

b) 19...♘xe3 20 ♕h5 h6 21 ♗xh6 with a crushing attack, e.g. 21...g6 22 ♕h3 e5 23 g4!.

14 ♘e4 ♕c7 15 c3 ♘f5 16 ♕f3

White has a comfortable position, Mäki-Feller, Novi Sad OL 1990.

D422)

6...a6 7 ♗f1

Now Black can choose between:

D4221: 7...d6   78
D4222: 7...♘g6!   78

D4221)

7...d6 8 b3! ♘g6 9 ♗b2 ♗d7 10 ♘e2 e5! 11 h3 ♗e7 12 ♘c3 0-0

12...♘f4 13 ♔h2 and now Black can try:

a) 13...c4!? 14 ♘d5 ♘xd5 (after 14...♕xf2 15 ♘c7+ ♔d8 16 ♘xa8 ♗xh3 17 ♖e2 ♘xe2 18 ♕xe2 White remains a piece to the good) 15 exd5 ♘d8 16 ♗xc4 ♕xf2 17 ♗d4! exd4 18 ♖e2 traps the black queen.

b) 13...0-0 14 g3 ♘e6 15 ♘d5 ♕d8 16 ♗g2 f5 17 exf5 ♖xf5 18 c3 ♘g5 (necessary to stop White's break of d2-d4) 19 ♘xg5 ♗xg5 20 ♕e2 with approximately equal chances.

13 ♘d5 ♕d8 14 c3 ♖e8 15 d4 ♗f8 16 ♕d2

Instead of 16 dxc5?!, which was equal in Marosi-Honfi, Hungary 1993.

16...cxd4 17 cxd4 ♘xd4 18 ♘xd4 exd4 19 ♕xd4

White has the edge thanks to his better pawn-structure and more active pieces.

D4222)

7...♘g6! 8 b3! ♗e7 9 ♗b2 0-0 10 ♘a4! ♕c7 11 c4 d6 12 d4 cxd4 13 ♘xd4 ♗d7

13...♘xd4 14 ♗xd4 gives White an edge on account of the weakness at b6. Up to now we have been following the game Kiss-Nemeth, Hungarian Cht 1993 where White played 14 ♖c1!? and there followed 14...♘xd4 15 ♗xd4 ♗xa4 16 bxa4 with approximate equality.

14 ♘c3!

We have reached a sort of Maroczy Bind where White has more space but Black is very solid and resilient. Black should aim for a timely break with either ...d5 or ...b5 and White should aim to put his rooks on c1 and d1 and try to clamp down on the position.

14...♘xd4

14...♗f6 15 ♘c2 ♘a5 16 ♘e3 b5 17 ♘g4! bxc4 18 ♘xf6+ gxf6 19 ♕f3 and White has good chances along the a1-h8 diagonal.

15 ♕xd4 ♗f6 16 ♕d2 ♗c6 17 ♖ac1! ♖ac8 18 ♖ed1

Now Black has to decide on how best to defend the d-pawn as 18...♖fd8 19 ♘d5! exd5 20 ♗xf6 gxf6 21 cxd5 is better for White and 18...♗e5 19 g3! is hardly inspiring while 18...♗e7 concedes the long diagonal.

D43)

5...a6 6 ♗xc6 ♕xc6 7 ♖e1 *(D)*

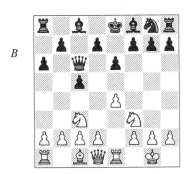

Now:

7...d6 8 d4 cxd4 9 ♘d5 transposes to Line D2.

D431)

7...♗e7?! 8 d4 cxd4 9 ♕xd4 ♘f6 10 e5 ♗c5

10...♘d5? 11 ♘xd5 exd5 12 c3 0-0 13 ♖d1 and Black will not be able to prove enough compensation for the d-pawn falling.

11 ♕h4 ♘d5 12 ♘e4 b5 13 a4!

A typical queenside 'softening-up' thrust.

13...bxa4

13...♗b7 14 ♘d4! with the following possibilities:

a) 14...♗xd4!? 15 axb5 ♕xc2 (not 15...axb5?? 16 ♘d6+ ♔f8 17 ♖xa8+ ♗xa8 18 ♕d8#) 16 ♘d6+ ♔f8 17 ♕xd4 axb5 18 ♖xa8+ ♗xa8 19 ♗g5 and White has plenty of play for the pawn.

b) 14...♕c7 15 axb5 ♕xe5 16 ♘f3 ♕c7 17 bxa6 ♖xa6 18 ♖xa6 ♗xa6 19 ♘xc5 ♕xc5 20 ♕g3 is very awkward for Black to meet.

14 ♖xa4 ♗e7 15 ♗g5! f6

15...♕xc2? 16 ♗xe7 ♘xe7 17 ♘d6+ ♔f8 18 ♖f4! ♕g6 19 ♖xf7+ ♕xf7 20 ♘xf7 ♔xf7 21 ♘g5+ ♔e8 22 ♕h5+ g6 23 ♕f3 ♖b8 24 ♕f7+ ♔d8 25 ♖d1! winning easily or 15...0-0? 16 ♗xe7 ♘xe7 17 ♘f6+! gxf6 18 ♖g4+ ♘g6 19 ♕h6! and Black is powerless to stop the oncoming threats.

16 exf6 gxf6 17 ♖c4! ♕b5 18 ♗xf6 ♘xf6 19 ♘xf6+ ♗xf6 20 ♕xf6 ♖f8 21 ♕d4

Black's position is sad, Barua-Donguines, Cebu 1992.

D432)

7...b5 8 d4 cxd4 9 ♘d5! ♘f6!?

a) 9...♕c5? 10 b4! ♕a7 11 ♗b2 exd5 12 exd5+ ♔d8 13 ♗xd4 ♕b8 14

♕e2 and White has masses of compensation for the piece.

b) 9...♕b7 10 ♘xd4 exd5 (not for the faint hearted!) 11 exd5+ ♔d8 12 ♕h5! ♘f6 13 ♕xf7 ♕xd5 14 ♖e8+! ♔c7 15 ♘e6+! ♔b6 16 ♗e3+ ♔b7 17 ♘d8+ ♔b8 18 ♗f4+ with a draw by perpetual as 18...d6 19 ♕xd5 ♘xd5 20 ♖xf8 ♖xf8 21 ♗xd6+ ♔a7 22 ♗xf8 wins.

10 ♘xd4 ♕b7 11 ♘xf6+ gxf6 12 ♕f3 ♗e7

12...♖g8 13 ♕h5! is unpleasant to meet.

13 ♕g3

White is better.

D433)

7...♕c7 8 d4 cxd4 9 ♘xd4 b5 10 ♗g5 ♗b4

10...b4? is refuted by 11 ♘d5! exd5 12 exd5+ ♗e7 13 ♗xe7 ♘xe7 14 ♖xe7+ ♔xe7 15 d6+!.

11 ♘f5! exf5

11...f6 12 ♗d2! ♗xc3 13 ♗xc3 exf5 14 exf5+ ♔d8 (14...♘e7? 15 ♗b4 wins) 15 ♕d5! ♗b7 16 ♕f7 and Black's position falls apart.

12 exf5+ ♔f8

12...♘e7? loses to 13 ♗xe7 ♗xe7 14 ♖xe7+ ♔xe7 15 ♘d5+.

13 ♘d5 ♕a5 14 ♘xb4 ♕xb4 15 ♕d5 ♖a7 16 c3!

White wins as the black queen can no longer cover d6.

E)

3...♘a5?!

If this strange move can be justified it is only due to the time Black will gain by playing ...a6.

4 c3 a6

After 4...♘f6?! 5 e5 ♘d5 6 d4 cxd4 7 ♕xd4 we have reached a type of 2 c3 Sicilian (1 e4 c5 2 c3 ♘f6 3 e5 ♘d5 4 d4 cxd4 5 ♕xd4 e6 6 ♘f3) where Black seems to be tempi down in that the knight on a5 must be a liability rather than an asset.

5 ♗e2! *(D)*

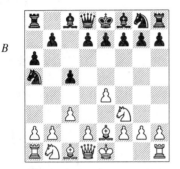

White's intention is to show that the 'gain' of tempo by Black in getting his knight to a5 is in fact a loss of time. Black has now tried:

a) 5...♕c7?! 6 d4 d6 7 0-0 e5 8 b4! ♘c6 9 bxc5 dxc5 10 d5 and White has gained so much time that although Black is still solid White holds a lasting initiative.

b) 5...b5 6 0-0 ♘f6 7 a4! ♘xe4 8 axb5 c4 (8...axb5? 9 b4 wins material) 9 d3 ♘b3 10 dxe4 ♘xa1 11 ♗xc4 ♗b7 12 b6! ♗xe4 13 ♗e3 d5 (13...♘c2? 14 ♘g5 d5 15 ♗b3 wins, while after 13...♗c2?!, 14 ♕e2! is simple and good) 14 ♘e5! and Black has no answers to the problems set.

c) 5...d6?! 6 d4 cxd4 7 cxd4 g6 8 ♗d2 ♗d7 9 ♗c3! ♗g7 10 ♕d2 ♘c6 11 d5 ♘e5 12 ♘xe5 dxe5 13 ♘a3 and White is well placed, Shtyrenkov-Lysenko, Russian Club Ch 1993.

d) 5...d5?! 6 exd5 ♕xd5 7 d4 c4 (7...cxd4 8 cxd4 is a favourable version of a 2 c3 Sicilian) 8 0-0 ♘f6 9 ♘e5 ♗d7 10 ♗e3 e6 11 b4! cxb3 12 axb3 ♘c6 13 ♗f3 ♕d6 (13...♕b5 14 c4 ♕b4 15 ♘xd7 ♘xd7 16 ♖a4 ♕d6 17 ♘c3 and with a lead in development, more space and the bishop-pair, White is well placed) 14 ♗f4 ♘xe5 15 ♗xb7! ♖a7 16 ♗xe5 and Black is a pawn down for nothing, T.Horvath-Rabovszky, Zalakaros 1994.

e) 5...e6 6 d4 cxd4 (6...d5?! 7 exd5 exd5 8 dxc5 is good for White) 7 cxd4 d5 8 exd5 exd5 (8...♕xd5 9 ♘c3 once again leads to a favourable 2 c3 Sicilian in that Black's knight is not well placed on a5) 9 0-0 and White is a little better due to his lead in development.

f) 5...♘f6?! 6 e5 ♘d5 7 d4 cxd4 8 ♕xd4 and similarly to the note to Black's 4th move we have reached a favourable line of a 2 c3 Sicilian.

F)

3...e5

Black occupies the centre, realizing that 4 ♗xc6 dxc6 5 ♘xe5? leads to nothing after 5...♕d4.

4 0-0

Now Black should choose between:

F1: 4...d6   80
F2: 4...♘ge7   82

F1)

4...d6 5 c3 *(D)*
5...♘ge7

Or:

a) 5...♕b6 6 ♘a3! does little to help Black's cause.

b) 5...♗e7?! 6 d4 exd4 7 cxd4 ♗d7 8 ♘c3 cxd4 9 ♘xd4 ♘f6 10 ♗f4 and

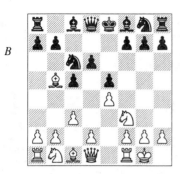

B

White has an edge due to Black's disrupted pawn-structure, Lendwai-Fauland, Austrian League 1990/1.

c) 5...♗g4?! 6 h3 and now:

c1) 6...♗h5 7 d4 cxd4 8 cxd4 exd4 9 g4!? ♗g6 10 ♘xd4 ♘ge7 (but not 10...♗xe4? 11 ♖e1) 11 ♘c3 a6 12 ♗a4 h5 (12...b5 13 ♘dxb5! axb5 14 ♘xb5! is very hard for Black to meet, e.g. 14...♔d7 {14...♖xa4? 15 ♘xd6+ ♔d7 16 ♘xf7+ wins} 15 ♘xd6 ♔c7 16 ♗f4 winning) 13 ♗g5 f6 14 ♗f4 ♖c8 (14...hxg4 15 ♘e6 ♕d7 16 ♕xd6 ♕xd6 17 ♗xd6 ♔d7 18 ♘xf8+ ♖axf8 19 ♗xe7 ♔xe7 20 hxg4 and Black must prove compensation for the pawn) 15 ♘e6 ♕d7 16 ♕xd6 hxg4? (16...♕xd6 transposes to the previous note) 17 ♕xd7+ ♔xd7 18 ♘c5+ 1-0 Lukin-Kozlov, Yaroslavl 1990.

c2) 6...♗xf3 7 ♕xf3 ♘f6 8 a4 and White is already better thanks to the bishop-pair and his control of the central light squares, Stefanov-Susterman, Odorheiu Secuiesc 1993.

d) 5...♘f6 6 d4 exd4 (after 6...♗d7 7 dxc5 dxc5 8 ♕e2 White has the edge due to Black's long-term weakness on d5 and the potential weakness along the a2-g8 diagonal, Glek-Rabiega, Hamburg 1993) 7 cxd4 ♕b6 (7...♕c7? 8 d5

a6 9 ♕a4! axb5 10 ♕xa8 ♘b4 11 ♘c3 and Black has little to show for being the exchange down) 8 ♘c3 ♗d7 9 d5 ♘e5 10 ♗xd7+ leads to a favourable Benoni type position.

e) 5...a6?! 6 ♗xc6+ bxc6 7 ♕a4!. It is typical of lines where Black plays an ...a7-a6 at some stage that he obtains the bishop-pair but at too high a price. White has a significant lead in development, good squares to put his pieces on and a superior pawn-structure. After 7...♗d7 8 ♘a3 ♘f6 9 d3 ♗e7 10 ♘c4, Domont-Jakoc, Swiss Cht 1993, White has a comfortable position and can aim to play a timely f4, place a knight on f5 to provoke further weaknesses or aim for h3, ♗e3, a3 and b4. Black on the other hand is solid but planless due to the immobility of his central pawns.

f) 5...♗d7 6 d4 ♕c7 (6...♗e7 7 dxc5 dxc5 8 ♕e2 ♕c7 9 ♗xc6!? ♗xc6 10 c4 ♘f6 11 ♘c3 0-0 12 ♗g5 ♖fe8 13 ♖fd1 h6 14 ♗xf6 ♗xf6 15 ♘d5 ♗xd5 16 ♖xd5 and White is a little better in view of his superior control of the d-file and potentially better minor piece, Schubert-Bialas, Bundesliga 1980; Black's central pawns are stagnant on the dark squares) 7 d5 ♘ce7 8 a4 seems fine for White.

6 d4 a6 7 ♗c4 b5

Or:

a) 7...♗g4?? 8 ♗xf7+ ♔xf7 9 ♘g5+ is obviously extremely strong for White.

b) 7...♕c7?! 8 dxc5 dxc5 9 ♗e3 ♘d8 10 a4 ♘ec6 11 ♘bd2 ♗e7 12 ♗d5! (occupying the centre whilst making way for the knight on c4) 12...a5 13 h3 0-0 14 ♘c4 gives White everything that she could want in terms of development and piece placement while Black's position looks cluttered and disjointed, Kovalevskaya-Strutinskaya, Russian wom Ch 1995.

8 ♗b3 c4 9 ♗c2

Although Black seems to have gained some time, his queenside pawns are likely to come under pressure while White maintains superior development especially as Black has yet to develop his dark-squared bishop in preparation for castling. For example after 9...♗g4 10 d5 ♘b8 11 ♗e3 ♘d7 12 h3 ♗h5 13 a4 White has a pleasant position.

F2)
4...♘ge7 5 c3 g6 *(D)*

Other moves are of little significance, e.g. 5...♕b6?! 6 ♘a3 ♘g6 7 d3 a6 8 ♗c4 ♗e7 9 ♗d5 d6 10 ♘c4 ♕d8 11 a4 h6 12 a5 0-0 13 ♕b3 and White has a strong bind, Kroeze-Bark, Dutch Ch 1996.

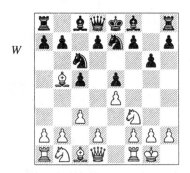

6 d4 cxd4 7 cxd4 exd4 8 ♗f4 ♗g7
8...d6? 9 ♕xd4 ♖g8 10 ♘a3 a6 11 ♘c4! ♗g7 (11...axb5 12 ♘xd6+ ♔d7 13 ♕d3! and Black is powerless against the threats) 12 ♘xd6+ ♔f8 13 ♕c4 ♗e6 14 ♘g5! ♘c8 (14...♗xc4?? 15

♘xh7#) 15 ♘xe6+ fxe6 16 ♕xe6 and White's position is overwhelming, Ulybin-E.Peicheva, Oakham jr 1990.

9 ♘a3 0-0 10 ♗d6! ♖e8 11 ♘g5 ♘a5?!

11...h6?? 12 ♘xf7 ♔xf7 13 ♗c4+ is killing.

12 b4 h6 13 ♘xf7 ♔xf7 14 bxa5 ♔g8 15 f4

White has a terrific bind, Mahdy-E.Csom, Budapest 1990.

G)
3...♘f6

An underestimated reply. Black develops a piece and puts the question to White of how best to proceed.

4 ♘c3 *(D)*

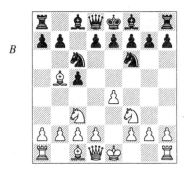

We have now reached a reversed Four Knights English (1 c4 e5 2 ♘c3 ♘f6 3 ♘f3 ♘c6) with the extra tempo ♗f1-b5, a fairly standard move in that variation. In theory at least this should be quite satisfactory. We will now look at the possibilities available for Black:

G1: 4...e5	83
G2: 4...♕c7	83
G3: 4...a6?!	84
G4: 4...♘d4	84
G5: 4...g6	85

Or:

a) 4...d5?! 5 exd5 ♘xd5 6 0-0 ♗g4 (6...♘xc3 7 bxc3 and White is already ahead in development) 7 h3 ♗h5 8 g4 ♗g6 9 ♘e5 is awkward for Black to meet.

b) 4...d6 will transpose into a line discussed in Part 2 of this chapter via the move-order 1 e4 c5 2 ♘f3 d6 3 d4 cxd4 4 ♕xd4 ♘c6 5 ♗b5 ♘f6 6 ♘c3.

G1)

4...e5 5 ♗xc6 dxc6 6 ♘xe5 ♘xe4! 7 ♘xe4 ♕d5

7...♕d4 will transpose after 8 0-0 ♕xe5.

8 0-0 ♕xe5

8...♕xe4? 9 ♖e1 is just asking for trouble.

9 ♖e1 ♗e7

9...♗e6?! 10 d3 0-0-0 11 ♘g5 ♕f5 12 ♘xe6 fxe6 13 ♕e2 ♖e8 14 a4! (the real point of this move doesn't become apparent until move 16) 14...♗d6 15 a5 h5 16 ♖a4! gives White a strong positional advantage due to the weakness of the black pawn-structure, Brajović-Knežević, Yugoslav Cht 1995.

10 d4!?

With the following possibilities:

a) 10...♕xd4 11 ♗g5! ♗e6 (not 11...♗xg5?? 12 ♘xc5+ winning outright; 11...♕xd1 12 ♖axd1 ♗e6 13 ♗xe7 ♔xe7 14 ♘xc5 ♖hd8 with equality) 12 ♗xe7 ♔xe7 (12...♕xd1 13 ♖axd1 transposes to 11...♕xd1) 13 ♕h5 b6 (13...♕d5?! 14 ♘g5 g6 15 ♕h4 with very good play for the pawn) 14 ♘g5 (White is threatening ♕xf7+) 14...g6 (14...♕f6 15 ♖e3 g6 16 ♕h6 ♕xb2 17 ♖ae1 is very uncomfortable for Black) 15 ♕f3 ♕f6 16 ♘xe6! fxe6

(16...♕xf3?? 17 ♘d4+ winning) 17 ♕xc6 with advantage.

b) 10...cxd4 11 ♗g5! 0-0 12 ♘f6+ ♗xf6 13 ♖xe5 ♗xe5. Although technically difficult White has a small advantage, Jansa-Tomczak, Bundesliga 1990/1.

G2)

4...♕c7 5 0-0 *(D)*

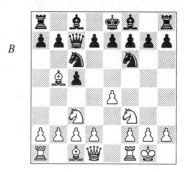

Now:
G21: 5...e5?! 83
G22: 5...♘d4 84

5...e6 6 ♖e1 d6 7 d4 cxd4 8 ♘d5! transposes to Line C3.

G21)

5...e5?!

Although this stops White playing d2-d4, the move is inconsistent with ...♕c7 as it invites White to make use of the d5-square.

6 d3

White aims for ♗g5 followed by ♗xf6 and ♘d5. To prevent this Black must spend a tempo with ...h6, but this just tempts White to aim for f2-f4 instead, provoking further weaknesses.

6...h6 7 ♘h4

White doesn't fear ...♘d4 in the slightest as this would just lead to him improving his light-squared bishop with ♗c4, when it would exert maximum pressure on the a2-g8 diagonal.

7...g5 8 ♘f5 ♘d4 9 ♘xd4 cxd4 10 ♘e2

Although Black has prevented White's plans, at least temporarily, he now has inherent weaknesses in his position, a lack of development and his king still in the centre.

10...a6 11 ♗a4 ♗g7 12 ♘g3 b5 13 ♗b3 d6 14 a4!

White has a little 'probe' on the queenside knowing that Black must keep his light-squared bishop covering the f5-square.

14...♖b8 15 axb5 axb5 16 ♗d2 0-0 17 h4!

Now it is time to 'probe' on the kingside.

17...gxh4 18 ♘h5 h3 19 ♘xf6+ ♗xf6 20 ♕h5 ♗g7 21 ♗xh6 ♕e7 22 ♖a7!

1-0 Glek-Brendel, Krumbach 1991. Black resigned in view of 22...♖b7 (22...♕xa7?? 23 ♕g6 with mate to follow) 23 ♖xb7 ♗xb7 24 ♕g6 ♕f6 25 ♕xf6 ♗xf6 26 ♗xf8 ♔xf8 27 ♖a1 with a fatal penetration of the rook down the a-file.

G22)

5...♘d4

This continues the theme of following a reversed Four Knights English.

6 ♖e1 a6 7 ♗c4 e6

7...b5?! 8 ♘d5! is strong, e.g. 8...♘xd5 9 ♗xd5 ♗b7 10 c3 ♘xf3+ 11 ♕xf3 ♗xd5 12 exd5, when Black will have problems due to his lack of development and White has pressure down the e-file.

8 e5 d5!? 9 exf6 dxc4 10 ♘e4 ♗d7 11 d3 0-0-0 12 ♘xd4 cxd4 13 fxg7 ♗xg7 14 ♗g5 ♖dg8 15 ♕h5

Despite his bishop-pair Black has problems due to the looseness of his queenside, Jansa-Mrva, Czechoslovak Ch 1992.

G3)

4...a6?! 5 ♗xc6

Now:

a) 5...bxc6 6 ♕e2 e6 7 d3 d5 8 0-0 ♗e7 9 b3! 0-0 10 ♗b2 a5 11 ♘e5 ♕c7 12 ♘a4 ♗a6 13 c4 gives White a pleasant edge due to the weakness of Black's doubled c-pawns and the lack of scope for his light-squared bishop combined with White's potential kingside play, Ibraev-Dos Santos, Guarapuava U-18 Wch 1995.

b) 5...dxc6 6 e5 ♘d5 7 ♘e4 c4!? 8 0-0 ♗g4 9 h3 ♗h5 10 e6! fxe6 11 ♘eg5 h6?! 12 ♘xe6 ♕d6 13 ♖e1 (White has a terrific bind thanks to his monster knight on e6) 13...♗f7 14 ♘fd4 c5? 15 ♘f5 and Black is in deep trouble, Kondou-Cincar, Komotini 1993.

G4)

4...♘d4 5 e5 ♘xb5 6 ♘xb5 ♘d5 7 ♘g5!? (D)

Why put one knight out on a limb when you can place two!? Now Black has these choices:

a) 7...h6?! 8 ♘xf7 ♔xf7 9 ♕f3+ ♘f6 (9...♔e6 10 c4! ♘b4 {10...♘b6 11 d4! d5 12 dxc5 ♘a4? 13 ♘d4+ ♔d7 14 e6+ ♔c7 15 ♕f4+ winning} 11 a3 ♘c2+ 12 ♔d1 and Black is in big trouble, e.g. 12...♘xa1 13 g4! and

B

Black is powerless to stop mate) 10 exf6 exf6 11 ♕d5+ and White is obviously a little better.

b) 7...f6 8 ♕h5+ g6 9 ♕f3 fxg5 (9...♘b4?! 10 exf6 ♘xc2+? {10...exf6 11 ♕e4+ ♕e7 12 ♘d6+ ♔d8 13 ♘gf7+ ♔c7 14 ♔d1! ♖g8 15 d4 ♕xe4 16 ♘xe4 and Black has problems untangling} 11 ♔d1 exf6 12 ♔xc2 fxg5 13 ♖e1+ winning) 10 ♕xd5 a6 11 ♘a3 e6 12 ♕f3 and White is a little better, e.g. 12...d5 13 exd6 ♗xd6 14 ♘c4 and Black is awkwardly placed due to his disrupted pawn-structure and his difficulty in castling.

c) 7...f5 8 0-0 e6 9 d4! ♕b6 10 c4 cxd4 11 ♕a4 a6 12 ♘xe6! ♕xe6 13 cxd5 ♕xe5 14 ♗g5 ♕b8 15 ♕c2! g6 16 ♘c7+ ♔f7 17 d6 1-0 Minasian-S.Schmidt, Leningrad 1990.

d) 7...♘c7 8 ♕h5! g6 9 ♕f3 f6 10 exf6 ♗h6 (10...exf6? 11 ♘xc7+ ♕xc7 12 ♕xf6 wins) 11 f7+ ♔f8 12 d4 ♗g7 13 ♘xc7 ♕xc7 14 ♗f4 ♕a5+ 15 ♗d2 and White is better, Brynell-F.Rayner, Haifa Echt 1989.

e) 7...♕b6 8 ♕f3 f6 9 ♕xd5 fxg5 10 c4 a6 11 ♘c3 e6 12 ♕f3 ♗e7 13 0-0 is similar to variation 'b'. In the game Kulish-Ciuksyte, Kishinev wom IZ 1995 White was a little better due to

Black's inability to castle and finish her development conveniently.

G5)

4...g6 5 e5!? ♘g4 6 ♗xc6 dxc6 7 h3 ♘h6 8 g4

White hopes to gain the initiative by controlling f5, thus limiting the scope of both Black's light-squared bishop and his knight on h6.

8...♗g7 9 d3 f5

Necessary as 9...0-0? would allow White to play 10 ♗e3, which not only hits the pawn on c5 but threatens ♕d2 winning the knight on h6. Black hopes instead not only to make a 'bolt-hole' for his knight but to lure forward White's g-pawn hoping to undermine it later with a timely ...h6.

10 g5 ♘f7 11 ♗f4 ♗e6 12 ♕e2 ♕a5 13 ♗d2 ♕c7 14 0-0-0 0-0-0

Curiously enough this position had been reached before, in J.Polgar-Ochoa, New York Open 1991. There White went on to win after 15 ♖de1 b5!? although Black may have been roughly equal.

15 ♖he1!

The idea of this is to keep a rook on d1 to assist the future advance of d3-d4.

15...h6 16 gxh6 ♗xh6 17 ♗xh6 ♖xh6 18 h4!

Necessary to restrict Black on the kingside.

18...♗d5 19 ♘xd5 ♖xd5 20 c4 ♖d8 21 ♕e3 b6 22 e6 f4 23 ♕e4 ♘h8 24 d4!

After this White is definitely better.

24...cxd4 25 ♖xd4 ♖xd4 26 ♕xd4

Black is badly tied up and must avoid a fatal penetration both on the kingside and down the d-file, Sanz Alonso-Frois, Oviedo rpd 1991.

H)

3...e6

This and 3...g6 are the most common replies to 3 ♗b5. Which of the two Black chooses is more a matter of style and taste than anything else.

4 0-0 *(D)*

As an alternative to 4 0-0 I am showing the possibilities of 4 ♘c3 in Part 3 of this chapter from the move-order 1 e4 c5 2 ♘f3 e6 3 ♘c3 ♘c6 4 ♗b5!?.

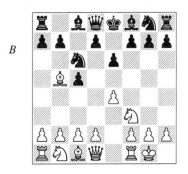

4...♘ge7

Almost an automatic response but let us first of all look at alternatives.

a) 4...a6?! 5 ♗xc6 dxc6 (5...bxc6 transposes to Line A13) 6 d3 ♕c7 7 e5! (gaining space and at the same time restricting Black from playing ...e5 freeing his light-squared bishop) 7...f5!? 8 a4 a5 9 ♘a3 ♘e7 10 ♘c4 ♘d5 11 ♖e1 ♘b6 12 ♘xb6 ♕xb6 13 b3 and White is better in view of Black's lack of development and potentially weak queenside structure, Hort-Kurajica, Vinkovci 1976.

b) 4...♕c7 transposes to Line C5.

c) 4...♘d4?! transposes to Line B after 5 ♘xd4 cxd4 6 d3.

d) 4...♕b6 5 ♘c3 transposes to Line D4.

e) 4...d6?! 5 c3 with the following possibilities:

e1) 5...a6?! 6 ♗xc6+ bxc6 7 d4 cxd4 8 cxd4 ♘e7 9 ♘c3 d5 10 e5 (we have now reached almost a French-type position where Black's inability to play the freeing move ...c6-c5 gives him little chance of equality) 10...♘g6 11 ♘a4! a5 12 ♕c2 ♕c7 13 h4 ♗a6 14 ♖e1 ♗b4 15 ♗d2 ♗b5 16 ♗xb4 axb4 17 ♘c5 0-0 18 ♘g5! and White's advantage is obvious, Friedgood-Volpert, South Africa 1967.

e2) 5...♗e7?! 6 d4 cxd4 7 cxd4 ♗d7 8 ♘c3 ♘f6 9 d5 exd5 10 exd5 ♘b8 11 ♘d4 0-0 12 ♗xd7 ♕xd7 13 ♕f3 g6 14 ♖e1 and White's extra space and lead in development together with Black's dark-squared weaknesses on the kingside guarantee White the advantage, Csoke-Balazs, Hungarian Cht 1993.

e3) 5...♗d7 6 d4 and now:

e31) 6...cxd4 7 cxd4 a6 8 ♗a4 ♘a7 9 ♗b3 ♘e7 10 ♗g5! h6 11 ♗h4 ♕a5 12 ♘bd2 ♘ec8 13 d5! (once again the thematic move d4-d5 seems the best to ensure an advantage in gaining space and restricting Black) 13...e5 14 ♘c4 ♕c7 15 ♖c1 and White's lead in development, better piece placement and extra space guarantee him the edge, Darcyl-Bonsignore, Buenos Aires 1990.

e32) 6...♘f6 7 ♖e1 ♗e7 8 a4 0-0 9 d5! exd5 10 exd5 ♘b8 11 ♘a3 reaches a Schmid Benoni type of position where Black has lost time due to the

...♘b8-c6-b8 manoeuvre. White can therefore expect to enjoy a pleasant advantage.

e4) 5...♘f6 6 d4! cxd4 (6...♘xe4?! 7 d5 ♕b6 8 ♘a3 exd5 9 ♕xd5 ♘f6 10 ♖e1+ ♗e6 11 ♖xe6+! fxe6 12 ♕xe6+ ♔d8 {12...♗e7 13 ♘c4 ♕c7 14 ♗f4 is difficult for Black to meet} 13 ♗g5 ♗e7 14 ♘h4! offers White a lot of play for the material invested) 7 cxd4 d5 8 e5 ♘d7 9 ♘c3 leaves Black with an inferior type of French position as he has released the tension in the centre prematurely.

f) 4...♗e7 5 d3! (opting for the more closed approach) 5...♕c7 6 ♘c3 b6 7 ♗xc6! dxc6 (7...♕xc6?! 8 ♘e5 ♕c7 9 ♗f4 d6 10 ♘b5 ♕d8 11 ♘c6 ♕d7 12 ♘xe7 ♕xb5 13 ♘xc8 ♖xc8 14 b3 ♕d7 15 ♕g4 is a little better for White due to his lead in development and more active position) 8 e5! (thematic in variations where White exchanges on c6, the move e4-e5 not only gains space but restricts Black's activity – especially that of his light-squared bishop) 8...♗a6 9 ♕e2 ♖d8 10 ♖e1 ♖d7 11 ♘e4 and White is better mainly due to the congested situation of Black's kingside, Khamatgaleev-Kosyrev, Russian Club Ch 1993.

g) 4...♗d6?! 5 ♖e1 f6 6 c3 ♕c7 7 d4 cxd4 8 cxd4 ♘ge7 9 ♘c3 0-0 10 ♗e3 b6 11 ♖c1 a6 12 ♗d3 gives White an advantage due to his extra space and classical centre leaving him with more options to make a break with a timely d4-d5 or e4-e5, El Ghaidi-Grolemund, Lucerne OL 1982.

h) 4...g6?! 5 ♗xc6! bxc6 6 e5! ♗g7 7 d3 f6 8 ♖e1 ♘e7 9 exf6 ♗xf6

10 ♘c3 d6 11 d4 cxd4 12 ♘xd4 ♗xd4 (12...e5? 13 ♘e4! ♗g7 14 ♘xc6 ♘xc6 15 ♘xd6+ is very strong in view of Black's loose knight on c6) 13 ♕xd4 0-0 14 ♗g5 and White has the edge due to Black's long-term weaknesses, C.Müller-Jannsen, German U-20 Ch (Hamburg) 1993.

5 ♖e1 *(D)*

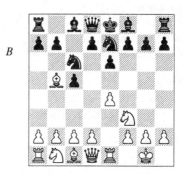

Now Black can choose between the following moves:

H1: 5...♘d4   88
H2: 5...♘g6   88
H3: 5...a6   88

Other possibilities are:

a) 5...♕b6 6 ♘c3 transposes to Line D42.

b) 5...d5?! 6 exd5 ♘xd5 (6...♕xd5 7 ♘c3 ♕h5 8 ♘e4! is better for White, while 6...exd5 7 ♘c3 is similar to the lines in Chapter 6, Part 1, Line A – a French line that favours White) 7 ♗xc6+ bxc6 8 d3 ♗e7 9 ♘bd2 0-0 10 ♘c4 f6 11 ♘fd2! e5 12 ♘e4 ♗e6 (12...f5? 13 ♘ed2! e4 14 dxe4 fxe4 15 ♘xe4 and Black has no real compensation for the pawn deficit) 13 b3 ♕d7 14 ♗a3 ♘b4 15 ♕d2 and White is a little better due to the inflexibility of the black position, Spassky-Ortega, Sochi Chigorin mem 1966.

c) 5...g6 6 ♗xc6! dxc6 (6...♘xc6 7 d4 cxd4 8 ♘xd4 is fine for White in view of the dark-squared weaknesses in Black's position) 7 e5 ♗g7 8 ♘c3 ♕c7? 9 ♘e4 ♗xe5 10 ♘xe5 ♕xe5 11 d4 cxd4? (11...♕xd4!? 12 ♗d2! 0-0 13 ♗c3 ♕xd1 14 ♘f6+ ♔g7 15 ♖axd1 gives White very good compensation for the pawn) 12 ♗g5! ♕c7 13 ♘f6+ ♔d8 14 ♕xd4+ ♗d7 15 ♘xd7 1-0 Adorjan-Reuben, England 1973.

H1)

5...♘d4 6 ♘xd4 cxd4 7 c4!

A new approach in this position. Instead of aiming to put pressure on d4 with c2-c3 or attempting to block the position with d2-d3 (when c2 can come under pressure in the long term) White first aims for queenside expansion.

7...♘c6

After 7...a6 8 ♗a4 ♖b8 9 d3 b5 10 cxb5 axb5 11 ♗b3 White may already be better because of his lead in development and gaps that may appear in Black's queenside, e.g. 11...d5 12 ♗f4 ♖a8 13 exd5! ♘xd5 14 ♗e5 ♘f6 15 ♕f3.

8 d3 d6 9 b4!

Black has still to find a plan while White has plenty of natural moves available, e.g. ♘d2, f4, ♘f3, a3, etc.

H2)

5...♘g6 6 ♘c3 ♗e7

6...a6 7 ♗f1 ♗e7 is likely to transpose.

7 d4 cxd4 8 ♘xd4 0-0 9 ♗e3 a6 10 ♗f1 b5 11 a4!

A typical 'softening up' type of move as after Black's reply the c4-square is permanently available for White to occupy.

11...b4 12 ♘xc6 dxc6 13 ♕xd8 ♖xd8 14 ♘a2 c5 15 ♘c1 ♗b7 16 f3 a5 17 ♘b3 ♖dc8 18 ♘d2!

This knight has gone the route b1-c3-a2-c1-b3-d2 eventually controlling that all-important c4-square.

18...♘e5 19 ♗f4 ♗f6 20 ♗xe5 ♗xe5

J.Polgar-Hajkova, Thessaloniki wom OL 1988. Despite having the bishop-pair Black is a little worse. Firstly her light-squared bishop is a poor piece, secondly her a- and c-pawns are both backward and may become vulnerable and thirdly White's knight may eventually hop into Black's position via c4.

H3)

5...a6 6 ♗xc6 ♘xc6

6...bxc6?! seems strange: playing ...e6, ...♘ge7 and ...a6 only to recapture on c6 with a pawn after all! 7 e5! (the usual thematic response) 7...♘g6 8 b3 ♗e7 9 ♗a3 0-0 10 d4 cxd4 11 ♕xd4 leaves White a little better due to the potentially weak dark squares in Black's position and his bad light-squared bishop, Tal-R.Byrne, Moscow 1971.

7 d4 cxd4 8 ♘xd4 *(D)*

Now Black can choose between:

H31: 8...♗e7   89
H32: 8...d6   89

Alternatives:

a) 8...♕f6?! 9 ♘xc6 dxc6 10 e5! and Black will find it hard to achieve

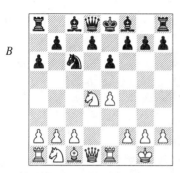

equality, e.g. 10...♕f5 11 ♘d2 ♗c5 (11...♗e7 12 ♘c4 0-0 13 ♘d6! ♕g6 14 ♖e3! and White has a strong bind on the position) 12 ♘e4! ♕xe5 13 ♗g5! and Black has big problems.

b) 8...♗b4?! 9 c3 ♗c5 10 ♗e3 ♘xd4 11 ♗xd4 ♗xd4 12 ♕xd4 0-0 and now rather than 13 c4?! (Ivkov-B.Ivanović, Sveti Sava 1994) White could have secured a definite advantage by 13 ♘d2, e.g. 13...b5 14 ♘b3 ♕c7 15 ♖ad1 ♖d8 16 ♕d6.

c) 8...♕b6 9 ♘xc6 ♕xc6 10 ♘c3 ♗b4? 11 ♕d4! ♗xc3 12 bxc3 f6 (12...0-0 13 ♗a3 ♖e8 14 c4! is better for White) 13 ♗a3 b5 14 ♕b4! d6 15 ♖ad1 ♔f7 16 ♖xd6 ♕c7 17 ♖ed1 and White is clearly well on top, Andersson-Forintos, Wijk aan Zee 1970.

d) 8...♘xd4?! 9 ♕xd4 b5 10 ♘c3 ♗b7 11 ♗f4! (again exploiting the central dark squares, in particular d6) 11...f6 (11...d6 12 ♗g3 and Black has problems with the long-term defence of d6) 12 ♗d6 ♗xd6 13 ♕xd6 ♕b8 14 ♕c5 ♕e5 15 ♘d5! and Black has problems, Ermenkov-L.Spasov, Varna 1973.

H31)

8...♗e7 9 ♘xc6 bxc6

9...dxc6 10 ♕xd8+ ♗xd8 11 e5! ♗c7 (11...c5!?) 12 a4 b5 13 ♘d2 f6 14 exf6 gxf6 15 ♘e4 ♔f7 16 ♖a3! and White has the advantage due to his superior pawn-structure, Nikolenko-Frolov, Berlin 1994.

10 ♕g4

Now:

a) 10...♔f8 11 e5 d6 (11...c5!? 12 ♘d2 ♗b7 13 ♘c4 h5 14 ♕f4 is a little better for White) 12 exd6 ♗xd6 13 ♘d2 e5 14 ♕h5 ♗e6 15 ♘e4 ♗c7 16 ♘g5 ♕e7 17 b3 f6 18 ♗a3! ♗d6 19 ♗xd6 ♕xd6 20 ♖ad1 ♕e7 21 ♘xe6+ ♕xe6 22 f4 e4 23 ♕c5+ 1-0 Glek-Richter, Bad Ragaz 1994.

b) 10...d6?! 11 ♕xg7 ♗f6 12 ♕h6 ♗b7 13 ♘d2 ♕e7 14 ♘c4 0-0-0 15 a4 ♖hg8 16 ♖a3 and Black has insufficient compensation for the pawn, Sisniega-Remon, Cuba 1980.

c) 10...g6 11 ♗h6 ♕a5?! 12 ♘d2 ♕h5 13 ♕xh5 gxh5 14 e5 ♖g8 15 ♖ad1 c5 16 ♘e4 ♗b7 17 f3 ♖g6 18 ♗c1 and White is a little better due to his superior pawn-structure, Mi.Tseitlin-Larsen, Palma de Mallorca 1989.

H32)

8...d6 9 ♘c3 ♗e7

Or:

a) 9...g6?! 10 ♗e3 ♗g7 11 ♘xc6 bxc6 12 ♕d2 0-0 13 ♖ad1 d5 14 ♗h6 and White has the edge.

b) 9...♗d7 10 ♘xc6 and now:

b1) 10...bxc6 11 ♖e3! ♗e7 12 b3! d5 13 ♗b2 0-0 14 ♕h5 with attacking chances, T.Horvath-Podlesnik, Gleisdorf 1996.

b2) 10...♗xc6?! 11 ♘d5! ♗e7 12 ♗f4 exd5 (12...e5 13 ♗e3 is better for White) 13 exd5 ♗b5 (13...0-0? 14

dxc6 bxc6 15 ♖xe7 ♕xe7 16 ♗xd6 and White will be a sound pawn ahead) 14 a4 ♗c4 15 ♕d4! ♖c8 (15...♕c7 16 ♖e4!) 16 ♕xg7 ♖f8 (16...♘d7 17 ♕xf7 ♖f8 18 ♕e6+ ♔e8 19 ♗xd6 is just too much for Black to cope with) 17 ♖ad1! (a quiet move of the type that is very easy to miss; now Black is under extreme pressure) 17...a5 18 ♗h6 ♔d7 19 ♕xh7 ♖h8 20 ♕f5+ ♔c7 (20...♔e8 21 ♖xe7+! mating) 21 ♕xf7 and Black is in all sorts of trouble.

10 ♘xc6 bxc6 11 ♕g4 ♔f8

Practice has shown 11...g6 12 e5 d5 13 ♗h6 is a little better for White.

11...♗f6? is bad due to 12 e5:

a) 12...♗xe5 13 ♖xe5 dxe5 14 ♕xg7 ♖f8 15 ♗h6 ♕e7 16 ♕xe5 ♖g8 (16...f6 17 ♗xf8 is very good for White) 17 ♘e4 winning.

b) 12...h5 13 ♕g3 h4 14 ♕g4 dxe5 15 ♘e4 is very strong for White.

c) 12...dxe5 13 ♘e4 0-0 14 ♖d1 h5 (14...♕e7 15 ♗e3 and Black cannot stop the threats) 15 ♕xh5 ♕e7 16 ♗g5 ♖d8 17 ♗xf6 gxf6 18 ♕h6 winning outright, Kostyra-Kaliszewski, Warsaw 1993.

12 b3 d5

12...e5 13 ♕g3 h5 14 h3 g5 15 ♗a3 ♕a5 16 ♘a4 ♗e6 17 ♖ad1 ♖d8 18 ♖e2 f6 19 ♕e3 ♔f7 20 ♖ed2 ♕c7 is unclear, Yuldashev-Anastasian, Lucerne Wcht 1993.

12...h5?! 13 ♕e2 h4 14 ♗a3 e5 15 ♖ad1 gives White an edge, Glek-Kishnev, Dortmund 1992.

13 ♕g3 h5?!

Or: 13...♗h4 14 ♕d3 d4 15 ♗a3+ ♔g8 16 ♘a4 e5 17 c3 with an edge for White; or 13...f6!? 14 e5 f5?! (14...♔f7! gives balanced chances) 15

♘a4 c5 16 ♗a3 ♕c7 17 ♕c3 and White is better.

14 ♘a4 h4 15 ♕c3! ♖b8

15...♗f6 16 ♗a3+ ♔g8 17 e5 is awkward for Black to meet.

16 ♗e3 h3

16...♗b4 17 ♗c5+ is good for White.

17 g3 ♖b4 18 ♗d4! e5

18...f6 19 e5 f5 (19...♔f7 20 exf6 gxf6 21 ♗xf6 d4 22 ♕xb4! winning) 20 ♗c5 and White has the advantage.

19 ♗xe5 d4 20 ♕d3 f6 21 ♗f4

White is obviously better, Yudasin-Greenfeld, Haifa 1995 (notes based on those by Svidler).

I)

3...g6 4 0-0 ♗g7 5 ♖e1 *(D)*

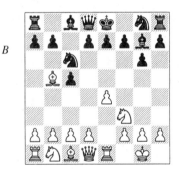

Probably the most common position arising from 3 ♗b5. Once again Black has many options. 5...♕c7 transposes to Line C1, while the others are:

I1:	5...♘h6?!	91
I2:	5...♘d4?!	91
I3:	5...e6?!	91
I4:	5...a6?!	91
I5:	5...d6?!	91
I6:	5...♕b6	92
I7:	5...e5	92
I8:	5...♘f6	95

I1)

5...♘h6?! 6 c3 0-0 7 d4 cxd4

7...d5?! 8 dxc5 dxe4 9 ♕xd8 ♖xd8 10 ♖xe4 and Black has little to show for the pawn deficit, Kholmov-Ciocaltea, Bucharest 1954.

8 cxd4 d6

8...d5 9 exd5 ♘b4 (9...♕xd5 10 ♘c3 ♕d6 11 d5 is awkward for Black) 10 ♗c4! maintains White's advantage due to the weakness on e7.

9 d5 ♘b8 10 ♘c3 ♘a6 11 h3 ♘c7 12 ♗f1

White is better, especially with the h6-knight looking misplaced, Galyas-H.Lehmann, Budapest 1994.

I2)

5...♘d4?! 6 ♘xd4 cxd4 7 c3

With the following possibilities:

a) 7...e6?! 8 ♕a4! ♕b6 9 e5 is good for White.

b) 7...e5?! 8 cxd4 exd4 9 d3 ♘e7 10 ♗g5 0-0 11 ♘d2 d6 12 ♗c4 with advantage to White, Zagema-Pieczka, Dortmund 1992.

c) 7...♕b6 8 ♘a3 a6 9 ♗a4 ♘f6 10 e5 ♘d5 11 ♗b3 ♘c7 12 ♘c4 ♕a7 13 a4 b5 14 axb5 ♘xb5 15 d3 dxc3 16 ♗e3 ♕c7 17 bxc3 with advantage to White, Vasiukov-Zinn, Berlin Lasker mem 1968, especially as 17...♘xc3?! 18 ♕f3 is very strong due to the threat of ♘d6+.

I3)

5...e6?! 6 ♗xc6!

Now:

a) 6...bxc6 7 e5 ♘e7 (7...f6 8 d3 transposes to note 'h' to Black's 4th move in Line H) 8 d3 0-0 9 ♘c3 ♕b6 10 ♘a4 ♕a5 11 b3 f6 12 ♗a3 fxe5 13

♗xc5 ♕d8 14 ♗d6 e4 15 dxe4 ♗xa1 16 ♕xa1 and White has excellent compensation for the small material deficit, Timman-Gamarra, Buenos Aires OL 1978.

b) 6...dxc6 7 e5 ♘e7 (7...♕c7? 8 ♘c3 ♘e7 transposes to note 'c' to Black's 5th move in Line H) 8 ♘c3 ♘f5 9 ♘e4 b6 10 d3 h6 11 g4! ♘d4 12 ♘xd4 cxd4 (12...♕xd4? 13 ♘d6+ ♔f8 14 ♖e4 wins the queen) 13 ♘d6+ ♔f8 14 ♕f3 ♕c7 15 ♕e4 and the d-pawn falls, Glek-Vedder, Bussum 1995.

I4)

5...a6?! 6 ♗xc6

Now:

a) 6...dxc6 7 e5 ♗g4 8 h3 ♗xf3 9 ♕xf3 e6 10 ♘c3 ♘e7 11 ♘e4! ♗xe5?! 12 ♘g5 f6 (12...0-0 13 ♖xe5 f6 14 ♘xh7 fxe5 {14...♔xh7 15 ♖xe6 ♘f5 16 ♖e4! leaves Black in difficulties} 15 ♘xf8 ♕xf8 16 ♕b3 is good for White) 13 ♖xe5 and Black has nothing better than to transpose into the previous note with 13...0-0.

b) 6...bxc6 7 e5! ♘h6 8 ♘c3 0-0 9 d3 d6 10 ♗f4 d5 11 ♘a4 ♕a5 12 b3 and White is slightly better, e.g. 12...♗g4 (12...c4? 13 ♕c1 ♘f5 14 g4 is good for White) 13 h3 ♗xf3 14 ♕xf3 ♘f5 15 c3, Popelka-Liska, Czechoslovak Cht 1987/8.

I5)

5...d6?! 6 e5! d5

6...♘h6?! 7 ♗xc6+ bxc6 8 exd6 ♕xd6 9 d3 0-0 10 ♘bd2 ♘f5 11 ♘e4 ♕d5 12 c4 ♕d8 13 ♘xc5 and Black has little to show for being a pawn down, Søbjerg-Clerico, Denmark 1997.

7 d4 c4?!

7...♕a5 8 ♘c3 a6 9 ♗xc6+ bxc6 10 dxc5 ♕xc5 11 ♗e3 ♕b4 12 ♗d4! with an edge to White.

8 b3 cxb3 9 axb3 ♗d7 10 c4

White is better, Vetemaa-Hamers, Vlissingen 1996.

I6)

5...♕b6 6 ♘a3!? d6

Or:

a) 6...♘f6 7 c3 0-0 8 e5 ♘d5 9 ♗c4 ♘c7 10 d4 and White is a little better.

b) 6...a6 7 ♗f1 ♕c7 8 c3 d6 9 d4! ♗g4 10 d5 ♘e5 11 ♗e2 ♗xf3 12 ♗xf3 ♘xf3+ 13 ♕xf3 and White is more comfortably placed, e.g. 13...b5 (13...♘f6 14 ♗f4 0-0 15 e5 with an edge) 14 ♗f4 ♘f6 15 e5 dxe5 16 ♗xe5 ♕b6 17 d6 is strong.

7 e5! d5

7...♗g4? 8 exd6 e6 9 d7+ is good for White.

8 d4 cxd4

8...♗g4? 9 dxc5 ♕xc5 10 ♗e3 ♗xf3 11 ♕xf3 d4 12 ♗xd4! is strong.

9 ♘xd4 ♗d7 10 ♗e3! ♘xe5? 11 ♘f5 ♕f6 12 ♘xg7+ ♕xg7 13 ♗d4

Black is in a real mess.

I7)

5...e5 6 ♗xc6 *(D)*

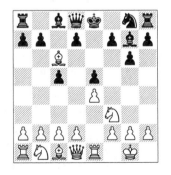

This obviously leaves Black with two options:

I71: 6...bxc6   92
I72: 6...dxc6   94

I71)

6...bxc6 7 c3 ♘e7

Or:

a) 7...♕c7 8 d4 cxd4 9 cxd4 exd4 10 ♘xd4 ♘f6 11 ♘c3 d6 12 ♕c2 0-0 13 ♘cb5! ♕b8 14 ♕xc6 d5 and now, instead of 15 ♗f4!?, which led to very unclear play in Franzen-Svensson, corr. 1977, White could have played simply for an advantage with 15 ♘d6, e.g. 15...dxe4 16 ♘xe4 ♘g4 17 ♘f3 ♗b7 18 ♕a4 ♖e8 19 h3 ♘e5 20 ♘xe5 ♗xe5 (20...♕xe5 21 ♘f6+! is very strong) 21 ♗f4!, when White is on top.

b) 7...♕b6 8 ♘a3 ♗a6 9 ♕a4! ♘e7 10 ♘c4 ♗xc4 11 ♕xc4 and now:

b1) 11...d5 12 ♕a4 dxe4 13 ♕xe4 f6 (13...f5 14 ♕e2 e4 15 d3 is difficult for Black to meet) 14 d4 f5 (14...cxd4 15 ♘xd4 f5 16 ♕h4 c5 17 ♘b3 and White has an edge) 15 ♕h4 e4 16 dxc5 ♕xc5 17 ♗e3 ♕b5 18 ♗d4 ♗xd4 19 ♘xd4 ♕xb2 20 ♘xc6!.

b2) 11...0-0 12 d3 d6 (12...d5 13 ♕a4 ♖ad8 14 exd5 ♖xd5 15 c4! ♖xd3 16 ♘xe5 ♗xe5 17 ♖xe5 ♖fd8 18 ♖e1 and White is a little better thanks to his superior pawn-structure) 13 ♖b1 a5 14 ♗e3 ♕b5 15 ♕xb5 cxb5 16 a4! c4!? 17 axb5 cxd3 18 c4 and White has the edge, Wahls-Bancod, Biel 1993.

c) 7...d6 8 d4 cxd4 9 cxd4 ♘e7?! (9...♗g4 10 dxe5 dxe5 11 ♘bd2 ♘e7 12 h3 ♗e6 13 ♘g5 ♗c8 14 ♘c4 0-0 15 ♗e3 ♗a6 16 ♕c2 ♕c7 17 ♗c5 ♗f6 18 ♘f3 ♖fd8 19 ♖ad1 and White has an edge due to his better pawn-structure and more active pieces, Hecht-Radulov, Siegen OL 1970) 10 dxe5 dxe5 11 ♕xd8+ ♔xd8 12 ♘c3 f6 13 b3 ♗e6 14 ♗a3 ♘c8 15 ♖ed1+ ♔e8 16 ♘a4 and White is slightly better due to Black's disrupted pawn-structure and hole on c5, Ma.Tseitlin-Ronin, 1983.

8 d4 cxd4 9 cxd4 exd4 10 ♘xd4 0-0

10...♕b6 11 ♘b3 0-0 12 ♘c3 f5? 13 ♗g5 ♖f7 14 ♗xe7 ♖xe7 15 ♘d5! cxd5 16 ♕xd5+ 1-0 A.Davies-Thinnsen, Lone Pine 1981.

11 ♘c3 (D)

The crucial position in this variation.

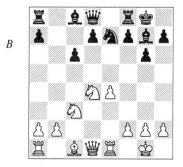

B

11...♖b8

Other possibilities for Black in this position:

a) 11...d6 12 ♗f4 ♕c7 13 ♖c1 ♕b8 (necessary because of the potential threats down the c-file) 14 ♕d2 with approximate equality although Black's position appears more loose with c6 and d6 being targets.

b) 11...♕c7?! 12 ♗g5! ♖e8 13 ♖c1 f6 14 ♗e3 d6 15 ♘cb5 ♕d7 16 ♘xc6! and White wins a pawn.

c) 11...♗b7 12 ♗g5 h6 (12...♔h8 13 ♕d2 f6 14 ♗f4 ♖e8 15 ♖ad1 ♘c8

16 ♘b3 ♘b6 17 ♘c5 ♗c8 18 ♕d3 d5 19 ♕g3 is pleasant for White, Kulish-S.Ivanova, Yalta wom 1996) 13 ♗h4 g5 14 ♗g3 d5?! 15 exd5 ♘xd5 16 ♘e4 and White has the upper hand, Smyslov-Zsu.Polgar, Monaco 1994.

d) 11...♖e8 12 ♗f4 ♗a6 13 ♕d2 d5 14 exd5 cxd5 15 ♗e5 ♕d7 16 ♗xg7 ♔xg7 and White is better due to his better pawn-structure and Black's dark-squared weaknesses, Titov-Plachetka, Bardejov 1991.

e) 11...h6 12 ♗f4 d6 13 ♕d2 ♔h7 (13...g5 14 ♗g3 ♗e5 15 f4! gxf4 16 ♗xf4 ♗xf4 {16...♕b6 17 ♗e3 with an edge to White} 17 ♕xf4 and White is a little better) 14 ♖ad1 a5 15 ♕c2 d5!? 16 exd5 cxd5 17 ♘cb5! ♘f5 (17...♗g4 18 f3 ♗f5 19 ♕c5! is pleasant for White) 18 ♘c6 ♕h4 19 ♗e5 ♗xe5 20 ♖xe5 and White is better, Hecht-de Castro, Dubai OL 1986.

f) 11...♕b6 12 ♘b3 a5 13 ♗e3 ♕c7 14 ♗c5! ♖e8 15 ♗d6 ♕a7 16 ♘a4 ♗a6 17 ♗c5 ♕b7 (17...♕c7? 18 ♗b6 ♕c8 19 ♗xa5 and Black has little to show for the pawn, Saulin-Erendzhanov, Russian Ch 1995) 18 ♗d4 and White is a little better, Illescas-Martin Manzano, Oviedo rpd 1993.

12 ♘b3

Now:

a) 12...d6 13 ♗f4 ♗e5 14 ♗xe5 dxe5 15 ♕c2 ♕d6 16 ♘a4 ♗e6 17 ♘bc5 ♖b4 18 ♖ad1 ♖d4 19 ♖xd4 exd4 20 b3 with approximate equality because Black's passed pawn may become a source of weakness as much as strength, Bezgodov-Scherbin, Russian Club Ch 1993.

b) 12...♕c7 13 ♗g5 d6 14 ♖c1 ♗a6 15 ♕d2 f6 16 ♗f4 ♘c8 17 ♘c5!

♕b6 18 ♘3a4 ♕b5 19 ♘d7 winning the exchange, Zagrebelny-Dolgener, Budapest 1993.

c) 12...d5 13 ♗e3 and then:

c1) 13...dxe4 14 ♗c5 ♖b7 15 ♖xe4 ♕xd1+ (15...♗e6 16 ♘d4! is pleasant for White) 16 ♖xd1 ♖e8 (16...♗e6 17 ♘a5! ♖xb2 18 ♘a4! ♖xa2 19 ♗xe7 is strong for White) 17 ♘a5 is good for White.

c2) 13...♖b7 14 ♗d4 dxe4 15 ♗xg7 ♔xg7 16 ♘xe4 ♕xd1 17 ♖axd1 ♗e6 18 ♘ec5 ♗xb3 19 ♘xb7 ♗xd1 20 ♖xe7 and White has a marginal edge in the ensuing ending, Pavasović-Ig.Jelen, Slovenian Ch 1993.

I72)
6...dxc6 7 d3 *(D)*

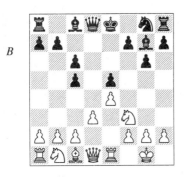

Now:

a) 7...♘h6?! 8 ♗e3 (8 ♗xh6? ♗xh6 9 ♘xe5 ♗g7 is fine for Black) 8...b6 9 ♕c1 ♘g4 10 ♗g5 ♕c7 11 h3 ♘f6 (11...h6 12 ♗d2 ♘f6 13 a4 gives White a positional advantage, especially as Black cannot castle due to the fact that h6 is hanging, for example 13...♗e6 14 ♘a3 0-0-0 15 b4! with an edge to White) 12 ♗h6 is better for White.

b) 7...♗e6 8 ♗e3 ♕d6 9 ♘bd2 ♘f6 10 a4 0-0 11 b3 h6 12 h3 ♔h7 13 ♘c4! ♗xc4 14 bxc4 leaves White a little better in view of his ability to use the b-file, B.Kristensen-Borge, Espergærde 1992.

c) 7...♗g4?! 8 h3 ♗d7 (I don't see the purpose to ...♗g4 if after h3 Black doesn't exchange – unless he intends to show the h3-pawn to be a weakness) 9 ♘bd2 ♕e7 10 ♘c4 f6 11 a4 ♘h6 12 a5 0-0 13 ♗d2 ♗e6 14 b3 and White has a comfortable position, Gizynska-Kawaciukova, Prague wom 1989.

d) 7...f6 8 ♗e3 ♕e7 9 ♕d2 ♗g4 10 ♕c3 b6 (10...♗xf3 11 ♗xc5 ♕d7 12 gxf3 ♕h3 13 d4! ♗h6 14 ♘d2 exd4 15 ♗xd4 ♗xd2 16 ♕xd2 ♕xf3 17 ♕c3 ♕g4+ 18 ♕g3 h5 19 ♖ad1 with advantage to White) 11 ♘bd2 and White is a little better.

e) 7...b6 8 ♘bd2 and now:

e1) 8...♕c7 9 ♘c4 ♗e6 10 ♗d2 and now, rather than 10...♘e7? 11 ♘cxe5 0-0-0 (11...♗xe5? 12 ♘xe5 ♕xe5 13 ♗c3 winning material) 12 ♗f4, when Black is a pawn down for nothing, Suetin-Gauglitz, Debrecen 1987, Black should play 10...♗xc4! 11 dxc4 ♘e7 12 ♗c3 0-0 13 ♕e2 with approximate equality.

e2) 8...♗e6 9 b3 f6 10 ♗b2 ♘e7 11 ♕e2 g5!? 12 ♘c4 ♘g6 13 g3 ♕d7 (13...g4 14 ♘h4! ♘xh4 15 gxh4 ♕d7 16 a4 and White is a little better) 14 ♘e3 h5 15 ♖ad1 0-0-0 16 c3 h4?! (16...g4 17 ♘h4 ♘xh4 18 gxh4 ♔b7 19 d4 cxd4 20 cxd4 exd4 21 ♗xd4 with an edge to White) 17 d4 hxg3 18 fxg3 g4 19 dxc5! ♕b7? (19...gxf3? 20 ♖xd7 fxe2 21 ♖xg7 is very strong for

White; 19...♕e7 20 ♕a6+ ♔b8 21 ♘d2! ♕xc5 22 ♗a3 ♕xc3 23 ♘dc4 ♖xd1 24 ♖xd1 ♗xc4 25 ♘xc4 c5 26 ♗xc5, with good attacking chances) 20 ♘d2 b5 21 ♘df1 ♖xd1 22 ♖xd1 ♗f8 23 b4 ♖g8 24 a3 ♕h7 25 ♕f2! ♗e7 26 ♘f5 and White has the edge, Nikitin-Kulashko, St Petersburg 1995.

f) 7...♘e7 8 ♘bd2 and then:

f1) 8...♕c7 9 a4 0-0 10 a5 ♗g4 11 h3 ♗e6 12 b3 h6 13 ♘c4 f5 14 ♗a3 fxe4 15 ♖xe4 ♗d5 16 ♗xc5! ♖ad8 17 ♕e2 ♗xe4 18 dxe4 and White has good compensation for the exchange as a7 or e5 will fall as well, Van der Wiel-Corbin, Novi Sad OL 1990.

f2) 8...0-0 9 ♘c4 f6 (9...♕c7 10 ♗d2 ♗e6 11 ♗c3 f6 12 a4 ♗xc4! 13 dxc4 a5 14 g3 b6 15 ♘h4 ♖ad8 16 ♕e2 ♘c8 17 b3 with equality, Kengis-Angskog, Gausdal Peer Gynt 1991) 10 ♗e3 b6 11 a4 a5 12 c3 ♗e6 13 ♕e2 ♘c8 14 d4! cxd4 15 cxd4 ♗g4 16 dxe5 ♗xf3 17 ♕xf3 ♕d3!? (17...fxe5 18 ♕h3! and White is better) 18 ♕e2 ♕xe4 19 ♗xb6 ♕xe2 20 ♖xe2 ♘xb6 21 ♘xb6 with advantage to White, Belikov-Granovsky, Moscow 1996.

g) 7...♕c7 8 ♗e3 b6 9 a3! ♘f6 10 b4 cxb4 11 axb4 0-0 (11...♗g4!? 12 ♘bd2 ♘d7 13 h3 ♗xf3 14 ♘xf3 and White is a little better) 12 h3! ♘h5 13 ♘c3 ♘f4 14 ♗xf4! exf4 15 ♕d2 h6?! (15...♗b7! 16 e5 c5! with chances for both sides) 16 e5! g5 17 d4 ♗f5?! 18 ♘e4 ♖ad8 19 c4! ♗xe4 (19...♗e6 20 ♕c3 with an edge for White as he plans to play c4-c5; 19...f6 20 ♘xf6+ ♗xf6 21 exf6 ♖xf6 22 ♖e5 is pleasant for White) 20 ♖xe4 f5 21 exf6 ♗xf6 22 ♕e2 and White has the edge, Shirov-Illescas, Madrid 1996.

h) 7...♕e7 8 a4 maintains maximum flexibility with White's minor-piece set-up while attempting to expand on the queenside *(D)*:

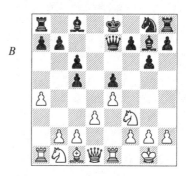

B

h1) 8...a5 9 ♘a3 f6 10 ♘c4 ♗e6 11 b3 ♕c7 12 ♗e3 b6 13 ♕d2 and White has a small advantage due to his grip on the position and his flexibility to opt for kingside expansion by preparing f2-f4.

h2) 8...♘f6 9 ♘bd2 0-0 10 ♘c4 ♘e8 11 ♗e3 ♘c7 12 b3 f6 13 h3 with a balanced position requiring patience from both sides.

h3) 8...♘h6 9 a5 f6 10 ♘c3! (the idea is to build up some pressure against Black's queenside with such moves as ♗e3 and ♘a4) 10...♖b8 11 h3 ♘f7 12 ♘a4 b5 13 axb6 axb6 14 ♗e3 (intending b4) 14...♘h6!? 15 ♕d2 ♗xe3 16 ♕xe3 0-0 17 b4! cxb4 18 ♘xb6 and White has the edge due to his superior control of the a-file, Miliutin-Mikhailov, corr. 1977.

I8)
5...♘f6 6 e5

The most natural and direct move. It not only gains space in the centre but also attacks Black's knight on f6.

6...♘d5

6...♘g4?! is met by 7 d4!:

a) 7...♕b6 8 ♘c3 cxd4 (8...♕xf2? 9 ♔xf2 cxd4 10 ♘d5 and White is a piece up as the b5-bishop is taboo; 8...♘xd4 9 ♘d5! wins material) 9 ♘d5 ♕d8 10 ♗g5 h6 11 ♗h4 leaves Black under some pressure.

b) 7...cxd4 8 ♗f4 and now:

b1) 8...♕b6 9 ♘a3 d3!? (9...0-0 10 h3 ♘h6 11 ♕c1! ♘f5 12 g4 and Black obtains insufficient compensation for the piece) 10 ♕d2 dxc2 11 ♖ac1 a6 12 ♗xc6 dxc6 13 h3 ♕xb2 14 ♘c4 ♕b5 15 ♖xc2 and Black is in trouble.

b2) 8...0-0 9 h3 ♘h6 10 ♕d2 ♘f5 11 g4 d6 (11...♕b6 12 ♘a3! a6 13 ♗d3 ♕xb2 14 ♘c4 and again Black loses a piece) 12 ♗xc6 bxc6 13 gxf5 and White has 'won' the opening, Faibisovich-Kupreichik, USSR Cht 1969.

7 ♘c3 ♘c7

7...♘xc3 8 dxc3 0-0 (8...♕c7?! 9 ♗f4 a6 10 ♗c4 b5? 11 ♗xf7+ ♔xf7 12 e6+ dxe6 13 ♗xc7 winning, Zapolskis-Balogh, Budapest 1992) 9 ♗g5 and then:

a) 9...♕c7 10 ♕d2 a6 11 ♗f1 ♖d8 (11...♘xe5 12 ♗xe7 ♘xf3+ 13 gxf3 ♖e8 14 ♗d6 is strong for White, e.g. 14...♕d8 15 ♖xe8+ ♕xe8 16 ♖e1 ♕d8 17 ♗c4!) 12 ♖ad1 d6 13 exd6 ♖xd6 14 ♕xd6! exd6 15 ♖e8+ ♗f8 16 ♗h6 ♗e6 17 ♖xa8 ♘d8 18 ♗g5! ♗e7 19 ♗xe7 ♕xe7 20 b4! with an unclear position that probably favours White.

b) 9...a6 10 ♗xc6 bxc6 (10...dxc6? 11 ♕xd8 ♖xd8 12 ♗xe7 wins a pawn for nothing) 11 ♕d2 f6 12 exf6 exf6 (12...♗xf6 13 ♗xf6 ♖xf6 14 ♕e3! is better for White) 13 ♗e3 c4!? 14 ♗c5

♖f7 15 ♕e2 ♗b7 (15...d5 16 ♕e8+ ♕xe8 17 ♖xe8+ ♗f8 18 ♘d4 ♗b7 19 ♖ae1 is grim for Black) 16 ♕xc4 and White is a sound pawn to the good, Fries Nielsen-Nilsson, Copenhagen Politiken Cup 1996.

8 ♗xc6 dxc6

8...bxc6?! 9 d4! cxd4 10 ♕xd4 d5!? 11 ♕h4 ♘e6 (11...h6 12 b3! ♘e6 13 ♗a3 is a little awkward for Black to meet) 12 ♗h6 ♗xh6 13 ♕xh6 ♕b6! 14 b3 ♕b4 15 ♘e2 and White has the edge, Lukin-Sveshnikov, USSR Ch select 1975.

9 ♘e4 *(D)*

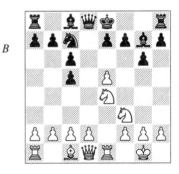

Now Black should choose between:

I81: 9...b6   97
I82: 9...♘e6   97

Others:

a) 9...c4?! 10 ♘f6+! ♔f8 11 ♘e4 ♗g4 (11...h6 12 b3!) 12 ♘c3 ♘e6 13 h3 ♗xf3 14 ♕xf3 h6 15 b3! is a little uncomfortable for Black.

b) 9...♗g4?! 10 ♘xc5 ♕d5 11 d4 0-0 12 c3 ♘e6 13 ♘e4 ♖fd8 (13...c5?! 14 h3 ♗xf3 15 ♕xf3 ♖fd8 {15...cxd4?? 16 ♘f6+ winning the queen} 16 ♗g5! and White is doing well) 14 h3 and Black has insufficient compensation for the pawn, Janssen-Atalik, Wijk aan Zee 1997.

I81)

9...b6 10 ♘f6+ ♚f8

10...♗xf6!? 11 exf6 e6 12 d4 cxd4 (12...♕xf6?! 13 ♗g5 ♕g7 14 dxc5 is better for White) 13 ♕xd4 ♕xd4 14 ♘xd4 ♗b7 15 c4 c5 16 ♘e2 0-0-0 17 ♗f4 with an approximately equal position, Khamatgaleev-Sorokin, Russia Cup (Perm) 1997.

11 ♘e4 ♗g4

11...h6 12 b3 ♚g8 13 ♗b2 ♚h7 14 d3 ♖f8 15 ♕d2 ♘e6 16 a4 a5 17 h4 ♗b7 18 ♕e3 ♕c7 19 h5 ♖ad8 20 ♘f6+ exf6 21 exf6 ♖de8 22 fxg7 ♘xg7 23 hxg6+ fxg6 24 ♕d2 with an edge for White, Biyiasas-Zaltsman, Lone Pine 1980.

12 d3 ♗xe5

12...♘e6 13 ♘ed2 ♕d5 14 h3 ♗xf3 15 ♘xf3 ♖d8 16 ♕e2 with some advantage to White, Lutz-Piket, Wijk aan Zee 1995.

13 ♘xe5!? ♗xd1 14 ♗h6+ ♚g8

14...♚e8? 15 ♘xc6 f5 (15...♕c8 16 ♘f6#) 16 ♖axd1 fxe4 17 ♘xd8 and White is very much on top.

15 ♘xc6 ♗xc2

15...♕d7 16 ♘f6+ exf6 17 ♘e7+ ♕xe7 18 ♖xe7 ♘d5 (18...♗xc2 19 ♖xc7 ♗xd3 20 ♖d1 ♖e8 21 h4 ♗f5 22 ♖xa7 and White is a little better because Black's kingside is so congested) 19 ♖d7 ♗xc2 20 ♖xd5 ♖e8 21 ♚f1 ♗a4 22 ♖e1 and Black has problems.

16 ♘xd8

An improvement on 16 ♘c3, which was played in Timman-Kramnik, Riga Tal mem 1995.

16...♖xd8 17 b4! ♗xd3!

17...cxb4 18 ♖ac1 ♗xd3 19 ♖xc7 ♗xe4 20 ♖xe7 ♘c6 21 ♖xa7 and White is doing well.

17...♘e6 18 bxc5 bxc5 19 ♖ac1 ♗xd3 20 ♘xc5 ♘xc5 21 ♖xc5 and White is better.

18 bxc5 ♗xe4 19 ♖xe4 ♘e6 20 cxb6 axb6 21 ♖b4

Black has yet to obtain equality. Analysis based on that by Ftačnik.

I82)

9...♘e6 10 d3 0-0

Alternatives:

a) 10...♕c7?! 11 ♗d2 b6 12 ♕c1 h6 13 ♗c3 ♕d7 14 ♕d2 ♗b7 15 ♘f6+ exf6 16 exf6 ♗f8 17 ♖xe6+ ♕xe6 (17...fxe6 18 f7+ ♕xf7 19 ♗xh8 and White has a nice position) 18 ♖e1 ♗c8 19 ♕f4 ♕xe1+ 20 ♗xe1 and White is clearly better thanks to Black's lack of coordination and development, together with White's threat of infiltration with ♕f4-c7, Wells-Pachow, Berlin 1995.

b) 10...h6 11 ♗e3 b6 12 ♕d2 ♗b7 (12...a5!?, with the idea of ...♖a7-d7, may be Black's best attempt to reach equality) 13 a4 and White has an edge since Black has to look at castling queenside, Biyiasas-Kagan, Petropolis IZ 1973.

11 ♗e3 b6

11...♕b6?! is strongly met by 12 ♖b1! intending b4.

12 ♕d2 *(D)*

Now:

a) 12...♖e8 (a move designed to maintain the bishop-pair) 13 ♗h6 ♗h8 14 c3 f5!? (14...♗a6 15 ♖ad1 ♕d7 16 b3 ♖ad8 17 c4 ♗c8 18 h3 ♕c7 19 ♘g3 ♘d4 20 ♘xd4 ♖xd4 21 ♕e3 a5

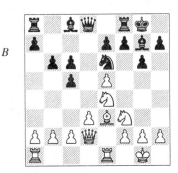

B

22 f4 and White has a marginal advantage, Breyther-Mi.Tseitlin, Budapest 1996) 15 ♘eg5 ♕d5 16 c4 ♕d8 17 ♘xe6 ♗xe6 18 ♖ad1 with a small advantage to White based on his bind on the kingside and the ineffectiveness of Black's dark-squared bishop, Sobianov-Egorov, Russia Cup (Smolensk) 1997.

b) 12...a5 13 ♗h6 ♖a7 14 ♗xg7 ♔xg7 15 ♘eg5 h6 16 ♘xe6+ ♗xe6 17 ♕c3 with an equal position, Steinbacher-Weindl, Lugano 1989.

c) 12...♘d4 13 ♘xd4 cxd4 14 ♗h6 and now:

c1) 14...♗xe5!? 15 ♗xf8 ♕xf8 16 a4 a5 17 b4 f5 (17...♕d8!?) 18 ♘g5 ♗d6 19 bxa5 ♖xa5 20 c3 ♕f6 (20...♕h6!? 21 f4 dxc3 22 ♕xc3 ♖c5 23 ♕d4 ♖d5 24 ♕c4 ♗d7 25 ♖ab1 e6 26 ♘xe6 ♗xe6 27 ♖xe6 is better for White) 21 ♕a2+ ♖d5 22 c4 ♖c5 23 ♘f3 and Black's compensation may not be enough, Golubović-Grabert, Bled 1997.

c2) 14...f6?! (14...f5?! 15 exf6 transposes) 15 exf6 exf6 16 ♗xg7 ♔xg7 17 ♕f4 with an edge to White, Van den Doel-De Wachter, Zagan jr Wch 1997.

c3) 14...♕c7 15 ♗xg7 ♔xg7 16 ♕g5 c5 17 h4 with equal chances.

c4) 14...♗f5?! 15 ♘g3 ♗xh6 16 ♕xh6 ♕d7 17 ♘xf5 gxf5 (17...♕xf5 18 ♖e4 ♖ad8 19 g4! is better for White, e.g. 19...♕f3 20 g5 ♕h5 21 ♕xh5 gxh5 22 ♖h4) 18 e6 fxe6 19 ♕xe6+ ♕xe6 20 ♖xe6 ♔f7 21 ♖ae1 ♖fe8 22 ♖xc6 ♖ac8 23 ♖ee6 ♖ed8 and White is clearly better, Nikolenko-Schoen, Pardubice 1995.

c5) 14...♗e6 15 ♘g3 ♕d7 16 h4 f5?! 17 h5 ♖f7 18 hxg6 hxg6 19 ♗xg7 ♖xg7 20 ♕g5 ♔f7 21 ♘e2! c5 22 b3 ♖h8 23 ♘f4 and White is a little better on account of his bind on the kingside, Rosenzweig-Hlavac, Czechoslovak corr. Ch 1988.

c6) 14...c5 15 ♗xg7 ♔xg7 16 ♕g5 ♗b7 (16...♕c7 transposes into note 'c3') 17 h4 with approximately equal chances, Lukin-Kaplun, USSR Ch select 1977.

d) 12...f5 13 exf6 exf6 14 ♗h6 a5 15 ♗xg7 ♔xg7 16 ♖e2 ♖a7 17 ♖ae1 ♖af7 18 h4 h5 with equality, Kramnik-Kasparov, Moscow 1996.

Part 2

1 e4 c5 2 ♘f3 d6 3 d4 cxd4

Black can play 3...♘f6, hoping to go into normal lines after 4 ♘c3 cxd4 5 ♘xd4. However, this is quite rare, as White also has useful extra options, notably 4 dxc5 and 4 ♗b5+. However, I suggest 4 ♘c3 cxd4 5 ♕xd4, which, as some games by Movsesian have shown, is not so easy for Black:

a) 5...♘c6 6 ♗b5 transposes to Line B, note 'e' to Black's 5th move.

b) 5...♗d7 6 e5 ♘c6 7 ♕f4 dxe5 8 ♘xe5 ♘xe5 9 ♕xe5 ♘g4?! 10 ♕g3 g6 11 ♗e2 ♘f6 12 ♗e3 ♗g7 13 ♗f3 keeps Black's queenside under some pressure, Karklins-Czuhai, Chicago 1990.

c) 5...a6 (preparing ...♘c6, and satisfactory according to *ECO*) 6 e5!? ♘c6 7 ♕a4 and now:

c1) 7...♘d7 8 exd6 ♘c5 9 ♕f4 e6 10 ♗e3 ♕xd6 11 ♕xd6 ♗xd6 12 0-0-0 and White keeps the initiative, Votava-Cao Sang, Budapest 1995.

c2) 7...♘g4 8 exd6 ♕xd6 9 h3 ♘f6 10 ♗f4 ♕b4 11 0-0-0! e6 12 a3 ♕xa4 13 ♘xa4 ♘d7 14 c4 f6 15 ♗c7 with a nice bind, Movsesian-Cvek, Prague 1995.

c3) 7...dxe5 8 ♘xe5 ♗d7 9 ♘xd7 ♕xd7 10 ♗d2 e6 11 0-0-0 ♕c8 12 ♗g5 (12 g4!?) 12...♗e7 13 ♗d3 h6 14 ♗xf6 ♗xf6 15 ♘e4 ♗e7 16 ♘g3 0-0 17 ♕e4 f5 18 ♕e2 ♘d4 19 ♕d2 ♕c6 20 ♔b1 ♖ac8 21 ♖he1 ♕xg2 22 ♕e3 ♗c5 23 ♘e2 ♕d5 24 ♘f4 ♕c6 25 ♕h3 with good play for the pawn, Movsesian-Khachian, Armenian Ch (Erevan) 1996.

4 ♕xd4!? *(D)*

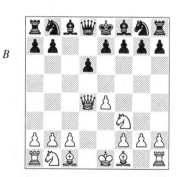

White's queen is surprisingly well-placed on d4. Now Black must answer the question of how best to tackle the situation: should he directly attack the queen with ...♘c6 or ...e5, should he prepare ...♘c6 first with ...a6 or ...♗d7 anticipating that the immediate ...♘c6 is going to be answered by White with the pinning move ♗b5? Or should he abandon the idea of attacking the white queen (at least temporarily) and opt for another idea altogether? This part of the chapter splits into sections accordingly:

A: 4...e5?!	99
B: 4...♘c6	100
C: 4...♗d7	106
D: 4...a6	108
E: 4...♘f6	113

4...♗g4!? has no independent significance as after 5 ♘c3 Black has nothing other than to transpose by 5...♘c6 5 ♗b5 to note 'd' to Black's 5th move in Line B.

4...e6!? 5 c4 will lead into the type of Maroczy Bind positions considered in Line C (note to Black's 6th move).

A)

4...e5?!

This is a relatively unusual response – and with good reason. Black gives up control of d5 and leaves himself with a backward d-pawn. Although this is the trend in some variations of the Sicilian, it proves a little premature in this exact position.

5 ♗b5+! ♘c6

5...♗d7?! is a bad idea as after the exchange of light-squared bishops Black will find it hard to cope with the light-squared weaknesses, particularly d5. 5...♘d7?! blocks the light-squared bishop and Black will soon have to move the knight again to free it.

6 ♕d3 ♘f6

6...♗e7 7 0-0 ♘f6 8 ♗g5 h6 9 ♗xf6 gxf6 10 ♘c3 a6 11 ♗a4 ♗e6 12 ♘d5 ♖c8 13 ♖ad1 b5 14 ♗b3 ♘a5 15 ♘h4! is a positional disaster for Black, Lopez-Rios, Ciego de Avila 1996.

7 ♘c3 a6 8 ♗c4 ♗e6

After 8...b5 9 ♗b3 ♘a5 10 0-0 ♗b7 11 ♗g5 ♗e7 12 ♖fd1 the weakness on d6 is starting to tell.

9 0-0 ♗xc4 10 ♕xc4 ♖c8 11 ♗g5 h6

11...♘d4 12 ♕a4+! ♕d7 13 ♘xd4 ♕xa4 14 ♘xa4 and now:

a) 14...♘xe4 15 ♘b6 ♖c7 (15...♖c5 16 ♘b3 ♖c6 17 ♗e3 and Black has no real compensation for the piece) 16 ♗h4 exd4 17 ♖ae1 f5 18 f3 and again Black has insufficient compensation.

b) 14...exd4 15 ♗xf6 gxf6 16 c3! b5 17 ♘b6 ♖c6 18 ♘d5 and Black's position is a mess due to his pawn-structure and lack of development.

12 ♗xf6 gxf6

After 12...♕xf6 13 ♘d5, White's knight on d5, better pawn-structure and lead in development give him a lasting advantage.

13 ♖ad1 b5 14 ♕e2 h5 15 a4

White's position has everything going for it, Conquest-Vinyet, Olot 1994.

B)

4...♘c6

The better of the two direct approaches and the most popular move against 4 ♕xd4!?.

5 ♗b5 (D)

The key position. Black has several options of which three are of most theoretical importance:

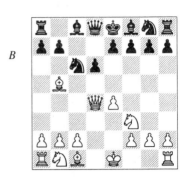

B1:	**5...♕a5+**	101
B2:	**5...♕d7**	102
B3:	**5...♗d7**	102

Others:

a) 5...e5?! transposes to Line A (4...e5?!).

b) 5...♕c7?! is not necessarily a bad move in itself but after 6 ♘c3 Black has done nothing to further his cause and therefore loses flexibility.

c) 5...e6 6 ♗g5 ♕c7 7 c4 ♘ge7 8 ♘c3 a6 9 ♕d2! and now:

c1) 9...axb5? 10 ♘xb5 ♕a5 11 b4! and then:

c11) 11...♘xb4 12 ♘xd6+ ♔d7 13 ♘e5+ (13 ♘xb7+?? ♘d3+ and Black has turned the tables) 13...♔c7 14 ♘b5+ ♔b6 15 ♕d6+ ♘bc6+ 16 ♗d2! and Black is not long for this world.

c12) 11...♕xb4 12 ♘c7+ ♔d8 13 ♘xa8 and Black has nothing to show for the material loss.

c2) 9...♗d7 10 0-0 ♘g6 11 ♗xc6 ♗xc6 (11...bxc6 12 ♖fd1 and Black is quite restricted) 12 ♖ac1 f6 13 ♗e3 ♔f7 14 ♘d5! and White is on top as 14...♕d8 (14...exd5 15 cxd5 ♘e7 16 ♘d4 is hardly appealing) 15 ♗b6 ♕d7 16 ♘d4 and White is well placed, Romanov-Lepeshkin, Sochi 1968.

d) 5...♗g4!? 6 ♘c3 with three variations:

d1) 6...♗xf3 7 gxf3 ♘f6 8 ♕a4 g6 9 ♗g5 ♘d7 10 0-0-0 ♕c8 11 ♘d5 and White has a nice position, Panchenko-Vitolinš, Moldova 1979.

d2) 6...e6 7 ♗g5 ♕a5 8 ♕c4 ♖c8 9 ♘d4 ♕c7 10 h3 ♗h5 11 g4 ♗g6 12 h4 h6 13 ♘xe6! ♕d7 14 ♘xf8 ♔xf8 15 ♗f4 ♕xg4 16 ♗xd6+ ♘ce7 17 ♕d5 and White clearly has a favourable position, Jazbinsek-Nardin, Nova Gorica 1997.

d3) 6...♘f6 7 e5! ♗xf3 (7...dxe5!? 8 ♕xd8+ ♖xd8 9 ♘xe5 ♗d7 10 ♘xd7 ♖xd7 is slightly better for White thanks to the bishop-pair) 8 exf6 e5 9 ♕c4 a6 10 ♗a4 ♗xg2 (10...b5 11 gxf3! ♕d7 {11...♘d4 12 ♘xb5 axb5 13 ♗xb5+ ♘xb5 14 ♕c6+! is winning} 12 ♘xb5 axb5 13 ♗xb5 ♖c8 14 fxg7 ♗xg7 15 ♕d5 and White is well on top) 11 ♖g1 and Black is in deep trouble as the bishop can't move from g2 due to fxg7.

e) 5...♘f6 has little independent significance as after 6 ♘c3, 6...♗d7 7 ♗xc6 ♗xc6 transposes to Line B32. Instead 6...♗d7!? 7 ♕c4! ♘b6 (after 7...♗c5 8 ♗e3 e6 9 ♖d1 ♕c7 10 0-0 ♗e7 11 ♗f4! a6 12 ♕xc5 dxc5 13 ♗xc7 axb5 14 a3 b4 15 ♘b5 White is slightly better) 8 ♕e2 gives White a slight lead in space and development. Alternatively White can play 6 e5 transposing to Line E.

f) 5...a6!? 6 ♗xc6+ bxc6 7 ♗g5! ♕c7 8 ♘c3 ♖b8 9 b3 e6 10 ♖d1 a5 11 0-0 f6 (at last Black does something about White's bishop on g5!) 12 ♗e3 ♗a6 13 ♖fe1 e5 14 ♕d2 ♗c8 15 h3 ♗e6 16 ♘h4! and White's vastly

superior development and the opportunity to exploit the f5-square gives him the edge despite the solid nature of Black's position, M.Fischer-Fabian, Bad Wörishofen 1992.

B1)
5...♕a5+ 6 ♘c3 *(D)*

6...♕xb5

6...♗d7 7 ♗xc6 and now:

a) 7...♗xc6 8 0-0 ♕c5 9 ♕d3 ♘f6 10 ♗g5 e6 11 ♗xf6 gxf6 12 ♘d4 a6 13 ♔h1 ♖g8 14 f4 f5 15 ♘xc6 ♕xc6 16 ♕h3 fxe4 17 f5 with interesting attacking chances, Shteinberg-Shamis, USSR Ch (Kharkov) 1967.

b) 7...bxc6 8 0-0 e5 9 ♕d3 and here:

b1) 9...♗c8?! 10 ♘d2 ♗a6 11 ♘c4 ♗xc4 12 ♕xc4 and having lost one of his 'compensations' (the bishop-pair) Black is worse.

b2) 9...♕c7 10 b3 ♗e7 11 ♖d1 ♗e6 (11...♘f6 12 ♗a3! ♕a5 13 ♘b1 c5 14 ♘fd2! is better for White) 12 ♘g5 and then:

b21) 12...♗g4 13 ♘e2 ♘f6 14 h3 ♗c8 (14...h6 15 ♘f3 d5! 16 hxg4 dxe4 17 ♕e3 exf3 18 ♕xf3 e4 19 ♕g3 ♕xg3 20 ♘xg3 ♖d8 21 ♖xd8+ ♗xd8 22

♗b2 and White is better) 15 c4 with an edge.

b22) 12...♗xg5 13 ♗xg5 is better for White as he is left with the better bishop and a lead in development.

7 ♘xb5 ♘xd4 8 ♘fxd4 ♔d8

8...♔d7?! 9 c4 a6 10 ♘c3 ♘f6 11 f3 e6 12 b3 and White is a little better due to his extra space, e.g. 12...♗e7 13 ♗b2 b6 14 ♖d1 ♗b7 15 ♘a4 ♗d8 16 e5! dxe5 (16...♘e8 17 exd6 ♘xd6 18 ♗a3 ♗c7 19 ♘c2 is strong due to the threat of ♘xb6+) 17 ♘f5+ is good for White.

9 c4 ♘f6

After 9...a6?! White can play a similar set-up to the previous note and anticipate a small initiative due to his extra space.

10 f3 ♗d7 11 a4 e6

11...♗xb5?! would be a poor positional move as it would concede the bishop-pair and leave White not only with a space advantage but the open a-file to work on, e.g. 12 axb5 e6 13 ♔e2 d5?! 14 ♖d1! ♗c5 15 ♗g5 is good for White.

12 ♗e3 a6 13 ♘c3 ♖c8 14 b3 ♗e7 15 ♔f2 ♔c7 16 ♖hd1

Again White has a small advantage due to his extra space, Holzhäuer-P.David, 2nd Bundesliga 1993.

B2)

5...♕d7 6 ♕e3!

After this move White can retain his bishop-pair and with careful play maintain an edge.

6...a6 7 ♗e2! ♘f6 8 0-0 ♕c7 9 c4 e6 10 ♘c3 ♗e7 11 h3 0-0 12 ♖d1 b6 13 b3 ♖d8 14 ♗b2 ♗d7 15 ♖ac1

With the idea of ♘d5 or ♘b5.

15...♕b7 16 ♖d2 ♗e8 17 ♖cd1 ♕c7 18 ♗f1 ♖ab8 19 ♗a3

Black is solid and needs to find a break with ...b5 or ...d5. However, if White can prevent these he has an edge due to his extra space, Short-Sigurjonsson, Brighton 1981.

B3)

5...♗d7

A more logical approach to unpinning the knight on c6 than ...♕d7, and more or less forcing White to give up the bishop-pair.

6 ♗xc6 (D)

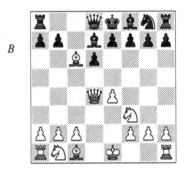

Black has a choice between:

B31)

6...bxc6 7 0-0 e5 8 ♕d3

With the following possibilities:

a) 8...f6!? 9 c4 ♘e7 10 ♖d1 (10 ♕xd6?? ♘d5 traps the queen) 10...♗e6 11 ♘c3 ♕c7 12 ♗e3 (it is best to develop this bishop on the c1-h6 diagonal in this variation so as to keep the f4-square covered; if White were to develop the bishop on b2 then ...♘g6-f4 could be embarrassing) 12...♖d8 13 b4! uses White's lead in development to start a queenside expansion and so maintains an edge, Braga-Ceschia, Reggio Emilia 1990/1.

b) 8...♗e7 9 ♖d1 h6?! 10 ♘bd2! ♘f6 (10...♗e6 11 ♘c4 ♗xc4 12 ♕xc4 and White is better as he has eliminated Black's bishop-pair) 11 ♘c4 d5 12 ♘cxe5 ♘xe4 (12...dxe4? 13 ♕c4 0-0 {13...♘d5 14 ♘xd7 ♕xd7 15 ♘e5 ♕d6 16 ♕xc6+ ♕xc6 17 ♘xc6 and White is well on top} 14 ♘xc6 is obviously strong) 13 c4 ♘f6 14 cxd5 cxd5 15 ♘d4 and White has a pleasant position.

c) 8...♘f6 9 c4 ♕c7 10 ♘c3 ♗e7 11 ♖d1 ♖d8 12 ♗g5 ♗e6 13 ♖ac1 ♕b8 14 b3 0-0 with approximate equality.

B32)
6...♗xc6 (D)

The most common recapture.
7 ♘c3 ♘f6
Alternatives:

a) 7...e5 8 ♕d3 and now:

a1) 8...♘f6 9 ♗g5 ♗e7 10 0-0-0 and then:

a11) 10...♕c7 11 ♗xf6 gxf6 12 ♘h4! 0-0-0 13 ♘f5 ♖he8 14 ♘d5 ♗xd5 15 ♕xd5 and White is very

well placed, Goldman-Kallas, Moscow 1967.

a12) 10...♘g4!? 11 ♗xe7 ♕xe7 12 ♖d2 ♖d8 (12...0-0 13 h3 ♘f6 14 ♕xd6 ♕xd6 15 ♖xd6 ♘xe4 16 ♖xc6 ♘xf2 17 ♖f1 bxc6 18 ♖xf2 with advantage to White) 13 ♘d5 ♗xd5 14 ♕xd5 ♘f6 15 ♕b5+! ♕d7 16 ♕b4! 0-0 17 ♖hd1 with an edge to White.

a2) 8...h6 9 ♘d5! ♗xd5 10 ♕xd5 ♕b6 11 0-0 ♘f6 12 ♕d3 ♕c6 13 ♘d2 and then:

a21) 13...♗e7 14 c4 0-0 15 b3 with an edge to White thanks to Black's backward d-pawn, Schöneberg-Gutman, Bundesliga 1991/2.

2a22) 13...d5! 14 exd5 ♕xd5 15 ♖e1! 0-0-0! 16 ♘c4 and here Black should avoid 16...e4 17 ♕c3 ♕c6 18 ♗f4 ♘d5 19 ♕h3+, with advantage for White, in favour of 16...♕xd3 17 cxd3 ♗b4 18 ♖xe5 ♖xd3 19 ♗e3 ♖hd8 (19...♘g4 20 ♗xa7! ♘xe5 21 ♘xe5 is very good for White due to the additional threat of 22 ♖c1+ ♔d8 23 ♘xf7+) 20 h3 with equality.

b) 7...e6 8 ♗g5 f6 (8...♘f6 transposes back to the main line) 9 ♗e3 ♘e7 10 0-0-0 and here:

b1) 10...d5!? 11 exd5 ♘xd5 12 ♖he1 ♔f7 13 ♕g4 h5!? 14 ♕h3 ♕c7 15 ♘d4 ♘xc3 (15...♘f4 16 ♕g3 ♗d6 17 ♘xe6! with advantage, for example 17...♘d3+ 18 ♖xd3 ♗xg3 19 ♘xc7 ♗xc7 20 g3) 16 ♕xe6+ ♔g6 17 bxc3 ♗a3+ 18 ♔b1 ♕b6+ 19 ♕b3 with advantage to White.

b2) 10...♘g6 11 ♕c4 ♕d7 12 ♘d4 ♔f7 (12...d5?! 13 exd5 exd5 14 ♕e2 with a positional edge for White; 12...e5 13 ♘e6! ♖c8 14 ♖d2 and Black has problems) 13 f4 and now:

b21) 13...d5 14 ♘xc6 bxc6 (White wins after 14...♕xc6 15 ♕b3 dxe4 16 f5 ♘h4 17 fxe6+ ♕xe6 18 ♖d7+ ♗e7 19 ♖xe7+! ♔xe7 20 ♕xb7+ ♕d7 21 ♘d5+) 15 f5! with an advantage for White.

b22) 13...♗e7 14 f5 ♘f8 15 ♖hf1 ♖c8 16 fxe6+ ♘xe6 17 ♕xe6+ ♕xe6 18 ♘xe6 ♔xe6 19 ♗xa7 with advantage to White, Laplaza-Larrarte, Argentina 1995.

8 ♗g5 e6 9 0-0-0 (D)

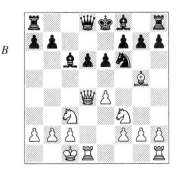

Now:

B321: 9...h6   104
B322: 9...♗e7   104

9...♕a5 10 ♗xf6!? gxf6 11 ♕xf6 ♖g8 12 ♕h4 ♖xg2 13 ♖hg1 ♖xg1 (13...♗e7? 14 ♕xh7 leaves Black with problems) 14 ♖xg1 and Black's king is awkwardly placed.

B321)
9...h6
This is an attempt by Black to avoid the line I am going to advocate in Line B322. However, by inserting the moves 9...h6 10 ♗h4 White gains an additional option on move eleven.

10 ♗h4 ♗e7 11 ♗g3!?

This interesting novelty requires Black to play carefully.

11...0-0

Or:

a) 11...♕a5? 12 ♗xd6 ♗xd6 (after 12...♖d8 13 e5 Black has little to show for the pawn) 13 ♕xd6 ♘xe4 14 ♘xe4 ♗xe4 15 ♘e5! ♕b5 16 ♖d4!! ♗c6 (16...♗d5 17 ♖b4! wins) 17 a4 ♕a6 18 ♘g6!! fxg6 19 ♕xe6+ ♔f8 20 ♖f4#.

b) 11...d5!? 12 exd5 ♘xd5 13 ♘xd5 ♗xd5 14 ♕a4+ ♔f8 (14...♕d7?! 15 ♕xd7+ ♔xd7 16 c4 ♖hc8 17 ♔b1 ♖xc4 18 ♘e5+ ♔e8 19 ♘xc4 ♗xc4 and White is better although there is a long technical battle ahead) 15 ♔b1 with a double-edged position.

12 ♖he1 e5

12...♘e8! 13 ♕d3 is roughly equal.

13 ♕d3

With an edge to White due to the holes on d5 and f5.

B322)
9...♗e7 10 ♖he1 0-0 11 e5
At one time this move had gone out of favour but recently White has been doing well with it.

11...dxe5

11...♘d5!? 12 ♗xe7 ♕xe7 13 exd6 ♕xd6 14 ♘e5 and White maintains a slight initiative.

12 ♕h4 (D)
12...♕c7

Others:

a) 12...♕e8!? 13 ♘xe5 h6 14 ♗xh6!? gxh6 15 ♕xh6 and then:

a1) 15...♖d8? 16 ♖e3 ♖xd1+ 17 ♔xd1! and now Black's only defence against ♖g3+ is 17...♘g4 (intending 18...♕d8+ and 19...♗g5), but White emerges two pawns up.

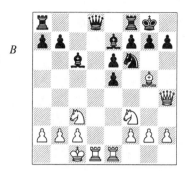

B

a2) 15...♘h7 16 f4 ♔h8 (16...♖d8?! 17 ♖e3 ♖xd1+ 18 ♔xd1 ♕d8+ 19 ♔c1 ♕d4 20 ♖h3 ♕g1+ 21 ♘d1 ♗e4 22 ♖g3+ wins) 17 ♕h5 ♖g8 (17...♗xg2? 18 ♖g1 ♗c6 19 ♖d3! and Black has big problems; 17...♗b4? 18 ♖d3 ♗xg2 19 ♖g1 ♗xc3 20 ♖xg2 ♗xb2+ 21 ♔b1! and Black cannot avoid mate) 18 ♘xf7+ ♔g7 19 ♕h6+ ♔xf7 20 ♕xh7+ ♖g7 21 ♕h5+ ♔g8 (21...♔f8?! 22 ♕h8+ ♔f7 23 ♕h3 ♗f6 24 g4 ♗xc3 25 ♕xc3 ♖xg4 26 f5 is awkward for Black to face) 22 ♕e5! (a new move) 22...♕f7 23 g3 ♗f6 24 ♕xe6 ♕xe6 25 ♖xe6 ♗xc3 26 bxc3 is tricky to assess but White should be no worse.

b) 12...♕a5 13 ♘xe5 h6 (13...♘fc8 14 ♘g4 ♘xg4 15 ♗xe7 ♘e5 16 ♗b4! favours White) 14 ♗xh6 gxh6 15 ♕xh6 ♘h7 16 f4 ♖ad8 17 ♖xd8 ♕xd8 (17...♖xd8 18 ♘xf7! ♔xf7 19 ♕xe6+ ♔g7 20 ♕xe7+ ♔h8 21 g4 ♖e8 22 ♕h4 and although White needs to be careful he is for choice; 17...♗xd8? 18 ♖e3 and Black has no satisfactory answer to ♖g3+) 18 ♖e3 ♕d4 19 ♖h3 transposes to the note to Black's 16th move in 'a2' with the move numbers decreased by one.

c) 12...♕b6?! 13 ♘xe5 ♖ac8 14 ♘g4! ♘xg4 15 ♗xe7 ♖fe8 (15...♘xf2

16 ♖d2! ♖fe8 17 ♗g5 and Black's knight remains trapped) 16 ♗g5! is good for White.

13 ♘xe5 (D)

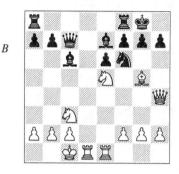

B

With the following possibilities:

a) 13...b5? 14 ♘g4 ♘d5 (but not 14...♘xg4? 15 ♗xe7 ♘xf2 16 ♖d2 ♖fe8 17 ♗d6 winning) 15 ♖xd5! b4 16 ♗xe7 bxc3 17 ♘f6+ 1-0 Radchenko-Shofman, USSR 1959.

b) 13...♖ac8? 14 ♘g4! ♘xg4 (or 14...♘d5?! 15 ♖xd5! f6 16 ♗xf6 ♖xf6 17 ♖d2 is good for White) 15 ♗xe7 ♕f4+ 16 ♖d2 ♖fe8 17 f3! ♖xe7 18 ♕xe7 and White is the exchange up for nothing, Radu-Ionescu, Bucharest 1991.

c) 13...♖fd8! 14 ♘g4 ♘xg4 (after 14...♖xd1+ 15 ♖xd1 ♘xg4 16 ♗xe7 ♕f4+ {16...♘xf2? 17 ♗d8! is very strong but 16...♘e5! 17 ♗d6 ♘g6 is equal} 17 ♖d2 ♕f5 {17...♕c4! 18 f3 ♘e3 19 ♕xc4 ♘xc4 20 ♖d3 is equal} 18 f3 ♘f6 19 ♗xf6 ♕xf6 20 ♕xf6 gxf6 21 b4 White has a small edge, Antunes-Garcia Martinez, Santa Clara 1990) 15 ♗xe7 ♕f4+ 16 ♔b1 ♖xd1+ 17 ♖xd1 ♕f5 18 f3 ♘e3 19 ♖d2 h6 20 ♕d4 ♘d5 21 ♘xd5 ½-½ Adorjan-Tal, Sochi 1977.

d) 13...♖fe8!? 14 ♖d3 ♘d5 15
♗xe7 ♘xe7 (after 15...♘xc3 16 ♖xc3
♖xe7 17 ♘xc6 bxc6 18 ♖d1 White has
a slight advantage on account of his
superior pawn-structure and better
control of the open d-file) 16 ♖h3 h6
17 g4! ♗g2!? 18 ♖g3 ♗d5 19 ♕h5
♘c6 (19...f6?! 20 ♕f7+ ♔h8 21 g5!
fxg5 {after 21...fxe5?? 22 gxh6 Black
cannot avoid mate} 22 f4! with an excellent attack) 20 ♘b5 ♕e7 21 g5
♘xe5 22 ♖xe5 ♖ac8 23 ♘c3 and
White has much the better attacking
chances.

e) 13...♘d5 14 ♗xe7 ♘xe7 (or
14...♕xe7?! 15 ♕xe7 ♘xe7 16 ♘xc6
♘xc6 17 ♖d7 ♘a5 18 b3! and White
has a pleasant edge due to his rook on
the seventh and Black's knight being
out of play, Antonio-Ru.Rodriguez,
Bacolod 1991) 15 ♖d7! (for the sacrifice of the exchange White builds up
massive positional pressure combined
with attacking chances on the kingside)
15...♗xd7 16 ♕xe7 ♖ad8 (16...♕d8?!
17 ♕xd7 ♕g5+ 18 ♕d2 ♕xg2 19 f4
♕xd2+ 20 ♔xd2 ♖fd8+ 21 ♘d3 and
White has the better of the ending,
Vasiukov-Dementiev, Vilnius 1972) 17
♖e3 ♕c8 (17...b6 18 b4! a6 19 f4 ♕c8
20 ♘e4 ♗a4 21 ♖c3! ♕a8 22 ♘f6+
♔h8 23 ♕xf7 ♗xc2 24 ♕g8+! 1-0
Onoprienko-Jaracz, Boleslav 1994) 18
♘e4 ♗c6 19 ♘f6+! ♔h8 20 ♖h3 h6
21 ♘g6+ 1-0 Oparaugo-Flogaus,
Württemberg Cht 1994.

f) 13...h6 14 ♗xh6 *(D)* and here:
f1) 14...♘e4 15 ♕h5 and then:
f11) 15...♗f6!? 16 ♘xe4 ♗xe5
(16...♕xe5!? 17 ♘xf6+ ♕xf6 18 ♗e3
♗xg2 19 ♖d4 ♗f3 20 ♕h3 e5 21 ♖h4
g6 22 ♖h7 ♖fd8 23 ♕h6 and the threat

B

of ♗g5 is very strong) 17 ♗d2 is
slightly better for White, for example
17...♖fc8 18 ♘c3 ♗f6 19 f3 b5 20
♕g4! b4 21 ♘e4.

f12) 15...♘xc3 16 ♗xg7 ♘xa2+
17 ♔b1 and now 17...♘c3+ was Gips-
lis-Tukmakov, Uzhgorod 1972, while
17...♔xg7 18 ♕g4+ is also a draw by
perpetual.

f2) 14...gxh6 15 ♕xh6 and now:
f21) 15...♘e4!? 16 ♘xe4 ♕xe5 17
♖d3 ♗xe4 18 ♖g3+ ♕xg3 19 fxg3
♗g6 20 ♖xe6! fxe6 21 ♕xg6+ ♔h8
22 ♕h6+ with a draw by perpetual.

f22) 15...♘h7 16 f4 ♗f6 17 ♖d3
♗xe5 18 ♖xe5 f6 19 ♖xe6 ♖ae8 20 f5!
and White has sufficient compensation
for the piece, for example 20...♖d8
(20...♕g7? 21 ♖g3 ♘g5 22 ♕xg7+
♔xg7 23 h4 is obviously good for
White) 21 ♖de3 ♕d7 22 b3!.

C)

4...♗d7 5 c4 ♘c6

5...♘f6 6 ♘c3 and here:

a) 6...♘c6 is likely to transpose
back to the main line.

b) After 6...g6!? 7 ♗g5 ♗g7 8 ♕d2
♘c6 9 h3 0-0 10 ♗e2 we have reached
a Maroczy Bind type position where
White is doing fine.

c) After 6...e5?!, if White can develop freely then he can expect a long-term advantage due to the weakness on d5 and the potential weak pawn on d6. 7 ♕d2 ♗c6 (7...♗e7 8 ♗d3 0-0 9 0-0 ♗g4 10 ♘e1 ♘c6 11 f3 ♗e6 12 ♘c2 ♕b6+ 13 ♘e3 ♘d4 14 b3 ♖ac8 15 ♗b2 leaves White better as his control of d5 and f5 is more important than Black's temporary control of d4) 8 ♗d3 ♘a6 9 0-0 and then:

c1) 9...♘c5 10 ♖e1 ♘xd3 11 ♕xd3 ♗e7 12 b4 0-0 13 ♗g5 h6?! (13...♘d7 14 ♗xe7 ♕xe7 15 c5! dxc5 16 b5 c4 17 ♕e3 winning material) 14 ♗xf6 ♗xf6 15 ♖ad1 ♗e7 16 b5 ♗e8 17 ♘d5 ♗g5 18 ♕a3 and White is well placed despite Black's two bishops.

c2) 9...♗e7 10 ♖e1 0-0 11 b3 ♘c5 12 ♗b2 and White is a bit better.

6 ♕d2 g6

If Black opts for a different type of set-up White can maintain an edge, e.g. after 6...♖c8!? 7 b3 ♘f6 8 ♘c3 e6 9 ♗b2 ♗e7 10 ♗d3 a6 11 0-0 h6 12 ♖ad1 Black is solid but providing White can stop the breaks ...b5 and ...d5 he has the better prospects, J.Schaefer-Barlag, NRW-Liga II 1991.

6...♘f6 is a common move in this position but after 7 ♘c3 g6 8 ♗e2 ♗g7 9 0-0 we have transposed to the main line.

7 ♗e2!

The purpose of this move-order is to avoid 7 ♘c3 ♗h6!, when White has to put his queen on an inferior square before Black then plays ...♗h6-g7!.

7...♗g7 *(D)*

7...♗h6!? 8 ♕c3! ♕a5! 9 ♕xa5 ♘xa5 10 ♘c3 ♖c8 11 ♗xh6 ♘xh6 12 b3 and then:

a) 12...♘c6 13 ♖d1 f5!? (13...♗g4 14 ♘g5 f6 15 ♗xg4 ♘xg4 16 ♘e6 ♔f7 17 ♘f4 with approximate equality) 14 ♘g5! 0-0 15 0-0 ♘f7 16 ♘xf7 ♖xf7 17 f4 fxe4 18 ♘xe4 with a roughly equal position but one in which I would prefer to be White.

b) 12...f6 13 0-0 e6?! 14 ♖fd1 ♘f7 15 ♘d4 a6 16 ♖ac1 0-0 17 ♗g4!? ♖ce8 (17...f5!? 18 exf5 gxf5 19 ♗h5 with a small edge to White) 18 f4 and White is slightly better, Knox-Holloway, Morecambe 1975.

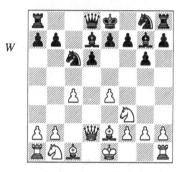

W

8 0-0 ♘f6 9 ♘c3 0-0 10 ♖b1 a6 11 b3 ♕a5

11...♖b8!? 12 ♗b2 b5 13 ♕f4! ♕a5 14 ♕h4 gives White some attacking chances, e.g. 14...bxc4 15 ♗xc4 ♗g4 16 ♘g5 h6 17 ♘d5 with unclear complications.

12 ♗b2 ♖fc8 13 ♖fd1 ♗g4

13...b5!? 14 cxb5 axb5 15 ♗xb5 ♘xe4 16 ♘xe4 ♕xb5 17 ♗xg7 ♔xg7 18 ♕b2+ and then:

a) 18...f6!? 19 ♖bc1 ♗g4 20 ♖xd6!? ♗xf3 (20...exd6 21 ♕xf6+ ♔g8 22 ♘xd6 ♕d5 23 ♘xc8 ♖xc8 24 ♘g5 with a double-edged position) 21 gxf3 exd6 22 ♕xf6+ ♔g8 23 ♘xd6 ♕d5 24 ♘xc8 ♖xc8 25 b4 ♘e7 26 ♖xc8+

♘xc8 27 a4 and White may well be better.

b) 18...♔g8 19 ♖xd6! exd6 20 ♘f6+ ♔f8 21 ♘xh7+ ♔e7 22 ♕f6+ ♔e8 23 ♕xd6!! ♔d8 (23...♘e7 24 ♘f6+ ♔d8 25 ♘d4! ♕b7 26 ♖e1 and Black has gone) 24 ♖e1 and Black cannot stop the threat of ♖e8+!.

14 ♕e3 ♘d7 15 ♘d5 ♗xb2

15...♕xa2?! 16 ♗xg7 ♔xg7 17 ♕c3+ ♘f6 18 ♘d2! ♗xe2 19 ♖a1 and Black probably has insufficient compensation for the queen.

16 ♖xb2 ♗xf3 17 ♗xf3 e6 18 ♘c3

White has the advantage due to his extra space and Black's weakness on d6, Anand-Kasparov, Moscow 1995.

D)

4...a6 5 ♗e3 *(D)*

It is necessary to vary from 5 c4 as after 5...♗g4 we can easily transpose to positions similar to Line C where Black has played ...♗c8-g4 rather than ...♗c8-d7-g4, thus gaining a tempo.

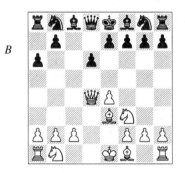

Now Black can choose between:

Other possibilities include:

a) 5...b5?? 6 ♕d5 ♕c7 7 ♕xa8 ♘c6 8 ♘c3 e6 9 ♘xb5 1-0 Veröci-Kondou, Thessaloniki wom OL 1984.

b) 5...♗g4?! 6 ♘c3 (White ignores ...♗xf3 as he intends to castle queenside anyway in which case he will be left with the two bishops and a gain in developmental time) 6...e6 7 ♕d2 ♘f6 8 0-0-0 ♘bd7 9 h3 ♗h5 (9...♗xf3?! 10 gxf3 ♕c7 11 f4 and White is well placed, for example 11...♗e7 12 ♖g1 g6 13 f5!) 10 g4 ♗g6 11 ♗d3 ♖c8 12 g5 ♘h5 (12...♗h5?! 13 ♗e2 ♘g8 14 ♘d4 ♗xe2 15 ♕xe2 and White has a nice position) 13 ♘h4 ♘c5 14 f4 ♘g3 (14...♘xd3+ 15 ♕xd3 ♘g3 16 ♘xg6 hxg6 17 ♖hg1 ♘h5 {17...♖xh3? 18 ♗d2 wins material} 18 f5 and White is well on top) 15 ♗xc5 ♖xc5 16 ♖hg1 ♖xc3 17 ♕xc3 ♘xe4 18 ♕d4 ♘c5 19 f5! ♗h5 20 ♖de1 and Black is in trouble, Kobas-Sunye Neto, Zenica 1986.

c) 5...♘d7 6 ♘c3 ♘gf6 transposes to Line D21.

D1)

5...e5 6 ♕b6!

Now that Black has weakened the d5-square this move becomes quite attractive.

6...♕xb6 7 ♗xb6 ♗e6 8 ♘c3 ♘d7 9 ♗e3 ♘gf6 10 ♖d1 ♖c8 11 ♘g5! ♗c4 12 ♗xc4 ♖xc4 13 f3

White has the better prospects because not only is the d5-square weak and Black's d-pawn backward but his dark-squared bishop is not a great piece either, Skripchenko-Tatai, Cannes 1997.

D2)

5...♘f6 6 ♘c3 *(D)*

Now Black has two main options:

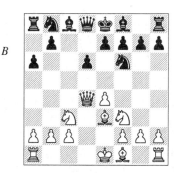

B

D21: 6...♘bd7!? 109
D22: 6...♘c6 109

Other possibilities:

a) 6...e5?! 7 ♕d2 ♘bd7 (7...♘c6 8 ♗c4 ♗e7 9 a4 0-0 10 h3 and White has a pleasant position, Perdomo-Farago, Budapest 1995) 8 a4 b6 9 ♗c4 h6 10 ♕d3 ♗b7 11 h3 b5 12 ♗b3 ♕a5 13 0-0 and White has quite a nice grip on the position, e.g. 13...b4 14 ♘d5 ♗xd5 15 ♗xd5 ♘xd5 16 exd5 ♘f6 17 ♖fd1 ♖c8 18 ♘d2 ♕xd5 19 ♕xa6 and White's a-pawn is very strong especially as Black has yet to develop his kingside, L.Cooper-Dragojlović, Cannes 1992.

b) 6...♘g4!? 7 0-0-0 ♘c6 8 ♕b6 ♘xe3 9 ♕xe3 e6 10 h4! and White's lead in development compensates for Black's bishop-pair, Grabarczyk-Kempinski, Koszalin 1997.

c) 6...♗g4?! 7 e5! ♘c6 (7...♗xf3?! 8 exf6 e5 9 ♕h4 ♗c6 10 fxg7! ♗xg7 11 ♕xd8+ ♔xd8 12 0-0-0 ♔e7 13 ♗c4 with an edge to White) 8 ♕a4 b5 (8...dxe5?! 9 ♘xe5 ♕c8 10 ♗c4 e6 11 ♘xc6 with advantage to White thanks to his better pawn-structure) 9 ♗xb5 axb5 10 ♕xb5 ♕c8 11 exf6 and White is better, Vasiukov-Grigorian, Vilnius 1975.

d) 6...e6 7 0-0-0 and here:

d1) 7...♗e7 8 e5! dxe5 (8...♘c6 9 ♕a4! is hard for Black to meet) 9 ♕xe5! ♘bd7 10 ♕g3 0-0 (10...♘h5 11 ♕g4 g6 12 ♗c4 0-0 13 ♖he1 and White has the edge due to his activity) 11 ♗d3 and all of White's pieces are pointing in the right direction.

d2) 7...♘c6 8 ♕b6! ♕xb6 9 ♗xb6 ♗d7 10 h3 ♖c8 11 ♗e2 ♗e7 12 ♔b1 0-0 13 ♖d2 ♗e8 14 ♖hd1 ♘d7 15 ♗e3 f6 (15...b5! 16 ♗f4 ♘de5 with a tense struggle ahead) 16 ♘d4 ♗f7 17 f4 b5 and White is a little better, for example 18 ♗g4 ♘xd4 19 ♖xd4 ♖c7 20 f5 e5 21 ♖4d2 and White's control of d5 combined with the potential weakness at d6 gives him the advantage, Gogichaishvili-Berg Hansen, Gausdal 1992.

D21)

6...♘bd7!? 7 0-0-0 e5!? 8 ♕a4 ♗e7

8...♖b8!? 9 ♗g5!? b5 10 ♕b3 ♘c5 11 ♕b4 d5!? 12 ♘xd5 ♘xd5 13 exd5! f6 (13...♘d3+? 14 ♗xd3 ♕xg5+ 15 ♘xg5 ♗xb4 16 ♗xh7! ♗e7 17 h4! and White is well-placed) 14 ♕e1! ♗b7 15 ♘xe5! ♕e7 (15...♗e7 16 d6 fxg5 17 ♕e3! and Black has all sorts of problems) 16 ♗e3 fxe5 17 ♗xc5 ♕xc5 18 ♕xe5+ winning for White.

9 ♗g5 0-0 10 ♗xf6 gxf6 11 ♘h4 b5 12 ♕b4!? ♘c5 13 ♘d5 a5 14 ♕e1 ♖b8 15 ♗d3 ♗e6 16 ♔b1 b4 17 ♕e3 ♔h8 18 ♖he1

White has the advantage, Gagarin-Kruglov, Moscow 1987.

D22)

6...♘c6 7 ♕d2 *(D)*

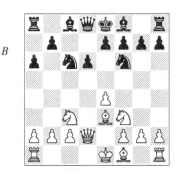

Black's main two moves now are:

D221: 7...g6   110
D222: 7...e6   111

Others:

a) 7...♗g4 8 0-0-0 e6 9 h3 and here:

a1) 9...♗h5 10 g4 ♗g6 11 ♗d3 and White has the edge, e.g. 11...♖c8 12 ♘d4 and now:

a11) 12...♗b4!? 13 ♔b1 ♕a5 (both 13...d5 14 e5! ♘xd3 15 cxd3 ♘d7 16 f4 and 13...♘xd3 14 cxd3 ♗e7 15 f4 e5 16 f5! exd4 17 ♗xd4 0-0 18 fxg6 are good for White) 14 ♘b3 is fine for White.

a12) 12...♘xd4 13 ♗xd4 d5 14 ♗xf6 ♕xf6 15 exd5 ♗xd3 (15...♗b4 16 g5 ♕e7 17 ♗xg6 hxg6 18 d6 ♕d7 19 ♕d4 ♗xc3 20 bxc3 and White is on top) 16 ♕xd3 is obviously good for White.

a2) 9...♗xf3 10 gxf3 ♖c8 11 f4 ♕a5 12 ♔b1 ♘b4 13 a3 and White is a little better.

b) 7...♗d7 8 0-0-0 b5 9 ♘d4 and now:

b1) 9...b4?! 10 ♘d5 and then:

b11) 10...♕a5? 11 ♘b3! ♕xa2 (not 11...♘xe4? 12 ♘xa5 ♘xd2 13 ♘c7+ ♔d8 14 ♘xa8 ♘xf1 15 ♖hxf1 ♘xa5

16 ♗b6+ and Black is a rook down) 12 ♘c7+ ♔d8 13 ♘xa8 and Black has insufficient chances for the lost material.

b12) 10...♘xe4 11 ♘xc6 ♗xc6 (11...♘xd2? 12 ♘xd8 ♘xf1 13 ♗b6! and White comes out material ahead) 12 ♕xb4 and White is well placed.

b2) 9...e6 10 f3 ♘e5 11 g4 and then:

b21) 11...b4!? 12 ♘b1 ♕a5 13 g5 ♘h5 (13...♘g8 14 f4 ♘g4 15 ♗g1! is strong for White) 14 f4 ♘g4 15 ♗e2 e5 16 fxe5 ♕xe5 (16...dxe5? 17 ♘f5! wins) 17 ♗xg4 ♗xg4 18 ♕xb4 ♕xe4 (18...♗xd1?? 19 ♕a4+ wins Black's queen) 19 ♖de1 with good chances for White.

b22) 11...h6 12 h4 ♕c7 13 ♗e2! (13 g5?! hxg5 14 ♗xg5 ♖c8 is a small edge for White, T.Horvath-Pavlov, Trnava 1981) 13...♖c8 (13...b4!? 14 ♘b1 d5 15 g5! and White is on top) 14 g5 ♘h5 (14...hxg5?! 15 hxg5 ♘h5 16 f4 ♘c4 17 ♗xc4 ♕xc4 18 g6! fxg6 19 ♕g2 ♔f7 20 ♘f3! and White has the better chances) 15 gxh6 g6 16 ♖hg1 ♗e7 17 ♗g5! is better for White.

c) 7...b5 8 ♘d4 ♗b7 9 f3 e6 10 0-0-0 ♕a5 11 ♔b1 ♗e7 12 g4 0-0?! 13 ♘xc6 ♗xc6 14 ♘d5! (a common tactical motif) 14...♕d8 15 ♘xe7+ ♕xe7 16 ♕xd6 and White is clearly better, Vydeslaver-Mihalyfi, Ajka 1992.

D221)

7...g6 8 0-0-0 ♗g7 9 ♗h6 0-0

9...♗xh6 10 ♕xh6 ♗g4 11 h3! ♗xf3 12 gxf3 ♕a5 13 f4 ♖c8 14 ♔b1 d5!? 15 e5 d4 (15...♘e4?! 16 ♘xe4 dxe4 17 ♕g7 ♖f8 18 e6! and White is doing well) 16 exf6 dxc3 17 ♗c4!

with excellent attacking chances, e.g.
17...♖f8 (17...cxb2? 18 ♕g7 ♖f8 19
♗xf7+ ♖xf7 20 ♕g8+ ♖f8 21 f7#) 18
♕xh7 exf6 (18...♕f5! 19 ♕h4 cxb2
{19...♕xf6 20 ♕xf6 exf6 21 ♖he1+
♘e7 22 ♗d5 ♖h8 23 ♖d3 with advantage to White} 20 ♖he1 is good for
White) 19 ♗xf7+ ♖xf7 20 ♕g8+ ♖f8
21 ♕xg6+ ♖f7 22 ♕g8+ ♖f8 23 ♕e6+
♘e7 24 ♖d7 ♕b4 25 ♖xe7+ and White
is winning.

10 ♗xg7 ♔xg7 11 h4 h5

11...♗g4!? 12 ♗e2 ♖c8 13 ♘g1
♗xe2 14 ♘gxe2 with mutual attacking chances.

**12 ♘g5 ♕a5 13 f3 b5 14 ♔b1 ♘e5
15 g4 hxg4**

15...b4?! 16 ♘d5 ♘xd5 17 exd5
and White has excellent prospects.

16 h5!

White must make his attack count
before Black can consolidate.

16...gxh5?!

16...♘xh5!? 17 ♗e2! ♖b8 18 f4
♘c4 19 ♕d4+ f6 20 ♘d5 with unclear
complications, e.g. 20...♖b7 21 f5!
♘e5 22 fxg6 ♘g3 23 ♖h7+ ♔g8
(23...♔xg6? 24 ♘f4+ ♔xg5 25 ♘e6+
♗xe6 26 ♕e3+ ♔g6 27 ♕h6#) 24
♘xe7+ ♖xe7 25 ♖xe7 winning.

16...b4? 17 hxg6! ♘xg6 (17...bxc3?
18 ♘e6+! ♔g8 19 ♖h8+ ♔xh8 20
♕h6+ with mate next move) 18 ♘h7
♖h8 19 ♕h6+ ♔g8 20 ♗c4 ♖xh7 21
♕xg6+ ♔f8 (21...♔h8 22 ♕xf7! is
too strong for Black to meet) 22 ♗xf7
and Black is in serious trouble.

**17 f4 ♘c4 18 ♗xc4 bxc4 19 ♕d4
♗b7 20 ♖xh5! e5 21 ♕g1 ♘xh5 22
♕xg4 ♖h8 23 ♘h7+!! ♔xh7 24 ♖h1
exf4 25 ♘d5**

Winning.

D222)
7...e6 8 0-0-0 *(D)*

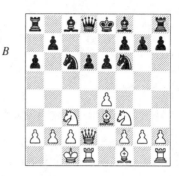

B

8...b5

a) 8...♘g4!? 9 ♗f4 ♕b6 10 ♗g3
♗e7 11 ♘d4 ♕xd4 12 ♕xd4 ♘xd4 13
♖xd4 b5 14 a4! bxa4 15 ♗e2 ♘e5 16
♖xa4 0-0 and White has a slight edge
due to the weaknesses on a6 and d6,
Kreiman-D.Gurevich, Chicago 1993.

b) 8...♕a5 9 ♔b1 ♗e7 10 ♘d4
♗d7 11 f3 b5 12 ♘b3 ♕c7 13 ♗xb5!
axb5 14 ♘xb5 ♕b8 15 ♘xd6+ ♗xd6
16 ♕xd6 gives White good compensation for the piece, Zso.Polgar-Zecević,
Portorož 1994.

c) 8...♗e7 9 ♗f4 and then:

c1) 9...e5?! 10 ♗g5 ♗g4 11 ♗xf6
♗xf3? (11...♗xf6?! 12 ♕xd6 ♕xd6
13 ♖xd6 ♗xf3 14 gxf3 and White is a
pawn up but still has a long technical
test ahead; 11...gxf6 12 ♘d5 ♖c8 13
♕h6! and White has a pleasant position) 12 ♗xe7 ♕xe7 13 gxf3 and White
is a piece up for nothing, Dostan-
Czekus, Budapest 1995.

c2) 9...♘g4 10 h3 ♘ge5 11 ♘d4
♕c7 12 ♘xc6 bxc6 13 ♗g5! ♗xg5 14
♕xg5 0-0 15 f4 and White has the
better chances, Glueck-Rohde, USA
1989.

d) 8...♕c7 9 ♗f4 and then:

d1) 9...♘e5? 10 ♘xe5 dxe5 11 ♗xe5! ♕a5 (11...♕xe5?? 12 ♕d8#) 12 ♗d6 ♗xd6 13 ♕xd6 and Black has the worse position as well as being a pawn down.

d2) 9...♘g4 10 ♗g3 ♗e7 11 ♗e2 ♘ge5 12 ♘xe5 dxe5 13 f4 0-0 (13...exf4?! 14 ♗xf4 ♕a5 {14...♘e5 loses a move by comparison with Schweber-Quinteros} 15 ♔b1 ♗b4 16 ♗d6 ♗xc3 17 bxc3 and White's bishop-pair and lead in development more than compensate for his disrupted pawn-structure) 14 fxe5 ♘xe5 15 ♕d4 ♗f6 16 ♖hf1 b5 17 ♖xf6! gxf6 18 ♕f2 with a very strong attack for the material invested, e.g. 18...♕a7 19 ♕xf6 ♘g6 20 ♗d6 ♕e3+ 21 ♔b1 b4 22 ♗h5 ♗d7 (22...bxc3?? 23 ♗xf8 ♘xf8 24 ♗xf7#) 23 ♗xb4 is winning for White, Schweber-Quinteros, Argentina 1969.

d3) 9...e5!? 10 ♗e3! and White may have a small initiative, e.g. 10...b5 11 ♔b1 h6 12 ♘d5 ♘xd5 13 exd5 ♘e7 14 ♘xe5! dxe5 15 d6 ♕d7 16 dxe7 ♗xe7 17 ♗e2 and White has a slight edge due to his lead in development and the gaps that may appear in Black's queenside.

9 e5!? dxe5

9...♘g4 10 exd6 ♘xe3 11 ♕xe3 and White is clearly better.

10 ♕xd8+ ♘xd8 11 ♘xb5!! axb5 12 ♗xb5+ ♗d7

12...♘d7 13 ♘xe5 ♖xa2 14 ♔b1 ♖a5 15 ♗xd7+ ♗xd7 16 ♘xd7 and Black is in deep trouble.

13 ♖xd7! ♘xd7 14 ♖d1 ♖a5

14...♖xa2?! 15 ♖xd7 ♖a1+ (15...♖a5 16 ♖xd8+ ♔xd8 17 ♗b6+ ♔c8 18

♗xa5 f6 19 b4 and White is well on top) 16 ♔d2 ♗b4+ 17 c3 ♗a5 18 ♗c5 is winning for White.

15 ♗xd7+ ♔e7 16 c4!

Better than 16 ♗b6, Yermolinsky-Shabalov, USA Ch 1993.

16...f6

16...e4?! 17 ♘g5! ♘b7 18 ♗c6 ♘d6 19 c5 ♘f5 20 ♘xe4 ♖a7 21 ♗f4 f6 22 ♗b8 1-0 Malaniuk-Mordassov, Alma-Ata 1980.

17 ♗b6 ♖xa2 18 ♔b1 ♖a6 19 c5 ♖a8 20 ♗b5!

Black has problems coping with White's queenside advance.

D3)

5...♘c6 6 ♕d2 e6 *(D)*

Instead:

a) 6...♘f6 7 ♘c3 transposes to Line D22.

b) 6...♗g4 7 ♘c3 ♘f6 transposes to note 'a' to Black's 7th move in Line D22.

c) 6...♗d7 7 ♘c3 ♘f6 transposes to note 'b' to Black's 7th move in Line D22.

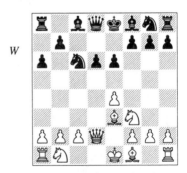

7 ♘c3 ♗e7 8 0-0-0 ♕c7

8...♘f6 transposes into lines already considered.

9 ♗f4 ♘e5 10 ♕d4 f6

10...♘xf3?! 11 gxf3 e5 12 ♘d5 ♕b8 13 ♕c3! and now White threatens ♘c7+, while 13...exf4? 14 ♕xg7 wins for White.

11 ♕a4+ ♗d7 12 ♗b5! ♘c6 13 ♕a3! e5 14 ♘d5 ♕b8 15 ♗e3 ♗d8 16 ♗e2

White is well placed, Ma.Tseitlin-Zaichik, Krasnoiarsk 1981.

E)

4...♘f6 5 e5 ♘c6

5...dxe5? 6 ♕xd8+ ♔xd8 7 ♘xe5 and White is already a little better, e.g. 7...♔e8 8 ♘c3 a6 9 ♗e2! (ready to occupy the long diagonal h1-a8) 9...e6 10 ♗f3 ♘bd7 11 ♘c4 ♖a7 12 ♗f4 b5 13 ♘a5 e5 14 0-0-0! with a dominating position, for example 14...♗c5 (14...exf4? 15 ♖he1+ ♗e7 16 ♘c6 ♖c7 17 ♖xe7+ ♔f8 18 ♖de1 g5 19 ♘d8 winning) 15 ♗g3 ♘g8 16 ♘c6 f6 17 b4! ♗b6 18 ♘e4 1-0 (as after 18...♖c7, 19 ♘d6+ ♔f8 20 ♘xc8 ♖xc8 21 ♖xd7 wins outright) Rausis-Djurhuus, Gausdal 1993.

6 ♗b5 ♕a5+

Or:

a) 6...♘g4? 7 exd6 ♕xd6 8 ♕xd6 exd6 9 0-0 and White is already better in view of Black's disrupted pawn-structure, Vescovi-Nalbandian, Matinhos U-20 Wch 1994.

b) 6...♘d7 7 ♗xc6 bxc6 8 exd6 exd6 9 0-0 ♘c5 (9...♘f6 10 ♖e1+ ♗e7 11 ♗f4 0-0? {11...♗e6 12 ♘g5! ♕d7 13 c4 and White is slightly better} 12 ♖xe7! ♕xe7 13 ♗xd6 and Black is a pawn down with the worse position) 10 ♗g5! gives White an edge, especially since after 10...♘e6? 11 ♗xd8

♘xd4 12 ♘xd4 ♔xd8 13 ♘xc6+ Black's bishop-pair constitutes insufficient compensation for the pawn.

7 ♘c3 ♕xb5

7...dxe5!? 8 ♗xc6+ bxc6 9 ♘xe5 ♗b7 10 0-0 ♖d8 11 ♕f4 e6 12 ♘c4 and White should be able to maintain a slight advantage thanks to his better pawn-structure, A.David-Janssen, Wijk aan Zee 1997.

8 ♘xb5 ♘xd4 9 ♘fxd4 dxe5 10 ♘c7+ (D)

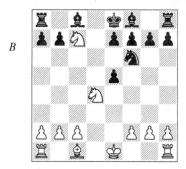

Now:

E1: 10...♔d8   113
E2: 10...♔d7!   114

E1)

10...♔d8 11 ♘xa8 exd4 12 ♗f4 ♘d5

12...e5!? 13 ♗xe5 ♗b4+ 14 ♔f1 ♖e8 15 ♗xd4 b6 with massive complications which should favour White, Szabo-Larsen, Hastings 1956.

13 ♗b8 ♗g4?

Also bad is 13...♘b4? 14 0-0-0 ♘c6 15 ♗xa7! ♘xa7 16 ♖xd4+ ♗d7 17 ♖hd1 winning, but Black has to try 13...b5! 14 a4! ♗b7 15 axb5 ♗xa8 16 ♗xa7 ♗b7 17 ♗xd4 with a messy position that should favour White.

14 h3 ♗f5 15 0-0-0 ♔c8 16 ♖xd4
1-0 A.David-Balje, Amsterdam 1996.

E2)
10...♔d7!
After this move Black can achieve full equality with careful play.

11 ♘xa8 exd4 12 ♗f4 ♘d5 13 0-0-0 e6 14 ♖xd4 ♗c5 15 ♖c4 b6 16 ♗g3 ♗b7 17 ♘c7 ♘xc7 18 ♗xc7 ♗d5 19 ♖xc5 bxc5 20 ♗f4 c4

½-½ Dmitriev-Zilbershtein, Smolensk 1984.

Part 3

1 e4 c5 2 ♘f3 e6 3 ♘c3 *(D)*

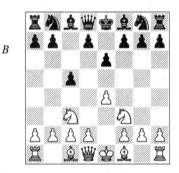

The basic plan I wish to play for White is g3, ♗g2, 0-0 and ♖e1, only playing d4 should Black adopt a set-up in which opening up the centre would be regarded as advantageous. The benefit of playing it this way is avoiding the vast amounts of theory you would need to know by playing d4 too early, when Black could switch back to one of several Sicilian lines, each of which demand extensive preparation. The only time when the set-up

I am suggesting is not especially viable is against 3...♘c6, thanks to the fact that 4 g3 d5! appears to equalize comfortably and so instead I am recommending 4 ♗b5!?. Black's main options against 3 ♘c3 are:

A: 3...a6   114
B: 3...d6   119
C: 3...♘c6   120

Others:

a) 3...d5? transposes to Line A of Part 1 of Chapter 6 (from the move-order 1 e4 e6 2 ♘f3 d5 3 ♘c3 c5?).

b) 3...♘f6 4 e5 transposes to a line covered in Part 4 of this chapter from the move-order 1 e4 c5 2 ♘f3 ♘f6 3 e5 ♘d5 4 ♘c3 e6.

c) 3...g6? should be regarded as a mistake and an ideal example of when White should change tack and play 4 d4, transposing into an Open Sicilian position where the moves ...e6 and ...g6 combine poorly at such an early stage.

d) 3...♛c7 is unlikely to have any independent significance as after 4 g3, 4...a6 is likely to be played, transposing into a position which will be covered in Line A.

A)
3...a6 4 g3 *(D)*
Black can now choose from the following:
A1: 4...d5?!   115
A2: 4...♘c6   115
A3: 4...b5   119

4...♘e7 5 ♗g2 ♘bc6 will be covered in A2 from the move-order 4...♘c6 5 ♗g2 ♘ge7.

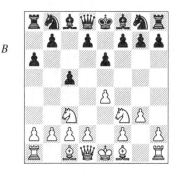

A1)

4...d5?!

The main move that Black can play to try to punish White for his move-order and get away from the 'normal' early Sicilian type moves.

5 exd5 exd5 6 d4!

Black is going to end up with an isolated d-pawn position but without the dynamic piece-play that he could expect to get in compensation from, for example, the Tarrasch (1 d4 d5 2 c4 e6 3 ♘c3 c5!?).

6...♘f6 7 ♗g2 ♗g4

Black delays developing his dark-squared bishop because White would play dxc5 and after ...♗e7/d6xc5 be a tempo up compared to the main line.

8 dxc5 ♗xc5 9 0-0 0-0 10 ♗g5 ♘c6

Now we have reached that Tarrasch QGD type position except that White has a pawn on c2 rather than e2, a factor that appears to favour White.

11 ♕d3!? ♘b4

After 11...♖e8? 12 ♗xf6 ♕xf6 13 ♘xd5 White will remain a good pawn up due to his additional threat of ♘c7.

12 ♗xf6! ♕xf6

12...♘xd3? 13 ♗xd8 ♗xf3 (not 13...♘xf2? 14 ♗c7 and Black has nothing special in terms of discovered

checks, e.g. 14...♘h3+ 15 ♔h1 ♘f2+ 16 ♖xf2 ♗xf2 17 ♘xd5 and White has two pieces for the rook) 14 ♗xf3 ♘e5 15 ♗g2! ♖axd8 16 ♘xd5 and although there is still a lot of work to do it is a thankless task for Black.

13 ♘xd5 ♕xb2

13...♘xd5? 14 ♕xd5 and White is a sound pawn ahead.

14 ♘xb4 ♕xb4

14...♗xb4?! 15 ♘g5 g6 (15...f5? 16 ♕c4+ ♔h8 17 ♘f7+ wins the exchange) 16 ♖ab1 ♕c3? (16...♕e5 17 ♖xb4 ♕xg5 18 ♖xb7 and White has a good position as well as being a pawn ahead) 17 ♕e4! wins material.

15 ♘g5 g6 16 ♖ab1 ♗f5 17 ♗e4!

White is very much on top, Benjamin-Manik, Philadelphia 1993.

A2)

4...♘c6 *(D)*

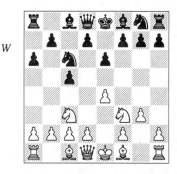

In the course of moves 4-7 Black can play ...♘c6, ...d6, ...♘f6, and ...♕c7 in virtually any order to reach the main line quoted. Therefore alternatives discussed after each move concentrate on moves that will alter Black's set-up from this.

5 ♗g2

Black can now play:

5...b5 will be covered in A3 from the move-order 4...b5 5 ♗g2 ♘c6.

A21)

5...g6 6 d4 cxd4 7 ♘xd4 ♗g7 8 ♗e3 ♘ge7 9 0-0 0-0

9...d6?! 10 ♕d2 is fine for White as if Black tries to occupy c4 with a knight White can always play b3 and Black's pawn on d6 will constantly be a target.

10 ♕d2 ♕c7 11 ♘xc6 bxc6

11...dxc6 12 ♖ad1 e5 13 ♗c5! leaves White with a positional edge, e.g. 13...♗g4?! 14 f3 ♗e6 (14...♖ad8?? 15 ♕g5 wins material) 15 ♕d6 and Black's dark-squared weaknesses around c5, b6, d6, e7, etc. will begin to tell.

12 ♘a4! d5 13 ♗b6 ♕b7 14 c4 ♖e8 15 ♖ac1

White has a very pleasant positional edge, Kveinys-Briffel, Manila OL 1992.

A22)

5...♘ge7 6 0-0 *(D)*

With the following possibilities:

A221)

6...g6 7 e5! ♗g7

7...♕c7 8 ♘e4! ♘xe5 9 ♘xe5 ♕xe5 10 d4! cxd4 (10...♕c7? 11 ♗f4 wins; 10...♕g7 11 ♗h6!! ♕xh6 12 ♘d6+

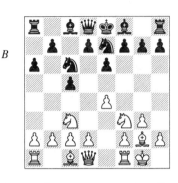

B

♔d8 13 ♘xf7+ wins) 11 ♗f4 ♕g7 12 ♗h6!! ♕e5 13 f4 ♕c7 14 ♕xd4 and White has a winning advantage.

8 ♘e4 ♘xe5 9 ♘d6+ ♔f8 10 d4 cxd4

10...♘xf3+?! 11 ♕xf3 ♘f5 12 ♘xb7! ♗xb7 13 ♕xb7 and White is better.

11 ♘xe5 ♗xe5 12 ♖e1! ♗g7

12...♗xd6?! 13 ♕xd4 ♗g8 14 ♕xd6 and White has plenty of compensation with the bishop-pair and control of the dark squares for the pawn.

12...♕c7 13 ♗h6+ ♔g8 (13...♗g7? 14 ♕xd4! ♖g8 15 ♗xg7+ ♖xg7 16 ♕xg7+ ♔xg7 17 ♘e8+ wins) 14 ♘e8! and then 14...♕d8 15 ♖xe5 ♕xe8 16 ♕xd4 f6 17 ♖c5 gives White good compensation, for example 17...♔f7 (17...♘f5?? 18 ♖xf5 wins outright) 18 ♗d2!; or 14...♕b8 15 ♖xe5! ♕xe5 16 ♗g7, which is very dangerous for Black to face.

13 ♘xb7 ♕c7

13...♗xb7 14 ♗xb7 ♖a7 15 ♗g2 with chances for both sides.

14 ♘d6 ♖b8

14...♘c6?! 15 ♗f4 e5 16 ♗xc6 ♕xc6 17 ♖xe5! ♗xe5 18 ♗xe5 ♖g8 19 ♕xd4 is very strong for White as 19...♗b7 20 ♘xb7 ♕xb7 21 ♗d6+ ♔e8 22 ♕h4 is mating.

15 &f4 &xb2

15...e5 16 &xe5 &xe5 17 &xe5 is good for White.

16 &xf7 &xc2 17 &xc2 &xc2 18 &xh8 &xh8 19 &ac1! &c3

19...&xa2? 20 &d6 wins.

20 &d2 &xc1 21 &xc1

White has the better chances.

A222)

6...&d4!? 7 &xd4 cxd4 8 &e2 &c6

8...&b6 9 c3 dxc3 10 &xc3! &c6 11 d3 is pleasant for White, for example 11...&e7 12 &a4! and Black will find it hard to stop White infiltrating on b6 and playing d3-d4 with advantage.

9 c3 dxc3

9...d3!? 10 &d4 &c5 11 &a4 &xd4 12 cxd4 b5 13 &b3 &xd4 14 &xd3 and White has an edge, while 9...&c5 10 b4! &a7 11 &b2 dxc3 12 &xc3 0-0 13 a4! also gives White a pleasant position.

10 dxc3 &c5 11 &f4 0-0 12 &d6 &xd6 13 &xd6

White has the advantage.

A223)

6...d6 7 &e2! &d7

7...d5?! 8 exd5 &xd5 (8...exd5?! 9 d4 &f5 10 &e1! &e6 11 &f4 &fxd4 12 &xd4 &xd4 13 c3 is very strong for White) 9 d4 b5 10 b3! and White has a comfortable position.

8 c3 c4!? 9 b3 b5 10 d4 cxd3 11 &xd3 &c8 12 &d1 &e7 13 e5!

White has the edge, since after 13...dxe5 14 &xe5 &xe5 15 &e4, 15...&c6? loses to 16 &xc6 &xc6 17 &xc6+, and 15...&b6 16 &xe5 &f6

17 &d6 &e7 18 &f4 &a7 19 &e3 is pleasant for White.

A224)

6...&g6 7 d4 cxd4 8 &xd4 &e7 9 &e3 0-0 10 f4

White is a little better, e.g. 10...f6 11 &e2 &c7 12 &ad1 &b8 13 h4!, Kupreichik-Bischoff, Slovenia 1989.

A23)

5...d6 6 0-0 &f6

6...&e7 and 6...&d7 are likely to transpose back to the main-line variations. Other alternatives:

a) 6...&ge7 transposes to A223.

b) 6...g6?! 7 d4 cxd4 8 &xd4 &ge7 9 &e3 &g7 10 &d2 &e5 11 &e2! &c7 12 f4 &c4 13 &db5! axb5 14 &xb5 &c6 15 &xc4 and White is a pawn ahead with the better position, Duncan-Kunte, London 1994.

c) 6...&b6!? is an unusual try, and now 7 d3 &f6 8 &d2 &e7 (8...&d4 9 &c4 &c7 10 a4 is slightly better for White) 9 &c4 &c7 10 a4 gives White an edge.

7 d4 cxd4 8 &xd4 *(D)*

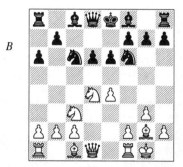

At this point Black can choose from:

A231: 8...♗e7?!   118
A232: 8...♕c7   118
A233: 8...♗d7   118

A231)

8...♗e7?! 9 ♘xc6! bxc6 10 e5 ♘d5 11 ♘xd5 cxd5 12 c4! dxe5 (D)

After 12...♗b7? 13 cxd5 ♗xd5 14 ♗xd5 exd5 15 ♕xd5 White is a pawn to the good.

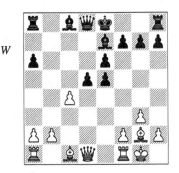

13 cxd5 exd5 14 ♗xd5 ♖b8 15 ♗c6+ ♗d7 16 ♕d5

This is awkward for Black to meet.

A232)

8...♕c7 9 ♘xc6 bxc6 10 ♘a4 ♗e7

10...♖b8 11 c4 c5 12 ♕e2 ♗e7 13 b3 and White may be a little better although Black is certainly very solid. It is difficult to predict exact move-orders here but the game could continue 13...♘d7 14 ♗b2 0-0 (14...♗f6 15 ♗xf6 ♘xf6 16 ♕e3 and White is better due to the idea of e4-e5) 15 ♖ad1 ♗b7 16 ♗c3! ♗c6 17 ♘b2 ♗f6 18 ♗xf6 ♘xf6 19 f4 with approximate equality.

11 c4 e5!? 12 ♗e3

Now that the a1-h8 diagonal is closed, White's dark-squared bishop

is better off on the c1-h6 and/or g1-a7 diagonals.

12...♗e6 13 b3 ♖b8 14 h3 ♕c8 15 ♔h2 h5!? 16 ♖c1

Preparing a future c4-c5 advance.

16...h4 17 g4

Since 17...♗xg4 18 hxg4 ♘xg4+ 19 ♔h1! leaves Black with insufficient play for the piece, White should have a slight advantage, Kavalek-Plachetka, Ostrava 1994.

A233)

8...♗d7

The main idea of this is not only to assist with development but to look at playing ...♘xd4, ...♗c6 and ...b5. Also if White exchanges on c6 Black has the option of recapturing with the bishop.

9 a4 ♗e7

Others:

a) 9...♕c7 10 ♘b3 ♗e7 11 f4! (11 a5 ♘e5! and Black gets counterplay) 11...0-0 12 ♔h1 ♘b4 13 a5 d5!? 14 e5 ♘e4 15 ♘xe4 dxe4 16 c3 ♗b5!? (16...♘d3 17 ♗xe4 ♘xc1 18 ♘d4! and White is better) 17 cxb4 ♖fd8 18 ♗d2! e3 19 ♕c1 and Black is in trouble.

b) 9...♖c8 10 ♘xc6 ♗xc6 11 a5 d5! 12 exd5 ♘xd5 13 ♘xd5 ♗xd5 14 ♗xd5 ♕xd5 15 ♕xd5 exd5 16 c3 and White may be marginally better due to his better pawn-structure, Hebden-I.Gurevich, London 1994.

10 ♘b3

With the following possibilities:

a) 10...♘a5!? 11 ♘xa5 ♕xa5 12 ♗f4 ♕c5 13 ♕d2 ♗c6 14 ♖ad1 ♖d8 15 ♖fe1 0-0 16 ♗e3! ♕b4 17 ♘d5 ♘xd5 18 exd5 ♕xd2 19 ♖xd2 ♗xa4

(19...exd5 20 ♗xd5 ♗xa4 21 ♗xb7
♖b8 22 ♗xa6 is good for White as
22...♖xb2? 23 ♗d4 wins material) 20
dxe6 fxe6 21 ♗b6! with an edge to
White.

b) 10...b6 11 f4 0-0 12 ♕e2 ♕c7 13
♗e3 ♖fc8 with approximate equality,
Ezersky-Emelin, St Petersburg 1996.

c) 10...♖c8 11 a5 ♕c7?! 12 ♗e3!
with an edge to White as he can play
♗b6 restricting Black's queenside and
leaving him a little cramped.

d) 10...0-0 11 f4! (more to prevent
...♘c6-e5-c4 than anything else)
11...♕c7 12 ♗e3 b6! (anticipating a4-
a5; 12...♘a5 13 ♘xa5 ♕xa5 14 ♕d2
♕b4 15 ♕d4! with a small advantage
to White) 13 ♕e2 and White may have
an edge due to his extra space.

A3)

4...b5 5 ♗g2 ♗b7 6 d3 d6

Other possibilities:

a) 6...d5?! 7 exd5 exd5 8 0-0 ♘f6 9
♖e1+ ♗e7 10 d4! and White has an
edge as Black has too many long-term
weaknesses, for example at f5.

b) 6...♘e7?! 7 ♗e3 ♘g6 8 0-0 d5
(8...b4 9 ♘e2 d5 10 exd5 exd5
{10...♗xd5 11 c4 bxc3 12 ♘xc3! and
White is better due to his lead in devel-
opment} 11 d4! is fine for White) 9
exd5 exd5 10 ♖e1! and Black has big
problems.

7 0-0

Now:

a) 7...♘d7 8 ♗f4 ♗e7 9 e5 dxe5 10
♘xe5 ♗xg2 11 ♔xg2 with a slight
edge to White, Timman-Torre, Bad
Lauterberg 1977.

b) 7...♗e7 8 e5 dxe5 (8...d5 9 ♘e2
h5!? 10 h4 ♘h6 11 c3 ♘c6 12 d4 cxd4

13 cxd4 ♕b6 14 ♗g5 and White is a
little better, Hecht-Timman, Helsinki
1972) 9 ♘xe5 ♗xg2 10 ♔xg2 ♘f6 11
♕f3 ♖a7 12 a4 b4 13 ♘e4 0-0 with a
slight advantage to White in view of
Black's backward c-pawn and potential weakness on c6, Ivanchuk-Polu-
gaevsky, Monaco 1992.

c) 7...♘f6 8 e5 dxe5 9 ♘xe5 ♗xg2
10 ♔xg2 ♘bd7 11 ♘xd7 ♕xd7 12 a4
b4 13 ♕f3 with equal chances.

B)

3...d6

For the purposes of this variation
we will only consider moves that do
not transpose back to Line A.

4 g3

Now:

B1: 4...♘c6   119
B2: 4...♘f6   119

B1)

4...♘c6 5 ♗g2 ♘f6

5...e5?! 6 d3 g6 7 0-0 ♗g7 and we
have reached a Closed Sicilian with
Black a tempo down.

**6 0-0 ♗e7 7 d4 cxd4 8 ♘xd4 ♗d7
9 a4 0-0 10 ♔h1!? ♘xd4 11 ♕xd4
♗c6 12 h3**

12 f4?! Short-Smirin, Tilburg 1992.

12...a6 13 ♗e3

With a small edge to White.

B2)

4...♘f6 5 ♗g2 ♗e7

5...♘c6 transposes back to B1.

6 0-0 0-0 7 d4 cxd4 8 ♘xd4 a6

8...♘bd7 9 b3! is pleasant for
White in that Black must still sort out
his queenside development.

9 a4 ♘c6 10 ♘b3 (D)

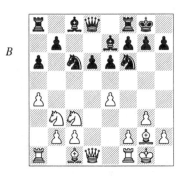

With the following lines:

a) 10...♖b8 11 a5 b5 12 axb6 ♕xb6 13 ♗e3 ♕c7 14 f4 (not so much played to expand immediately on the king-side as to keep Black's knight out of c4) 14...♖d8 15 ♕e2 d5!? (at last Black attempts to break free) 16 e5 ♘d7 17 ♗xd5! ♘dxe5 (17...exd5? 18 ♘xd5 ♕b7 19 ♘a5 ♘xa5 20 ♘xe7+ ♔f8 21 ♘xc8 ♖bxc8 22 ♖xa5 ♕xb2 23 ♖f2 and White remains a pawn to the good) 18 ♗e4 ♘d7 (18...♘g6 19 ♕c4! ♖d6! { 19...♗b7 20 ♘a5 is better for White} 20 ♖fe1 and White has a slight edge) 19 ♖fd1 with a tense position.

b) 10...♕c7 11 a5 ♘e5 (11...b6 12 axb6 ♕xb6 13 ♗e3 ♕c7 14 ♘a4 ♗b7 is unclear) 12 ♕e2 ♗d7 13 f4 ♘g6 (13...♘c4 14 g4!? ♖fc8 15 g5 ♘e8 16 f5 gave White attacking chances in Kindermann-Lau, Altensteig 1989) 14 ♗e3 ♖fe8 15 ♗b6 ♕c8 16 ♖ae1!? ♗c6 17 ♘d4 and White has an edge.

c) 10...♘a5 11 ♘xa5 ♕xa5 12 ♗d2 ♕c7 13 a5 ♗d7 14 ♗e3 ♖ac8 15 ♖e1 ♗c6 16 ♗b6 ♕b8 17 ♘d5 ♗xd5 (17...exd5 18 exd5 ♘xd5 19 ♗xd5 ♗f6 20 c3 ♖fe8 and White has the advantage) 18 exd5 e5 19 ♗h3 ♖ce8 20 c4 and White has a pleasant position,

L.Bronstein-Restifa, Buenos Aires 1990.

d) 10...♘b4!? 11 a5! e5 (11...d5 12 e5 ♘d7 13 f4 b5! 14 ♘d4 ♗b7 15 ♗e3 with a hard battle ahead) 12 ♖a4 is better for White.

C)

3...♘c6 4 ♗b5 (D)

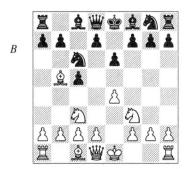

At this point Black has a number of options:

C1: 4...♘a5?!	120
C2: 4...a6?!	121
C3: 4...d6	121
C4: 4...♕c7	121
C5: 4...♘ge7	122
C6: 4...♘d4	124

4...♕b6 transposes into Line D4 of Part 1 of this chapter.

C1)

4...♘a5?! 5 0-0 a6 6 ♗e2 b5

A move consistent with ...♘a5 so that Black can develop his light-squared bishop along the a8-h1 diagonal.

7 d4 cxd4 8 ♕xd4 ♘c6

8...d6 9 a4! ♘c6 10 ♕d3 b4 11 ♘d1 and White is better as he plans to occupy c4 with his knight.

9 ♕d3 ♘ge7 10 ♗g5 f6 11 ♗f4 ♘g6

11...b4 12 ♘a4 ♕a5 (12...d5 13 ♗e3! is strong for White) 13 b3 d5 (13...e5 14 ♗e3 d5 15 ♗b6 dxe4 16 ♕xe4 ♕d5 17 ♕h4 ♘f5 18 c4!! with an edge to White) 14 c4 and White is a little better, e.g. 14...dxe4 15 ♕xe4 e5 16 ♗e3 ♗f5 17 ♕h4 g5 18 ♕h5+ ♗g6 19 ♕h3 and Black must deal with the threat of ♗b6.

12 ♗g3 ♗e7 13 a4

An improvement on 13 ♕d2?!, Landa-Fominykh, Noiabrsk 1995.

13...b4 14 ♘d1 ♗b7 15 ♘e3

White is better.

C2)

4...a6?! 5 ♗xc6 bxc6

A more consistent move than 5...dxc6, the plans against which were covered in depth in Part 1 of this chapter after the moves 1 e4 c5 2 ♘f3 ♘c6 3 ♗b5 a6?!.

6 0-0 d5 7 d3 ♘f6 8 ♕e2 ♗e7 9 b3!

The position now resembles a type of reversed Nimzo-Indian with an extra tempo.

9...♕c7 10 ♗a3 ♘d7 11 ♘a4 h5!? 12 c4!

Tying down the weakness on c5.

12...♗b7 13 ♖ac1 g5 14 cxd5 cxd5 15 ♗xc5! ♘xc5 16 ♘xc5 ♗xc5 17 b4

White is doing well, e.g. 17...g4 (17...dxe4 18 dxe4 ♕f4 19 ♖xc5 g4 20 ♘g5!) 18 ♖xc5 gxf3? 19 ♕b2, winning, Spraggett-Costa, Loures 1996.

C3)

4...d6 5 ♗xc6+ bxc6 6 0-0 ♘e7 7 e5! d5 8 b3 ♘g6 9 ♗a3 ♗a6 10 ♖e1 ♗e7

10...♕a5!? 11 ♕c1 ♘f4 12 g3 d4 13 ♗b2! ♘h3+ 14 ♔g2 ♘xf2 15 ♔xf2 dxc3 16 ♗xc3 with an edge to White.

11 d3 ♗b5 12 ♘b1 ♕a5 13 c4

Here White has a good positional advantage, Alexandria-Furman, USSR 1971.

C4)

4...♕c7 5 0-0 *(D)*

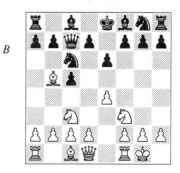

5...a6

Or:

a) 5...♘f6 6 ♖e1 transposes to C3 in Part 1 of this chapter.

b) 5...d6 has little independent significance after 6 ♖e1 as it is likely to transpose into 5...♘f6 lines or into 5...a6 lines.

c) 5...♘ge7 will transpose into positions to be discussed next in Line C5.

6 ♗xc6 ♕xc6 7 ♖e1 ♕c7 8 d4 cxd4 9 ♕xd4 d6

9...♘f6? 10 e5 ♗c5 11 ♕h4 and Black is worse.

9...♘e7 10 ♗e3! ♘c6 11 ♕b6 gives White a nice position.

10 ♗g5! ♗d7

10...h6 11 ♗h4 ♘e7 12 ♖ad1 ♘c6 13 ♕d2 and Black will have long-term problems with his d-pawn.

11 ℤad1 ♗c6 12 ♘d5! ♕b8

12...♗xd5 13 exd5 e5 14 ♘xe5! dxe5 15 ℤxe5+ ♗e7 (15...♔d7 16 ♕g4+ ♔d6 17 ♗f4 winning) 16 d6 and Black's position is grim.

13 ♕b6 ♗xd5 14 exd5 e5 15 ♘xe5! dxe5 16 d6 ♔d7 17 ℤxe5 f6

Or 17...♘f6 18 ♗f4! with a winning attack.

18 ℤc5 ♗xd6 19 ♗f4 ♕a7 20 ♕xd6+ ♔e8 21 ♕d7+

1-0 Paal-Kovacs, Debrecen 1997.

C5)
4...♘ge7 5 0-0 *(D)*

Black can now choose between the following moves:

C51)
5...g6 6 d3 ♗g7 7 ♗f4 d6 8 ♕d2 a6 9 ♗h6 0-0

9...♗xh6 10 ♗xc6+ ♘xc6 11 ♕xh6 and White is a little better on the grounds that it is not going to be easy to get the black king to safety.

10 ♗xc6 ♘xc6 11 ♗xg7 ♔xg7 12 d4!

Black will find it difficult to obtain full equality, e.g. 12...cxd4 13 ♘xd4 ♘xd4 (13...♘e5 14 b3! followed by f2-f4) 14 ♕xd4+ e5 15 ♕b4 a5 16 ♕a3 f5 17 ℤad1 ℤa6 18 ℤd2 with an edge to White.

C52)
5...♕c7 6 ℤe1 ♘d4

6...♘g6 7 d4!.

7 ♗f1 ♘ec6 8 ♘xd4 cxd4

8...♘xd4 9 ♘b1! ♗d6?! (9...♗e7 10 c3 ♘c6 11 d4 and White has an edge) 10 g3 ♘c6 11 c3 and White has a nice position.

9 ♘b5 ♕e5 10 a4! ♗e7 11 d3 a6 12 ♘a3 ♕c7 13 g3 0-0 14 ♘c4

White is a little better, Vonthron-Bischoff, Bundesliga 1989/90.

C53)
5...♘g6 6 d4 cxd4 7 ♘xd4 ♗e7

7...a6 8 ♘xc6 bxc6 (8...dxc6 9 ♕xd8+ ♔xd8 10 ℤd1+ ♔c7 11 ♗f1 and Black will have an upward struggle to achieve equality due to his dark-square weaknesses, lack of development and space) 9 ♗d3 and White is comfortable.

8 ♗e3 0-0 9 f4 a6 10 ♗xc6 bxc6 11 ♕h5 c5

11...f6 12 ℤf3 ℤf7!? 13 f5! and White has the better attacking chances, Liao-Tisdall, Thessaloniki OL 1988.

12 ♘b3 f5

With chances for both sides, Tal-Stein, Tallinn 1977.

C54)
5...♘d4 6 ♗d3 *(D)*

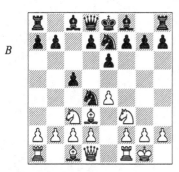

B

6...$\diagdown$ec6

6...d5 7 b3 dxe4 8 $\diagdown$xe4 $\diagdown$ec6 9 $\triangle$a3 $\triangledown$a5 10 $\triangle$b2 and White is well placed, Gipslis-Heine Nielsen, Gausdal 1992.

7 b3 g6

The alternative 7...$\diagdown$b4!? 8 $\triangle$a3 $\diagdown$xd3 9 cxd3 d6 10 b4! gives chances for both sides, Gipslis-Maliutin, Minsk 1993.

8 $\diagdown$xd4 cxd4

8...$\diagdown$xd4 9 $\triangle$b2 $\triangle$g7 10 $\diagdown$b5 0-0 11 $\diagdown$xd4 cxd4 12 f4 f5 13 exf5 gxf5 14 $\triangledown$f3 and White has a slight edge, Gipslis-Fustlu, Berlin 1991.

9 $\diagdown$e2 $\triangle$g7 10 $\triangle$a3 d6 11 f4 f5 12 exf5 exf5

12...gxf5 13 $\diagdown$g3 with attacking chances.

13 $\triangle$c4! d5 14 $\triangle$b5 $\triangledown$b6

14...$\diamond$f7 15 $\triangle$xc6 bxc6 16 $\triangle$c5 and White has a slight edge.

15 Ξe1 $\diamond$f7

15...d3+ 16 $\diamond$h1 dxe2 17 $\triangledown$xe2+ $\diamond$f7 18 $\triangle$xc6 winning.

16 $\triangle$xc6 bxc6 17 $\diagdown$c1! d3+ 18 $\diamond$h1 $\triangle$xa1 19 Ξe7+ $\diamond$g8

19...$\diamond$f6 20 $\triangledown$e1 g5 (20...h6 21 $\diagdown$xd3 with the idea of $\triangledown$h4 winning) 21 $\diagdown$xd3 $\triangle$d4 22 fxg5+ $\diamond$xg5 23 $\triangledown$g3+ $\diamond$h6 24 $\triangledown$h4+ $\diamond$g6 25 $\diagdown$f4#.

19...$\diamond$f8 20 Ξxa7+ is also very strong for White.

20 Ξe8+ $\diamond$g7 21 Ξe7+ $\diamond$g8

Not 21...$\diamond$h6? 22 $\triangledown$f3.

Now, as an improvement over Gipslis-Sveshnikov, Podolsk 1992, Blatny provided the following analysis: 22 c3 $\triangle$d7 (22...Ξa6? 23 $\triangledown$e1 c5 24 $\triangledown$e5 mating) 23 $\triangledown$e1 $\triangledown$d8 (23...$\triangledown$c7? 24 $\diagdown$xd3 with the idea of $\diagdown$c5-e6 winning) 24 $\triangledown$e5! $\triangledown$f8 (24...$\triangledown$xe7 25 $\triangle$xe7 and Black's in big trouble) 25 Ξxd7! Ξe8 26 Ξg7+! forcing mate.

C55)

5...a6 6 $\triangle$d3 $\diagdown$d4 7 $\diagdown$xd4 cxd4 8 $\diagdown$e2 *(D)*

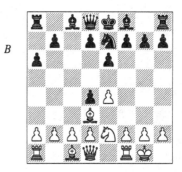

B

Black now has a choice between:
C551: 8...d5   123
C552: 8...$\diagdown$c6   124

C551)

8...d5 9 exd5 $\triangledown$xd5

9...$\diagdown$xd5!? 10 c3 dxc3 11 dxc3 and White's lead in development and pieces pointing towards Black's kingside should ensure an edge.

10 c3 $\diagdown$c6

Black wants to avoid exchanging on c3 if convenient since after White recaptures with his c-pawn it releases his only problem piece – his dark-squared bishop.

11 ♕c2 f5!?

Aiming to control the e4-square. After 11...♗d6 12 ♖e1! Black has to find an active plan to stop ♗e4 (the immediate 12 ♗e4? with the idea of ♗xc6+ and ♘xd4 falls into 12...♗xh2+ 13 ♔xh2 ♕h5+ 14 ♔g1 ♕xe2 15 ♗xc6+ bxc6 16 ♕a4 ♕e4 17 d3 ♕d5, when Black has full equality).

12 cxd4 b5

12...♘b4 13 ♕c4 ♘xd3 14 ♕xd3 and despite White's pawn-structure Black has problems.

12...♘xd4 13 ♘xd4 ♕xd4 14 ♗xa6!! is a bolt from the blue that keeps White well on top.

13 ♖e1 ♘b4 14 ♕c3 ♘xd3 15 ♕xd3 ♗c5!? 16 b3! 0-0

16...♗b7? 17 ♘f4 leaves Black with serious problems.

17 ♗b2 ♗b6

17...e5 18 ♘f4! exf4 19 ♖e5 and White is well placed.

18 ♕g3 ♕d7 19 d5!

Returning the pawn in order to open up the a1-h8 diagonal.

19...exd5 20 ♘f4 d4

♘xd5 was threatened.

21 ♗a3 ♖f7

After 21...♖e8? 22 ♘h5! Black can no longer defend against the threats.

22 ♘d5 ♗d8 23 ♖e5 f4 24 ♖ae1 ♗e7 25 ♘xe7+ ♖xe7 26 ♕xf4

1-0 Svidler-Zyla, Groningen 1993.

C552)

8...♘c6 9 c3 ♗c5 10 b4 ♗a7

10...♗b6, while quite possible, is not likely to affect the general nature

of the assessment of this position but is less flexible as it blocks Black's b-pawn.

11 ♗b2! dxc3

11...e5 12 cxd4 exd4 13 ♗c4 0-0 14 a4 d6 15 d3 and White has a nice position, P.Schmidt-Beblik, West German jr Ch 1988.

11...0-0 12 ♕b3 dxc3 (12...♕f6 13 c4! d6 14 f4 and White has the better chances) 13 ♕xc3 with a small edge for White.

12 dxc3 0-0 13 ♕d2 d6 14 c4

White has a comfortable position, Westerinen-Brodsky, Helsinki 1992.

C6)

4...♘d4 5 ♗d3

Now the only line that is independent from C54 and C55 is:

5...♘xf3+ 6 ♕xf3 ♗d6

6...d6 7 0-0 ♘f6 8 ♗b5+ ♗d7 9 e5! with an edge to White.

7 ♕e3!? e5 8 ♘b5 ♕e7 9 b4 cxb4 10 ♕g3 ♗b8 11 ♕xg7 ♕f6 12 ♕xf6 ♘xf6 13 a3!

With advantage to White, e.g. 13...d5 (13...a6? 14 axb4) 14 f3 ♖g8 15 g3 ♗h3 16 exd5 ♗g2 17 ♖g1 ♗xf3 18 d6, Bronstein-A.Zaitsev, Berlin Lasker mem 1968.

Part 4

This covers more unusual lines for Black after **1 e4 c5 2 ♘f3**, namely:

A: 2...a6   124
B: 2...♘f6   126
C: 2...g6   128

A)

2...a6

Known as the O'Kelly after the late Belgian grandmaster. The basic idea is that White cannot gain an advantage after 3 d4 (a move we do not want to play in the Sicilian lines I have recommended anyway!) because of 3...cxd4 4 ♘xd4 ♘f6 5 ♘c3 e5, when Black has a favourable version of a Najdorf as his dark-squared bishop can be developed on b4 or c5 rather than inside the pawn-chain, as would be the case had Black already played ...d6.

3 c4 *(D)*

B

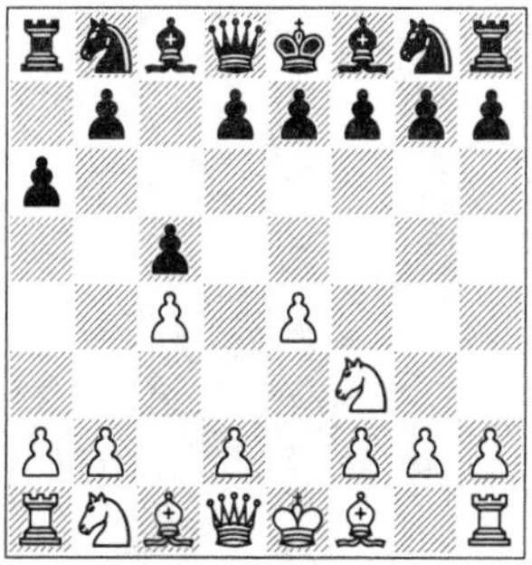

Now Black can try:

A1: 3...d6 125
A2: 3...e6 125
A3: 3...♘c6 126

A1)

3...d6

This changes the style of the position to more that of a Hedgehog set-up.

4 d4 cxd4

4...♗g4 5 dxc5! and Black will have to lose time recovering the pawn. 4...♘d7 5 d5 g6 6 ♘c3 ♗g7 7 ♗e2 ♘gf6 8 0-0 b5 9 cxb5 0-0 10 a4 axb5 11 ♗xb5, and by transposition we have reached a line from the Benko Gambit where White seems to be under no pressure for the extra pawn, A.Martin-M.Franklin, London 1996.

5 ♘xd4 ♘f6 6 ♘c3 b6 7 ♗d3 ♗b7 8 ♕e2

More accurate than 8 0-0 ♘bd7 9 ♕e2 ♘e5!?, which is unclear as 10 ♗c2 ♖c8 11 ♗a4+ ♘fd7 gives Black counterchances.

8...♘bd7 9 b3 e6 10 0-0 ♕c7 11 ♗b2 ♕c5?!

11...♗e7 followed by ...0-0 seems more natural.

12 ♖ae1! b5

12...♕xd4? allows 13 ♘a4 trapping the queen, while after 12...♕h5 13 ♕d2 g6 (13...g5 14 ♘d5!) 14 f4 ♗h6 15 ♕f2 g5 16 ♗e2 g4 17 ♕g3 ♖g8 18 ♗d1! White has a good position, Nunn-M.Franklin, London 1977.

13 cxb5! ♕xd4 14 bxa6 ♗c6 15 ♘b5 ♕b6 16 ♗d4 ♕b8 17 ♖c1 ♘c5 18 a4!

White has tremendous play for the piece with b3-b4 looming.

A2)

3...e6 4 ♘c3 ♘c6 5 d4 cxd4 6 ♘xd4 ♗b4!?

6...♘f6 or 6...♕c7 is met by 7 ♘c2!.

7 ♘xc6 bxc6

7...dxc6!? 8 ♕xd8+ ♔xd8 9 ♗f4 and White has the edge as he plans to play 0-0-0+ followed by ♘a4 exploiting Black's weak dark squares on c5 and b6 while if Black exchanges on c3 White has the perfect square of d6 for his dark-squared bishop.

8 ♕d4!

This is awkward for Black as both 8...♘f6 and 8...♕f6 can be met by 9 e5!.

A3)

3...♘c6 4 d4 cxd4 5 ♘xd4 ♘f6

Or: 5...e6 6 ♘c2 is still good for White; 5...g6? 6 ♘xc6 bxc6 7 ♕d4! is strong for White; 5...e5 6 ♘f5 d5 (6...♘f6 7 ♘c3 transposes back to the main line) 7 cxd5 ♗xf5 8 exf5 ♘d4 9 ♘c3 ♘e7 (again 9...♘f6 transposes back) 10 ♗d3 ♘exf5 11 0-0 ♗d6 12 f4! and Black has problems.

6 ♘c3 e5 7 ♘f5 d5

7...d6 8 ♗g5 ♗xf5 9 exf5 ♘d4 10 ♗d3 and White is well placed with the bishop-pair and light-squared central dominance.

8 cxd5 ♗xf5 9 exf5 ♘d4 10 ♗d3 ♘xd5 11 0-0 ♗b4

Others:

a) 11...♘xc3?! 12 bxc3 ♘c6 and now that Black's best piece has had to move Black's position is not good, e.g. 13 ♖b1 ♖b8 14 ♕f3 ♕c7 15 ♗e4 Ravinsky-Kliascicki, USSR 1966.

b) 11...♘f6 12 ♖e1 ♘c6 13 ♕b3 ♗b4 14 ♖d1 ♕e7 15 ♗g5 and Black has failed to equalize, Rogacovski-Konovalov, corr. 1972.

c) 11...♗e7 12 ♗e4 ♘xc3 13 bxc3 ♘c6 14 ♖b1 ♕c8 15 ♕g4 and White is on top, Matanović-Perez, Belgrade 1961.

12 ♗e4! ♘xc3 13 bxc3 ♗xc3 14 ♖b1 0-0

14...♖b8 is too greedy as after 15 ♕g4 g6 16 ♗g5 gxf5 17 ♗xf5 f6 18 ♕h5+ White is winning, Altshuler-Fink, corr. 1960.

15 ♖xb7

This simple move, threatening ♗a3 as after Black's rook leaves f8 White can play ♕h5 hitting f7 and keeping f5-f6! in reserve, was accredited to

Gligorić and Sokolov. The older continuation, 15 ♕g4, leads to an unclear position.

15...♕d6?

15...♖b8!? 16 ♖xb8 ♕xb8 17 f6 gives White a strong attack.

16 ♖b3!

Winning material, Nunn-Surtees, Basingstoke 1977.

B)

2...♘f6

This move is much better than its reputation. White needs to be well-versed in the tactical complications that ensue if he is to prove an advantage.

3 e5 ♘d5 4 ♘c3 *(D)*

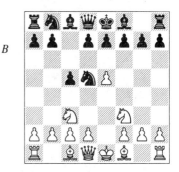

Black can now play:

B1: 4...♘xc3   126
B2: 4...e6   127

4...♘b4 5 ♗c4! and 4...♘c7 5 d4 cxd4 6 ♕xd4 ♘c6 7 ♕e4 are good for White.

B1)

4...♘xc3 5 dxc3

With the following possibilities:

a) 5...d5 6 exd6 ♕xd6 (6...exd6 7 ♗c4 ♗e7 8 ♗f4 0-0 9 ♕d2 and after

White plays 0-0-0 Black's backward d-pawn will come under severe pressure) 7 ♕xd6 exd6 8 ♗f4 ♗g4 (8...d5 9 0-0-0 ♗e6 10 ♘g5 and Black is worse) 9 0-0-0 ♘d7 10 ♗c4! followed by ♗xd6 is good for White.

b) 5...♘c6 6 ♗f4 e6 (6...♕b6 is met by 7 b3) 7 ♕d2 ♕c7 (...h6 is always going to be met by h4) 8 0-0-0 h6 9 h4 b6 10 ♗c4 ♗b7 11 ♕e2 and White has a strong initiative.

c) 5...g6 6 ♗c4 ♗g7 7 ♗f4 0-0 8 ♕d2 and White has a strong attack by following up with 0-0-0 and h4.

d) 5...b6? is weak due to 6 e6! dxe6 (6...fxe6 and 6...f6 are both met by 7 ♘e5!) 7 ♕xd8+ ♔xd8 8 ♘e5 ♔e8 9 ♗b5+ ♗d7 10 ♘xd7 ♘xd7 11 ♗f4 and Black is close to being busted.

B2)
4...e6 5 ♘xd5 exd5 6 d4 ♘c6

6...d6 fails to equalize after 7 ♗b5+:

a) 7...♗d7 8 ♗xd7+ ♕xd7 (not 8...♘xd7? 9 dxc5) 9 0-0 ♘c6 10 exd6 ♗xd6 (10...♕xd6 11 dxc5 ♕xc5 12 ♗e3 is good for White) 11 ♖e1+ ♘e7 12 dxc5 ♗xc5 13 ♗g5 0-0 14 ♕d3 f6 (14...h6 15 ♗xe7 ♗xe7 16 ♖ad1 ♖ad8 17 c4 ♗f6 18 cxd5 ♗xb2 19 d6 with a dangerous passed pawn) 15 ♗e3 and White is better due to Black's pawn-structure.

b) 7...♘c6 8 0-0 ♗e7 9 c4 ♗e6 (9...dxc4 10 exd6 ♕xd6 11 d5 a6 12 ♗xc4 and White is much better; 9...a6 10 ♗xc6+ bxc6 11 cxd5 cxd5 12 exd6 ♕xd6 13 dxc5 ♕xc5 14 ♗e3 and Black is in trouble) 10 ♗e3 ♕b6 (necessary as exd6 was threatened) 11 a4 a6 12 a5 ♕c7 13 exd6 ♕xd6 14 dxc5 ♕d8 15 ♗xc6+ bxc6 16 ♘e5 ♕c7 17

♕a4 and Black is struggling, Unzicker-Pomar, Bad Aibling 1968.

7 dxc5 ♗xc5 8 ♕xd5 *(D)*

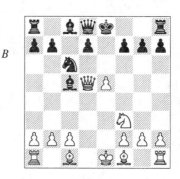

This is the critical position for the whole variation.

8...♕b6

8...d6!? 9 exd6 ♕b6 (Black sacrifices a second pawn to mobilize his forces quickly) 10 ♗c4 ♗xf2+ 11 ♔e2! 0-0 12 ♖d1 ♗e6 13 ♕e4 ♖ae8 14 ♔f1 ♗d7 15 ♕f4! leaves White better, Hübner-Heidrich, Bundesliga 1984/5.

9 ♗c4 ♗xf2+ 10 ♔e2 0-0 11 ♖f1 ♗c5 12 ♘g5 ♘d4+

12...d6? 13 ♖xf7! ♘d4+ 14 ♔d1 ♗g4+ 15 ♖f3+ ♔h8 16 ♕g8+ ♖xg8 17 ♘f7#.

12...♘xe5? 13 ♕xe5 d5 14 ♕xd5 ♖e8+ (14...♗g4+ 15 ♖f3 ♗g1 16 ♔f1 ♖ad8 17 ♕e4 is winning for White, Prokopchuk-Kuznetsov, USSR 1972) 15 ♔f3 ♕f6+ 16 ♔g3 ♗d6+ 17 ♖f4! and White's attack takes over, Spassky-Cirić, Marianske Lazne 1962.

13 ♔d1 ♘e6 14 ♘e4 d6

14...♗e7?! 15 c3 d6 16 exd6 ♖d8 17 ♔c2 ♗xd6 18 ♖xf7! ♔xf7 19 ♘g5+ ♔e8 (19...♔g8 20 ♕e4 h6 21 ♗e3 ♕a5 22 ♗xe6+ ♗xe6 23 ♕h7+ ♔f8 24 ♖f1+ winning) 20 ♘xe6 ♕f2+

21 ♔b3 ♛b6+ 22 ♗b5+ ♗d7 23 ♘c7+! wins.

14...♗e3 15 ♗xe3 ♛xe3 16 ♘d6 keeps Black under a lot of pressure.

15 exd6 ♖d8

15...♗xd6? 16 ♘xd6 ♖d8 17 ♗f4 ♘xf4 18 ♛xf7+ ♔h8 19 ♛g8+ Unzicker-Sarapu, Siegen OL 1970.

16 ♗d3 ♗xd6 17 ♛h5 f5 18 ♘xd6 ♛xd6

18...♖xd6?! 19 ♛xf5 forces Black to give up the exchange.

19 ♛xf5 ♛xh2

19...g6 20 ♛f7+ ♔h8 21 ♛f6+ ♔g8 22 ♗f4 and White will remain a sound pawn ahead.

20 ♛f7+ ♔h8 21 ♗g5 ♖g8 22 ♗e3! ♛xg2

22...♘d8 23 ♛f4! ♛xf4 (23...♛xg2 24 ♖g1 ♛d5 25 ♔d2 with the idea of ♖h1) 24 ♖xf4 with a good ending for White.

23 ♖f2!? ♛g4+

23...♛h1+ 24 ♔d2 ♛h4 (and not 24...♛xa1? 25 ♖h2 mating) 25 ♖g1 with good play for the pawn.

24 ♔c1!?

White has good practical chances in this unclear position.

C)

2...g6

The Hyper-Accelerated Dragon. As we are playing 3 ♗b5 after 1 e4 c5 2 ♘f3 ♘c6 this is the only move-order by which Black can attempt to reach a Dragon set-up. However, we are not going to give in to Black's whims that easily!

3 d4

At this point Black can choose between:

C1: 3...cxd4   128
C2: 3...♗g7   129

C1)

3...cxd4

Black is aiming to steer the game back into Dragon lines by 4 ♘xd4 ♗g7 5 ♘c3 (5 c4 leads into a Maroczy Bind) 5...♘c6 6 ♗e3 ♘f6, etc.

4 ♛xd4!

Denying Black his wish, and leading to interesting play.

4...♘f6 5 ♗b5 (D)

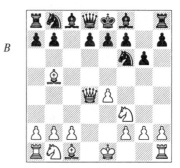

5...♘c6

Or:

a) 5...a6!? 6 e5 axb5 7 exf6 ♘c6 (7...exf6 8 0-0 ♗e7 9 ♗h6! ♘c6 10 ♛e3 gives White tremendous play for the pawn, for example 10...♘b4 11 ♘d4 d6 12 ♘c3 and now White has the open e-file to work on as well as threatening Black's b-pawn directly and his pawn on f6 by playing ♗g7 so as to meet ...♖g8 with ♗xf6) 8 fxe7 and now:

a1) 8...♛a5+!? 9 ♛d2!? (9 b4!? ♘xd4 10 exf8♛+ ♖xf8 11 bxa5 ♘xc2+ 12 ♔d1 ♘xa1 13 ♖e1+ ♔d8 14 ♗e3! d6 15 ♗b6+ ♔d7 16 ♔c1 ♖e8 17 ♖xe8 ♔xe8 18 ♔b2 may well be better for

White) 9...♗xe7 (9...♕xd2+ 10 ♗xd2 ♗g7 11 ♗c3 f6! 12 b4 ♔xe7 13 ♘bd2 ♖e8 14 0-0 with approximate equality) 10 ♘c3! 0-0 11 0-0 and White has a lovely outpost on d5 for his knight as well as some dark squares around Black's kingside to work on.

a2) 8...♕xe7+ 9 ♕e3 and then:

a21) 9...♘b4 10 ♘d4 ♗g7 (or 10...♕xe3+ 11 ♗xe3 ♗g7 12 ♔d2 and White is a little better on account of Black's shattered pawns) 11 0-0 ♕xe3 12 ♗xe3 ♗xd4 13 ♗xd4 ♘xc2 14 ♗xh8 ♘xa1 15 ♘a3! b4 16 ♘b5 ♖xa2 17 ♖e1+ ♔f8 18 ♘d6 with mate next move.

a22) 9...b4 10 0-0 and White is a little better, Kudrin-Dzindzichashvili, USA 1997.

b) 5...♕a5+?! 6 ♕c3! (a key tactical point) 6...♘c6 (6...♕xc3+ 7 ♘xc3 ♘c6 8 ♗g5! ♗g7 9 ♗xf6 ♗xf6 10 ♘d5 with an edge to White) 7 ♕xa5 ♘xa5 8 ♘c3 ♗g7 (8...a6?! 9 e5 ♘g4 10 ♘d5 ♖b8 11 h3 e6 12 hxg4 exd5 13 ♗e2 with advantage to White, Kavalek-Lehmann, Bundesliga 1985) 9 ♗g5 a6 10 ♗d3 d6 11 ♗xf6 followed by 12 ♘d5 secures a permanent structural superiority.

6 ♗xc6 bxc6

6...dxc6 7 ♕xd8+ ♔xd8 8 ♘c3 and White maintains a small edge because Black has problems placing his king in a safe position.

7 e5 ♘d5

7...♘g8 8 0-0 ♗g7 9 ♘c3 and Black has difficulty activating his pieces while White has the simple plan of constricting Black by maintaining his e5-pawn and bringing his rooks to the centre.

8 0-0 ♗g7 9 ♕h4 f6!? 10 c4 ♘c7 11 ♗h6 0-0 12 ♗xg7 ♔xg7 13 ♘c3 ♘e6 14 ♖ad1

White has the more comfortable position, Sax-Tatai, Rome 1986.

C2)

3...♗g7 4 dxc5 ♕a5+ 5 c3 ♕xc5 6 ♗e3 ♕c7

6...♕a5?! 7 ♘bd2 ♘c6 8 ♗e2 d6 9 0-0 gives White a comfortable advantage due to his lead in development.

7 ♘a3 *(D)*

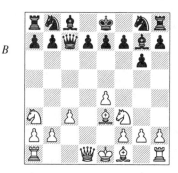

B

7...♘c6

7...♗xc3+?! 8 bxc3 ♕xc3+ 9 ♘d2 ♕xa3 10 ♖c1 ♘c6 11 ♘c4 ♕b4+ (11...♕xa2?? 12 ♖a1 traps the queen) 12 ♗d2 ♕c5 13 ♘e3 with excellent play for the material invested, for example 13...♕d4 14 ♖c4 ♕d6 15 ♘d5.

8 ♘b5 ♕b8

8...♕d8 9 ♕b3! with the threat of ♘xa7!.

9 ♕a4 a6

Necessary since ♗b6!! was threatened, for example 9...d6 10 ♗b6!! axb6 11 ♕xa8 ♕xa8 12 ♘c7+ and White is well on top.

10 ♘bd4

White has a comfortable game.

6 French Defence

Against the French I recommend the Two Knights Variation:

1 e4 e6 2 ♘f3 d5 3 ♘c3 *(D)*

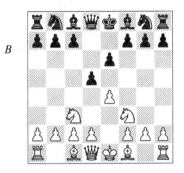

Still far from common, this variation can lead to highly original positions or else transpose back to more main-line positions depending on how both players handle it. The nice thing about the Two Knights, though, is the amount of time you can expect to gain on the clock within just a few moves! Especially if Black is normally a well-prepared Winawer player (1 e4 e6 2 d4 d5 3 ♘c3 ♗b4), he finds it difficult to adjust to the type of positions to which this variation leads. I have better results against the French than any other major defence and I put this down to better preparation and understanding than my opponent of what is still a relatively uncommon and unexplored variation.

After 1 e4 e6 I recommend the move-order 2 ♘f3 followed by 3 ♘c3 since it avoids considering lines for White if Black plays 2...♗b4 against 2 ♘c3. Note that 2...c5 transposes to a Sicilian line that is within our repertoire.

For practical purposes then the game will start 1 e4 e6 2 ♘f3 d5 3 ♘c3 and from here the chapter will be divided into three parts: Part 1 deals with lines other than 3...♘f6 4 e5 ♘fd7, Part 2 covers variations up to 5 d4 c5 6 dxc5 ♘c6 7 ♗f4 ♗xc5 8 ♗d3 f6 9 exf6 without 9...♘xf6 and Part 3 discusses the main line, 9...♘xf6.

Part 1

1 e4 e6 2 ♘f3 d5 3 ♘c3

At this point it is already time for Black to make a big decision! Does he steer the game back into French-style positions by 3...dxe4 or 3...♘f6 or try to exploit White's move-order with some other continuation? We will thus consider the following:

A: 3...c5?	130
B: 3...♗b4	131
C: 3...d4	131
D: 3...dxe4	132
E: 3...♘f6 4 e5 ♘e4	135

A)

3...c5? *(D)*

This sensible-looking move aims to gain space in the centre but can be easily dealt with. After 4 exd5 exd5 White

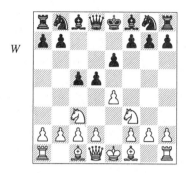

can either play 5 d4! with an edge (compare this with the move-order 1 e4 e6 2 d4 d5 3 ♘c3 c5? 4 exd5 exd5 5 ♘f3) or go for rapid piece development by 5 ♗b5+ ♘c6 (5...♗d7 and 5...♘d7 allow 6 ♕e2+ and 7 ♘xd5 winning a pawn) 6 ♕e2+ after which Black soon gets in a tangle, e.g. 6...♗e7 7 0-0 ♘f6 8 ♖e1 ♗g4 (8...h6 9 ♘e5 ♗e6 10 ♘g6!) 9 d3 and now Black finds it difficult to castle in view of the tactical possibility of ♗xc6 and ♕xe7, while 9...♗xf3 10 ♕xf3 0-0 11 ♗xc6 bxc6 12 ♗f4 gives White a pleasant edge.

B)

3...♗b4 (D)

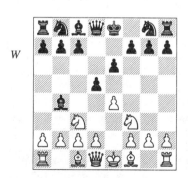

This move at once puts pressure on White's centre while developing a piece. However, with careful play White soon gains time with a favourable position. After 4 e5 c5 (best as 4...♗xc3 5 bxc3 c5 6 d4 is simply good for White; compare this to the Winawer variation from the move-order 1 e4 e6 2 d4 d5 3 ♘c3 ♗b4 4 e5 c5 5 a3 ♗xc3+ 6 bxc3 – White already has a knight developed on f3 and can develop his dark-squared bishop to a3 with a preliminary a4 gaining a tempo as he hasn't played an earlier a2-a3) 5 ♘e2 ♘e7 6 c3 ♗a5 7 d4 0-0 8 a3 ♗c7 9 ♘g3 cxd4 10 cxd4 ♘bc6 11 ♗d3 White has better piece placement and more space.

C)

3...d4

Black lunges forward in the centre with gain of time.

4 ♘e2 c5 5 c3 (D)

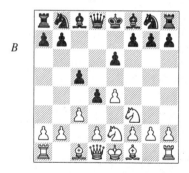

Black now has four choices:

a) 5...d3? is simply bad. 6 ♘f4 wins a pawn as 6...c4 is met by 7 ♕a4+ followed by ♕xc4 (and d3 falls as well).

b) 5...♘f6 6 ♘g3 ♘c6 7 ♗c4 ♗e7 8 0-0 0-0 9 ♕e2 b6 10 e5 ♘d5 11 cxd4 cxd4 12 ♕e4 leaves White well placed as the pawn on d4 is weak and there are attacking possibilities towards the black king.

c) 5...dxc3 releases the tension and the game soon reaches a middlegame that slightly favours White. After 6 bxc3 ♘f6 7 ♘g3 ♘c6 8 d4 cxd4 9 cxd4 ♗b4+ 10 ♗d2 ♕a5 11 ♖b1! (threatening 12 ♖xb4 ♘xb4 13 ♕b1 ♕xa2 14 ♕xa2 ♘xa2 15 ♗c4) 11...♗xd2+ 12 ♕xd2 ♕xd2+ 13 ♔xd2 I prefer White due to his extra space, pressure down the b-file and well-placed king for the late middlegame/endgame.

d) 5...♘c6 develops a piece and at the same time protects Black's centre. However, White can put Black under a lot of pressure by the following forcing sequence: 6 cxd4 cxd4 7 ♕a4 ♗c5 (7...♘f6? 8 ♘exd4! ♗d7 9 ♘xc6! ♗xc6 10 ♗b5 and White won the ensuing ending in Baker-Whiteley, London 1994) 8 b4! ♗xb4 (8...♗b6 9 b5 wins a pawn) 9 ♘exd4 ♕a5 10 ♗b5 ♕xa4 11 ♗xa4 and White has the edge, e.g. 11...♗d7 12 ♘xc6 ♗xc6 13 ♗xc6+ bxc6 14 ♖b1 ♗a5 15 ♘e5! (this is an improvement on 15 ♗a3, as played in the game Baker-Gamble, Paignton 1997, although I won eventually) 15...♘e7 16 ♖b7 ♗b6 17 ♗a3! with a decisive advantage for White due to his powerfully placed dark-squared bishop on the a3-f8 diagonal, his rook on the seventh and knight on e5 pressurizing c6 and f7.

D)

3...dxe4 4 ♘xe4 *(D)*

Now Black has four choices, the first three of which transpose back to positions arising from the move-order 1 e4 e6 2 d4 d5 3 ♘c3/♘d2 dxe4 4

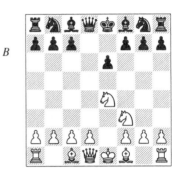

♘xe4 and finally 4...c5, leading to an independent variation.

D1)

4...♘f6 5 ♘xf6+ ♕xf6

5...gxf6 6 d4 b6 7 ♗f4 ♗b7 8 ♗b5+! (disrupting Black's development whilst reducing the effectiveness of the bishop on b7) 8...c6 9 ♗d3 ♘a6 10 a3 ♘c7 11 c4 ♕d7 12 ♕c2 h5 13 0-0-0 0-0-0 14 ♔b1 h4 15 d5?! (the simple 15 h3 gives White a pleasant spatial plus and better piece placement) 15...♗d6? (15...cxd5 16 cxd5 ♗xd5! seems to leave Black a pawn up for little compensation) 16 dxe6 fxe6 17 ♗e4 (now White is back on top) 17...♕e7 18 ♗e3 ♖dg8 19 ♘d4 ♗c5? 20 ♘xc6 ♗xc6 21 ♗xc6 ♗xe3 22 fxe3 ♕c5 23 ♗f3 f5 24 ♕a4 ♔b8 25 ♖d7 e5 26 ♖hd1 e4 27 ♖1d5 b5 28 ♖xc5 bxa4 29 ♖cxc7 exf3 30 gxf3 ♖h6 31 ♖b7+ ♔c8 32 ♖dc7+ ♔d8 33 ♖d7+ ♔c8 34 ♖dc7+ ♔d8 35 ♖f7 ♖g1+ 36 ♔c2 ♖g2+ 37 ♔c3 ♔e8 38 ♖xa7 ♖e6 39 ♖h7 1-0 Plachetka-Meyer, Odense 1993.

6 d4 h6 7 ♗d3 ♘c6 8 c3

8 0-0 ♗d7 9 c3 ♗d6 10 ♖e1 0-0-0 11 ♕e2 g5 12 ♘e5 ♗xe5 13 dxe5 ♕g7 14 a4 h5 15 a5 ♗e8 16 ♗c2?! (16 ♗c4! is better) 16...♘e7 (Black can equalize with 16...♖d5! putting pressure on the e5-pawn) 17 ♕e3 ♔b8 18 ♕xg5 ♕xg5 19 ♗xg5 ♖d7 20 ♗f6 ♖h6 21 ♗g7 ♖g6 22 ♗xg6 fxg6 23 ♖ad1 ♘f5 24 ♗f6 c5 25 ♖xd7 ♗xd7 26 f3 h4 27 ♖e4 ♗c6 28 ♖g4 1-0 Meszaros-Schnitchen, Hajduszoboszlo 1995.

8...♗d7 9 ♕e2 ♗d6 10 ♘d2 ♕e7 11 ♘c4 0-0-0 12 0-0 f5 13 b4! *(D)*

White's queenside play is far more convincing than Black's on the kingside.

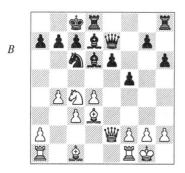

13...♖de8 14 b5 ♘d8 15 a4 e5 16 dxe5 ♗xe5 17 ♕e3 ♔b8 18 ♘xe5 ♕xe5 19 ♕xe5 ♖xe5 20 c4!

White has more space and, together with the bishop-pair, this ensures White a clear advantage for the endgame that follows. 20...♖ee8 21 ♗b2 ♖hg8 22 ♖ad1 c5 23 ♖fe1 g6 24 a5 ♖xe1+ 25 ♖xe1 ♖e8 26 ♖xe8 ♗xe8 27 ♗c1 h5 28 f3 ♘e6 29 ♔f2 ♔c7 30 g4 hxg4 31 fxg4 fxg4 32 ♔g3 b6 33 a6 ♗f7 34 ♔xg4 ♔d6 35 ♗b2 ♘d4 36 ♔g5 ♘f3+ 37 ♔f6 ♗e6 38 ♗c1 g5 39 ♗xg5 ♘xg5

40 ♔xg5 ♔e5 41 h4 ♗f7 42 ♗e2 ♗e8 43 ♗h5 ♗d7 44 ♗f7 ♔d6 45 h5 ♔e7 46 ♔g6 ♗g4 47 h6 1-0 Sanz Alonso-Pisa Ferrer, San Sebastian 1993.

Having adopted similar set-ups and then aiming for either ♘e5 or ♘c4 in both games quoted White had the opportunity of maintaining a lasting edge with careful play.

D2)

4...♗d7

Black aims for ...♗c6 to develop his problem 'French' bishop outside the light-squared pawn-chain. He may follow this up with a later ...♗xf3 and ...c6. Known as the 'Fort Knox' variation, Black is very solid but potentially passive. Here is an example to show how White should deal with this plan: 5 d4 ♗c6 6 ♗d3 ♘d7 7 0-0 ♘gf6 8 ♕e2 ♗e7 9 c3 0-0 10 ♘xf6+ ♘xf6 11 ♘e5 ♕d5 12 f3! (not only stopping threats against g2 but also taking control over the e4-square) 12...a6 13 ♔h1 b5 14 ♗g5! b4 15 ♗xf6 ♗xf6 16 ♘xc6 ♕xc6 17 ♗e4 (the point behind 14 ♗g5! – White now wins the exchange) 17...♕d6 18 ♗xa8 ♖xa8 19 ♕c4 ♖b8 20 ♖ac1 bxc3 21 bxc3 ♖b5 22 ♖b1 ♖h5 23 f4 g5 24 ♖b7 ♗d8 25 ♕c5 ♕xc5 26 dxc5 gxf4 27 ♖d1 ♗e7 28 c6 ♗d6 29 ♖xd6 1-0 Naiditch-Janko, Rimavska Sobota U-12 Ech 1996.

D3)

4...♘d7

This is the most common line following an early ...dxe4. White must play accurately to demonstrate any kind of real advantage.

5 d4

Many games – indeed the majority of those presented here – reach this position via the move-order 1 e4 e6 2 d4 d5 3 ♘c3 (or 3 ♘d2) 3...dxe4 4 ♘xe4 ♘d7 5 ♘f3.

5...♘gf6 6 ♗d3

I find this move and Anand's follow-up to be the most convincing. Others:

a) 6 ♗g5 c5?! (6...h6 or 6...♗e7 is far more consistent) 7 ♗xf6 gxf6 8 dxc5 ♗xc5 9 ♕d2! f5? (Black was already in trouble; this move just hastens the end) 10 ♘xc5 ♘xc5 11 ♕c3 1-0 R.Hennigan-Maduekwe, British League (4NCL) 1997.

b) 6 ♘xf6+ ♘xf6 7 ♗d3 and now:

b1) 7...c5 8 0-0 cxd4 9 ♘xd4 ♗e7 (9...♕xd4?? 10 ♗b5+ winning the queen) 10 c3 0-0 11 ♖e1 a6 12 ♕e2 ♖e8 13 ♗g5 h6 14 ♗h4 ♘d5 15 ♗g3 ♗d6 16 ♘f3 ♗xg3 17 hxg3 ♘f6 (Black is solid but lacks a plan and still has problems developing his light-squared bishop) 18 ♘e5 ♕c7 19 ♕e3! (preparing a kingside attack by g4 with g5 to follow) 19...b6 20 g4 ♗b7 21 g5 hxg5 22 ♕xg5 ♕e7 23 ♖e3 ♘d7 24 ♕h5 f5 25 ♖ae1 ♘f6 26 ♕g6 ♖ad8 27 ♖h3 b5 28 ♕g5 ♘h7 29 ♕h5 g5 30 ♘g4! ♕g7 31 ♗xf5 exf5 32 ♖xe8+ ♖xe8 33 ♕xe8+ 1-0 Mortensen-J.Fries Nielsen, Copenhagen 1995.

b2) 7...h6 8 ♕e2 ♗d6 9 ♘e5 a6 10 c3 c5 11 ♗e3 ♕e7 12 ♘c4! (eliminating Black's dark-squared bishop leaves him with too many weaknesses, which White exploits to the full) 12...cxd4 13 ♘xd6+ ♕xd6 14 ♗xd4 ♕e7 15 ♕e5! (stopping Black castling due to the threat of ♗c5) 15...♕d8 16 0-0-0 ♗d7

17 ♗c5 ♕b8 18 ♗d6 ♕a7 19 ♖d2 ♗c6 20 ♗g6 ♗d7 21 ♗c2 ♗c6 22 ♖hd1 b6 23 ♗a3 ♗d7 24 ♗e4 0-0-0 25 ♗e7 ♘xe4 26 ♕xe4 ♖he8 27 ♕c4+ ♔b8 28 ♗xd8 ♖xd8 29 ♕f4+ ♔c8 30 ♕xf7 g5 31 ♖xd7 1-0 J.Tan-D.Lopez, Greenhills 1997.

6...♘xe4 7 ♗xe4 ♘f6 8 ♗g5 (D)

The plan of White developing his dark-squared bishop to g5 before Black can get in ...h6 seems strong. If Black had played ...h6 prior to ...♘f6 White would have had time for c3 providing the c2-square for his light-squared bishop. This provides a useful tempo gain as White can now play ♗c2 directly after ...♘f6 from Black as opposed to ♗d3 with a later c3 and ♗c2. This plan is common for White in these lines. An important follow-up idea if Black castles kingside is ♕d3 launching a kingside attack or at least provoking weaknesses.

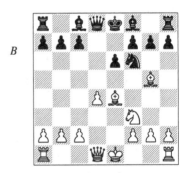

8...♗e7 9 ♗xf6 gxf6 10 ♕e2 c6 11 0-0 ♕b6 12 c4

White already has an advantage in space, better development and a safer king. Now Anand-Vaganian, Riga Tal mem 1995 saw Anand relentlessly turning on the pressure: 12...♗d7 13 c5

♕c7 14 ♖fd1 h5 15 ♘d2 ♖d8 16 ♘c4 ♗c8 17 ♕e3 b5 18 cxb6 axb6 19 ♖ac1 ♗b7 20 ♕f3 f5 21 ♘e5 fxe4?? (an incredible blunder that may have been played as a form of resignation as opposed to suffering on) 22 ♕xf7# (1-0).

D4)
4...c5

This is in my opinion the best of the more unusual replies to the Two Knights Variation. By exchanging off on e4 and then playing ...c5 Black has better central control and is very solid. In return White has a short-term lead in development. There is very little practical experience of this variation so here is a sample line: 5 ♗c4 ♘c6 6 0-0 ♗e7 7 ♕e2 ♘f6 8 d3 0-0 9 ♗g5 b6 10 ♖fe1 ♗b7 11 ♖ad1 ♘a5 12 a3 with equal chances. Generally Black should play ...♗e7 before ...♘f6 anticipating the possible exchange by White on f6 and also avoid exchanging on e4 as positions after dxe4 tend to favour White. There is a lot of scope for original analysis in this line for both players.

E)
3...♘f6 4 e5 ♘e4 (D)

While uncommon, ...♘e4 is not to be underestimated. The most testing move seems to be an immediate ♘e2 by White with the idea of gaining time back by next playing d2-d3. Black can cut across this plan by playing his bishop to c5 hitting f2, when White has to play d2-d4. Although Black must then lose time, at least the black knight on e4 is secure – at any rate temporarily.

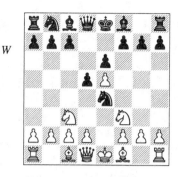

W

5 ♘e2 ♗c5

5...♗e7 6 d3 ♘c5 7 d4 ♘e4 is an odd transposition to the main line, but with the move-number increased by one.

6 d4 ♗e7

6...♗b6 7 ♘g3 c5 8 ♗d3 f5 9 exf6 ♘xf6 10 dxc5! (as in the main line it is better for White to capture early on c5 than to play c2-c3 and give Black the option of when to release the tension in the centre) 10...♗xc5 11 0-0 ♘c6 12 ♗g5 0-0 13 ♕e2 e5?! (13...♘b4 must be better than the text although White already has the edge) 14 ♘xe5 ♕b6 15 ♘xc6 bxc6 16 ♗e3 ♗g4 17 ♕d2 ♗xe3 18 ♕xe3 ♕xe3 19 fxe3 c5 (the question now is not if White is better but how much better) 20 b3 ♖fe8 21 ♖ae1 ♖e5 22 ♘f5 ♗xf5 23 ♖xf5 ♖xf5 24 ♗xf5 ♖e8 25 h3 c4 26 c3 g6 27 ♗c2 ♔g7 28 b4 g5 29 a4 g4 30 ♔f2 h5 31 ♔e2 d4 32 cxd4 ♘d5 33 e4 ♘xb4 34 ♔d2 a5 35 ♗b1 ♖f8 36 hxg4 hxg4 37 ♔c3 ♖f2 38 e5 ♖xg2 39 e6 ♔f6 40 ♔xc4 ♔e7 41 ♖e5 ♖b2 42 ♗e4 ♘a2 43 d5 ♖b8 44 ♖g5 ♖b4+ 45 ♔d3 ♘c1+ 46 ♔e3 ♔f6 47 ♖f5+ 1-0 Pcola-Sedlakova, Slovakian open Ch (Trenčin) 1995.

7 ♘g3 c5 8 dxc5! (D)

Better than 8 c3, which gives Black the choice of when to release the tension in the centre.

8 ♗d3 ♘xg3 9 hxg3 h6 10 c3 ♘c6 11 a3! (anticipating Black exchanging on d4 and then playing ...♘b4 with the idea of exchanging off White's light-squared bishop as retreating it to e2 allows ...♛c7 followed by ...♘c2+) 11...c4 12 ♗c2 ♔d7?! (a bold decision – not wanting to castle kingside, the black king seeks safety in the centre) 13 b3 b5 14 a4! ♗a6 15 axb5 ♗xb5 16 ♘d2 cxb3 17 ♗xb3 ♛b6 18 ♛g4 ♗d3 19 ♗xd5 ♗f5 20 ♛f3 ♘xd4? 21 cxd4 ♛xd4 22 ♗xa8 ♛xe5+ 23 ♗e4 (23 ♔d1! is even stronger) 23...♛xa1 24 ♛d3+ 1-0 Kaeser-O.Seidler, Baden-Baden 1988. Actually, this game lasted 25 moves as it came from the 5...♗e7 6 d3 ♘c5 7 d4 ♘e4 move-order.

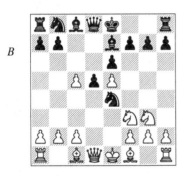

8...♘d7 9 ♗d3 ♘exc5 10 0-0 0-0 11 ♖e1 f6 12 exf6 ♗xf6 13 ♗f1 b6 14 ♘d4

Now the most natural move is 14...♘e5, when White enjoys a small but clear advantage. Instead 14...♔h8? 15 b4! ♘b8 16 bxc5 bxc5 17 ♘b3 ♗xa1 18 ♘xa1 ♛f6 19 ♗e3! d4 20 ♘e4 ♛f5 21 ♗c1 ♗b7 22 f3! ♛d5 23

♘b3 c4 24 ♘bc5 ♗c6 25 ♛e2 c3 26 ♛f2 e5 27 ♗d3 (White has slowly but surely gained control of the central light squares as Black's pawns have been committed to the stagnant occupation of c3, d4 and e5) 27...♘d7 28 ♛h4 ♖ae8 29 ♘xd7 ♛xd7 30 ♘c5 e4 31 ♘xd7 exf3 32 ♘xf8 1-0 was the game Matychenkov-Volkov, Smolensk 1991.

Part 2

1 e4 e6 2 ♘f3 d5 3 ♘c3 ♘f6 4 e5 ♘fd7 *(D)*

Around 90% of my French games start this way and proceed...

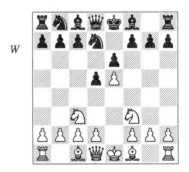

5 d4 c5

...by which we have transposed to the variation 1 e4 e6 2 d4 d5 3 ♘c3 ♘f6 4 e5 ♘fd7 5 ♘f3 c5. Before going any further we should consider what the implications of this transposition are. White has avoided the Winawer (1 e4 e6 2 d4 d5 3 ♘c3 ♗b4) but can no longer play 5 f4, which is considered to be the most testing move after 4...♘fd7. However, I believe through years of practical experience that White can demonstrate a lasting edge and that most players with Black are ill-prepared to meet this variation.

6 dxc5 ♘c6

6...♗xc5 7 ♗d3 ♘c6 8 ♗f4 transposes to Line D.

7 ♗f4

At this point Black can play:

A: 7...a6!?   137
B: 7...♘xc5   137
C: 7...♗e7   138
D: 7...♗xc5   139

A)

7...a6!? *(D)*

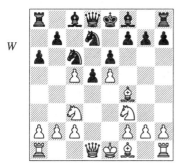

This semi-waiting move has the idea of seeing where White places his light-squared bishop before deciding which way to recapture on c5. Also in many lines ...a6 is a useful move for Black as it stops a white minor piece coming to b5 and prepares queenside expansion whilst also giving a bolt-hole for Black's dark-squared bishop from c5 in some variations.

8 ♗d3 ♗e7 9 0-0 ♘xc5 10 ♘e2!

Better than 10 ♗e2. White improves his knight from c3 via e2 to d4 where, covered by the other knight on f3, it will be difficult for Black to dislodge

and will exert considerable pressure on the central squares.

10...0-0 11 ♘ed4 f6

A natural and typical way for Black to strike back in the centre.

12 exf6 ♗xf6 13 ♘xc6 bxc6 14 ♗e5 ♘d7 15 ♖e1 ♘xe5 16 ♘xe5 ♗xe5 17 ♖xe5

These exchanges have left White with control of some important dark squares, in particular e5. Kaeser-Spiekermann, NWL-Liga II 1994 continued 17...♕f6 18 ♕e2 ♖b8 19 c4! ♖b4 20 b3 a5 21 ♖c1 ♗d7 22 ♖e3 a4 23 ♖f3 ♕e7 24 ♖xf8+ ♕xf8 25 bxa4! ♕f6 26 ♖b1 ♖xb1+ 27 ♗xb1 ♕a1 28 ♕c2 g6 29 a5 e5 30 a6!! ♗f5 31 ♕d1 ♗xb1 32 cxd5 cxd5 33 a4 ♕b2 34 ♕xd5+ ♔g7 35 ♕b7+ 1-0.

B)

7...♘xc5 *(D)*

Black plans to discourage White from putting a bishop on d3 and tries to get better control of e4.

8 ♗b5!?

White in turn tries to exploit Black's lack of control of d4 by pinning the c6-knight. Otherwise:

a) 8 ♗d3 is considered in Line C.

b) 8 ♗e2 ♗e7 9 0-0 a6 10 ♗g3 0-0 11 ♘d4 ♕b6 12 ♖b1 ♘d7 13 ♘f3 f6 14 exf6 ♘xf6 15 ♘e5 (we have now reached a position similar to one covered in Part 3 of this chapter although White's light-squared bishop is normally placed on the better square d3 and generally Black's queen is poorly placed on b6) 15...♘xe5 16 ♗xe5 ♗d6?! (it is generally wrong for Black to exchange off the dark-squared bishops if he cannot then safely play the freeing move ...e6-e5) 17 ♘a4?! (simpler is 17 ♗xd6 ♕xd6 18 ♗f3 with a lasting edge) 17...♕c7 18 ♗xd6 ♕xd6 19 c4 ♗d7 and Black has equalized, Sikora Gizynska-T.Berg, Aabybro wom tt 1989.

Both 8 ♗b5!? and 8 ♗e2 seem perfectly viable for White and it seems more a matter of style which you may prefer. I would recommend you look at Line C first, as 8 ♗d3 transposes to this, before deciding.

8...♕b6 9 0-0 a6 10 ♗xc6+ bxc6 11 ♖b1!

Not only protecting b2 but preparing the thematic advance b2-b4 controlling the c5-square.

11...a5!?

Stopping White's plan of b2-b4 but permanently weakening the b5-square if Black intends to follow up with a later ...c6-c5 advance.

12 ♘d4 ♘d7 13 ♖e1 ♗b7 14 ♘a4 ♕a7 15 c3 ♘c5 16 ♘xc5 ♕xc5 17 b4! ♕c4 18 bxa5 ♗a6 19 ♕g4!

Exploiting both Black's king still being in the centre and lack of development on the kingside. Birke-Klings, Germany 1994 continued 19...♔d7 20 h4?! (20 ♕h5! g6 21 ♕f3 maintains

the initiative) 20...c5 21 ♘f3 ♗e7 22 ♖b6 h6 23 ♖eb1 ♖hg8 24 ♘d2 ♕xc3 25 ♗xh6 ♕xa5 (25...gxh6 26 ♕a4+ ♔d8 27 ♖xa6! ♖xa6 28 ♖b7 wins) 26 ♗g5 c4? (26...♗xg5! 27 ♕xg5 ♕xa2 is better, when despite the dangerous piece placement it is not clear how White should proceed) 27 ♖b7+! ♗xb7 28 ♖xb7+ ♔c6 29 ♖xe7 ♖a7 30 ♖xf7! ♖e8 31 ♖xa7 ♕xa7 32 ♗e3 ♕xa2 33 ♕xg7 c3 34 ♕f7 ♕a8 35 ♘b3 ♔b5 36 ♘d4+ ♔c4 37 ♕f4 ♔d3 38 ♗c1 ♕a1 39 ♕e3+ ♔c4 40 ♘c2 ♕b1 41 ♘a3+ 1-0.

C)

7...♗e7 (D)

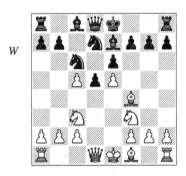

Black delays capturing on c5 until White commits his bishop to d3. This seems more logical than 7...♘xc5 and cuts down White's options. However, the only example of this is by transposition, with Black playing 7...♘xc5 meeting 8 ♗d3 with ...♗e7, viz. 7...♘xc5 8 ♗d3 ♗e7 9 0-0 0-0 10 ♖e1 f6 11 exf6 ♗xf6 12 ♗g3 ♕b6 13 ♖b1 ♗d7 14 ♕d2 ♖ae8 15 b4! ♘xd3 16 cxd3 (to maintain control of both c4 and e4) 16...♘d4 17 ♘e5 ♗c8 18 ♘a4 (18 ♕e3! gives Black more problems)

18...♕d8 19 b5 ♘f5 20 d4 ♗g5 21 ♕c3 ♖e7?! (21...♘xg3 22 hxg3 b6! and Black has equalized) 22 b6 (now White is back on top) 22...♕e8 23 ♘c5 axb6 24 ♖xb6 h5 25 ♘f3 ♗f6 26 ♗e5 ♕g6 27 a4 ♕h6 28 a5 g5 29 ♗xf6 ♕xf6 30 ♘e5 ♖c7 31 ♕d2 ♘g7 32 ♖b3 ♕f4 33 ♕b2 ♕f6 34 ♖c3 g4 35 ♖ec1 ♕h6 36 ♕b6 ♕f4 37 ♖3c2 ♘e8 38 ♘cd3 ♖xc2 39 ♖xc2 1-0 Drozhdov-Landenbergue, Budapest 1990.

D)

7...♗xc5 8 ♗d3 *(D)*

In this position Black has tried no fewer than eight different replies:

D1)

8...0-0? *(D)*

Not a move experienced French players are likely to make, as they are only too aware of possible sacrifices

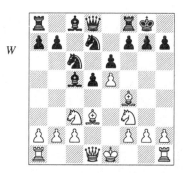

on h7! White can now gain a winning advantage although accurate play is necessary not to let Black off the hook.

9 ♗xh7+ ♔xh7 10 ♘g5+ ♔g6

On 10...♔g8 there follows 11 ♕h5 ♖e8 12 ♕xf7+ ♔h8 13 ♕h5+ ♔g8 14 ♕h7+ ♔f8 15 ♕h8+ ♔e7 16 ♕xg7#.

11 ♕d3+ f5 12 ♘xe6

The alternative 12 ♕g3 looks very strong but in fact Black has tactical resources of his own, a possible continuation being 12...♗xf2+! 13 ♔xf2 ♘dxe5 14 ♘xe6+ ♘g4+! 15 ♕xg4+ fxg4 16 ♘xd8 ♖xf4+ 17 ♔g3 ♖f8, when it would be difficult to demonstrate any real advantage for White.

12...♕b6 13 ♘xd5 ♗xf2+ 14 ♔f1

White is winning. Note that this idea is not only applicable after 8...0-0, but at any point over the next few moves if Black castles without taking adequate precautions.

D2)

8...♕b6? *(D)*

Black makes a direct attack on both f2 and b2. However, the b2-pawn is poisoned and with a ♘a4 looming, ...♕b6 achieves nothing.

9 0-0 ♕xb2

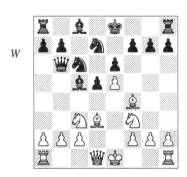

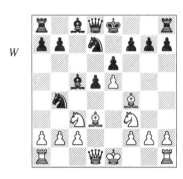

9...0-0? is of course answered by 10 ♗xh7+!.

10 ♘b5

Now:

a) 10...♖b8 11 ♗d2! a6 12 ♗c3 ♕xa1 13 ♘c7+ ♔d8 14 ♘xe6+ fxe6 15 ♗xa1 ♔c7 16 ♕e2 h6 17 ♘h4 g5 18 ♘g6 1-0 Jurković-Malivanek, Hradec Kralove 1992.

b) 10...♗b6 11 ♗d2! d4 12 ♖b1 ♕xa2 13 ♗c4 ♕xb1 14 ♕xb1 0-0 15 ♖e1 ♗c5 16 c3 dxc3 17 ♘xc3 ♘b6 18 ♘g5 g6 19 ♕e4 ♗e7 20 ♕h4 h5 21 ♗e2 ♔g7 22 ♗f3 ♗d7 23 ♗xc6 bxc6 24 ♘xe6+ ♗xe6 25 ♕xe7 ♘d7 26 ♕g5 ♖h8 27 ♘e4 ♖ab8 28 ♘f6 ♘c5 29 ♗e3 ♘d3 30 ♖d1 ♗f5 31 e6 ♘e5 32 ♗d4 ♖hd8 33 ♘d7 1-0 Carretero-Carrasco, Spanish Cht 1993.

In both cases Black suffered by taking on b2, with White's ♗d2! being the key move.

D3)

8...♘b4?! *(D)*

If Black wants to exchange off a knight for the bishop on d3 it seems more logical to do so with the knight from d7 by playing 7...♗e7 followed by 8...♘xc5 (Line C above). Now White can either ignore the plan and

take back on d3 with his queen, play ♘c3-e2-d4 and c3, or retreat the bishop to e2 and play a3 at a suitable moment, as in the following game: 9 ♗e2 b6 10 a3 ♘c6 11 0-0 h6?! (while the plan of 9...b6 is unusual it must still be more logical to play ...f6 to challenge the centre rather than ...h6?! if Black intends to castle kingside instead of trying for kingside expansion) 12 ♗g3 ♗b7 13 ♖e1 ♖c8 14 ♗d3 ♗e7 15 ♘b5! (with the familiar idea of occupying d4 with the knight from c3) 15...0-0 16 c3 a6 17 ♘bd4 ♖e8 18 ♗c2 ♘f8 19 ♗f4 f5 20 exf6 ♗xf6 21 ♘xc6 ♗xc6 22 ♘e5 ♗xe5 23 ♗xe5 (now White's two bishops and kingside attacking chances give him a distinct advantage) 23...♕g5 24 f4 ♕e7 25 ♖e3 ♕c5 26 ♗d4 ♕d6 27 ♖g3 ♖e7 28 ♕g4 ♕d7 29 ♕h5 ♖c7 30 ♕xh6 ♕e8 31 ♖e1 ♕d7 32 ♖e5 ♔f7 33 ♖xg7+ ♔e8 34 ♖g8 1-0 Medvegy-Pilardeu, Mamaia cadets Wch 1991.

D4)

8...♗e7?! *(D)*

The idea of this move is not to play ...♘c5 (as this would just lose a tempo compared to playing ...♘xc5 and ...♗e7 in the first place) but to support

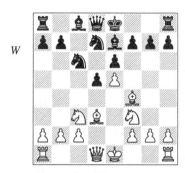

a ...g5 thrust. Whereas this idea is dangerous for White and he needs to react carefully, it is also risky for Black to open the kingside while his own king is still in the centre and castling queenside, even if desirable, is some way off.

9 ♗g3

9 0-0?! (White should not hurry to castle short in this variation) 9...g5 10 ♗g3 g4 11 ♘e1 ♘dxe5 12 ♕e2 ♗f6? (12...♗d6 is almost certainly an improvement, when it is difficult to justify White's investment of a pawn) 13 ♖d1 0-0 14 ♗b5 ♕b6 15 ♗xc6 ♘xc6 16 ♕xg4+ ♗g7 17 ♘d3 d4 18 ♘b1 ♕a5 19 ♘d2 ♕xa2 20 ♘b3 ♕a4 21 ♗d6 ♖d8 22 ♕g3 ♕b5 23 ♖fe1 ♕h5 24 ♗c7 ♖f8 25 ♘f4 ♕f5 26 ♘xd4 ♘xd4 27 ♖xd4 ♔h8 28 ♖d3 b6 29 ♖e5 ♗xe5 30 ♗xe5+ f6 31 ♘h5 ♕g6 32 ♗xf6+ ♔g8 33 ♕e5 1-0 Zimmermann-Heinicke, Bundesliga 1980/1.

9...g5 10 h3! h5 11 ♕e2

This plan seems to slow down Black's kingside expansion/kingside attack. After White castles, an advance of ...g4 allows hxg4 hxg4, ♘h2 when the pawn on g4 comes under pressure and the open h-file is difficult for Black to use to any effect.

D5)
8...a6!? (D)

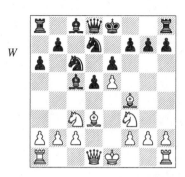

The idea is either to put the queen on c7 without worrying about ♘b5 happening at an unsuitable moment or to expand with ...b5.

9 0-0 ♕c7!?

While putting pressure on White's pawn on e5 it is always dangerous to put Black's queen on the same diagonal as White's dark-squared bishop as ♘xd5 and e6 can be 'in the air'. Others:

a) 9...0-0? allows White the standard attack without Black having any active counterplay: 10 ♗xh7+ ♔xh7 11 ♘g5+ ♔g6 12 ♕d3+ f5 13 ♕g3 ♕b6 14 ♘xe6+ ♔f7 15 ♘xd5 ♕a5 16 ♘dc7 ♖g8 17 ♕g5 g6 18 ♕h4 ♗f8 19 ♕h7+ ♗g7 20 ♘g5+ ♔e7 21 ♕xg8 1-0 Borg-Veer, Thessaloniki OL 1984.

b) 9...b5 10 ♖e1 ♗a7 11 a3 b4 12 axb4 ♘xb4 13 ♗f1 0-0 14 ♗g3 ♕c7 15 ♕d2 ♖b8 16 ♘b5! axb5 17 ♕xb4 ♗c5 18 ♕h4! (once again White plays for a kingside attack as Black's pieces are cluttered around the queenside) 18...b4 19 ♗d3 h6 20 ♗f4 ♕d8 21 ♕g3! ♔h8 22 ♕h3 ♖e8 23 ♗xh6 gxh6 24 ♕xh6+ ♔g8 1-0 Jahn-M.Horvath, Graz wom Z 1993.

c) 9...f6 may well transpose to Line B in Part 3.

10 ₩e2 ⌽d4 11 ⌽xd4 ⌽xd4 12 ⌤ae1 ⌽xc3 13 bxc3 ₩xc3 14 ₩g4 g6 15 ₩h4

Now 15...₩b2!? is relatively best, when White has the two bishops, a safer king and dark-square domination in return for a pawn. Instead Blaich-Holzinger, Ladenburg 1992 proceeded 15...f5?! 16 exf6 ₩xf6 17 ⌽g5 ₩f7 18 ₩b4! (without Black being able to castle White's advantage soon becomes apparent) 18...⌽f6 19 ⌤e3 (19 c4! breaking up Black's centre is even stronger) 19...h6 20 ⌽xf6 ₩xf6 21 ⌤f3 ₩g7 22 ⌤e1 b5 23 ₩d6 ⌤a7 24 ₩b8 ⌸d8 25 ⌤xe6 (White, now having recovered his modest material investment, has a dominating position) 25...₩c7 26 ⌤d6+ ⌸e7 27 ₩xc7+ ⌤xc7 28 ⌤xg6 a5 29 ⌤g7+ ⌸d8 30 ⌤xc7 ⌸xc7 31 ⌽xb5 ⌸b6 32 a4 ⌤h7 33 ⌤f6+ ⌸a7 34 ⌤d6 ⌤e7 35 ⌸f1 ⌤e5 36 f4 ⌤e4 37 g3 h5 38 ⌤xd5 h4 39 ⌸f2 h3 40 f5 ⌽b7 41 ⌤d7 ⌸b6 42 f6 ⌤e6 43 f7 ⌤f6+ 44 ⌸e3 1-0.

D6)
8...h6!? *(D)*

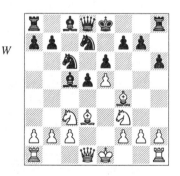

W

An unusual move, the idea being to prepare ...0-0 followed by, or in conjunction with, queenside expansion while maintaining the tension in the centre. As the following example shows though, White's kingside play is still not to be underestimated: 9 ⌽g3 a6 10 0-0 b5 11 ⌤e1 0-0 12 ⌽e2! (the thematic improvement of the knight from c3; this time it is heading for f4 to aid the forthcoming kingside attack) 12...b4 13 c3! (more to control the b4- and d4-squares than to exchange off Black's b4-pawn) 13...bxc3 14 bxc3 a5 15 ⌽f4 ⌽a6 16 ⌽c2 (not surprisingly White wants to keep his light-squared bishop to assist his attacking chances) 16...⌤c8 17 ₩d2 ⌤e8 18 ⌽h5 ⌽f8 19 ⌤ac1 ⌽e7 20 ⌽d4 ⌽c5 21 ⌽h4! (White takes the opportunity to swap off one of Black's more useful defensive pieces) 21...₩d7 22 ⌽xe7 ₩xe7 23 ⌤e3 ⌤ed8 24 ⌤g3 ⌸h8 25 ₩f4 ⌽d7 26 ⌽a4 ⌽xe5? 27 ₩xe5 ₩c7 28 ₩e3 e5 29 ⌽f3 e4 30 ₩d4! exf3 31 ⌤xg7 ₩c5 32 ₩g4 ⌤d6 33 ⌤g8+ ⌸h7 34 ⌽c2+ 1-0 Gufeld-Spassky, USSR Ch (Leningrad) 1960.

D7)
8...f5!? *(D)*

Logical in one way, to block the b1-h7 diagonal while expanding on the kingside, 8...f5!? leaves White with two choices: either to transpose to the main line with 9 exf6 or to try to exploit f5 immediately with 9 ⌽xf5?! exf5 10 ₩xd5. Then 10...⌽e7?! 11 ₩d3 ⌽b6 12 0-0-0 ⌽c5 13 ₩c4 ₩c7 14 ⌽b5 1-0 Edocs-Gorla, Bern 1991 was a great success for White, but after 10...₩b6! 11 ₩e6+ ⌽e7 White has

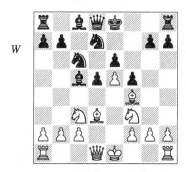

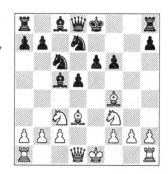

little for the piece. I would therefore recommend 9 exf6.

D8)
8...f6 *(D)*

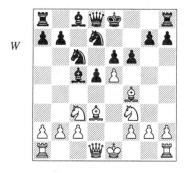

The normal continuation.
9 exf6
Black must again make a decision:
D81: 9...gxf6? 143
D82: 9...♕xf6!? 143

The main line, 9...♘xf6, is covered in Part 3.

D81)
9...gxf6? *(D)*
If Black could get away with ...gxf6 he would be well-placed in the long term with a mass of central pawns and

the open g-file to work on. However, the capture is premature and White can soon exploit the position of the black king: 10 ♘h4! ♕e7 11 ♕h5+ ♔d8 12 0-0-0 ♘de5?! (12...♗xf2!? asks for trouble but may well be the best way of asking White to 'prove' he has something concrete) 13 ♗b5 ♗d7 14 ♗xc6! bxc6 15 ♗xe5 fxe5 16 ♘g6 ♕e8 17 ♕g5+ ♔c8 18 ♘xe5?! (18 ♘xh8 ♕xh8 19 ♖he1 seems simplest and best) 18...♖g8 19 ♕h4 ♖xg2 20 ♘e4 ♗e7 21 ♕h3 ♕g8 22 ♕c3 ♕g7 (22...♗f6! 23 ♘xf6 ♕g5+ is the best try) 23 f4 ♗e8 1-0 (in view of 24 ♘xc6 ♕xc3 25 ♘xe7+ ♔d7 26 ♘xc3 ♔xe7 27 f5! when Black's position falls apart) Lukovnikov-Yachmenev, Voronezh 1991.

D82)
9...♕xf6!?
White has tried 10 ♗g5 in this position with little success and I therefore recommend a quieter move:
10 ♗g3 0-0 11 0-0 *(D)*
11...h6
Or:
a) 11...♘de5? 12 ♘xe5 ♘xe5 13 ♗xh7+! ♔xh7 14 ♕h5+ ♔g8 15 ♗xe5 ♗xf2+ 16 ♔h1 and Black is in trouble.

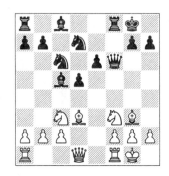

b) 11...g6 12 ♕e2 ♘b6 13 ♖ae1 a6 14 ♘e5 ♗d4 15 ♘d1 ♖e8 16 ♘g4 ♕f8 17 c3 ♗g7 18 f4 (a standard idea to strengthen White's grip on e5) 18...♗d7 19 h4 (an unusual but effective way to attack Black's kingside) 19...♕e7 20 ♘df2 ♕c5 21 h5 gxh5 22 ♘e5 ♘xe5 23 fxe5 ♗b5 24 ♔h2 ♖f8 25 ♕xh5 ♗xd3 26 ♘xd3 ♕c4 27 ♘f4 ♖f5 28 ♕g4 ♖af8 29 b3 ♕c6 30 ♘h5 ♖5f7 31 ♗h4 with a massive attack for White, U.Kaeser-P.Meyer, Sankt Augustin 1990.

c) 11...♘d4 12 ♘xd4 ♗xd4 and here White even has the luxury of a choice: 13 ♕d2 a6 14 ♖ad1 ♔h8 15 ♖fe1 ♘c5 16 ♗f1 ♗xc3 17 ♕xc3 ♕xc3 18 bxc3 ♘a4 19 c4 with a very attractive position for White, Pogosian-Shliakhtin, Moscow Alekhine mem 1992 or 13 ♕e2 ♘e5 14 ♘b5 ♘xd3 15 cxd3 ♗b6 16 ♘c7 ♗xc7 17 ♗xc7 ♗d7 18 ♗e5 ♕f5 19 ♕e3 ♗b5 20 ♖ad1 ♖f7 21 ♕d4 ♖c8 22 ♖d2 a6 23 h3 ♕g5 24 f4 and the presence of opposite-coloured bishops and major pieces allows White to launch a strong attack on the kingside dark squares, Lukin-Veinger, USSR Spartakiad (Leningrad) 1967.

12 ♕d2

This has been the preferred move in practice although 12 ♕e2 may well be the most thematic, taking control of the e5-square.

After 12 ♕d2 there are two examples *(D)*:

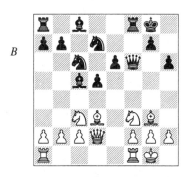

a) 12...♘de5 13 ♘xe5 ♘xe5 14 ♖ae1 ♘f7 15 ♕e2 ♗d7 16 ♕g4 ♕g5 17 ♕xg5 ♘xg5 18 h4 ♘f7 19 ♗b5 ♗c8 20 ♗d3 a6 21 ♘a4 ♗a7 22 ♗c7 ♗d7 23 ♘b6 ♗xb6 24 ♗xb6 e5 25 f3 and White has the better ending, Blimke-Kludacz, Polish wom Ch (Brzeg Dolny) 1996. The general plan is to force one of Black's central pawns forward.

b) 12...♗b4 13 a3 ♗e7 14 ♖fe1 a6 15 ♖e2 ♘c5 16 ♘e5 ♘xe5 17 ♗xe5 ♕f7 18 ♖ae1 ♗g5 19 ♕d1 ♗f4 20 ♗xf4 ♕xf4 21 g3 ♕f6 22 ♕d2 ♗d7 23 ♖e5 ♗c6 24 f4 consolidated White's positional advantage in Matychenkov-Galanov, USSR Cht (Naberezhnye Chelny) 1988.

In conclusion White seems to have good practical chances with careful play and therefore 9...♘xf6, covered next in Part 3, is the most common and possibly the best chance for Black to seek equality.

Part 3

1 e4 e6 2 ♘f3 d5 3 ♘c3 ♘f6 4 e5 ♘fd7 5 d4 c5 6 dxc5 ♘c6 7 ♗f4 ♗xc5 8 ♗d3 f6 9 exf6 ♘xf6

This is the main line.

10 0-0 0-0 11 ♘e5 *(D)*

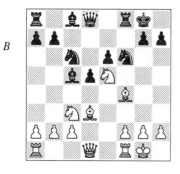

B

Black can choose between:

A:	**11...♘e4?!**	145
B:	**11...a6?!**	145
C:	**11...♗d6?**	146
D:	**11...♘xe5**	146
E:	**11...♗d7**	146
F:	**11...♕e8**	148

A)

11...♘e4?!

A strong-looking move both putting pressure on f2 and hitting the bishop on f4. However, due to a clever series of tactics White keeps a clear plus.

12 ♗xe4 ♖xf4 13 ♘d3 ♗xf2+

After 13...♗d6 14 ♘xf4 ♗xf4 Black has insufficient compensation for the exchange but White must be careful to consolidate his advantage in view of Black's central pawn majority and short-term initiative on the dark squares, a possible continuation being 15 ♗d3

♗e5 16 ♕h5 g6 17 ♕h6 ♕f6 18 ♕d2 ♗f4 19 ♕e1 ♗e5 20 f4! with a clear advantage for White.

14 ♖xf2 ♖xf2

Now:

a) 15 ♘xf2 dxe4 16 ♕xd8+ ♘xd8 17 ♖d1! ♘c6 18 ♘fxe4 e5 gives White a lasting edge in the endgame but one that may be difficult to convert for the full point.

b) 15 ♗xh7+ ♔xh7 16 ♕h5+ ♔g8 17 ♘xf2 e5 18 ♖d1 d4 19 ♘fe4 ♕e7 20 ♖f1!! dxc3 21 ♘g5 (winning) 21...♕xg5 22 ♕xg5 cxb2 23 ♖b1 ♗e6 24 ♖xb2 b6 25 ♕g6 ♗d7 26 c3 ♖e8 27 ♖d2 ♖e6 28 ♕g4 ♗c8 29 ♖f2 ♘e7 30 ♕a4 ♘c6 31 h4 ♗d7 32 h5 e4 33 ♖e2 e3 34 ♕f4 ♗c8 35 ♖xe3 1-0 Ljubojević-Bednarski, Skopje OL 1972.

B)

11...a6?! *(D)*

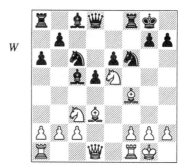

W

The type of move that can be difficult to assess. The plan of queenside expansion played in the following miniature worked out very badly but if instead 11...a6?! were to be used purely as a 'pass' to see how White plans to continue it may become a useful move, e.g. to stop a future ♘b5 or to give the bishop on c5 a useful retreat to a7 maintaining it on the a7-g1 diagonal.

12 ♕e2! (a common theme in such variations: White invites ...♘d4 'gaining a tempo' on the grounds that the black knight will be misplaced there) 12...♘d4 13 ♕d2 b5? 14 ♗e3 ♕b6 15 b4! (decisive) 15...♗xb4 16 ♗xd4 ♕c7 17 ♘xb5 ♗xd2 18 ♘xc7 ♖b8 19 ♖ab1 1-0 Baker-Spice, Cardiff 1997.

C)
11...♗d6? *(D)*

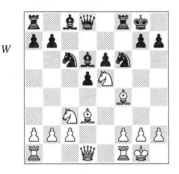

This move puts pressure on e5 but withdraws the bishop from the very useful a7-g1 diagonal and does nothing to improve Black's development. The following game shows how White can best exploit this inaccuracy: 12 ♕e2! (maintaining control of the vital e5-square) 12...♘e4?! (conceding control of the dark squares) 13 ♘xe4 ♖xf4 14 ♘xd6 ♕xd6 15 ♖ae1 ♘xe5 16 ♕xe5 ♕xe5 17 ♖xe5 ♗d7 18 g3 ♖d4 19 f4 g6 20 ♔f2 ♖a4 21 a3 ♔f7 22 ♖fe1 b5 23 f5 gxf5 24 ♗xf5 b4 25 ♗xe6+ ♗xe6 26 ♖xe6 bxa3 27 ♖e7+ ♔g8 28 bxa3 ♖xa3 1-0 Bezsilko-Vareille, French Ch (Val Thorens) 1988.

D)
11...♘xe5 12 ♗xe5 ♗d7 *(D)*

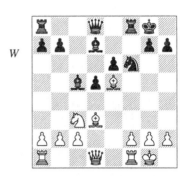

Solid, but uninspiring. Black would do better to play ...♗d7 before capturing on e5 (as in variation E) to see how White intends to follow up 11 ♘e5.

Now:

a) 13 ♕f3 is an alternative idea, when 13...♕b6?! 14 ♔h1! gives White a definite advantage now the f2-pawn is no longer pinned and doesn't fall with check in crucial lines. However, 13...♘e4 14 ♕g4 ♕g5! 15 ♕xg5 ♘xg5 yields equality.

b) The game I.Rogers-Calderwood, London Lloyds Bank 1991 shows that White has the opportunity to get in the thematic moves ♔h1 and f4 without Black getting any active counterplay: 13 ♕e2 a6 14 a3 ♕b6 15 ♔h1 ♖ae8 16 f4 ♗c6 17 ♖ae1 ♖f7 18 ♘d1 ♘e4 19 c3 ♖d8 20 ♕g4 ♖e8 21 ♖f3 ♗d6 22 ♗xd6 ♘xd6 23 ♖xe6 ♖xe6 24 ♕xe6 ♘e4 25 ♖e3 ♕b3 26 ♖e1 ♗d7 27 ♕e5 ♖f5 28 ♕e7 ♗c6 29 ♕e6+ 1-0.

E)
11...♗d7 *(D)*

More consistent than an immediate ...♘xe5, Black is not afraid of giving

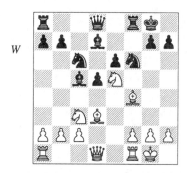

up the bishop-pair, so instead completes his development and looks to see how White intends to make progress.

12 ♕e2

This appears to be the best plan for White. We have seen this theme in previous variations: White overprotects the e5-square, continues to stop ...♘h5 and does not fear ...♘d4 'winning a tempo' as after ♕d2 the knight on d4 becomes a real liability. Other moves:

a) 12 ♕f3 ♘xe5 (12...♕b6? allows White a good position after 13 ♔h1!) 13 ♗xe5 transposes to note 'a' in Line D, where 13...♘e4 14 ♕g4 ♕g5! leads to equality.

b) 12 ♕d2!? ♘xe5 13 ♗xe5 ♘g4 (with the queen now on d2 as opposed to e2 this now becomes possible) 14 ♗g3 h5?! (better is 14...♕b6) 15 ♗e2 ♗c6 16 ♗xg4 hxg4 17 ♕e2 ♕f6 18 ♕xg4 ♖ae8 19 ♖ad1 ♕f5 20 ♕xf5 ♖xf5 21 ♖fe1 (despite White's extra pawn, Black's two bishops and central pawn majority make it a difficult technical task for White) 21...b5 22 a3 a5 23 ♘e2 e5 24 ♘c1 ♗b6 25 ♘d3 e4 26 ♘c1 ♖ef8 27 ♘e2? (27 ♖e2 maintains an edge) 27...♖xf2 28 ♗xf2 ♖xf2? (the simple 28...♗xf2+ appears to

give Black a perfectly respectable position) 29 ♔h1 d4 30 ♘xd4 ♗b7 31 c3 e3 32 ♖e2 ♗xg2+ 33 ♔g1 ♗f3 34 ♖xe3 ♖g2+ 35 ♔f1 ♗d5 36 ♖e5 ♗f3 37 ♘xf3 ♖f2+ 38 ♔e1 ♖xf3 1-0 Macieja-Kujawski, Polish Ch 1991.

12...♕e7

12...♘xe5 13 ♗xe5 ♕b6 14 a4! a6 15 a5 ♕b4 16 h3 ♖ae8 17 ♔h1 g6 18 f4! (the thematic follow-up to ♔h1; it both maintains a tight grip on e5 and in effect strengthens what was the potentially weak f2-square) 18...♘h5 19 ♕g4! (playing as usual for the kingside attack) 19...♖f7 20 ♗xg6 hxg6 21 ♕xg6+ ♘g7 22 f5 ♖ef8 23 ♖f4!? (23 f6! wins more easily) 23...♕xf4 (at this point White accepted Black's draw offer to win the tournament outright but after 24 ♗xf4 ♖xf5 25 ♗h6 ♖f1+ 26 ♖xf1 ♖xf1+ 27 ♔h2 ♗g1+ 28 ♔g3 ♗f2+ 29 ♔f3 White is in a winning position) ½-½ Baker-Gunter, Paignton 1997.

13 ♖ae1 ♖ae8

13...♖ae8 14 ♗g3 ♘xe5 15 ♗xe5 ♗c6 16 ♔h1 ♗d6?! (as we have already seen repeatedly it is inaccurate for Black to exchange off the dark-squared bishops without the freeing move ...e6-e5 being available) 17 ♘b5?! (17 f4! is more thematic and the way to obtain the advantage in this type of position) 17...♗xe5 18 ♕xe5 ♘d7 19 ♕h5 (19 ♕c7!?) 19...g6 20 ♕h3 ♗xb5! 21 ♗xb5 a6 and Black has equalized, I.Rogers-Thorhallsson, Gausdal Troll 1996.

14 a3 a6 15 ♗g3 ♗d4!? 16 ♘d1

Now 16...b5 is relatively best. Instead Drozhdov-Castañeda, Russian club Ch (Briansk) 1995 continued 16...♘e4?

17 ♗xe4 ♘xe5 18 ♗xe5 ♗xe5 19 ♗xh7+ (the move missed when Black played 16...♘e4?) 19...♔xh7 20 ♕h5+ ♔g8 21 ♖xe5 ♗a4 22 ♘c3 ♗c6 23 ♖d1 (the rest is now just technique) 23...♕f6 24 ♕e2 ♕g6 25 ♖d4 ♕h6 26 ♕d2 ♕g6 27 ♘e2 ♕f6 28 ♕e3 ♕g6 29 ♖d2 ♖f6 30 ♘d4 ♗d7 31 ♖e2 ♖c8 32 h3 ♖e8 33 ♔h2 ♖ef8 34 c3 ♖e8 35 f4! ♔h8 36 f5 exf5 37 ♖xe8+ ♕xe8 38 ♕xe8+ ♗xe8 1-0.

F)

11...♕e8 *(D)*

Black prepares ...♘h5 indirectly fighting for control of the e5-square. White can keep the game under control provided he does not respond mechanically.

12 ♘xc6! bxc6

12...♕xc6 13 ♗e5 ♗d6 14 ♖e1 ♗xe5 15 ♖xe5 ♕b6 16 ♖b1 ♘e4 17 ♘xe4 dxe4 18 ♗xe4 ♖xf2 19 ♔h1 with an edge to White.

13 ♘a4

Having relinquished occupation of e5, White seeks to drive the bishop from the useful a7-g1 diagonal back to e7. The effect of this will be to stop the advance ...e6-e5 by interfering with the e8-queen's support for this push.

13...♗e7

Or 13...e5 14 ♘xc5 exf4 15 ♖e1 ♕f7 16 ♕f3 g5? 17 ♖e5! h6 18 h3 ♖b8 19 b3 with advantage for White.

14 c4 ♗a6

On 14...♕h5?!, 15 ♖e1 ♘g4 16 ♖e5! is strong.

15 ♕e2

White's position is better.

To conclude, the Two Knights' Variation may not be to everyone's taste but it can lead to some exciting and original chess. It has given me consistently good results against the French Defence over the years and I have yet to be convinced that Black can demonstrate a clear route to equality.

7 Caro-Kann Defence

1 e4 c6 2 d4 d5 3 ♘c3 (D)

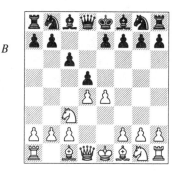

B

The Caro-Kann has a reputation of being rather boring. This can in fact be far from the truth. Although some lines tend to lead to quiet positions, this is as much from White's choice as Black's.

The logic of the Caro is quite straightforward. Black aims to stop White obtaining a sustainable classical centre and at the same time give himself flexibility on where and when to develop his minor pieces.

I am recommending that White play 3 ♘c3, at which point Black must show his 'true colours' by committing himself to a course of action. In Part 1 we will look at lines where Black plays **3...g6**. The other parts of this chapter will consider plans for Black after **3...dxe4 4 ♘xe4**, namely **4...♘f6!?** (Part 2), the classical **4...♗f5** (Part 3) and the modern preference **4...♘d7** (Part 4).

Part 1

1 e4 c6 2 d4 d5 3 ♘c3 g6

Black's idea is to maintain the tension in the centre, at least temporarily, and to fianchetto his dark-squared bishop. Black could try to get to the same type of positions by the move-order 1 e4 g6 2 d4 ♗g7 3 ♘c3 c6 and so resulting positions from this variation tend to be a cross between a Caro-Kann and a Modern Defence.

4 ♘f3 (D)

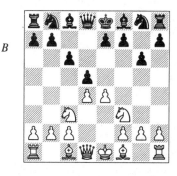

B

Note that the Caro-Kann move-order commits Black to 2...d5, so he cannot transpose to a Classical Pirc or Modern Defence. Lines where Black tries to get White to commit himself to playing an early f4 before playing ...d5 are dealt with in Line B of Chapter 9.

4...♗g7

The logical move. Others fail to offer any realistic chances of equality:

a) 4...♘f6? is rare, since 5 e5 gives Black problems: 5...♘h5 (5...♘e4? 6 ♘xe4 dxe4 7 ♘g5 and Black has a bad position) 6 ♗e2 f6 7 0-0 ♘d7 8 ♘h4! ♘g7 9 exf6! is pleasant for White, for example 9...exf6 10 ♖e1 and with his lack of development, weakened kingside pawn-structure and king still in the centre Black's position is unenviable; or 9...♘xf6 10 ♗f4, where with his development incomplete and backward e-pawn Black is worse.

b) 4...♘h6?! fails to give Black equality on precise play: 5 ♗f4! (better than 5 e5, which would justify Black's action, this move prepares ♕d2 hitting the knight on h6) 5...f6 6 ♕d2 ♘f7 7 e5 ♗g7 8 h3! (preventing Black from developing his light-squared bishop to a decent square) 8...0-0 9 ♗d3 b6 10 0-0 and although Black is still solid, White has completed his development and with his pieces on sensible squares he can enjoy an advantage, Kotz-Pfaffel, Graz 1994.

c) 4...dxe4?! (unnecessarily releasing the tension) 5 ♘xe4 and now:

c1) 5...♗f5 6 ♗d3 ♗xe4 7 ♗xe4 ♘f6 8 ♗d3 ♗g7 9 0-0-0-0 gives White a comfortable edge due to his bishop-pair, Vogt-Lechtynsky, Trnava 1983.

c2) 5...♘d7 6 ♗c4 ♗g7? 7 ♗xf7+! ♔xf7 8 ♘eg5+ ♔e8 9 ♘e6 ♕b6 10 ♘xg7+ ♔f7 11 ♘e6 ♔xe6 12 ♘g5+ ♔d6 13 ♗f4+ e5 14 dxe5+ 1-0 Borngässer-Lodes, Bundesliga 1988/9.

d) 4...♗g4 5 exd5! cxd5 6 h3 ♗xf3 (6...♗f5 7 ♗b5+ ♘c6 8 ♘e5 is nice for White) 7 ♕xf3 e6 (7...♘f6 8 ♗g5!; perhaps Black should try 7...♘c6!?) 8 ♗f4! ♘c6 9 0-0-0 (White's position is already preferable) 9...a6 10 h4 h5 11

♗d3 ♗h6 12 ♖he1 ♗xf4+ 13 ♕xf4 ♘ge7 14 ♘a4! ♕a5 15 ♘c5 ♕xa2 16 ♕f6! 0-0-0 17 ♕xf7 ♗b8 18 ♕xe6 ♖he8 19 c3 b6 20 ♔c2 ♘f5 21 ♕xc6 bxc5 1-0 Hansen-Lauritsen, Denmark 1996.

5 h3 *(D)*

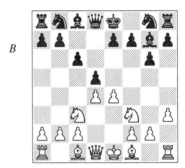

This is the most consistent move as it still leaves Black the problem of how to develop his light-squared bishop. Black has the flexibility to try a number of different plans:

A: **5...a6?!**   150
B: **5...h5?**   151
C: **5...e6?!**   151
D: **5...♘f6**   151
E: **5...♘h6**   153
F: **5...dxe4**   154

A)

5...a6?!

Black aims to expand on the queenside but, as the sole practical example shows, his pieces get cramped and it is White who has the option of when to open the position up. 6 ♗e2 b5 7 a3 ♘f6 8 e5 ♘fd7 9 0-0 e6 10 b4! f6 11 exf6 ♘xf6 12 a4! gives Black a poor position, e.g. 12...c5 13 bxc5 b4 14 ♘b1 ♘e4 15 c3 bxc3 16 ♖a3 ♘c6 17

♘xc3 0-0 18 ♗e3 and White is a sound pawn ahead, Feher-Lenart, Hungarian Cht 1992.

B)

5...h5?

An inappropriate move as White hasn't yet played e4-e5. The following miniature shows how to deal with inaccurate play with natural moves: 6 ♗d3 dxe4 7 ♘xe4 ♗f5 8 c3 ♕c7 9 0-0 ♘d7 10 ♖e1 ♗xe4 11 ♗xe4 0-0-0 12 ♕a4 ♔b8 13 ♘g5 ♘h6 14 ♕b3 e6 15 ♗xg6 c5 16 ♗xf7 ♘e5 17 dxe5 ♘xf7 18 ♘xe6 1-0 Hebden-Blanco Corzo, Seville 1987.

C)

5...e6?!

This solid-looking move leaves Black with the problem of how to develop his light-squared bishop and the need to retain his dark-squared bishop at all costs to avoid too many dark-squared weaknesses, especially around the kingside. 6 ♗f4! (preparing ♕d2 and ♗h6 – an exchange Black cannot afford to allow) 6...♘e7 7 ♕d2 h6 8 0-0-0 g5 9 ♗e5 f6 10 ♗h2 and White has the edge, Anka-Ireneusz, Geneva 1995.

D)

5...♘f6 6 ♗d3 dxe4 7 ♘xe4 ♘xe4

Best since the natural 7...0-0 works out badly, for example 8 0-0 ♘bd7 9 ♘xf6+ ♘xf6 10 c3 ♕c7 11 ♖e1 ♖e8 12 ♘e5 ♗e6 13 ♗f4 ♘h5 14 ♗h2 ♕c8 and with his greater space and more harmoniously developed pieces White has the advantage, Kasparov-Lputian, Tbilisi 1976.

8 ♗xe4 (D)

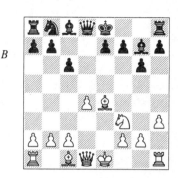

The critical position. Now:

D1: 8...♗e6?! 151
D2: 8...♗f5 151
D3: 8...♘d7 152

8...0-0 9 0-0 ♘d7 10 c3 transposes to D3.

D1)

8...♗e6?!

Black intends to solve the problem of his light-squared bishop by playing ...♗d5 and exchanging it off. However, this takes time and leaves White with a spatial edge and Black with dark-squared weaknesses: 9 0-0 ♗d5 10 ♕e2 ♗xe4 11 ♕xe4 ♕d5 12 ♕h4 ♘d7 13 ♖e1 e6 14 c3.

D2)

8...♗f5

A clever attempt to gain equality by immediately exchanging off the light-squared bishops.

9 ♗xf5 ♕a5+! 10 c3 ♕xf5 11 0-0 0-0

11...♘d7?! 12 ♖e1 e6 13 ♕b3 b6 14 ♕a3! gave Black problems castling in Lobron-Grünfeld, Lucerne 1979, as

14...♗f8 15 ♕a6! is unpleasant for Black to meet.

12 ♖e1!

Developing the rook to a natural square while tying down the black rook to a passive one.

12...♖e8 13 ♗g5 e6 14 ♕b3 b5 15 a4! ♘d7 16 axb5 cxb5

16...♕xb5?! 17 ♕c2 leaves Black with a fairly miserable position.

17 ♖a5!

White has a good position with play against b5 and along the a-file.

D3)

8...♘d7 9 c3 0-0 10 0-0

Now:

D31: 10...♕c7?!   152
D32: 10...c5   152
D33: 10...e5!   153

D31)

10...♕c7?! 11 ♖e1 c5 12 ♗c2 e6 13 d5! exd5 14 ♕xd5 ♘f6 15 ♕g5!

An original way of bringing the queen back into play.

15...♗d7 16 ♕h4 ♖ae8 17 ♗g5 *(D)*

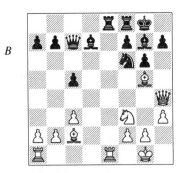

White has a good position due to his potential attacking chances. When Black tried to relieve this with exchanges White was left with a 'pressure game' which, in Adams-Stangl, Garmisch-Partenkirchen 1994, Adams exploited to the full with some exemplary play: 17...♖xe1+ 18 ♖xe1 ♕b6 19 ♗b3 ♖e8 20 ♖xe8+ ♗xe8 21 ♕f4 ♕d8 22 ♘e5 ♕e7 23 ♕e3 ♔f8 24 a4 ♕d6 25 ♘c4 ♕e7 26 ♗f4 ♕xe3 27 ♗xe3 b6 28 ♗f4 ♗c6 29 ♗b8 ♘d7 30 ♗xa7 ♗d5 31 ♘d2 ♗xb3 32 ♘xb3 ♔e7 33 a5 bxa5 34 ♗xc5+ ♔e6 35 ♗e3 a4 36 ♘d2 ♘e5 1-0.

D32)

10...c5 11 ♗g5 ♕c7 12 ♕e2 ♘f6 13 ♗c2 b6 14 ♖fe1 e6 15 dxc5! ♕xc5 16 ♘e5! *(D)*

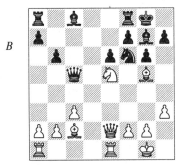

Black is horribly tied up as natural developing moves meet with tactical refutations.

16...h6?

16...♗b7? is no better: 17 ♗xf6 ♗xf6 18 ♘d7, for example 18...♕c6? 19 ♘xf6+ ♔g7 20 ♗e4!.

17 ♗xf6 ♗xf6 18 ♕f3 ♗xe5 19 ♕xa8

White is the exchange ahead for nothing, Knazovcik-Cerny, Pardubice 1992.

D33)

10...e5!

Undoubtedly the best way to strike back at the centre.

11 ♗g5

Now:

a) 11...♕c7 12 ♖e1 f5 13 ♗c2 e4 14 ♗b3+ ♔h8 15 ♘h4 is good for White.

b) 11...f6?! 12 ♕b3+ ♔h8 13 ♗h4 is better for White.

c) 11...♕b6 12 ♘xe5 ♘xe5 (after 12...♕xb2 13 ♘xd7 ♗xd7 14 ♕b3 White has a small edge) 13 dxe5 ♗xe5 14 ♕e2 ♖e8 15 ♖ad1 with approximate equality.

E)

5...♘h6 6 ♗f4

Now Black can choose between:

E1: 6...♕b6!?   153
E2: 6...dxe4   153
E3: 6...0-0   153
E4: 6...f6   153

E1)

6...♕b6!? 7 ♕c1 dxe4 8 ♘xe4 ♘f5 9 c3 ♗e6 10 ♗d3 ♗d5 11 0-0 0-0 12 ♖e1 ♘d7 13 ♘ed2 ♖fe8 14 ♗xf5 gxf5

White is better due to her control of e5 and better pawn-structure, Xie Jun-Gaprindashvili, Novi Sad wom OL 1990.

E2)

6...dxe4 7 ♘xe4 ♘f5 8 c3 0-0 9 ♗d3 b6

After 9...♘d6 10 ♘xd6 exd6 11 0-0 d5 12 ♕d2 ♘d7 13 ♖ae1 ♘f6 14 ♘e5 White is comfortably better due to his lead in development.

10 ♕e2 a5 11 ♘e5 a4 12 0-0 ♗b7 13 ♘g5 ♘d6 14 ♕g4 *(D)*

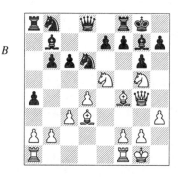

White has excellent attacking prospects, Tischbierek-Broemel, East German Ch 1988.

E3)

6...0-0 7 ♕d2 dxe4 8 ♘xe4 ♘f5 9 c3 ♘d7

9...♘d6 10 ♘xd6 exd6 11 ♗e2 ♖e8 12 0-0 with an edge for White in view of his superior development.

10 g4! ♘d6 11 ♘xd6 exd6 12 ♗xd6 ♖e8+ 13 ♗e2

White is a sound pawn to the good.

E4)

6...f6

The most consistent way to follow up 5...♘h6.

7 ♕d2 ♘f7 8 0-0-0 0-0 9 e5! b5

9...♘a6?! 10 ♗xa6! bxa6 11 ♘a4 fxe5 12 ♘xe5 ♘xe5 13 ♗xe5 ♗xe5 14 dxe5 e6 15 h4! and with the better pawn-structure, better minor piece and greater attacking chances White has a distinct edge, Baker-Chaplin, Bristol League 1998.

10 ♖e1 a5 11 h4 a4 12 ♗d3 b4 13 ♘b1 ♗a6 14 e6 ♘d6 15 h5

White has the better attacking chances, e.g. 15...♗xd3 16 cxd3 ♕e8 17 hxg6 ♕xg6 18 ♘h4 ♕e8 19 ♗xd6 exd6 20 ♘f5 ♖a7 21 e7 1-0 Friedrich-Broemel, Germany 1993.

F)
5...dxe4 6 ♘xe4 *(D)*

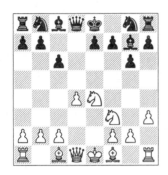

Black can now choose between:
F1: 6...♗f5   154
F2: 6...♘d7   154
F3: 6...♘f6   155

F1)
6...♗f5

This is a more logical time to play ...♗f5 than after 1 e4 c6 2 d4 d5 3 ♘c3 g6 4 ♘f3 dxe4?! 5 ♘xe4 ♗f5 as the extra move each are White having played h3 and Black ...♗g7. Whereas h3 is a useful move Black's ...♗g7 is a natural developing move.

7 ♘g3

7 ♗d3? is not as attractive as in the aforementioned line due to 7...♗xd4! 8 ♘xd4 ♕xd4 9 ♗d2?! ♗xe4! 10 ♗c3 ♕d5 11 ♗xh8 ♗xg2 12 ♖h2 ♗f3, when Black is clearly better.

7...♘f6

Others are less inspiring:

a) 7...♕d7?! 8 ♘xf5 ♕xf5 9 ♗d3 gives White an edge in view of his bishop-pair.

b) 7...♗e6?! 8 c3 ♘f6 9 ♗d3 0-0 10 0-0 and then:

b1) 10...c5 11 ♖e1 ♘c6 12 dxc5 ♕d5 13 ♗e3 ♖fe8 14 ♗c2 ♕xd1 15 ♖exd1 ♗d5 16 ♘g5 and Black has insufficient compensation for the minus pawn, Huysman-Sphinx Galaxy Computer, Dieren 1988.

b2) 10...♕c7 11 ♖e1 c5 12 ♖xe6!? (12 ♘g5!) 12...fxe6 13 ♘g5 c4 (13...♕c6 14 ♕e2 cxd4 15 ♘xe6 and White is doing well, e.g. 15...dxc3 16 ♘xf8 ♔xf8 17 bxc3) 14 ♗f1 ♖c8 15 ♘xe6 ♕d7 16 ♕e2 with good compensation for the exchange, Landenbergue-Gerber, Swiss Ch 1995.

8 ♘xf5 gxf5

8...♕a5+?! 9 c3 ♕xf5 10 ♕b3! ♕c8 11 ♗c4 e6 12 0-0 0-0 13 ♖e1 ♘bd7 14 ♗f4 and White's advantage is obvious, Matthey-Kuna, Germany 1994.

9 ♗d3 e6 10 ♕e2 c5!? 11 ♗xf5 cxd4 12 0-0 ♘c6 13 ♖e1 0-0 14 ♗d3 ♘b4?!

14...♕b6?! 15 ♗g5! ♕xb2 16 ♗xf6 ♗xf6 17 ♕e4 ♖fb8 18 ♕xh7+ ♔f8 19 a4! gives White a pleasant position.

15 ♗g5 ♖c8

Now instead of 16 ♖ad1?! (Sherzer-I.Ivanov, USA Ch 1992), 16 a3 ♘xd3 17 ♕xd3 ♕b6 18 ♘e5 is good for White.

F2)
6...♘d7

A natural move so as to play ...♘gf6 and recapture with a knight after the exchange of pieces.

7 ♗c4 ♘gf6 8 ♘xf6+ ♘xf6 9 0-0 0-0 10 ♖e1 *(D)*

This is the critical position after 6...♘d7. Black has tried a number of

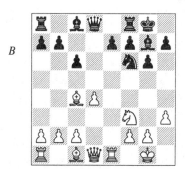

B

different moves in this position without managing to find equality:

a) 10...♘d5?! 11 ♗b3! ♖e8 12 c4 ♘c7 13 ♗f4 ♘e6 14 ♗e5 ♗xe5 15 ♖xe5 leaves Black with an unpleasant task ahead, Moen-Tjomsland, Gausdal 1997.

b) 10...h6?! 11 ♕e2 b5 12 ♗b3 ♘d5 13 a4 a6 14 ♘e5 ♗b7 15 c3 e6 gives White the superior position, for example 16 ♘d3 ♖e8 17 ♘c5 ♗c8 18 ♕f3, Grzesik-Lehmann, Bundesliga 1987/8.

c) 10...e6?! 11 ♗g5 h6 12 ♗f4 ♕b6 13 ♗b3 ♘d5 14 ♗d6! ♖e8 15 c4 ♕d8 16 ♗g3 ♘f6 17 ♕e2 ♗d7 18 ♖ad1 b5 19 c5! gives White a terrific bind, Veröci-J.Miles, Dubai wom OL 1986.

d) 10...b6!? 11 ♕e2 e6 (11...♘d5!? 12 ♗g5 ♖e8 13 ♘e5 ♕d6 14 ♗h4 ♗b7, Stenner-Schulz, Germany 1993, 15 ♕f3! is good for White) 12 ♗g5 ♗b7 13 ♖ad1 ♕c7 14 ♘e5 h6 15 ♗h4 ♘h5 16 ♕e3! ♔h7 17 ♗e2 ♘f6 18 c4 gives White the upper hand, Renet-Spiridonov, French Cht 1995.

e) 10...♗f5 11 ♗f4 ♗e4!? 12 c3 ♗d5 13 ♗b3 ♖e8 14 ♗e5 ♗xb3 15 axb3 ♘d7 16 ♗xg7 ♔xg7 17 d5! cxd5 18 ♕xd5 ♕c7 19 ♖xa7! ♖xa7 20 ♕d4+ e5 21 ♕xa7 and Black is a pawn

down with no compensation, Kuijf-Lau, Wijk aan Zee 1989.

F3)

6...♘f6 7 ♘xf6+ exf6!

7...♗xf6?! 8 ♗h6 c5 9 c3 cxd4 10 ♘xd4 ♘c6 11 ♘xc6! ♕xd1+ 12 ♖xd1 bxc6 13 ♗e2 ♗d7 14 ♖d2 0-0-0 15 ♗c4! ♗e6 16 ♗xe6+ fxe6 and with four(!) pawn islands Black can expect little joy in the ensuing ending, Ma.Tseitlin-Podgaets, USSR 1970.

8 ♗d3 0-0 9 0-0 ♗e6 10 ♗e3 ♘d7 11 ♕d2 ♖e8 12 c4 ♘b6 13 ♖fc1 ♕d7 14 a4 ♖ad8 15 b4

White has the edge due to his extra space on the queenside, e.g. 15...f5 16 ♗f1 f4!? 17 ♗xf4 ♗xd4 18 ♘xd4 ♕xd4 19 ♕xd4 ♖xd4 20 ♗e3 and with the bishop-pair and everything under control White is doing well, S.Horvath-Van Gompel, Vlissingen 1997.

Part 2

1 e4 c6 2 d4 d5 3 ♘c3 dxe4 4 ♘xe4 ♘f6!? 5 ♘xf6+ *(D)*

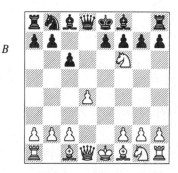

B

This section divides into two depending on how Black recaptures:

A: 5...exf6   156
B: 5...gxf6   159

A)

5...exf6

Black accepts an inferior pawn-structure and the latent possibility that White can create a passed pawn with his queenside majority with c2-c4 and d4-d5. In return Black hopes he will get a solid position with active piece-play.

6 c3

This is the most flexible and testing move. White is now directly supporting the pawn on d4.

6...♗d6

Alternatives fare badly:

a) 6...c5? prematurely releases the central tension, leaving Black with few prospects of obtaining full equality, e.g. 7 ♘f3 cxd4 8 ♕xd4 (8 ♘xd4!? may be even stronger) 8...♕xd4 9 ♘xd4 ♗c5 10 ♗e3 0-0 11 ♗d3 and White has a comfortable edge.

b) 6...♗f5?! (this attempts to 'improve' over 6...♗d6 7 ♗d3 by developing the c8-bishop before White has a chance to prevent it, but the bishop on f5 is more a target and liability than an asset) 7 ♘e2 ♗d6 8 ♘g3 ♗g6 (8...♕e7+!? 9 ♗e3 ♗g6 10 ♕f3 ♕e6 11 ♗e2 h5 12 h4! ♗xg3 13 ♕xg3 ♘d7 14 c4 0-0 15 0-0 ♘b6 16 b3 and White has everything under control, Duncker-Bandza, Giessen 1994) 9 ♗c4 0-0 10 0-0 ♖e8 11 f4! b5 12 ♗b3 ♗e4 13 ♕h5 ♕d7 14 ♘xe4 ♖xe4 15 ♗c2 g6 16 ♕h4 ♖e8 17 f5! ♗e7 18 ♖f3 g5 19 ♕h5 ♗d8 20 ♗xg5! 1-0 Nunn-K.Arkell, London Lloyds Bank 1987.

c) 6...♗e6?! (again I don't see the point of committing this piece prior to playing ...♗d6; with careful play White soon gets the upper hand) 7 ♘e2! (with the idea of coming to f4) 7...♗c4 8 b3 ♗a6 9 c4 ♗b4+ 10 ♗d2 ♗xd2+ 11 ♕xd2 0-0 12 ♘g3 ♖e8+ 13 ♗e2 ♘d7 14 0-0 and with the better pawn-structure and minor piece placement, White can enjoy a pleasant edge, Popović-Mirković, Novi Sad 1992.

7 ♗d3 (D)

This is best, as White will generally wish to develop his knight from g1 to e2 and so naturally wants first to develop his light-squared bishop to its most active square.

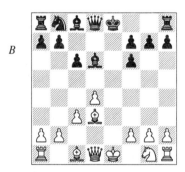

7...0-0

This is the normal move; alternatives:

a) 7...c5?! 8 ♘e2 ♘c6 9 ♗e3 ♕e7 10 0-0 ♗g4 and now instead of 11 ♕a4?! (Schaefer-Engqvist, Budapest 1991), 11 dxc5 ♗xc5 12 ♗xc5 ♕xc5 13 ♕a4! ♗xe2 14 ♕e4+ ♕e5 15 ♕xe2 gives White a lasting edge due to his queenside majority and better minor piece.

b) 7...♘d7?! 8 ♘e2 ♘f8 9 ♗f4 ♘e6 10 ♗g3 g6 11 ♕d2 ♕c7 12 0-0

0-0 13 ♖fe1 ♗d7 14 ♕h6 leaves White better as Black's pieces are cramped and he has weaknesses that will last throughout the game, Leko-Lenart, Hungarian Cht 1994.

c) 7...♗e6?! 8 ♘e2 ♕c7 9 ♕c2 ♘d7 10 c4 c5! 11 d5 ♗g4 12 h3 ♗xe2 13 ♕xe2+ ♔f8 14 0-0 ♖e8 15 ♕c2 h5 16 f4! and now that Black is unable to occupy e5 he is left with a miserable position, Watson-Hodgson, Kuala Lumpur 1992.

d) 7...♕c7!? is the main alternative, and has been played by Smyslov on more than one occasion but with little success, for example 8 ♘e2 ♘d7 (8...♗g4?! is no better as 9 ♗e3 ♘d7 10 ♕d2 ♗xe2 11 ♕xe2 0-0-0 12 0-0-0 ♔b8 13 ♔b1 ♘b6 14 g3 ♔a8 15 ♕f3 ♘d5 16 ♗c1 leaves White with all the pluses, Karpov-Smyslov, Tilburg 1979) 9 ♘g3 0-0 10 ♘f5 ♖e8+ 11 ♗e3 ♘f8 12 ♘xd6 ♕xd6 13 0-0 ♗e6 14 a4! ♖ad8 15 a5 a6 16 ♖e1 ♘g6 17 ♕c2 c5 18 b3! and White has a nagging edge, Ivanchuk-Smyslov, Tilburg 1994.

8 ♕c2

White generally plays ♕c2 and ♘e2 in one order or the other. I prefer the text-move as it cuts down on Black's options.

8...♖e8+

Alternatives tend to transpose as if he deals with the threat on h7 first White will still play ♘e2, with ...♖e8 being the most natural response.

9 ♘e2

At this point Black must choose between:

A1)
9...♔h8

This is the least popular way of dealing with the threat of ♗xh7+. 10 ♗e3 is most common reply now. However, I believe that **10 ♗d2!** may be more accurate as it allows White to contest the open e-file before Black is fully developed. The following game is instructive as it shows how White can enter an ending where he plays it as though he is a pawn up based on his active queenside majority compared to Black's relatively stagnant kingside. de Firmian-Borst, Antwerp 1994 went: 10...♗g4 11 f3 ♗h5 12 0-0-0 ♗g6 13 ♗xg6 fxg6 14 ♘g3 f5! 15 ♖de1 ♘d7 16 ♖xe8+ ♕xe8 17 ♕b3 ♘b6 18 ♖e1 ♕g8 19 ♕xg8+ ♔xg8 20 b3 c5 21 dxc5 ♗xc5 22 ♔c2 ♔f7 23 c4 ♗d4 24 ♘e2 ♗e5 25 h3 ♖c8 26 ♘c3 ♗xc3 27 ♗xc3 ♘d7 28 ♖d1 ♘f6 29 ♗xf6 ♔xf6 30 ♖d7 (the rest, as they say, is mere technique) 30...b5?! (30...♖b8 is a better practical chance of holding the position) 31 ♖xa7 bxc4 32 b4 g5 33 ♔c3 h5 34 b5 g4 35 hxg4 fxg4 36 fxg4 h4 37 a4 g6 38 b6 ♔g5 1-0.

A2)
9...g6

While looking solid, this move invites a kingside thrust. Black has few defending pieces and White's 'bits' are all pointing in the right direction.

10 h4! *(D)*

10...♗e6

Black hopes to develop his light-squared bishop to an active square prior to stabilizing his kingside with ...♘d7-f8. However, this in effect gives

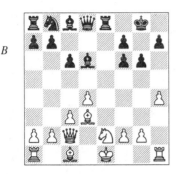

White an extra tempo for his attack. Others:

a) 10...f5? is just asking for trouble: 11 h5 ♘d7 12 hxg6! fxg6? (12...hxg6 13 g4! is extremely powerful) 13 ♕b3+ ♔g7 14 ♗h6+ ♔f6 15 f4 and Black must give up material to stop the threats, Ernst-Liberec, Osterskan 1994.

b) 10...♘d7 is certainly more logical than 10...f5? as Black intends to put the knight on f8, where it will prove an excellent defender. However, White's position still looks the more threatening, for example 11 h5 ♘f8 12 hxg6! fxg6 13 ♗h6 ♗e6 14 0-0-0 b5 (14...f5?! is no better, e.g. 15 ♔b1 b5 16 ♘c1 ♕f6 17 f4! and White has a definite bind, Pilnik-Golombek, Amsterdam 1950) 15 ♘f4 ♗xf4+ 16 ♗xf4 ♕d7 and with the bishop-pair, the open h-file to work on and more space, White has the better chances, Beliavsky-Boersma, Tilburg 1993.

11 h5 f5

11...♕c7?? 12 hxg6 fxg6 13 ♗xg6 ♖e7 14 ♗xh7+ 1-0 Brustman-Bouton, Cappelle la Grande 1997.

12 hxg6!

It is important to exchange off the h-pawn now as 12 ♗h6?? is well met by 12...g5!, as in A.Pereira-Hodgson, Almada 1988 and Abramović-Hodgson, London 1988 – in both cases Black won quickly.

12...fxg6 13 ♗h6 ♘d7 14 g4 ♗d5 15 0-0-0!! ♗xh1 16 ♖xh1 ♗f8 17 ♗d2

With the open h-file and Black's kingside being ripped to shreds White has enormous compensation for the exchange.

17...fxg4 18 ♕b3+ ♔g7 19 ♖xh7+ ♔xh7 20 ♕f7+ ♔h8 21 ♘f4

1-0 Kudrin-King, London 1988.

A3)
9...h6

Although this may look odd it is a far safer way of stopping the threat of ♗xh7+ as a kingside pawn thrust is no longer attractive. White now needs to change tack and rely on the positional elements at hand.

10 0-0 ♕c7

10...♘d7 is gaining popularity but after 11 ♗e3 ♘f8 12 ♘g3 White can enjoy a lasting edge.

11 ♘g3 c5 12 dxc5 ♗xc5 13 ♕a4 ♘d7 14 ♗f4 ♕b6

Now:

a) After 15 ♖ad1?!, Guyot-A.Spielmann, France 1989 went 15...♖d8? 16 b4! and White was much better. However, after 15...♕xb2! White has to prove he has enough for the pawn because 16 ♗f5 is answered by 16...b5! and 16 ♗b5 is adequately met by 16...♘b6.

b) 15 b4! is the recommended move. White is a lot better due to his lead in development, well-placed pieces and active queenside majority.

B)
5...gxf6 *(D)*

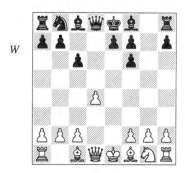

This is much more popular and dynamic than 5...exf6. Black hopes that the open g-file, active piece-play and the underlying imbalancing qualities of the position will compensate for his disrupted pawn-structure. White has looked at a number of different moves here but the most reliable and consistent is...

6 c3

...against which Black has tried no fewer than eight different replies:

B1: **6...e5?**   159
B2: **6...e6?!**   159
B3: **6...♖g8?!**   160
B4: **6...h5!?**   160
B5: **6...♕c7?!**   161
B6: **6...♘d7**   161
B7: **6...♕d5**   162
B8: **6...♗f5**   163

B1)
6...e5?

Not surprisingly, as it is strategically very poor, the only experience of this move I could find was between computers. Providing White does not oblige and exchange on e5 then the doubled pawns will later become weak. Moreover, the new weaknesses created at f7 and f5 are there for exploitation. Logically with this in mind and the fact that ...e7-e5 does nothing to assist Black's development it is not a move I would expect you to have to meet on any kind of regular basis. However, so as to give you an idea of how best to deal with it I give you the following as reference: 7 ♗e3 ♗d6 8 ♗c4 ♕c7 9 ♕h5! exd4 10 ♗xd4 ♗e5 11 ♗e3 ♘a6 12 ♖d1! Mephisto Polgar 5 MHz-Conchess 2 MHz, 1990. Black is in real trouble: it has a poor pawn-structure, its pieces are badly placed and f7 is very weak. The only thing that I find at all surprising about this is not how bad Black's position is so quickly after 6...e5? but how well the computer as White has played positionally to exploit it.

B2)
6...e6?!

Not a good move as it leaves Black with the long-term problem of how to deploy his light-squared bishop. Moreover, it does nothing to aid Black's development, and the only thing you can say in its favour is that it is relatively solid. The only master example of this move in practice dates back to the 1940s and although the game was eventually drawn White was well on top for a lot of it. I will quote some of the game together with suggestions on how White could have improved still further.

7 ♘e2 ♘d7 8 ♘g3 ♘b6 9 ♗d3 ♕d5 10 0-0 h5 11 ♗e4 ♕d8 12 ♘xh5 f5 13 ♗f3 ♗d6 14 g3?!

Both 14 ♖e1! and 14 ♗f4! are better as they continue with natural development without creating any potential weaknesses.

14...♗d7 15 ♖e1 ♔f8 16 ♕e2

Again 16 ♗f4! seems best. Certainly Black should want to avoid exchanging off the bishops as this would leave him with permanent dark-squared weaknesses.

After the text-move, the game O.Bernstein-Flohr, Groningen 1946 continued 16...♕c7 17 ♗g5 ♗e7 18 ♕d2 ♕d8 19 ♗xe7+ ♕xe7 20 b3 ♖d8 21 c4 ♗e8 22 ♕e3 ♘d7 23 d5 cxd5 24 cxd5 f6 25 ♕xe6 ♕xe6 26 dxe6 ♘e5 27 e7+ ♔xe7 28 ♘f4 b6 29 ♗g2 ♗f7 30 ♖e2 (30 ♖ad1 looks the most logical, when with the better piece placement and a good extra passed pawn, the rest should be mere technique) 30...♔f8 31 h4 ♔g7 32 ♗h3? (this is just trying to 'gild the lily', which is dangerous while Black's pieces are still actively placed) 32...♖d6 33 ♗xf5? (33 ♖c1 would still keep White well on top) 33...♘f3+ 34 ♔f1 ♘d4 (all of White's hard work has been in vain) 35 ♗d3 ♘xe2 36 ♔xe2 and the position is now approximately equal.

B3)

6...♖g8?!

Whereas it is in some ways logical to attempt to use the half-open g-file for his rook this foregoes any ideas of castling kingside and leaves the h-pawn weak for exploitation. As the following line shows, the move is premature.

7 ♘f3 ♗g4 8 ♗e2 ♕c7 9 ♕c2 ♘d7 10 ♕xh7 ♖g7 11 ♕c2?!

11 ♕e4!, with the idea of meeting 11...f5 with 12 ♕f4, seems best.

11...e6 12 g3 0-0-0 13 ♗h6 ♖g8 14 ♗xf8 ♖dxf8 15 0-0-0 ♕a5 16 ♔b1 b5? 17 d5! ♗xf3

After 17...exd5 18 ♘d4 ♗xe2 19 ♕xe2 ♔b7 20 ♘f5 White is much better as he has an outpost for his knight, which looks at jumping in to some of Black's dark-squared weaknesses, together with a healthy passed h-pawn.

18 dxe6! ♗xh1 19 exd7+ ♔b7 20 ♖xh1

With a bishop and two passed pawns for a rook together with the safer king, White is winning, Gabrielsen-G.Hansen, Copenhagen 1996.

B4)

6...h5!?

Although this move looks strange, White must be calm and not over-react, because otherwise Black may be able to create an initiative on the kingside.

7 ♗e2!

Better than the more obvious 7 ♗c4 as Black tends to gain a tempo with a timely ...b5.

7...h4 8 ♗f4 ♗f5 9 ♘f3 e6

9...h3?! 10 g3 gains nothing for Black other than leaving him with a stagnant long-term weakness.

10 ♕b3 ♕b6 11 ♘d2! c5 12 ♘c4 ♕xb3 13 axb3 ♘c6

13...cxd4?? drops material to 14 ♘b6.

14 dxc5 ♖g8 15 b4! e5

15...♖xg2? allows 16 ♘e3, forking rook and bishop.

16 ♗e3 ♖xg2 17 ♗f3 ♖g8 18 b5

White's mobile queenside majority is just too much for Black to cope with.

18...♞d8 19 ♞b6 ♜b8 20 ♞d5 ♜g6 21 ♜xa7 ♝d3 22 c6 bxc6 23 ♞c7+

1-0 Yanovsky-Mi.Tseitlin, Hastings Challengers 1991.

B5)

6...♛c7?!

Not a common line. The main idea appears to be to stop White playing a convenient ♝f4 while otherwise both developing his queen to a sensible square and almost 'passing' to see what White will do next. Experience of this move is limited.

7 ♝c4

I quite like the idea 7 ♛h5! to meet 7...♝e6 with 8 ♞h3! while 7...e6 transposes to the main line without allowing 7...♝f5 after 7 ♝c4.

7...e6

As just suggested, 7...♝f5 is preferable.

8 ♛h5 c5 9 d5! e5 10 ♞e2 ♝d6 11 f4 ♞d7 12 0-0 a6 13 b3 ♞b6?

13...b5 needs to be played, though White's position is still preferable.

14 fxe5 fxe5 15 ♞g3

Exploiting the weaknesses on e4, f5 and, less apparent for the moment, f7 to the full.

15...♞xc4 16 bxc4 b6 17 ♞e4 ♜a7 18 ♜xf7!

1-0 Kaplan-Rossolimo, Puerto Rico 1967.

B6)

6...♞d7

The first of the sensible moves available for Black.

7 g3

In my opinion this is the best for White. The move solidifies the g-file while developing the light-squared bishop on g2, from where it may later influence and put pressure on the h1-a8 diagonal.

7...♞b6 8 ♝g2 ♝f5 9 ♞f3 ♛d7 10 0-0 *(D)*

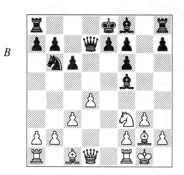

Now Black has tried:

B61: 10...h5?! 161
B62: 10...♝h3 162

B61)

10...h5?! 11 a4! ♝h3?

After 11...0-0-0? White is better with the natural advance a5-a6.

11...a5 is the best try but after the continuation 12 ♛b3 ♜a6 13 ♜e1 ♝h3 14 ♝xh3 ♛xh3 15 c4 White has a clear advantage.

12 ♝xh3 ♛xh3 13 a5 ♞c8

13...♞d5 14 c4 ♞c7 (14...♞b4? 15 ♛b3 e6 16 ♝d2 and Black's position collapses) 15 ♝f4, and after 15...♞e6 16 ♝e3 Black's queenside is under pressure.

14 a6 b6

After 14...♛d7 15 axb7 ♛xb7 16 ♜e1 e6 17 b4 White has a pleasant edge, with the better pawn-structure, superior development and safer king.

15 d5 c5

15...♕d7? 16 dxc6 ♕xc6 17 ♘d4 ♕d7 18 ♕f3 wins material, while 15...cxd5 16 ♕xd5 ♖b8 17 ♕b7!! produces a pretty win.

16 ♖e1 ♕d7

After 16...♘d6 17 ♗f4 0-0-0 18 b4! the oncoming attack is too much for Black to handle.

17 ♘h4!? ♕g4

17...♗h6? 18 ♕xh5 is simple and good.

17...♘d6 18 ♗f4 0-0-0 19 b4! c4 20 ♗xd6 ♕xd6 21 ♘f5 ♕c7 22 d6! exd6 23 ♕d5 and with moves like ♖e4 in the air Black is in dire straits.

18 ♕c2 ♕d7

After 18...♘d6 19 ♗f4 0-0-0 20 ♗xd6 ♖xd6 21 ♘f5 ♖d7 22 ♖a4 Black has severe problems finding active counterplay to meet White's forthcoming attack.

19 ♗f4 ♗h6

After 19...♘d6 20 ♗xd6 ♕xd6 21 ♘f5 ♕d7 22 ♖e2 0-0-0 23 ♖ae1 ♖e8 24 b4! Black can do little more than sit and wait.

19...♕xd5? 20 ♖ad1 ♕c6 21 ♕d3 and Black must give up heavy material to avoid mate.

20 ♘g6!

White is winning as the knight is taboo, e.g. 20...fxg6 21 ♕xg6+ ♔d8 (21...♔f8 22 ♗xh6+ ♖xh6 23 ♕xh6+) 22 ♗xh6 ♕g4 23 ♕f7 and Black is busted, Campora-Morozevich, Moscow OL 1994.

B62)

10...♗h3 11 ♗xh3 ♕xh3 12 a4 *(D)*

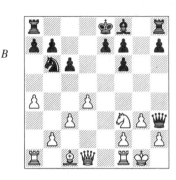

We now have the following possibilities:

a) 12...♕d7!? 13 a5 ♘c8 and White has an edge.

b) 12...a5?! 13 ♕b3 ♖a6 14 c4 ♕d7 15 ♗e3 e6 16 d5! ♗b4 17 dxe6 fxe6 18 ♗xb6 ♖xb6 19 ♕e3! leaves White comfortably better, Kruppa-Cvorović, Pula 1994.

c) 12...0-0-0? 13 a5 ♘d5 14 a6 b6 15 c4 ♘c7 16 ♕e2! and White's attack has gained too much momentum.

d) 12...♕f5?! 13 a5 ♘d5 14 c4 ♘c7 15 ♗f4 ♘a6 16 d5! is good for White, e.g. 16...0-0-0 17 ♘d4 ♕d7 18 dxc6! ♕xd4 19 cxb7+ ♔xb7 20 ♕f3+ winning.

e) 12...♕h5! 13 a5 ♘c4 14 b3 ♘d6 15 c4 e6 16 ♗a3! ♖d8 17 a6 b6 18 ♕e2 ♗e7 19 ♖fe1 0-0 and now 20 ♘h4! is a little better for White (and an improvement on 20 ♗b2?!, as in Popović-Korchnoi, Titograd 1984 and Popović-Damljanović, Yugoslav Ch 1985).

B7)

6...♕d5

This interesting idea makes it difficult for White to develop normally due to the pressure against g2. White has tried several moves here but the most direct seems to provide a lasting initiative:

7 c4! ♕e4+ 8 ♗e3 e5! 9 ♘e2 ♗b4+

9...♗g4 10 ♘c3!.

10 ♘c3 ♗xc3+

10...♗h3!? 11 ♖g1 ♖g8 12 ♕b1! gives White the edge.

11 bxc3 ♗f5

11...♗h3?! 12 ♕b1! is good, e.g. 12...♗xg2 13 ♗d3! ♕h4 14 ♕xb7 ♗xh1 15 ♕xa8 0-0 16 ♖b1 ♘d7 17 ♕xa7 and White is on top.

12 ♕d2 ♘d7 13 f3! ♕c2 14 ♕xc2 ♗xc2 15 ♔d2 ♗g6 16 ♗e2 0-0-0 17 ♖ae1

White is a little better due to his bishop-pair and more flexible pawn-structure.

B8)

6...♗f5 *(D)*

By far the most popular response for Black on move six. He quite naturally wishes to solve the problem of his light-squared bishop by developing it on the b1-h7 diagonal. The most consistent reply for White now is the simple...

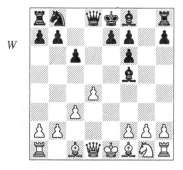

7 ♘f3

...after which the main three replies are:

B81: 7...♕c7 164
B82: 7...e6 164
B83: 7...♘d7 165

Others include:

a) 7...♗g7?! 8 ♗c4 ♕c7 9 ♘h4! ♗g6 10 ♕f3 e6 11 0-0 ♘d7 12 ♗f4 ♕d8 13 ♖fe1 0-0 and now instead of 14 ♖ad1? as in the game Ga.Hernandez-Christiansen, Saint John 1988, 14 ♕h3! would have kept White well on top.

b) 7...♖g8!? 8 g3 and now:

b1) 8...e6 9 ♗g2 ♗d6 10 0-0 ♘a6 11 ♘h4! ♗g4 12 ♕d3! f5 13 ♗xc6+ bxc6 14 ♕xa6 and Black has insufficient compensation for the pawn.

b2) 8...♕d7 9 ♗g2 ♘a6 10 0-0 0-0-0 11 ♕b3 e6 12 ♗e3 ♗e4?! 13 ♘e5 fxe5 14 ♗xe4 exd4 15 ♗xd4 ♘c5 16 ♗xc5 ♗xc5 17 ♖ad1 ♕c7 18 ♖xd8+ ♖xd8 19 ♗xh7 and White has the better prospects.

b3) 8...♗e4 9 ♗g2 ♘a6 10 0-0 e6 11 ♖e1 f5 12 ♗f4 ♗d6 13 ♗xd6 ♕xd6 14 ♘e5 and White is better.

c) 7...h5?! 8 ♘h4 ♗e4 (8...♗g4 9 f3! ♗c8 10 f4 f5 11 ♗c4 e6 12 ♘f3 ♘d7 13 0-0 ♘f6 14 ♘e5! and White is well placed) 9 ♕e2 ♕d5 10 f3 ♗h7 11 g3 e6 12 ♗g2 f5 13 f4 ♕d6 14 ♕xh5 and White is a good pawn ahead, Westerinen-Hodgson, Brighton 1983.

d) 7...♘a6?! 8 ♗c4 e6 9 0-0 ♘c7 10 ♖e1 ♕d7 11 ♘h4 ♗g6 12 a4 ♗g7 13 ♕f3 0-0 14 ♘xg6 hxg6 15 h4! gives White the advantage of the bishop-pair, more space and good attacking prospects, Benjamin-Dlugy, Manhattan 1983.

B81)

7...♕c7

Quite popular although to be honest not a move that I totally understand. Black commits his queen to a fairly passive square prior to finishing his minor-piece development. It does tend, however, to lead to transpositions as it seems to make little difference in what order Black plays the moves ...♕d7, ...♘d7 and ...e6.

8 g3 ♘d7 9 ♗g2 e6 10 0-0 (D)

We have arrived at the critical position.

10...♗d6

Or:

a) 10...e5?! 11 ♕a4 h5 12 ♖e1 ♗e7 13 dxe5 fxe5 14 ♘xe5! ♘xe5 15 ♕f4 and Black is in trouble, Krecmer-Urban, Czechoslovak Ch 1989.

b) 10...0-0-0 11 a4! ♗e4 12 a5 h5 13 ♖e1 ♗d5 14 ♕e2 h4 15 c4 ♗xf3 16 ♕xf3 hxg3 17 hxg3 ♗b4 18 ♖e3 a6 19 ♖a4 ♗xa5 20 c5! e5! 21 b4 exd4 22 ♖e7 ♖he8! 23 ♖xe8 ♖xe8 24 ♗d2 ♗b6! 25 cxb6 ♕xb6 26 ♗h3! ♕b5 27 ♖a1 ♕e2 28 ♕f4! ♖e4 29 ♕d6 1-0 Cuijpers-Metz, Bern 1993. This whole game is cut-and-thrust and very illustrative. It is worth playing through carefully to

appreciate the resources available to both players.

c) 10...♗g4 11 ♗f4! ♗d6 12 ♗xd6 ♕xd6 13 ♕b3 0-0-0 14 ♘d2 h5 15 h3 ♗f5 16 ♘c4 ♕c7 17 ♖ad1 ♖dg8 18 ♕a3! h4 19 ♘d6+ ♔b8 20 g4 ♗g6 21 c4 ♘b6 22 d5! exd5 23 cxd5 ♘xd5 24 ♗xd5 cxd5 25 ♖xd5 and Black has severe problems, Hecht-Miltner, Bundesliga 1986.

11 ♖e1 0-0-0 12 b4 e5

12...h5?! 13 ♘h4 ♗g4 14 ♕a4 ♔b8 15 c4 e5 16 c5 ♗f8 17 b5 cxb5 18 ♕xb5 a6 19 ♕b2 exd4 20 ♗f4 ♘e5 21 ♖xe5 1-0 Kudrin-Sowray, London Lloyds Bank 1987.

12...♗g4!? 13 ♕a4 ♗xf3 14 ♗xf3 h5 15 ♕xa7 h4 16 ♕a8+ ♘b8 17 b5 hxg3 18 hxg3 cxb5 19 ♖b1 ♖dg8 20 ♖xb5 gives White the better attacking chances, Ljubičić-Cvorović, Solin 1994.

13 a4 h5 14 b5! c5 15 ♘h4 ♗g6 16 a5 f5 17 ♗g5 ♖de8 18 b6! axb6 19 axb6 ♘xb6 20 ♗f6 ♖hg8 21 dxe5 ♗xe5 22 ♗xe5 ♖xe5 23 ♖xe5 ♕xe5 24 ♕b3! ♕e6 25 ♕b5 ♖d8 26 ♖a8+!! ♔c7 27 ♕xc5+ ♔d7 28 ♕d4+ ♘d5 29 ♖xd8+

1-0 Gallagher-Lematchko, Swiss Cht 1991.

B82)

7...e6 (D)

A solid choice.

8 g3

We will only consider moves here that do not transpose back to variations considered in Line B81.

8...♕d5

Seeking to cause trouble on the light squares. Others:

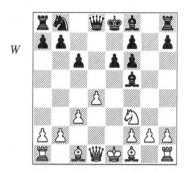

a) 8...♕b6?! 9 ♕e2 ♗d6 10 ♘h4!
♗g6 11 ♗e3 ♕c7 12 ♗g2 ♘d7 13 0-0
0-0-0 14 c4 c5 15 ♖ac1 ♔b8 16 ♖fd1
cxd4 17 ♗xd4 ♗e5 18 ♗e3 f5 19 f4!
♗f6 20 ♘xg6 hxg6 21 c5! and White's
attack is coming good while Black has
no real counterplay on the kingside.
Smagin-Heine Nielsen, Copenhagen
1991.

b) 8...h5!? 9 ♗g2 ♗e4 10 0-0 f5 11
♕b3 ♕b6 12 ♘e5 ♗xg2 13 ♔xg2
♘d7 14 ♘c4 ♕a6 15 ♗f4 gives White
an edge due to his better development
and safer king, Gelfand-Pieterse, Amsterdam 1988.

c) 8...♘d7 9 ♗g2 ♗g7?! 10 0-0 0-0
11 ♘h4 ♗g6 12 a4 a5 13 ♗f4 ♘b6 14
♕b3 ♗d3 15 ♖fd1 ♗c4 16 ♕c2 ♘d5
17 b3! ♘xf4 18 bxc4 ♘xg2 19 ♘xg2
♕c7 20 ♖ab1 b6 21 d5! and Black has
failed to equalize, Adams-Spraggett,
Hastings 1989.

d) 8...♗e4 9 ♗g2 h5!? 10 0-0 ♗e7
(10...f5?! 11 ♕b3! is hard to meet satisfactorily) 11 ♖e1 f5 12 ♗f4! ♘d7 13
♕e2 h4 14 ♘e5! ♗xg2 15 ♘xf7 ♔xf7
16 ♕xe6+ winning, Bofill-Mancebo,
Alicante 1989.

9 ♗g2

Now Black has to choose between
two replies:

e1) 9...♕e4+ 10 ♗e3 ♕c2 11 ♘h4
♕xd1+ 12 ♖xd1 ♗g6 (12...♗g4!? 13
f3 ♗h5 14 0-0 leaves White a little
better due to his lead in development
and superior pawn-structure) 13 ♘xg6
hxg6 14 0-0 ♘d7 15 c4 ♗d6 16 b4 a6
17 ♖b1 gives White an edge due to his
bishop-pair and extra space, Prand-
stetter-Plachetka, Czechoslovak Ch
1982.

e2) 9...♕c4!? (Black tries to maintain the pressure along the f1-a6 diagonal) 10 ♘h4 ♗d3 11 ♕d2! ♗g6 12
♘xg6 hxg6 13 b3 ♕b5 14 ♗b2 ♗h6
15 ♕c2 ♘d7 16 c4 ♕a5+ 17 ♗c3 ♕h5
18 f4! ♗g7 19 ♕d3 f5 20 ♗f3 ♕h6 21
♕e3 leaves White well-placed, Khol-
mov-Bronstein, Moscow 1987.

B83)
7...♘d7 *(D)*

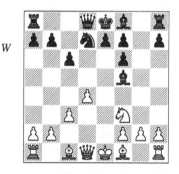

The most flexible reply.
8 g3

Again I recommend this idea, which
is probably best for White. Here we
will consider possibilities for Black
that do not transpose to positions already evaluated:

a) 8...♕b6?! 9 ♗c4 e6 10 ♕e2 ♗g6
11 ♗f4 ♕a5 12 0-0-0 0-0-0 13 ♗b3

♘b6 14 ♘h4 ♘d5 15 ♗d2 ♘c7 16 h3 ♗e7 17 f4 f5 18 ♘f3 ♗h5 19 g4! fxg4 20 ♘e5 f6 21 hxg4 ♗e8 22 ♘d3 and White is much better due to his extra space, more active pieces and pressure against e6, 'Quest'-Bronstein, The Hague 1996.

b) 8...♕a5 is relatively untried but 9 b4! may be critical, e.g. 9...♕d5 10 ♗g2 ♕c4 11 ♕b3 ♕d3 12 ♗e3 e6 13 ♖d1 with an edge for White.

c) 8...♗e4!? 9 ♗g2 e6 10 0-0 ♗g7 11 ♖e1 f5 12 ♘g5! ♘f6 13 ♕b3 ♕e7 14 ♘xe4 and White is a good pawn up.

Part 3

1 e4 c6 2 d4 d5 3 ♘c3 dxe4 4 ♘xe4 ♗f5 *(D)*

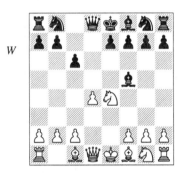

The Classical Variation. Black develops his light-squared bishop outside the pawn-chain before sealing it up with ...e6. He doesn't worry about the possible loss of time involved in moving the bishop maybe two or three more times over the next few moves but relies on the positional aspects of the variation and solidity of his pawn-structure to offer reasonable equalizing

chances. Many good works have been published in the past on the Classical main lines showing how White can with careful play maintain a small advantage all the way into the late middlegame or endings that ensue. For the purpose of 'startling' our opponents I am going to recommend a slightly less usual approach:

5 ♘g3 ♗g6 6 ♘1e2!? *(D)*

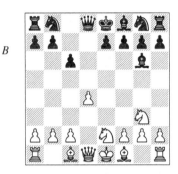

The main practical benefit of this variation is that it is necessary for Black to 'think on his feet' as he must react quickly by playing non-typical Caro moves.

It is quite obvious that White plans to follow up with ♘f4, but the sting in the tail is that then h4 would force a terrible weakness (for example ...h6, ♘xg6 fxg6). Black needs to resolve this immediately or disaster will strike! Black can now try the following:

A: 6...e5?   166
B: 6...h6?!   167
C: 6...♘d7   168
D: 6...e6   168
E: 6...♘f6   169

A)

    6...e5?

It would be nice for Black if he could solve the problem this easily!

7 dxe5

7 h4?! is best met by 7...exd4! as 8 h5 allows 8...♗xc2! 9 ♕xc2 d3, when Black is better.

7...♕a5+

Black doesn't get enough for the pawn after 7...♕xd1+?.

8 ♗d2

8 c3 ♕xe5 9 ♗f4 offers some advantage for White too.

8...♕xe5 9 ♗c3 ♕c7

9...♕e6 is the main alternative for Black. White should meet it with a similar plan of ♕d2, 0-0-0 and then maybe ♔b1 to guard his a-pawn. White will sooner or later gain a tempo back with a timely ♘f4.

10 ♕d2!

White has a lead in development and has managed to open up the centre. With this in mind he prepares a quick queenside castling, bringing the rook onto the open d-file at the same time.

10...f6?!

A typical Caro-Kann player's move. He wishes to be solid and stop any active play before completing development and getting his king to safety. However, due to the fact that the position is now open, this is definitely unwise.

11 0-0-0 ♘e7

Aiming for the d5 outpost but this attempt by Black to 'go solid' is easily parried.

12 ♘f4 ♗f7 13 ♕e3! ♘d7 14 ♘f5

Black is busted – he is unable to stop the knight coming into d6 with devastating effect.

14...♘e5 15 ♗xe5

1-0 Browne-Polstein, Atlantic City 1972.

B)

6...h6?!

Another typical Caro move – Black carries on with the 'business as usual' reaction, creating a hole to bury his bishop in. However, contrary to the main lines, after gaining a tempo with his knight White is not going to oblige and exchange off the light-squared bishops by ♗d3.

7 ♘f4 ♗h7 8 ♗c4

Now Black can choose between:

B1: 8...e6?!   167
B2: 8...♘f6   168

B1)

8...e6?!

Black carries on with thematic Caro-Kann moves, oblivious to his impending doom.

9 0-0 ♘f6 10 ♖e1 ♗e7

10...♘d5? 11 ♗xd5 cxd5 12 ♕h5! ♕g5? 13 ♖xe6+ ♔d8 14 ♕xf7 ♘c6 15 ♖e8# (1-0) Schindwein-Hugger, Badenweil 1990.

11 ♕e2 ♘d5!?

11...♕xd4? 12 ♘xe6 leads to a winning attack.

12 ♘gh5 0-0

12...♘xf4 13 ♗xf4 slightly reduces White's attacking chances but only at the expense of exchanging off Black's best piece.

13 ♗xd5 cxd5 14 ♘xg7!! ♔xg7 15 ♕e5+ ♔g8

Alternatives meet with a similar fate, e.g. 15...f6 16 ♘xe6+ ♔h8 17 ♕g3 ♖g8 18 ♘xd8 ♖xg3 19 hxg3

♗xd8 20 ♖e8+ winning; or 15...♗f6 16 ♘h5+ ♔g6 17 ♘xf6 ♕xf6 18 ♕g3+ ♔h5 19 ♕h3+ ♕h4 20 g4+ winning the queen.

16 ♘h5 f6 17 ♕xe6+ ♖f7 18 ♗xh6 ♕d7 19 ♘xf6+ ♗xf6 20 ♕e8+

Mate is forced.

B2)

8...♘f6 *(D)*

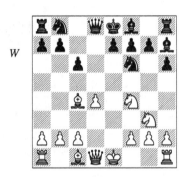

W

A more logical approach by Black, developing a piece and omitting ...e6 altogether.

9 0-0 ♘bd7

9...e6?! transposes to B1.

10 ♖e1 ♘b6 11 ♗b3 a5 12 a3 a4 13 ♗a2 ♘bd5 14 c4! ♘xf4 15 ♗xf4 g5 16 ♗e5 ♗g7 17 ♕f3

White is obviously better, Zhu Chunhui-Wu Shaobin, Beijing S.T.Lee Cup 1995.

C)

6...♘d7

A sensible-looking reply.

7 h4 h6

7...♘gf6 8 h5 ♗f5!? (8...♗e4 9 c4 e6 10 ♘c3 ♗b4 11 h6 g6 12 ♕b3 and White is better due to the rather awkward placing of Black's bishop on e4)

9 ♘xf5 ♕a5+ 10 ♘c3 ♕xf5 11 ♗d3 ♕a5 12 ♗d2 ♕b6 13 ♖h4! and with the bishop-pair, lead in development and more space White has the advantage.

8 ♘f4 ♗h7

8...e6?? 9 ♘xg6 fxg6 10 ♕g4! is just overwhelming for White, Moyano Morales-C.Pons, Palma de Mallorca 1991.

9 ♗c4 e5!? 10 ♕e2 ♕e7 11 dxe5 ♕xe5 12 ♗e3 ♗c5! 13 ♗xc5 ♕xe2+ 14 ♔xe2 ♘xc5 15 ♖he1 ♘f6 16 b4! ♘cd7 17 ♔f1+ ♔f8 18 ♗b3 g5 19 hxg5 hxg5 20 ♘h3

White has an edge due to his better command of the open d- and e-files and well-placed bishop on the a2-g8 diagonal, Tal-Botvinnik, Moscow Wch (7) 1960.

D)

6...e6 7 h4 h6 8 ♘f4 ♗h7 9 ♗c4 ♘f6

Others:

a) 9...♗d6?! 10 ♘gh5 and now 10...g6 11 ♘g3 (or 11 ♘g7+!?) is better for White, while 10...♔f8 11 ♕g4 g6 is hardly inspiring.

b) 9...♘a6!? 10 c3 ♘c7 11 ♘gh5 ♘f6 12 ♕f3! is a little better for White due to his minor-piece pressure.

10 0-0 ♘d5?!

10...♗d6!? 11 c3 (the brave at heart can try the sacrifice 11 ♘xe6!? fxe6 12 ♗xe6, e.g. 12...♔e7?! 13 ♖e1 ♖e8 14 ♗xh6 ♔f8? 15 ♘h5 gxh6 16 ♕f3 1-0 Barczay-A.Schneider, Hungarian Ch 1977, but I doubt its soundness) 11...0-0 12 ♖e1 ♕c7 13 ♕f3, when I prefer White's attacking chances.

11 ♗xd5 cxd5 12 ♕h5 ♕f6 13 ♖e1 ♔d8 14 ♘xd5! exd5 15 ♕xd5+ ♘d7

15...♔c7 16 ♘h5!.
16 ♗d2! ♖b8 17 ♘h5 ♕c6 18 ♗a5+
1-0 Hjorth-Tempone, Copenhagen 1982.

E)
6...♘f6
The best and most versatile reply.
7 ♘f4
Best as 7 h4 h6 8 ♘f4 ♗h7 9 ♗c4 e5! at least equalizes for Black.
7...e5 8 ♘xg6 hxg6 9 ♗e3! *(D)*

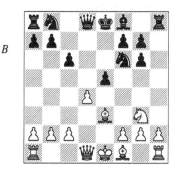

An important novelty when introduced by Slobodjan in 1995. The stem-game is still critical for the viability of this variation.
9...♘bd7
9...exd4 10 ♕xd4 ♕xd4 11 ♗xd4 ♘bd7 12 0-0-0 leaves White a little better due to the bishop-pair and the potential weakness of f7.
10 ♕d2 exd4
10...♘g4?! 11 0-0-0 ♗e7 (after 11...♘xe3?, 12 ♕xe3 is strong) 12 dxe5 ♘dxe5 13 ♕c3 ♕c7 14 h3 ♘xe3 15 ♕xe3 leaves White well placed due to the threat of f2-f4.
11 ♗xd4 ♗c5 12 0-0-0 0-0 13 h4!? ♗xd4 14 ♕xd4 ♕a5 15 h5!? gxh5

The alternative 15...♕xa2 leads to interesting complications after 16 hxg6, for example 16...♕a1+ 17 ♔d2 ♕a5+ 18 c3 ♕g5+ (18...♘e5 19 gxf7+ ♖xf7 20 ♔c2 leads to a slight plus for White) 19 ♔c2 ♕xg6+ 20 ♗d3 ♕g5 21 ♖h3 with good attacking prospects or 16...♘b6 17 gxf7+ ♖xf7 18 ♗d3, which is unclear.
15...♕g5+ 16 ♕d2 ♕xd2+ 17 ♖xd2 g5 18 ♘f5 is an edge for White.
16 ♘xh5 ♘xh5
16...♕xa2 17 ♘xf6+ ♘xf6 18 ♕h4 ♕a1+ 19 ♔d2 ♖fd8+ 20 ♗d3 ♕a5+ (20...♖xd3+? 21 ♔xd3 ♕a6+ 22 ♔c3 ♕a5+ 23 ♔b3 and Black's counter has run out of steam) 21 ♔c1! (21 b4 ♕g5+!! 22 ♕xg5 ♘e4+ 23 ♔c1 ♘xg5 and Black is a good pawn ahead) 21...♔f8 (21...♕a1+ is a draw) 22 ♔b1 with equal chances.
17 ♕xd7 ♖ad8?!
17...♕xa2 18 ♕g4 ♖fd8 19 ♗d3 ♘f6 20 ♕h4 (20 ♕h3? ♔f8 and Black has the better chances) 20...♕a1+ is equal.
18 ♕g4 ♖xd1+ 19 ♔xd1 ♖d8+ 20 ♗d3 g6 21 ♕h4 ♕d5 22 g4 ♕f3+ 23 ♔c1 ♖d4 24 ♖g1
24 ♗f5!? ♕f4+ 25 ♔b1 ♕f3 26 ♔c1 with chances for both sides.
24...♘f6
After 24...♔g7? 25 ♗xg6! fxg6 26 ♕e7+ ♕f7 27 ♕e3 Black is in difficulties, while 24...♘f4 25 ♖h1 ♘xd3+? (25...♘h5 with equality) 26 cxd3 ♕f4+ 27 ♔b1 ♕e5 (27...♔f8 28 ♖e1 ♔g7 29 ♖e8 winning) 28 f4! ♕g7 29 ♕e7 leaves Black with no escape from the threat of ♕e8+ as ...♕f8 is met by ♖h8+.
25 ♖h1 ♘h5 26 ♖g1 ♘f6 27 ♖h1

½-½ Slobodjan-Dautov, Altensteig 1995. A fascinating struggle with numerous chances for both sides to go wrong.

Part 4

1 e4 c6 2 d4 d5 3 ♘c3 dxe4 4 ♘xe4 ♘d7

The Modern variation. Black delays playing ...♘g8-f6 until he can recapture, if White exchanges on f6, with the other knight. This would free Black's pieces to a degree and release his light-squared bishop to be developed. True, White would still have a slight advantage in space but this sort of long-term minimal advantage is not for us. Instead I am recommending...

5 ♗c4 *(D)*

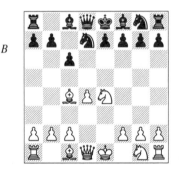

5...♘gf6

This is the logical follow-up to his previous move. Other possibilities:

a) 5...e6?! 6 ♘f3 ♘gf6 7 ♘xf6+ ♘xf6. The difference between this and 'normal' lines where a pair of knights have been exchanged on f6 is that now Black has committed himself to ...e6 thus blocking in his light-squared bishop. This gives him long-term

problems developing the piece. 8 0-0 and now:

a1) 8...♗d6 9 ♗g5 h6 10 ♗h4 ♕c7 11 ♖e1 ♘d5 12 ♗b3! (preparing expansion with c4) 12...♘f4 13 ♘e5 ♗xe5 14 dxe5 ♘g6 15 ♕g4 ♘xh4 (15...0-0 16 ♖ad1 ♘xe5? 17 ♕g3 f6 18 f4! and Black has no good retreat for the knight) 16 ♕xh4 ♕e7 17 ♕g3 (White delays the exchange of queens to exert maximum pressure) 17...♕g5 18 ♕c3 0-0 19 ♖ad1 ♖d8 20 h3 ♗d7 21 ♕b4 b6 22 h4! c5 (necessary as queen moves allow the killing reply ♕e7!) 23 hxg5 cxb4 24 gxh6 gxh6 25 ♖d4 (Black has great problems, not so much from the threat to his b-pawn but how to meet ♖ed1) 25...a5 26 ♖ed1 ♖a7 27 ♗c4 ♖c8 28 ♖g4+ 1-0 (Black could no longer face the suffering) Karpov-M.Grigorian, Poland simul 1997.

a2) 8...♗e7 is little better, for example 9 ♕e2 0-0 10 c3 b6 11 ♗f4 ♗b7 12 ♖ad1! (developing naturally while retarding Black's freeing manoeuvre ...c6-c5) 12...♕c8 13 ♘g5! (with the obvious threat of ♘xe6 to answer ...fxe6 with ♗xe6+, winning the queen) 13...♘d5 14 ♕d3 ♗xg5 15 ♗xg5 c5 now instead of 16 ♗b3, Lein-Benko, USA Ch 1978, 16 ♕g3! gains an advantage, e.g. 16...♔h8 17 ♕h4 ♕c6 (17...♗a6 18 dxc5 ♗xc4 19 ♕xc4 bxc5 20 ♖fe1 leaves White better due to the weak pawn at c5) 18 ♗d3 f5 19 f3! and White has the better position due to his bishop-pair and Black's weakness on the e-file.

b) 5...♘df6!? 6 ♘g5 ♘d5 (6...e6 7 ♘e2 h6 8 ♘f3 ♗d6 9 0-0 b5 10 ♗d3 ♘e7 11 a4! bxa4 {11...b4 12 ♗f4 0-0

13 a5 is pleasant for White} 12 罝xa4 0-0 13 奧f4! gives White has a comfortable edge due to his lead in development and better pawn-structure) 7 ②1f3 g6 (7...f6?! 8 ②e4 奧g4 9 0-0 ②h6 10 h3 奧f5 11 罝e1 ②f7 12 奧b3 ②d6 13 ②g3 奧g6 14 c4 ②c7 15 d5! and Black is horribly tied up, Berelovich-Poliansky, Russian club Ch 1996, while 7...h6?? meets an even worse fate after 8 ②xf7! 會xf7 9 ②e5+ 會e6 10 豐g4+ 會d6 11 ②f7+ 1-0 Voorema-Luik, Estonia 1962) 8 0-0 奧g7 9 罝e1 h6 (9...②gf6 10 ②e5 0-0 11 c3 h6 12 ②gf3 with an edge to White) 10 ②e4 奧g4 11 c3 ②gf6 12 ②c5! 豐c7 13 h3 奧xf3 14 豐xf3 0-0 15 奧b3!? (with the idea of c4) 15...b6 16 ②d3 b5 17 a4 a6 18 奧f4! ②xf4 (18...豐c8 19 奧e5 with good attacking chances) 19 ②xf4 with a pleasant advantage for White, Psakhis-Rodriguez, Sochi 1988, especially as 19...e6? can be met by 20 罝xe6!! fxe6 21 奧xe6+ 會h7 22 ②xg6 罝fe8 23 豐f5 (threatening 24 ②f8++ 會h8 25 豐h7+ ②xh7 26 ②g6#) 23...罝xe6 24 ②e5+ 會h8 25 豐xe6, which is very strong for White.

6 ②g5 e6 7 豐e2 ②b6

7...h6?? and 7...奧e7?? both allow 8 ②xf7! 會xf7 9 豐xe6+ 會g6 10 奧d3+ 會h5 11 豐h3#.

8 奧d3 h6

8...c5?! is inferior because later the knight on g5 can retreat to e4 rather than f3, e.g. 9 dxc5 奧xc5 10 ②1f3 h6 11 ②e4 ②xe4 12 豐xe4 豐d5 13 豐g4! (forcing weaknesses) 13...g6 14 0-0 ②d7 15 罝d1 ②f6 16 豐h4 奧e7 17 奧g5! ②g8 18 奧xe7 ②xe7 19 豐f6 (White dominates the dark squares around Black's king) 19...罝f8 20 ②e5

豐c5 21 ②xg6!! ②d5 22 奧b5+ 1-0 Rublevsky-Kataev, USSR Cht 1991.

8...豐xd4?! 9 ②1f3 豐d5 10 ②e5 豐xg2 11 罝f1 奧e7 12 ②ef3! is precarious for Black.

9 ②5f3 c5

Logically Black at last hits back in the centre in order to gain space and free his pieces. Other attempts fall short of the mark:

a) 9...豐c7?! 10 ②e5 奧d6 11 ②gf3 0-0 12 奧d2 c5 13 dxc5 豐xc5 14 0-0-0 ②bd7 15 ②c4 奧e7 16 罝hg1 b5 17 ②ce5 奧b7 18 g4! 奧xf3 19 ②xf3 ②d5 20 g5 and White's attack is already gaining momentum, Arnason-I.Wells, Manchester 1981.

b) 9...②bd5?! 10 a3 b5 11 ②e5 奧b7 12 奧d2 豐c7 13 f4 奧d6 14 ②gf3 a6 15 f5! 奧c8 16 fxe6 奧xe6 17 ②g6! 罝g8 18 0-0 and Black has a miserable position, de Firmian-Hort, Tunis IZ 1985.

10 dxc5 *(D)*

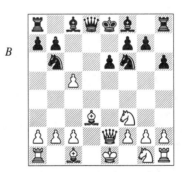

Black can choose between:

A: 10...②bd7 171
B: 10...奧xc5 173

A)

10...②bd7

This was once a popular choice as Black intends to redevelop his knight from b6 to recapture on c5 where it will have a greater influence on the centre while hitting White's precious bishop on d3.

11 b4! (D)

However, it requires nerves of steel to face this move.

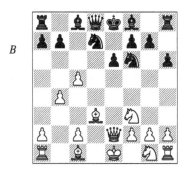

Black must now decide how best to obtain counterplay:

A1: 11...a5?!   172
A2: 11...♘d5!?   172
A3: 11...b6   172

A1)

11...a5?!

A speciality of Meduna.

12 c3 ♗e7 13 ♘d4 0-0 14 ♘gf3 e5!? 15 ♘xe5!

Better than 15 ♘f5!?, when Black gets adequate compensation with 15...e4!.

15...♘xe5

15...axb4? loses to 16 ♘ec6!.

16 ♕xe5

Black is struggling to justify his two-pawn investment.

On current evidence, 11...a5 does not look at all adequate for Black.

A2)

11...♘d5!? 12 ♗d2 ♕f6 13 ♖b1 a5 14 a3 g5 15 ♔f1!

Leading into interesting complications and asking Black to prove his compensation. Two lines:

a) 15...axb4 16 axb4 ♘c3 (16...g4?! 17 ♘e1 h5 18 h3! is good for White) 17 ♗xc3 ♕xc3 18 ♕d2! and Black still has counterplay but White is a good pawn ahead.

b) 15...♘c3 16 ♗xc3 ♕xc3 17 ♖b3 ♕a1+ 18 ♕e1 ♕xe1+ 19 ♘xe1 and White should have an edge but must first unravel his pieces.

A3)

11...b6 12 ♘d4 ♘xc5 (D)

Or:

a) 12...♕c7?! 13 ♘b5 ♕c6 14 ♕f3! ♘d5 15 ♗f4 is good for White.

b) 12...bxc5?? 13 ♘c6 ♕c7 14 ♕xe6+! 1-0 is both Gershon-Finkel, Spain 1997 and Perenyi-Eperjesi, Budapest 1974.

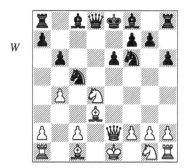

13 ♗b5+ ♘cd7 14 a3 ♗b7 15 ♘gf3 ♗e7 16 ♗b2 a6 17 ♗c4!?

17 ♗d3 is the safe way to maintain a slight advantage, Kasparov-Bagirov, Tbilisi 1978.

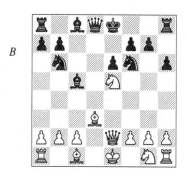

**17...b5 18 ♗xe6 fxe6 19 ♘xe6
♕b6 20 ♘xg7+ ♔f7 21 0-0-0**

White has perfectly good compensation for the piece, Sideif-Zade – A.Ivanov, USSR 1979.

B)
10...♗xc5 11 ♘e5 *(D)*

White intends at last to make space to develop his knight from g1.

11...♘bd7

The knight has done its job on b6 and so Black retreats to oppose White's well-placed knight on e5. Other possibilities for Black include:

a) 11...a6?! 12 ♘gf3 ♘bd5 13 a3 ♗d6 14 c4 ♘b6 15 0-0 ♘bd7 (at last Black's knight gets to where it should have aimed for in the first place) 16 ♗f4! gives White a strong position as 16...♘h5 fails to 17 ♘xf7.

b) 11...0-0 is likely to transpose to the main line after 12 ♘gf3 ♘bd7 while 12...♘bd5?! leads to an advantage for White after 13 a3! a5 14 0-0 b6 15 c4 ♘e7 16 ♖d1 ♕e8 17 ♗d2 a4 18 ♗c3, Hecht-Keene, Germany 1966.

c) 11...♕c7 has no independent significance after 12 ♘gf3 ♘bd7.

12 ♘gf3

Black should now choose between:

B1: 12...♘xe5   173
B2: 12...♕c7   174

12...0-0 is likely to transpose to one of the above options and offers little independent significance.

B1)
12...♘xe5

Black exchanges on e5 relieving the tension.

13 ♘xe5

Now:

B11: 13...♕c7?!   173
B12: 13...0-0   174

B11)
13...♕c7?! 14 ♗b5+! *(D)*

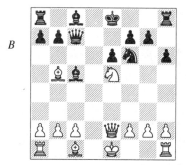

14...♗d7

Or 14...♘d7 15 ♗f4 ♗b4+ (15...a6 16 ♘xd7! ♕xf4 17 ♘xc5+ axb5 18 ♕xb5+ wins; 15...♗d6 16 ♘xd7 ♗xd7 17 ♗xd7+ ♕xd7 18 ♖d1 ♗b4+ 19 c3 winning) 16 c3! ♗xc3+ 17 bxc3 ♕xc3+ 18 ♕d2! ♕xa1+ 19 ♔e2 ♕xh1 20 ♗xd7+ ♔f8 (20...♔d8 21 ♕d6 wins outright; 20...♔e7 21 ♘g6+! ♔f6 22 ♗e5+! ♔xg6 23 ♕d3+ f5 24 ♕g3+ ♔h5 25 ♕xg7 ♕c1 26 ♕f7+ and Black's position falls apart) 21 ♕d6+

♔g8 22 ♗e8 ♕b1 (22...♕xg2 23 ♗xf7+ ♔h7 24 ♕d3+ g6 25 ♗xg6+ ♔g7 26 ♗e4 ♕g1 27 ♕d4! with a winning attack) 23 ♗xf7+ ♔h7 24 ♗g6+ ♕xg6 25 ♘xg6 ♔xg6 26 ♗e5 b6 27 ♕d3+ ♔f7 28 ♗e1! ♔g8 29 ♕g6 and Black can pack his bags.

15 0-0 0-0

15...♗xb5 16 ♕xb5+ ♔e7 17 ♗f4 ♗d6 18 ♖fd1 ♖hd8 19 ♖xd6 ♖xd6 20 ♘c4 ♖b6! 21 ♘xb6 ♕xb6 22 ♕xb6 axb6 23 c4 and White has the better endgame.

16 ♘xd7 ♘xd7 17 c3

White has the edge due to his bishop-pair and potentially more mobile pawn majority, Blatny-Adams, Adelaide jr Wch 1988.

B12)

13...0-0 14 ♗d2 ♕d5

14...♗d4?! 15 0-0-0 ♕d5 16 f4! ♕xa2 17 c3 ♗c5 18 g4 ♘d5 19 g5 gives White the superior attacking chances in compensation for the pawn, for example 19...♕a1+ 20 ♗b1 g6 21 gxh6 b5 22 ♕e4 ♗a3 23 ♕c2 ♗b7 24 ♖hg1 ♖fc8 25 ♖xg6+ ♔f8 26 h7 ♔e7 27 ♖g7 b4 28 ♖xf7+ ♔d6 29 ♖d7+ ♔c5 30 ♖xb7 1-0 Kirpichnikov-Lein, Moscow 1974.

15 f4! b5 16 ♗e3 ♗xe3 17 ♕xe3 ♗b7 18 ♖g1 ♖fd8 19 g4 ♕d4

19...♘e4!? is unclear.

20 ♕xd4 ♖xd4 21 g5 hxg5 22 fxg5 ♘h5

22...♘e4?! 23 ♖g4 a6 24 a4! with advantage.

23 0-0-0 ♖d5

Now 24 ♖de1! is an improvement on Shirazi-Dlugy, USA 1985, after which White can lay claim to a small

advantage due to his impending kingside pressure.

B2)

12...♕c7 13 0-0

Necessary since 13 ♗d2? allows 13...♘xe5 14 ♘xe5 ♗xf2+! 15 ♔xf2 ♕xe5 with advantage to Black. Please note this carefully, as the tactic is very easily overlooked.

13...0-0

Best, as exchanging a pair of knights on e5 first releases the tension prematurely and offers White a small but lasting advantage.

14 ♗f4 ♗d6 15 ♖fe1 ♘xe5

Or:

a) 15...♘c5 16 ♖ad1 b6 17 c3 ♗b7 18 ♗c2 ♖fd8 19 ♖d4 a5 20 c4 with a tense position in which White may have a slight edge.

b) 15...b6 16 ♘xd7 ♗xd7 17 ♗xd6 ♕xd6 18 ♘e5 ♖fd8 19 ♖ad1 ♕c7 20 ♕f3! leaves White a little better due to his more mobile majority, extra space and slightly better placed minor pieces.

16 ♘xe5 b6 17 ♕f3! ♗b7 18 ♕h3

Now we have:

B21: 18...♘d5?! 174
B22: 18...♖fd8 175

B21)

18...♘d5?! 19 ♗xh6! *(D)*

19...gxh6

Or 19...♗xe5 20 ♗xg7! with a winning attack.

20 ♕xh6 f6

After 20...f5 21 ♕xe6+, Black's position falls apart, while 20...♖fd8 21 ♗h7+ ♔h8 22 ♘xf7+ wins outright.

21 ♖e4!

White wins due to the following possibilities:

a) 21...♗xe5 22 ♖g4+ ♔f7 23 ♖g7+ ♔e8 24 ♗g6+ ♔d8 25 ♖xc7 ♔xc7 26 ♕g7+ ♔c6 27 c4 and Black can no longer defend.

b) 21...fxe5 22 ♕g6+ ♕g7 23 ♕xe6+ ♖f7 24 ♖g4:

b1) 24...♖d8 25 ♖xg7+ ♔xg7 26 ♗e4 ♘f6 27 ♗xb7 ♖xb7 28 ♖d1 ♖bd7 29 g4 ♘e4 30 h4 ♘c5 (after 30...♘xf2 31 ♖xd6 ♖xd6 32 ♕xe5+ ♔f7 33 ♔xf2 ♖d2+ 34 ♔g3 Black's rooks are powerless to stop White's queen and connected passed pawns) 31 ♕f5 e4 32 ♔g2 and the material imbalance in the position strongly favours White due to his safer king and the oncoming thrust of his passed pawns.

b2) 24...♕xg4 25 ♕xg4+ ♔f8 (25...♖g7 26 ♕e6+ ♔h8 27 ♕xd6 wins) and now 26 ♕h4! is very strong, e.g. 26...♘f4 27 ♗c4.

c) 21...♘e3!? 22 ♖h4 ♕g7 (both 22...♗xe5 23 ♕h8+ ♔f7 24 ♖h7+ ♔e8 25 ♗g6+ and 22...fxe5 23 fxe3 ♕g7 24 ♖g4! are winning for White) 23 ♗h7+ ♔h8 24 ♘g6+ ♕xg6 25 ♗xg6+ ♔g8 26 ♕h8#.

B22)

18...♖fd8 19 ♖ad1 ♘e4 20 ♗xe4 ♗xe4 21 ♘xf7 ♔xf7

21...♕xf7 22 ♖xd6 ♗xg2 23 ♕xg2 ♕xf4 24 ♖dxe6 is clearly better for White.

22 ♗xd6 ♖xd6 23 ♕h5+ g6 24 ♕e5 ♗d5 25 c4

White is on top.

8 Pirc Defence

1 e4 d6 2 d4 ♘f6 3 ♘c3 g6

Extremely popular, particularly at club level, the Pirc offers active piece-play while Black looks at the set-up White adopts before hitting back at the centre with a thematic ...c5 or ...e5 counter. Over the years many different systems have been adopted by White either to neutralize Black's dark-squared bishop, to make use of White's extra space or to maintain a small but lasting edge. The most aggressive option for White involves an early f4 (the Austrian Attack) by which any 'soft' approach is disregarded – White goes for the throat! Great care is needed by both sides as Black can get squashed if he doesn't react quickly enough; on the other hand White can overextend and leave permanent weaknesses for Black to exploit to his advantage. However, it is in these critical lines that I believe White can demonstrate a real advantage. The basic position is arrived at after...

4 f4 ♗g7 5 ♘f3 *(D)*

Now Black has two main options, which are dealt with in the first two parts of this chapter: **5...c5** (Part 1) or **5...0-0** (Part 2). There is also a third part of the chapter covering what I call the Jansa System, **1 e4 d6 2 d4 ♘f6 3 ♘c3 c6!?**, the objective of which is not for Black to develop his dark-squared bishop on g7 but to attack White's centre with active piece-play. This

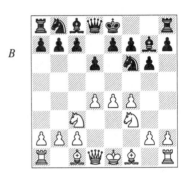

system is still relatively rare at club level it is growing in popularity and can catch the unwary. 3...e5 is considered on page 235.

Part 1

1 e4 d6 2 d4 ♘f6 3 ♘c3 g6 4 f4 ♗g7 5 ♘f3 c5 *(D)*

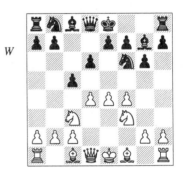

Black hits back at the centre immediately, forcing White to decide on a course of action.

6 ♗b5+ ♗d7

This is best as 6...♘c6?! leaves Black with problems after 7 dxc5! ♛a5 8 0-0 0-0 9 ♕e1! ♘d7 10 a4! a6 11 ♗xc6 ♛xc5+ 12 ♗e3 ♛xc6 13 ♘d5, e.g. 13...♖e8 14 ♘d4 ♗xd4 15 ♗xd4 ♛xc2 16 f5 b6 17 ♕h4 f6 18 fxg6 hxg6 19 ♖xf6! exf6 20 ♘xf6+ ♘xf6 21 ♕xf6 1-0 Mestel-Beaumont, British Ch (Plymouth) 1989.

7 e5 ♘g4

All of this is very well known and at this point White has at least three or four sensible options.

8 ♗xd7+

We are going to concentrate on this move, which leads to good fighting play.

8...♛xd7

After 8...♘xd7? White can immediately exploit the potentially loose black knight on g4 in conjunction with the light-square weaknesses around the black king, viz. 9 e6! fxe6 10 ♘g5 ♘gf6 11 ♘xe6 ♛c8 12 ♕e2 ♗h6 13 ♘b5! ♔f7 14 ♘g5+ ♗xg5 15 fxg5 a6 16 gxf6 (Black's position is on the verge of collapse) 16...♘xf6 17 ♘c3 cxd4 18 ♘e4 ♘xe4 19 ♕xe4 ♛c4 20 ♖f1+ ♔e8 21 ♗g5 1-0 R.Bellin-Kahn, Amsterdam 1995.

9 d5! dxe5

9...♘a6?! 10 h3 ♘h6 11 g4 0-0-0 12 ♗e3 e6 13 ♕e2 f5 14 0-0-0! ♘c7 15 dxe6 ♛xe6 16 ♘g5 leaves White well on top, Filipowicz-Heiberg, Gausdal 1977.

10 h3 e4!

Necessary to stop White from obtaining a sustainable big centre with extra space and active piece play. Black does not get enough for the piece after 10...exf4? 11 hxg4 ♗xc3+ 12 bxc3

♛xg4 13 ♕e2 g5 14 ♗b2, Pinto-Reading, USA Open 1991.

11 ♘xe4

Although 11 hxg4 is tempting Black gets a comfortable game after 11...exf3 12 ♕xf3 ♘a6 13 ♗d2 0-0-0 14 0-0-0 ♘c7.

11...♘f6 12 ♘xf6+

12 ♘e5 has been tried but Black appears to have good chances for equality after 12...♛a4!.

12...♗xf6

After 12...exf6?!, 13 ♕e2+ ♕e7 14 ♕xe7+ ♔xe7 15 f5! favours White.

13 0-0

Now Black has the choice between 13...c4?! and the more natural 13...0-0.

A: 13...c4?!   177
B: 13...0-0   178

A)

13...c4?! *(D)*

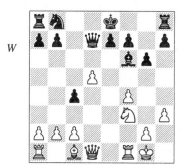

The idea behind 13...c4?! is to cut across White's plan of playing c4 himself and thereby securing the centre. However, by playing natural moves White gets a distinct advantage.

14 ♘e5 ♛b5

14...♛c7 is strongly met by 15 ♕e2!.

15 ♗e3 0-0

15...♘d7 16 a4! ♕xb2 17 ♗d4 c3 18 ♖b1! and White is well placed.

15...♕xb2 is well met by 16 ♖b1.

16 b3! c3

After 16...cxb3 17 axb3 Black can't stop c4 coming.

17 a4 ♕a6 18 ♕g4 ♖d8

18...♕d6 19 ♖ad1 ♗xe5 20 fxe5 ♕xe5 21 ♗h6 is strong.

19 ♖ad1 ♕d6 20 ♘c4 ♕d7 21 f5

White is now on top.

21...b5

After 21...♘a6!? both 22 ♗g5 and 22 ♗d4 are good.

22 axb5 ♕xb5 23 h4! ♘d7 24 h5 ♘f8 25 d6 ♕b7 26 ♗h6 ♔h8 27 fxg6

Stronger than 27 ♗xf8?! gxh5 28 ♕xh5 ♖xf8.

27...fxg6 28 ♗g5! gxh5 29 ♕xh5 ♗xg5 30 ♕xg5 ♘g6 31 ♘e5

1-0 Yusupov-Hodgson, Tilburg 1993. As 31...♘xe5 32 ♕xe5+ ♔g8 33 ♕g5+ ♔h8 34 ♖f7 is winning and 31...♖f8 32 ♘xg6+ hxg6 33 ♕h6+ ♔g8 34 ♕xg6+ ♔h8 35 ♖xf8+ ♖xf8 36 d7 ♖d8 (36...♕b8 37 ♖d3) 37 ♕e8+ is also decisive.

B)

13...0-0 (D)

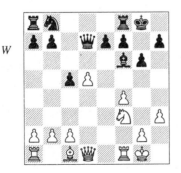

Black sensibly castles and awaits developments.

14 ♗e3

This is probably best although 14 ♘e5 and 14 c4 deserve serious consideration.

14...♘a6

14...e6 15 ♗xc5 ♖d8 16 ♗d4 ♗xd4+ 17 ♕xd4 ♕xd5 18 ♕xd5 ♖xd5 19 ♖ad1 ♘c6 20 ♖xd5 exd5 21 ♖d1 ♖d8 22 g4 f6 23 ♔f2 ♔f7 24 c3 with an edge to White, Dolmatov-Chernin, Sverdlovsk 1984.

15 ♘e5 ♕d6 16 ♘g4 ♗xb2

If 16...♗g7?! White can play the strong move 17 f5! with the idea of ♘h6+.

17 ♖b1 ♗g7 18 f5

18 ♖xb7?! e6! with equal chances.

18...♘c7

18...♘b4!? 19 c4 ♘xa2 20 ♖xb7 ♘c3 21 ♕d3 gxf5 22 ♖xf5 ♕g6 23 ♘e5 ♘e2+! 24 ♔f2 ♗xe5 25 ♖g5 ♘f4 26 ♖xg6+ fxg6 27 ♕e4 ♗d6 led to unclear complications in Yusupov-Hort, Bundesliga 1993/4.

19 ♖xb7!

19 c4 b5! gives Black what he wants.

19...♘xd5 20 f6 exf6

Or: 20...♗xf6 21 ♖xf6 ♘xf6 (on 21...exf6, 22 ♕xd5! is very strong) 22 ♕xd6 exd6 23 ♘xf6+ ♔g7 24 ♘g4! winning; 20...♘xf6 21 ♕xd6 exd6 22 ♘xf6+ ♗xf6 23 ♖xf6 wins; 20...♘xe3 21 ♕xd6 exd6 22 fxg7 wins.

21 c4 h5

21...f5? is poor due to 22 ♘h6+ ♗xh6 23 ♗xh6.

22 ♘h6+ ♔h7 23 ♘f5 gxf5

After 23...♘c6 24 ♕xd5 ♕xd5 25 cxd5 gxf5 26 ♗xc5 Black has problems.

24 cxd5 ♔g8

24...♔g6? loses to 25 ♕d3 ♕e5 26 ♖e7!.

25 ♖xf5 ♕a6 26 ♕b1 ♖fe8

Now, rather than 27 ♗f2, Yusupov-Adams, Dortmund 1994, Korchnoi shows that 27 ♗xc5 ♖e2 28 ♖b8+ ♖xb8 29 ♕xb8+ ♔h7 30 ♖xh5+ ♔g6 31 ♕g3+ ♔xh5 32 ♕xg7 wins.

Part 2

1 e4 d6 2 d4 ♘f6 3 ♘c3 g6 4 f4 ♗g7 5 ♘f3 0-0 *(D)*

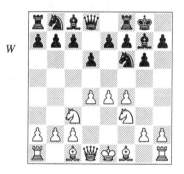

A sensible option. Black simply castles and awaits developments.

6 ♗e3

White has a number of other moves, but I like the flexible text-move. At this point Black has many possible set-ups:

A)

6...c6 *(D)*

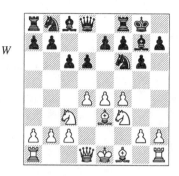

7 ♗d3 ♘bd7

This does not seem to lead to equality, but neither do any of the alternatives:

a) 7...♗g4?! 8 h3 ♗xf3 9 ♕xf3 and White already stands better, Plaskett-Afifi, Bahrain 1990.

b) 7...♘fd7? 8 ♕d2 e5 9 dxe5 dxe5 10 f5! ♖e8 11 g4 gives White an overwhelming space advantage, Lanka-Nill, Regensburg 1996.

c) 7...e5?! 8 fxe5 dxe5 9 ♘xe5 ♘h5 10 ♘f3 ♗g4 11 ♗e2 and Black has not got enough for the pawn, Falk-Bomert, Hessen 1992.

d) 7...♘a6!? 8 ♕d2 b5 9 h3! (not 9 a3? b4!, Brustman-Tseshkovsky, Poland 1997, when Black has active queenside counterplay) keeps everything under control and White can enjoy a long-term advantage.

e) 7...♕b6?! is too provocative, e.g. 8 ♖b1 a5 9 h3 a4 10 0-0 a3 11 b4 e5!? 12 fxe5 dxe5 13 ♘xe5 ♘xe4 14 ♘xe4 ♗xe5 15 ♗c4! leaves White very well placed with the light-squared bishop and the rook on f1 combining against f7, Mikhalchishin-Rakić, Yugoslav Cht 1994.

8 h3 e5 9 dxe5 dxe5 10 fxe5 ♘e8 11 ♗c4! ♘c7

11...♕e7 12 e6 fxe6 13 0-0 b5 14 ♗b3 with advantage to White, Beliavsky-Christiansen, Moscow IZ 1982.

12 0-0 ♘e6 13 ♗xe6 fxe6 14 ♕e2 ♘xe5 15 ♘xe5 ♗xe5

Now 16 ♗c5!, with a definite edge for White, is an improvement on 16 ♖ad1, as in Timmerman-Richardson, corr. 1986.

B)

6...♘a6 *(D)*

Black is preparing ...c5 and White must play forcefully to demonstrate an advantage, viz.:

7 e5 ♘g4 8 ♗g1 c5 9 h3 cxd4 10 ♕xd4 ♘h6 11 0-0-0 ♕a5 12 g4 ♗e6

12...♗d7 13 ♘d5! ♕xa2, Tseshkovsky-Vadasz, Malgrat de Mar-Calella 1978, is complicated, but White won with careful play in 26 moves.

13 ♕a4 ♕xa4 14 ♘xa4 dxe5 15 fxe5

White has a good position because Black is cramped and lacks an active plan, Bareev-Todorčević, Marseilles 1990.

C)

6...♘c6 *(D)*

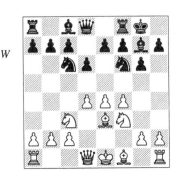

Again White can best meet this with an immediate central thrust:

7 e5

Black should now try for the ending:

7...dxe5 8 dxe5 ♘g4 9 ♗g1 f6 10 h3 ♕xd1+

10...♘h6?! 11 ♗c4+ ♔h8 12 ♕e2 gives White the initiative, Anand-C.Horvath, Oakham 1986.

11 ♖xd1 ♘h6

White is better placed for the ending, e.g. 12 exf6 exf6 13 ♘d5 ♖f7 14 g4 ♗e6 15 ♖h2.

D)

6...c5 *(D)*

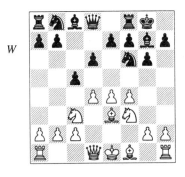

A bold attempt to strike at White's centre without further ado. However, White can maintain an edge:

7 dxc5 ♕a5 8 ♕d2 dxc5 9 ♘b5 ♕xd2+

9...♕a4 10 e5 ♘e4 11 ♕d3 ♕b4+ 12 ♘d2 ♗f5 13 ♘c7 ♘c6 14 ♘xa8 ♖d8 15 ♕a3 ♘xd2 16 0-0-0 and White emerges from the complications well on top, Beliavsky-Timman, Tilburg 1986.

10 ♘xd2 ♘a6 11 0-0-0 b6 12 ♗e2 ♗g4

White is slightly better, Baker-Harnett, Bristol League 1997/8.

E)

6...♘bd7 *(D)*

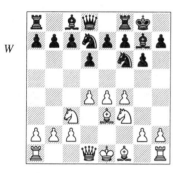

7 ♕d2

The direct 7 e5?! is insufficient for an advantage, so White has to take a less direct approach.

7...c5 8 0-0-0 b6

This is in my opinion a better try for Black to equalize than the more 'normal' 8...♘g4 discussed in 'b'. Black has tried the following alternatives:

a) 8...b5? (Black gets insufficient play for the pawn) 9 ♗xb5 ♖b8 10 ♗xd7 ♕xd7 11 e5 ♕b7 12 b3 ♘g4 13 dxc5 dxe5 14 fxe5 ♕a6 15 ♔b1 ♗b7 16 ♗d4 ♖fd8 17 ♕f4 ♗xf3 18 gxf3 ♘h6 19 ♕e4 ♘f5 20 f4 ♕a5 21 ♔b2

♖b4 22 ♘d5 ♖xd4 23 ♖xd4 ♘xd4 24 ♕xd4 e6 25 ♕b4 ♕xb4 26 ♘xb4 g5 27 ♘d3 gxf4 28 b4 f3 29 ♖f1 f6 30 exf6 ♗xf6+ 31 ♔b3 e5 32 ♖xf3 ♔g7 33 ♖e3 ♖e8 34 ♘f2 ♗g5 1-0 Campora-Todorčević, Biel 1991.

b) 8...♘g4 is regarded as best by most sources but I have my doubts. Following 9 ♗g1 cxd4 10 ♘xd4 e5, after 11 ♘de2?! Black has done well but I cannot see why White is not comfortably placed after 11 ♘db5!, when trying to exploit the h6-c1 diagonal with 11...♗h6 fails to 12 g3 exf4 13 gxf4 ♕f6 14 ♘d5, while after 11...exf4 12 ♘xd6 ♗h6 13 ♔b1 f3 14 ♕e1 it is difficult to see what Black has for the pawn.

9 e5 ♘g4 10 ♗g1 ♗b7 11 dxc5

11 e6!? may be White's best try for advantage, as in Campora-Todorčević, Cordoba 1991.

11...♘xc5 12 h3 ♘h6 13 exd6 exd6 14 ♗c4! ♘f5 15 ♗f2

The position is roughly equal.

F)

6...b6 *(D)*

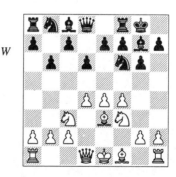

This is the most logical of Black's replies to 6 ♗e3. It gives maximum flexibility to continue development with ...♗b7 or to challenge in the centre with ...c5. White needs to expand in the centre first to cut across Black's plan.

7 e5 ♘g4 8 ♗g1 c5

8...♗b7 9 h3 ♘h6 10 ♗c4! is pleasant for White and after 8...dxe5 9 dxe5 ♗b7, 10 ♗c4! seems good (and an improvement on the game Balashov-Gufeld, USSR 1981).

9 h3 ♘h6 10 d5 *(D)*

An attempt to gain an advantage immediately with 10 dxc5?! (with the idea of meeting 10...dxc5? with 11 ♕d5! ♘c6 12 ♗b5, winning) fails to 10...bxc5!! 11 ♕d5 ♕b6 12 ♕xa8 ♗b7 13 ♘d5 ♕xb2 14 ♘xe7+ ♔h8 15 ♕xa7 ♕xa1+ 16 ♔f2 ♗xf3 17 gxf3 dxe5, when Black's position is preferable.

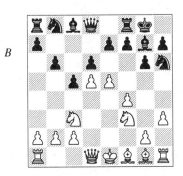

B

The critical position and one that needs careful play by White if he is to prove an edge. In practice Black has done quite well but with the improvements on accepted theory below I feel White is definitely better.

10...♘d7

Or:

a) 10...♘f5 11 ♗f2 dxe5 12 fxe5 ♘d7 13 ♕e2 ♗b7 14 0-0-0 ♕b8 15

g4! proved better for White in Balashov-Timman, Tilburg 1977.

b) 10...♘a6 11 ♕d2 ♘c7 12 0-0-0 ♗b7 13 ♗h2 a6 14 g4 e6 15 exd6 ♘xd5 16 ♘xd5 ♗xd5 17 ♗g2 with an edge for White, Grzesik-Kindermann, Dortmund 1983.

c) 10...♗b7 has done well when White has replied 11 ♕d2, but 11 ♗c4! looks promising, though it still needs a practical test.

11 ♗h2 ♕c7 *(D)*

11...♘f5!? 12 ♗b5 dxe5 13 fxe5 e6 and now 14 ♗c6 ♖b8 15 ♗f4! is good for White, and an improvement on 14 ♕d3? ♘d4! with equality, Cuartas-Nunn, England 1980.

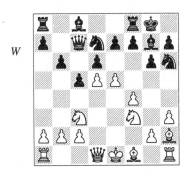

W

12 ♕d2! ♗b7

12...dxe5? 13 fxe5 ♘xe5 14 ♗xe5! ♗xe5 15 ♕xh6 wins.

13 ♗e2

This seems a solid approach to maintain a spatial advantage.

In conclusion, against the Austrian Attack, 5...c5 seems a little inflexible and unless improvements can be found White should do well with the line suggested in Part 1 of this chapter. After 5...0-0 6 ♗e3 Black's best seems to opt for variation E3 or F3/F4 where he may have to accept that he is a little worse but that White has no more than a normal opening edge. As with many lines suggested in this book the player who is better prepared in the variations given will get good practical results and make life difficult for his opponent.

Part 3

1 e4 d6 2 d4 ♘f6 3 ♘c3 c6!? *(D)*

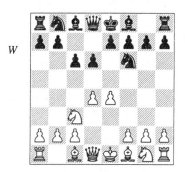

W

4 f4

This is the only real way for White to question the soundness of Black's opening. It is also consistent with the way we have chosen to meet the Pirc and Modern Defence. 4 ♘f3, if nothing else, would allow Black to transpose back to a Classical Pirc with 4...g6.

After 4 f4 Black has tried 4...♕b6 and 4...♕a5 (the original and best idea behind 3...c6!?).

A: 4...♕b6   184
B: 4...♕a5   184

There are a handful of 'others', which in the main are played for shock value or to get White 'out of book':

a) 4...d5?! 5 e5 ♘e4 (5...♘g8?! is likely to transpose to a Gurgenidze System {i.e. 1 e4 g6 2 d4 ♗g7 3 ♘c3 c6 4 f4 d5 5 e5} but with Black some tempi down) 6 ♘xe4 dxe4 7 ♘e2 f5 8 c4 e6 9 ♘c3 ♘a6 10 ♗e3 ♘c7 and although Black is solid and has a protected passed pawn he is worse as he lacks activity, Klovan-A.Ivanov, Beltsy 1977. A ...c5 break is likely to be met by White playing d5.

b) 4...e6?! is not so much downright bad, as just very passive. Sooner or later Black is likely to have to spend another tempo with a central pawn to gain a little space and activity, e.g. 5 ♘f3 ♘bd7 6 ♗d3 ♕c7 7 a4 e5 8 ♗e3 a5 9 ♕d2 and White has an edge mainly in view of Black's lost tempo in playing ...e7-e6 and then ...e6-e5, J.Přibyl-Hock, Prague 1990.

c) 4...♘bd7?! 5 e5 ♘d5 6 ♘f3 dxe5 7 fxe5 e6 8 ♘e4! ♗e7 9 c4 and White is better as Black must retreat the knight from d5 to b6, Gažik-Sazonov, Ceske Budejovice 1992, as 9...♗b4+? fails in view of 10 ♗d2! ♘e3 (10...♗xd2+ 11 ♕xd2 ♘5b6 12 ♘d6+ ♔f8 13 ♘g5 and Black's in big trouble) 11 ♗xb4 ♘xd1 12 ♘d6+ ♔f8 13 ♘xb7+ and White is coming out on top, e.g. 13...♔e8 (13...c5 14 ♘xd8 ♘e3 15 ♔d2 ♘xf1+ 16 ♖hxf1 cxb4 17 ♘g5 wins) 14 ♘xd8 ♘e3 15 ♔d2 ♘xf1+ 16 ♖hxf1 ♔xd8 17 ♘g5.

d) 4...♗g4?! 5 ♕d2! is strong for White, e.g. 5...d5 6 e5 ♘fd7 (6...♘e4 7 ♘xe4 dxe4 8 ♕e3 and eventually the pawn on e4 will become weak) 7 h3 ♗e6 8 ♘f3 and White is much better.

e) 4...b5 5 ♗d3 e6?! 6 ♘f3 ♗e7 7 0-0 0-0 8 e5 ♘d5 9 ♘xd5 exd5 10 f5!

dxe5 11 dxe5 ♕b6+ (11...♗c5+ 12 ♔h1 f6 13 e6 is still good for White as eventually he will get a kingside attack going) 12 ♔h1 c5 13 f6! (this is the sort of thing you can do to your opponent when he neglects development and king safety too long) 13...gxf6 14 ♗h6 ♖e8 15 ♘g5! fxg5 16 ♕h5 ♕e6 17 ♗xh7+ ♔h8 18 ♖xf7 ♗f6 19 ♗g7+ 1-0 Napoli-Cappelli, corr. 1991.

f) 4...g6 has no independent significance as after 5 ♗e3 ♗g7 it will transpose back to Part 2, Line A of this chapter.

A)

4...♕b6 5 e5 ♘d5 *(D)*

5...dxe5 6 fxe5 ♘d5 7 ♘xd5 cxd5 8 ♗d3 g6 9 c3 ♗g7 10 ♕f3 ♗e6 11 ♘e2 and White is a little better since ♘f4 will put pressure on d5 and e6, Skripchenko-Muresan, Romanian Cht 1994.

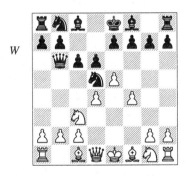

6 ♘xd5 cxd5 7 ♗d3 ♘c6

7...g6 8 c3 ♗f5?! (8...h5 9 ♕f3 ♗e6 10 ♘h3 ♗xh3 11 ♕xh3 e6 12 0-0 ♘c6 13 ♗xg6! fxg6 14 ♕xe6+ ♘e7 15 exd6 ♖d8 16 ♕e5 and Black is busted, Sion-Cabezas, Oropesa del Mar 1996) 9 ♗xf5 gxf5 10 ♕h5! (this ties down the black king to defend f7 as well as

preventing Black playing ...h5 and ...♗h6) 10...e6 11 ♘f3 ♘c6 12 ♘g5 ♘d8 13 g4! ♗e7 (13...fxg4?! 14 ♘xh7 ♗g7 {14...♗e7 15 ♕xg4! is good for White} 15 ♖g1 and with ♖xg4 coming Black is in deep trouble) 14 gxf5 exf5 15 ♘xf7! ♘xf7 16 e6 ♖f8 17 ♖g1 (now we can see another reason why White wanted to open up the g-file) 17...0-0-0 18 exf7 ♖d7 19 ♖g8 and White is nicely placed, Wells-Rashkovsky, London 1990.

8 c3 g6 9 ♕e2 h5

9...♗g7 10 ♗e3 0-0 11 ♘f3 f6 12 0-0 ♕c7 13 exf6 ♖xf6 14 ♖ae1 and White has a pleasant edge, Zuckerman-London, New York Open 1987.

10 h3!

White doesn't want to let Black trade his queen's bishop for the white knight, which could prove to be a very useful piece.

10...♗f5 11 ♗xf5 gxf5 12 e6 ♕a6 13 ♕e3 ♖h6 14 exf7+ ♔d7

14...♔xf7 15 ♘f3 e6 leaves Black with a permanent weakness. He would prefer to use the e6-square for a rook!

15 ♔f2 ♘d8 16 ♘f3 ♖e6 17 ♕d2 ♘xf7 18 ♕c2! ♗h6 19 ♗e3 ♖f6

White has the better long-term chances, Morozevich-Rivas, Pamplona 1994/5.

B)

4...♕a5 5 ♗d3 e5 6 ♘f3 ♗g4 *(D)*

6...exd4 7 ♘xd4 ♕b6 8 ♘b3 a5 9 ♕e2 a4 10 ♘d2 ♗e7 11 ♘c4 ♕c7 12 e5 dxe5 13 fxe5 ♗g4 14 ♕e3 gave White a substantial advantage in Wessels-Schulenburg, NRW-Liga II 1996.

7 ♗e3 ♘bd7

Or:

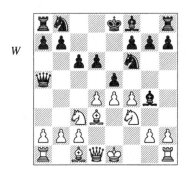

a) 7...exd4 8 ♗xd4 ♕b4 9 ♗e2! ♘xe4 10 0-0 d5 11 ♘xe4 dxe4 12 c3 ♕xb2 13 ♖e1! f5 14 a4 ♘d7 15 ♘g5 ♗c5 16 ♗xg4 ♕xc3 17 ♗xc5 ♕xc5+ 18 ♔h1 ♘f6 19 ♕b3 0-0-0 20 ♖ab1 with advantage to White, Glek-J.Přibyl, Bundesliga 1990/1.

b) 7...exf4 8 ♗xf4 ♕b6 9 ♘e2! ♗xf3 (9...♘bd7 10 0-0 and White has a slight plus) 10 gxf3 ♕xb2 11 ♖b1 ♕xa2 12 ♖xb7 ♕a5+ 13 ♗d2 ♕d8 14 ♕a1! (with the idea of both 15 ♗a5 and 15 ♖xa7) 14...a5 15 d5! ♕c8 (15...cxd5 16 ♗b5+ ♘bd7 17 e5 ♕c8 {17...dxe5 18 ♕xe5+ ♗e7 19 ♖g1 and Black has big problems} 18 exf6 with a very strong attack for White) 16 ♕b2 a4 (16...♗e7 17 ♘d4 and 16...cxd5 17 exd5 give White very strong attacking chances) 17 ♘d4 a3 18 ♕b3 a2 19 ♔f2 g6 (19...c5 20 ♘b5 ♘a6 21 ♘a7 winning; 19...cxd5 20 exd5 and Black has big problems) 20 dxc6 ♗e7 21 ♖a1 0-0 22 ♖xe7 ♘xc6 23 ♘xc6 ♕xc6 24 ♕c3 1-0 Shirov-Rivas, Manila OL 1992.

8 0-0 ♗e7 9 ♔h1!? exd4

9...0-0 10 dxe5 dxe5 11 f5 ♘c5 12 h3 ♗xf3 13 ♕xf3 and g4 is coming.

10 ♗xd4 ♘c5

10...0-0 11 h3 ♗xf3 12 ♕xf3 and White has a clear plus thanks to his bishop-pair, extra space and attacking chances.

11 ♕e1! ♘xd3

11...0-0?! 12 ♘d5! ♕d8 13 ♘xe7+ ♕xe7 14 ♗xc5 dxc5 15 e5 and Black has problems.

12 cxd3 ♗xf3

12...♕c7!? is worth considering, when White has just an edge.

13 ♖xf3 ♕b4 14 ♕g1

White has the advantage due to his attacking chances in the centre or on the kingside if Black castles, Smagin-Pekarek, Prague 1992. (Notes based on those by Stohl.)

9 Modern Defence

1 e4 g6 2 d4 ♗g7

This is the basic starting position of the Modern Defence. In some ways Black's strategy is very similar to the Pirc but in playing this move-order Black delays the development of his g8-knight. This gives White the option of playing 3 c4 now that his e-pawn is not under immediate pressure attack. However, for the purposes of this book we shall continue with...

3 ♘c3 (D)

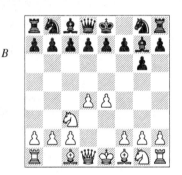

...and see what Black has in mind. This chapter divides as follows:

A)

3...c5!?

Now White has a few options. 4 ♘f3 cxd4 transposes to a form of Dragon, while 4 d5 transposes to a Schmid Benoni, neither of which are dealt with elsewhere in this book. So instead I am going to recommend:

4 dxc5

This also happens to be the most logical and critical reply.

4...♛a5

Black occasionally tries something else:

a) 4...♗xc3+?! 5 bxc3 ♛a5 6 ♘f3 ♛xc3+ 7 ♗d2 ♛xc5 and now either 8 ♖b1 or 8 ♗d3 followed by an early ♛e2 gives very good attacking chances for White. Black will miss his dark-squared bishop and rue his lack of development.

b) 4...♘a6?! 5 ♗xa6! bxa6 6 ♘ge2 ♘f6 7 0-0 and now:

b1) 7...0-0 8 f3 ♗b7 (8...♖b8 9 b3 ♛c7 10 ♗e3 and Black appears to be a pawn down for nothing) 9 ♗e3 and again Black has little to show for the pawn.

b2) 7...♛c7 8 ♗e3 ♘g4 (8...♗b7 9 f3 0-0 is similar to 'b1') 9 ♗f4 and then:

b21) 9...♛xc5 10 ♘d5 d6 (10...e5 11 ♗g3 transposes back to the main line; 10...0-0 11 b4 ♛c4 12 ♘xe7+ ♔h8 13 c3! is good for White since 13...♛xe4? allows 14 ♘xc8 with f3 to follow) 11 c3 with an edge for White, e.g. 11...♗b7 (11...♖b8 12 b4 ♛c4 13 ♘xe7! ♛xe4 14 ♘xc8 followed by f3) 12 ♛a4+.

b22) 9...e5 10 ♗g3 ♕xc5 (10...♖b8 11 b4! is good) 11 ♕d5 ♕xd5 (11...♕c6 12 h3 ♘h6 13 ♖ad1 ♗b7 14 ♕d6 and White is better) 12 ♘xd5 ♖b8 13 f3 ♘h6 14 b3 is strategically very good for White in that Black has a backward d-pawn, a weak square on d6 and disrupted queenside pawns. Black's bishop-pair is hardly adequate compensation for these factors.

c) 4...♘c6 5 ♗e3 ♘f6 6 f3 ♕a5 7 ♕d2 0-0 8 ♘b5! ♗b4 (8...♕xd2+ 9 ♗xd2 a6 10 ♘c7! and White has the advantage) 9 c3 ♘c6 10 b4 ♕d8 (after 10...♕a4 11 ♘d4 Black has little to show for the pawn) and White is better, Erben-Dekan, Wolfbusch-Marktheide 1986.

5 ♗d2! ♕xc5 6 ♘d5 *(D)*

Now we have:

A1: 6...b6   187
A2: 6...♘a6   189

A1)

6...b6 7 ♗e3 ♕c6

7...♕d6 8 ♗f4 and then:

a) 8...e5?! is positionally wrong, e.g. 9 ♗g5! ♕c5 (9...f6?? 10 ♘xf6+ wins; 9...♔f8?! 10 ♗c4 h6 11 ♗h4 and White has a comfortable edge; 9...♗f8

10 ♗c4 h6 11 ♘f6+ ♘xf6 12 ♕xd6 ♗xd6 13 ♗xf6 0-0 14 ♖d1 ♗c7 15 ♘f3 with advantage to White) 10 b4 ♕c6 11 ♗b5 ♕b7 12 c4 and White is better, e.g. 12...a6 13 ♗a4 h6 14 ♗e3 b5?! 15 cxb5 axb5 16 ♗xb5 ♘f6 17 ♘b6 ♘xe4 18 ♘xa8 ♘c3 19 ♘c7+! ♕xc7 20 ♖c1! and Black is in trouble.

b) 8...♗e5 9 ♗xe5 ♕xe5 10 ♘e2! (an improvement over 10 ♘f3?!, Acs-A.Horvath, Szombathely U-12 Ech 1993, which allows 10...♕xe4+ 11 ♗e2 ♘a6 and Black is doing fine) 10...♗b7 (10...♘c6 11 f4 ♕b8 12 ♕d2 and White is a little better) 11 f4 ♕d6 12 ♕d4 f6 (12...♘f6 13 ♘ec3! ♗xd5 14 ♘xd5 0-0 15 ♘xf6+ ♕xf6 16 ♕xf6 exf6 17 ♗c4 and White has the advantage, e.g. 17...♖e8 18 0-0-0! ♔f8 19 ♖d6 ♖xe4?! 20 ♗d5 ♖d4 21 c3 winning the exchange) 13 ♘ec3 ♘c6 (13...♘a6?! 14 ♗xa6 ♗xa6 15 ♕a4 is strong for White) 14 ♕a4 ♖c8 15 ♗a6 and White has a pleasant position.

8 ♗b5 ♕b7 9 ♗f4!!

My own innovation and, I hope, a good one! It leads to massive complications.

A11: 9...a6!?   188
A12: 9...♗xb2   188

Other possibilities are:

a) 9...♔d8?! 10 ♗c7+ ♔e8 11 ♗g3 and Black has a worse version of the main lines given below, as he has lost the right to castle and White's bishop is better on g3.

b) 9...♔f8 10 c3 and White maintains an edge due to the position of the black king, e.g. 10...♘f6!? 11 ♘f3 a6 12 ♘xf6 ♗xf6 (12...axb5 13 ♘d5 b4 14 ♗e5 ♗xe5 15 ♘xe5 d6 16 ♘c4 bxc3 17 ♕d4) 13 ♗d3 and White has a small edge.

A11)

9...a6!? 10 ♘c7+ *(D)*

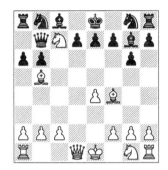

10...♔f8

10...♔d8 11 ♘xa8 ♕xe4+ (after 11...♕xa8 12 ♗d3 ♗xb2 13 ♖b1 ♗c3+ 14 ♗d2 White is the exchange for a pawn up) 12 ♗e3 and now:

a) 12...♕xg2 13 ♗xb6+ ♔e8 14 ♕f3! ♕xf3 (14...♗b7 15 ♕f4 and Black has problems, e.g. 15...e5 16 ♘c7+ ♔f8 17 ♗c5+ ♘e7 18 ♕h4 g5 19 ♗xe7+ ♔xe7 20 ♕b4+ d6 21 0-0-0 ♖d8 22 ♘e8!! and White has a powerful attack) 15 ♘xf3 and White has an edge, for example 15...axb5 (15...♗xb2 16 ♘c7+ ♔f8 17 ♖b1 ♗c3+ 18 ♔e2 axb5 19 ♖xb5) 16 ♘c7+ ♔f8 17 ♘d4! ♗b7 18 0-0 b4 19 a3 bxa3 20 ♖xa3.

b) 12...axb5 13 ♕d5!! ♗b7 14 ♕xf7! ♗h6 15 ♘e2 ♗xa8 16 ♗xb6+ ♔c8 17 ♕e8+ ♔b7 18 ♗d4 and White is winning.

11 ♘xa8 ♕xe4+

11...axb5!? 12 ♕d5 ♘c6 13 ♘c7 ♗xb2 14 ♖b1 ♗c3+ 15 ♔d1! ♘f6 16 ♕d3 b4 17 ♘d5 with a complex position that should favour White.

12 ♗e2 ♕xf4

12...♕xa8?! 13 c3! ♗b7 (certainly not 13...♕xg2?? 14 ♗f3 trapping the queen!) 14 ♘f3 and White is better.

12...♗xb2?! 13 ♖b1 ♗c3+ 14 ♗d2 ♗xd2+ 15 ♕xd2 ♕xa8 16 ♕c3 ♗b7 17 ♖xb6!! ♘f6 18 ♕b2 wins for White.

13 c3 ♗b7 14 ♗f3! ♕e5+

14...♗xa8 15 ♗xa8 ♘f6 16 ♘e2 and White is on top.

15 ♕e2 ♕xe2+ 16 ♔xe2

White is better.

A12)

9...♗xb2 10 ♖b1 ♗g7 *(D)*

10...e5 11 ♗g3 ♗d4 12 c3 is good for White.

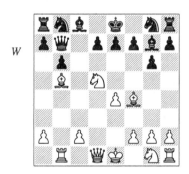

11 ♘f3 ♔f8

11...♔d8 12 0-0! d6 (12...♘f6 13 ♗c7+ ♔e8 14 ♗e5! ♘xd5 15 ♗xg7 ♖g8 16 exd5 ♖xg7 17 d6! and White has excellent play for the pawn) 13 e5 ♗e6 14 c4 a6 15 ♗a4 ♗xd5 16 cxd5 and White has a strong position.

12 ♘c7 ♕xe4+ 13 ♗e3 ♗c3+

Or 13...♗b7 14 0-0 ♘f6 15 ♖e1 and now:

a) 15...♕g4 16 h3 ♕h5 (16...♗xf3 17 ♕xf3 ♕xf3 18 gxf3 a6 19 ♘xa8 axb5 20 ♖xb5 and White is well on top) 17 ♗d4! d6 18 ♗c4 and White has an edge, e.g. 18...♘c6 19 ♖b5 e5 (19...♘xd4 20 ♖xh5 ♘xf3+ 21 gxf3 ♖c8! is unclear but White should be better, e.g. 22 ♘d5! ♘xh5 23 ♘xe7 ♖d8 24 ♗d5) 20 ♗xb6! axb6 21 ♕xd6+ ♔g8 22 ♘xa8 winning.

b) 15...♘d5 16 ♗d4 and Black is worse as 16...♘xc7 (16...♕xe1+ 17 ♕xe1 ♘xc7 18 ♗xg7+ ♔xg7 19 ♕e5+ wins; 16...♕f5 17 ♘xa8 ♗xa8 18 ♗xg7+ ♔xg7 19 ♖e5 is very good for White) 17 ♖xe4 ♗xe4 18 ♗xg7+ ♔xg7 19 ♕d4+ wins.

14 ♔f1 ♗b7

14...♘f6 15 ♖b3 ♗a5 16 ♗h6+ ♔g8 17 ♖e3 ♕b4 18 ♕d4 ♕xd4 (after 18...♕b1+ 19 ♘e1 Black has to contend with the threat of ♕xf6!!) 19 ♘xd4 ♗b7 (19...♘g4 20 ♖xe7 ♘xh6 21 ♘xa8 and White has a slight edge) 20 ♘xa8 and White is well placed.

15 ♘xa8 ♗xa8 16 ♖b3 ♗g7

16...♗f6! 17 ♕d2 with an unclear position.

17 ♗xd7 ♕d5

17...♗d5 18 ♗b5! ♘f6 19 ♕d3! and White is a little better; 17...♘f6 18 ♖c3 ♗c6 19 ♗xc6 ♘xc6 20 ♕d3 and White is better; 17...♕c4+ 18 ♕d3 and White has an edge, for example 18...♕xd3+ 19 ♖xd3 ♗e4 20 ♖d1! ♗xc2 21 ♖d2 ♗e4 22 ♗b5.

18 ♖d3 ♕c4

18...♕xa2 19 ♗b5! and Black has serious problems.

19 ♔g1

White is better.

A2)

6...♘a6 7 ♘f3 *(D)*

7...e6

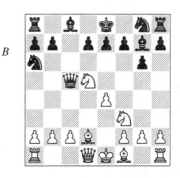

7...♗xb2? 8 ♖b1 ♗g7 9 ♗xa6 bxa6 10 0-0 a5 (10...e6 11 ♗b4 with a massive attack for White) 11 ♗e3 ♕c4 (11...♕c6 12 ♘d4! is very strong for White) 12 ♕d3 ♕xd3 13 cxd3 ♔d8 14 ♗d2 1-0 MChess Pro-Van der Pol, The Hague 1995.

7...♘f6? 8 b4! ♕d6 9 ♗f4 ♕e6 10 ♘g5 ♕c6 11 ♗e5!! (a big improvement on Bojković-Lelchuk, Yugoslav wom Cht 1993, which continued 11 b5 ♕c5 12 ♗e3 ♕a3!! with an unclear position) 11...d6 (11...h6?! 12 b5 ♕c5 13 ♗d4 ♕d6 {13...♘xd5!? 14 ♗xc5 ♗c3+ 15 ♔e2 ♘f4+ 16 ♔e3 ♘xc5 17 ♘f3 is good for White} 14 e5! ♕xd5 15 c4 winning) 12 b5 ♕d7 (12...♕c5 13 ♗d4! ♗g4 {13...♘xd5? 14 ♗xc5 ♗c3+ 15 ♔e2 ♘f4+ 16 ♔f3 and White is winning} 14 f3 and White will emerge a piece ahead) 13 bxa6 and Black cannot take on e5 because of ♗b5 winning the queen.

8 ♗c3 ♗xc3+

8...♔f8!? 9 ♗xg7+ ♔xg7 10 ♘c3 with approximate equality, Galyas-Shurygin, Budapest 1994.

9 ♘xc3 ♘f6

9...♘c7?! 10 e5! and 9...♘e7?! 10 ♕d2 0-0 11 e5! both favour White.

10 ♕d2 0-0 11 0-0-0

White has the advantage, Barle-Forintos, Maribor 1977.

B)

3...c6

Black plans ...d5, a system devised by Gurgenidze. The idea is for Black to develop his light-squared bishop to g4 or f5 at some time after the moves 4 f4 d5 5 e5 have been played. This way Black can then play ...e6 and reach a French-type position with his 'bad' bishop outside the pawn-chain. This variation tends to lead to long positional games where a battle rages to see if White can play g4 or if Black can stop this move. The importance of this move is that it would give White extra space, cramping Black and bringing in the possibility of a f4-f5 break.

Were I convinced Black would meet 4 ♘f3 with 4...d5, I would almost certainly play this way to transpose back to the system I recommended in the Caro-Kann chapter from the move-order 1 e4 c6 2 d4 d5 3 ♘c3 g6 4 ♘f3, etc. However, there is always the possibility Black will cross this plan and play 4...d6 and transpose back to a line of the Classical Pirc, circumventing our chosen repertoire. Therefore I am going to recommend a more radical approach:

4 ♗c4!? *(D)*

Black can choose between:

B1: 4...d5   190
B2: 4...b5   191
B3: 4...e6   194
B4: 4...d6   195

B1)

4...d5 5 exd5 b5

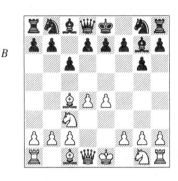

B

5...cxd5?! 6 ♘xd5 and now:

a) 6...♗e6 7 ♕f3 ♗xd4 8 ♘e2 ♘c6 9 0-0! ♘e5 10 ♕f4 ♗xd5 11 ♗b5+! ♗c6 (11...♘c6 12 ♘xd4 ♘f6 13 ♖d1 ♕d7 14 c4 ♗e4 15 f3 ♗f5 16 ♗e3 and Black's position looks decidedly ropy) 12 ♘xd4 ♕d5 13 ♘xc6 and with the bishop-pair White is well placed, e.g. 13...♘xc6 14 c4 ♕e6 15 ♗d2 0-0-0 16 ♗c3.

b) 6...e6 7 ♕e2 ♗xd4 (7...♘f8 8 ♘f4 ♕xd4 9 ♘f3 and White is better) 8 ♗f4 ♗b6 (8...♗xb2 9 ♖d1 ♕a5+ 10 ♔f1 and Black is in deep trouble) 9 0-0-0 ♘d7 (9...♗d7? 10 ♗e5 f6 11 ♘xf6+ ♘xf6 12 ♗xe6 and Black is busted) 10 ♘f3 ♔f8 11 ♘xb6 ♕xb6 (11...axb6? 12 ♘e5 gives Black insurmountable problems) 12 ♖d6 ♕c5 13 ♖hd1 ♕f5 14 ♕d2 ♘df6 15 ♖d8+ ♔g7 16 ♗e5 1-0 Kosten-Thierry, French Cht 1992.

6 ♗b3 b4 7 ♘ce2 cxd5 8 ♗d2! a5

Others:

a) 8...♘a6?! 9 a3 bxa3 10 ♖xa3 ♘c7 11 ♕a1! a6 12 ♗a5 ♘f6 13 ♗a4+ ♗d7 14 ♖c3 ♖c8 15 ♘f3 with advantage to White, Pritchett-Ristoja, Groningen 1969.

b) 8...♕d6?! 9 ♗f4 and Black has no useful square for the queen.

c) 8...♘c6? 9 ♗a4 and White will win a pawn for nothing, e.g. 9...♗d7 10 ♗xc6 ♗xc6 11 ♗xb4.

9 a3 bxa3

9...a4? 10 axb4! is just good for White.

10 ♖xa3 ♘c6

10...e6? 11 ♗a4+! ♗d7 12 ♗xd7+ ♕xd7 (after 12...♘xd7 13 ♕a1 ♖c8 {13...♕c8? 14 ♖xa5 ♖xa5 15 ♕xa5 ♕xc2?? 16 ♕a8+ ♔e7 17 ♗b4+ ♔f6 18 ♕d8+ mates} 14 ♗c3 ♕g5 15 ♘g3! Black will drop a pawn) 13 ♖xa5 ♖xa5 14 ♗xa5 and Black has little to show for the pawn, e.g. 14...♘c6 15 ♗c3 ♘f6 16 f3!, Sorokin-Maciejewski, Belgorod 1991.

11 ♘f3 ♘f6 12 ♘e5! ♘xe5 13 dxe5 ♘e4

13...♘g4 14 ♕a1! ♕b6 15 0-0 ♗xe5 16 h3 and White is on top.

14 ♗e3 e6 15 f3! *(D)*

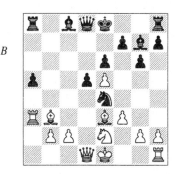

This leads to a long tactical sequence which favours White.

15...♕h4+ 16 g3 ♘xg3 17 ♗f2 ♕b4+ 18 c3 ♕xa3!? 19 bxa3 ♘xh1 20 ♗a4+! ♔f8

20...♗d7 21 ♗d4 and Black's knight on h1 remains trapped.

21 ♗c5+ ♔g8 22 ♔d2!

Picking up the knight on h1 and an obvious improvement on 22 ♗d6?, Ghinda-B.Schneider, Dortmund 1986, which is less clear.

B2)
4...b5 5 ♗b3 *(D)*

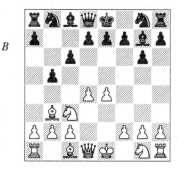

Now Black has played:
B21: 5...a5   191
B22: 5...b4   193

B21)
5...a5 6 a3

With the following possibilities:
B211: 6...♗a6   192
B212: 6...d6   192

Others:

a) 6...a4?! leaves Black somewhat inflexible on the queenside. 7 ♗a2 ♕b6 8 ♘f3 b4? 9 axb4 ♕xb4 10 0-0 a3 (this is a consistent approach after 6...a4?! and 8...b4? but with little in the way of development and king safety it is asking for trouble) 11 ♗b3! ♗h6 12 ♗xh6 ♘xh6 13 ♕d2 ♘g8 14 bxa3 ♖xa3? 15 ♖xa3 ♕xa3 16 ♕f4 1-0 (with threats on f7 and b8 Black does the right thing) Thorhallsson-Mirallès, Hartberg 1991.

b) 6...♕b6 7 ♘f3 e6?! 8 e5! d5 9 exd6 (Black is not going to find it easy to recover this pawn) 9...♘f6 10 0-0 0-0 11 ♗g5 ♘bd7 12 ♖e1 a4 13 ♗a2 b4 14 ♘e4 ♘xe4 15 ♖xe4 ♘f6 16 ♖f4 ♘d5 17 ♗xd5 exd5 18 ♗e7 and White is doing well, Hjartarson-G.Hansen, Copenhagen 1996.

c) 6...e6!? 7 e5 d5 8 exd6 ♕xd6 9 ♘e4 ♕c7 10 c3 and White has a comfortable position because of Black's long-term weaknesses on the dark squares.

B211)
6...♗a6 7 ♕f3 e6 8 e5 d6 *(D)*

After 8...f5!? 9 ♘ge2 White has a good chance of exploiting Black's kingside, e.g. 9...♘e7 10 ♘f4 0-0 11 h4 h6 (11...b4 12 ♘a4 is good for White as it brings his knight from c3 right back into the game) 12 ♕g3 ♕e8 13 ♗e3 and White is a little better because he can build up pressure on the kingside while Black is without any real activity.

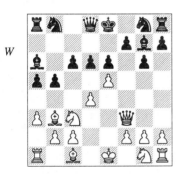

W

9 exd6 ♗xd4

9...♕xd6 10 ♗f4 ♕xd4? loses to 11 ♗xb8!.

10 ♘ge2 ♗e5

10...♕xd6 11 ♗f4 ♗e5 (11...e5 12 ♘e4 ♕e7 13 ♗xf7+! is strong for White) 12 ♘e4 ♕c7 13 0-0-0 and White has excellent compensation for the pawn, for example 13...♘d7 14 ♘d6+ ♗xd6 15 ♖xd6 ♕b7 16 ♖hd1 ♘gf6 17 ♗e5! ♔e7 18 ♖xd7+! ♘xd7 19 ♖xd7+!! ♔xd7 (19...♕xd7 20 ♕f6+ wins) 20 ♕xf7+ winning.

11 ♗f4 ♗g7

11...♕xd6 transposes to the previous note.

12 0-0-0 b4 13 ♘e4 bxa3 14 bxa3 ♘d7 15 ♘d4 c5

15...♕b6 16 ♗e3 ♗h6 (16...♕b7 17 ♘xc6!) 17 ♗xh6 ♘xh6 18 ♘xc6 is strong.

16 ♗xe6 ♗xd4

16...cxd4 17 ♗xf7+! ♔f8 (17...♔xf7 18 ♘g5+ ♔e8 19 ♖he1+ and Black falls apart) 18 ♘g5 ♘c5 19 ♗xg8 ♖xg8 20 ♗e5+, etc.

16...fxe6? 17 ♘xe6 and Black is defenceless.

17 ♗xf7+! ♔f8

17...♔xf7 18 ♘g5+ ♔xg5 19 ♗xg5+ ♘gf6 20 ♖he1 ♖ae8 21 c3 and White is well on top.

18 ♗d5 ♔g7

18...♗g7 19 ♗g5+ ♘gf6 20 ♘xf6 ♘xf6 21 ♗xa8 and Black is lost.

19 ♘g5

White wins.

B212)
6...d6 7 ♕f3 e6 8 ♘ge2 *(D)*

Now Black has tried the following:

a) 8...♘e7 9 h4 (trying to soften up Black's kingside) 9...h5 10 ♗g5 and White has an edge in terms of space and development, Shaked-A.Ivanov, USA Ch (Parsippany) 1996.

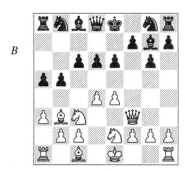

b) 8...♘d7 9 0-0 ♘b6 10 d5! b4 11 ♘a4 cxd5 12 exd5 ♗b7 (12...♘xd5!? 13 ♗xd5 exd5 14 ♕xd5 ♗e6 15 ♕f3 ♖c8 16 ♘f4 and White is better, e.g. 16...♖xc2 17 ♘xe6 fxe6 18 ♕e4 ♕c8 19 ♘b6 ♘f6 20 ♕e3) 13 ♘xb6 ♕xb6 14 axb4 axb4 (14...♕xb4?! 15 ♕e3 and White is better, for example 15...♗h6 16 ♕c3 ♕xc3 17 ♘xc3 e5 18 ♗xh6 ♘xh6 19 ♖a4 and Black's a-pawn is going) 15 ♗e3 ♕d8 16 ♕f4 ♗xb2 17 dxe6 fxe6 18 ♗a4+ ♔e7 (18...♖xa4 19 ♖xa4 ♗a3 20 ♗d4! is extremely strong) 19 ♕xb4 ♗xg2 20 ♕xb2 1-0 (Black quite rightly gives up the chase) Brinck-Claussen – G.Hansen, Danish League 1996.

c) 8...♗a6 9 d5 cxd5 10 exd5 e5 11 ♘e4 h6 (11...♕c7 12 c4! {a fine positional pawn sacrifice} 12...bxc4 13 ♗a4+ ♘d7 14 ♘2c3 ♔e7? 15 ♘xd6!! and White eventually won in the game J.Polgar-Shirov, Amsterdam Donner mem 1995) 12 g4! (an attempt to restrict Black's kingside expansion) 12...♘f6 13 ♘2g3 ♘xe4 (13...♗b7!? leads to complex play) 14 ♘xe4 0-0 15 ♕h3 f5 (15...♘d7? 16 ♗xh6 ♘c5 17 ♘g5 ♗f6 18 ♗g7!! 1-0 Zulfugarli-Bologan, Nikolaev Z 1995) 16 gxf5 ♗c8! 17 ♘g3 with chances for

both sides, Anand-Shirov, Dos Hermanas 1996.

B22)
5...b4 6 ♘ce2 ♘f6 *(D)*
Others:

a) 6...d5 7 exd5 cxd5 transposes to the main line in Line B1.

b) 6...d6 7 ♘f3 ♘f6 8 ♘g3 maintains a slight edge for White (and is far calmer than 8 e5!?). Now 8...0-0 9 ♗g5 ♕b6 10 0-0 ♗a6 (Black has waited until White had castled for this; otherwise White would have castled long and the bishop on a6 would have been left blocking an advance of Black's queenside pawns) 11 ♖e1 e6?! 12 ♕d2 (White has a space advantage and the more active pieces) 12...♖e8 13 ♕f4 leaves White clearly better, Nicolcea-Manu, Romanian Cht 1992.

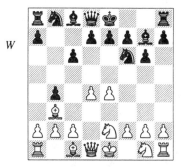

7 e5 ♘d5 8 ♘f4 ♘b6?!
Better chances for Black are:

a) 8...♘xf4 9 ♗xf4 0-0 10 h4 d6 11 ♕e2 a5 12 h5 and White has the better attacking chances, Adams-Z.Bašagić, Hastings Challengers 1987.

b) 8...e6 9 ♘f3 a5 10 ♘d3! (this blocks the f1-a6 diagonal, controls c5 and re-opens the c1-h6 diagonal)

10...♘a6 11 h4 h6 12 a3 ♗b7 13 ♘d2 d6 14 ♘e4 dxe5 15 dxe5 0-0 16 h5 and White has an edge, Hebden-Vaisman, Montpellier 1988.

9 a3 bxa3 10 ♖xa3 0-0 11 h4!

Again the thematic lunge to prise open Black's kingside.

11...e6 12 h5 d6?! 13 hxg6 dxe5?

13...hxg6 14 ♕g4! and White has massive attacking chances, for example 14...dxe5 15 dxe5 ♕c7 (15...♕d4 16 ♘xg6! ♕xg4 17 ♘e7#; 15...♗xe5 16 ♘xg6 fxg6 17 ♗xe6+ ♗xe6 18 ♕xe6+ ♖f7 19 ♕xe5 and Black is in big trouble) 16 ♘f3 ♖d8 (16...♘8d7? 17 ♘xe6 wins; 16...♗xe5 17 ♘xg6! fxg6 18 ♗xe6+ ♗xe6 19 ♕xe6+ ♕f7 20 ♕xe5 and Black is much worse) 17 ♕h4 ♔f8 (17...♗xe5 18 ♕h7+ ♔f8 19 ♘xg6+ fxg6 20 ♗h6+ ♔e8 21 ♕g8+ ♔e7 22 ♗g5+, etc.) 18 ♘d3 ♘d5 19 ♗g5 ♘e7 20 ♗f6 with a crushing attack.

14 gxh7+ ♔h8 15 ♘h5

Black is busted, Kelleher-Hanken, Philadelphia 1997.

B3)

4...e6 5 e5! *(D)*

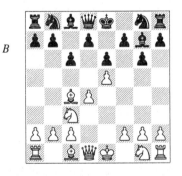

B

5...d5

5...f6? 6 ♘e4 fxe5 7 ♘d6+ ♔e7 (7...♔f8? 8 ♕f3+ ♔e7 9 ♕a3 wins) 8 ♗g5+ ♗f6 9 ♗xf6+ ♘xf6 (9...♔xf6 10 ♕f3+ ♔g7 {10...♔e7 11 dxe5! ♕a5+ 12 ♔f1 ♕xe5 13 ♘xc8+ ♔d8 14 ♕f8+ ♔c7 15 ♖d1 and Black has big problems} 11 ♕f7+ ♔h6 12 dxe5 with a massive position for White) 10 ♘xc8+ ♕xc8 11 dxe5 with a very promising position for White.

6 exd6 ♕xd6

6...♘f6!?.

7 ♘e4 ♕c7

7...♕b4+ 8 c3 ♕xc4?? 9 ♘d6+ wins the queen.

7...♕xd4?! 8 ♕xd4 ♗xd4 9 ♘d6+ ♔e7 10 ♘xc8+ ♔d7 11 ♘f3 ♗f6 12 ♘xa7 ♖xa7 and White has an edge thanks to the bishop-pair, Ulfarsson-Goganian, Duisburg U-16 Wch 1992.

8 ♕f3 f5

8...♗xd4 9 ♗f4 and now:

a) 9...♕a5+ 10 b4! ♕xb4+ 11 c3 ♕a5 (11...♕b2 12 ♖d1 and Black is in trouble) 12 ♘d6+ ♔d7 13 0-0-0!! is very powerful for White.

b) 9...e5 10 0-0-0 exf4 (10...♗xb2+ 11 ♔xb2 exf4 12 ♘d6+ is good for White) 11 ♖xd4 and Black has problems, e.g. 11...c5 12 ♘d6+ ♔f8 13 ♖d2 ♘d7 14 ♕xf4 and Black's position is falling apart.

9 ♘g5 ♗xd4

Black needs to be greedy as he has committed positional suicide by playing ...f5 leaving a backward e-pawn and masses of dark-square weaknesses.

10 ♘e2 ♗e5

10...♗f6 11 ♘xe6 ♗xe6 12 ♗xe6 and White has the bishop-pair and easy development as well as a monster light-squared bishop.

11 ♘f4 ♕e7 12 ♕e2 ♘d7

12...♕b4+ 13 c3 ♗xc3+ 14 ♔f1! and Black has problems.

13 ♘fxe6

Now White is well on top, Chatalbashev-Grigorov, Pazardzhik 1991.

B4)

4...d6 5 ♕f3

This is the way to steer the game into lines independent of the Classical Pirc.

5...e6 *(D)*

5...♘f6 6 e5 dxe5 (6...♗g4? 7 ♕f4 wins material) 7 dxe5 ♘d5 8 ♘xd5 cxd5 9 ♗xd5 0-0 10 ♗xb7 ♕a5+ 11 c3 ♗xb7 (after 11...♕xe5+?? 12 ♘e2 ♗xb7 13 ♕xb7 Black loses material, and 11...♘d7? 12 ♗xa8 ♘xe5 13 ♕d5! is obviously good for White) 12 ♕xb7 and here:

a) 12...♕b6 13 ♕xa8 (13 ♕xb6 is the safe way to play for an advantage; after 13...axb6 14 ♘f3 Black has little to show for being two pawns down) 13...♘c6 14 ♕xf8+ ♔xf8 15 ♘f3 ♘xe5 16 ♘xe5 ♗xe5 17 0-0 and White has two rooks and a pawn for a queen.

b) 12...♘a6 13 ♘f3 ♘c5 14 b4! ♘xb7 15 bxa5 ♘xa5 16 ♗e3 ♘c6 17 ♖b1 ♘xe5 18 ♘xe5 ♗xe5 19 c4 ♖ac8 20 c5 ♖fd8 21 ♔e2 ♗d4 22 ♖hc1 ♗xe3 23 ♔xe3 with a tight ending in which White may be marginally better due to his passed pawn, Leko-Hamdouchi, Cap d'Agde 1994.

6 ♘ge2

After which we have:

Others include:

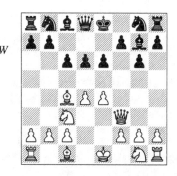

a) 6...h6 7 0-0 ♘e7 8 ♗b3 0-0 9 ♗f4 e5 10 dxe5 dxe5 11 ♖ad1 ♘d7 12 ♗e3 and White has a long-term edge because Black is a little cramped, B.Thipsay-Safranska, Moscow wom OL 1994.

b) 6...♘e7 7 0-0 b5 8 ♗b3 b4 9 ♘d1 0-0 10 a3 ♘a6 11 ♗g5 ♕c7 12 axb4 ♘xb4 13 c3 ♘a6 with an edge to White, Werner-Nikolova, Zagan girls Wch 1997.

c) 6...d5 7 ♗b3 ♘d7 (7...♘a6?! 8 ♗f4 ♘f6 9 0-0 and White has an edge as Black has some dark-square weaknesses and will find it difficult to complete his development satisfactorily) 8 0-0 ♘e7 9 ♕h3! 0-0 10 ♗h6 dxe4 11 ♗xg7 ♔xg7 12 ♘xe4 ♘d5?! 13 c4 ♘5f6 14 ♘d6 ♕c7 15 c5 e5 16 dxe5 ♘xe5 17 ♕c3 ♘ed7 18 ♗xf7! ♖xf7? 19 ♘e8+ 1-0 Nagy-Holfeuerova, Hlinsko 1993.

d) 6...b5 7 ♗b3 a5 8 a3 transposes into Line B212.

B41)

6...♕e7 7 a4!

A typical queenside restricting manoeuvre.

7...♘d7 8 0-0 ♘gf6 9 a5! e5 10 d5 c5

10...♘c5?! 11 b4 ♗g4 12 ♕e3 ♗xe2 13 ♕xe2 ♘cd7 14 a6 and White is well placed.

11 a6 bxa6 12 ♗xa6 0-0 13 ♘b5

White has the edge as his queenside initiative is growing while Black's kingside counterplay has yet to get underway, Glek-Niesel, Werfen 1991.

B42)

6...♘d7 7 a4

With the following possibilities:

a) 7...♕e7 8 0-0 transposes into Line B41.

b) 7...a5 8 h4 ♘gf6 9 ♗a2 h5!? 10 ♗g5 e5 11 0-0 ♕e7 12 ♕g3 exd4 (this releases the tension too early) 13 ♘xd4 ♕e5 14 ♘f5! gxf5 (14...♕xg3?! 15 ♘xg7+ ♔f8 16 fxg3 ♔xg7 17 ♖ad1 and White picks up the d-pawn) 15 ♗f4 and White has a good advantage, Ljubojević-Ciocaltea, Yugoslavia 1971.

c) 7...b6!? 8 0-0 ♗b7 9 ♕g3 ♕e7 10 d5! and Black has yet to equalize.

d) 7...♘gf6 8 ♗b3 0-0 9 0-0 reaches a balanced position, Madl-Feustel, Dubai wom OL 1986. If Black aims for ...e6-e5 he will reach a Classical Pirc a tempo down but on the other hand White's queen is not so well placed on f3. Otherwise White has a slight space advantage but Black is very solid and flexible.

C)

3...d6 4 f4 a6!?

Objectively this is not a very good move but against an unprepared player it has good shock value. It looks better than it really is as Black will get in ...b5 and possibly ...♗b7 quite quickly. However, White will aim to make a central thrust with e4-e5, when Black will miss not having his light-squared bishop covering the e6-square.

5 ♘f3 *(D)*

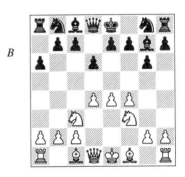

5...b5

Others:

a) 5...♗g4?! 6 ♗e2 and now:

a1) With 6...♘c6 Black hopes that White will overextend his centre but this is just not the case. 7 d5 ♘b8 8 0-0 c6 (8...c5 9 a4 and Black is tempi down on a Benoni-type position) 9 ♗e3 ♘f6 10 h3 ♗xf3 11 ♗xf3 and White has the bishop-pair and extra space.

a2) 6...♘f6 7 h3 ♗xf3 8 ♗xf3 c6 9 ♗e3 0-0 10 g4 and with the bishop-pair, a great deal of extra space, and the g4-g5 push at his disposal, White is already much better.

b) 5...e6?! is met by the restricting move 6 a4!, when Black is solid but cramped.

c) 5...♘d7 6 a4! and now after 6...c5 7 d5 we have reached a Schmid Benoni type position where Black will find it difficult to get in ...e6 and his knight on d7 blocks his light-squared bishop. White will develop normally and aim for a strong central thrust with e4-e5.

6 ♗d3

Now Black can choose from:

a) 6...b4 7 ♘e2 d5 8 e5 ♗g4 9 0-0 e6 10 a3 ♘c6 11 ♗d2 ♗f5 12 ♗xb4 ♗f8 13 ♗xf8 and Black has no compensation for the pawn, Inkiov-Arnaudov, Sofia 1977.

b) 6...♗b7 7 a4 b4 8 ♘e2 ♘d7 (8...♘f6 9 ♘g3 0-0 10 0-0 e6 11 c4 and White has a spatial advantage, Luther-Pähtz, East German Ch 1988) 9 c3 bxc3 10 bxc3 c5 11 ♖b1 ♖b8 12 0-0 cxd4 13 cxd4 ♘gf6 14 e5 ♘d5 15 ♘g5! e6 16 ♘e4! is very good for White, Ljubojević-Sznapik, Buenos Aires OL 1978.

c) 6...♘d7 7 a4 b4 8 ♘e2 e5 9 fxe5 dxe5 10 c3 c5 11 ♗e3 bxc3 12 bxc3 ♕c7 13 0-0 ♘gf6 14 h3 0-0 15 d5 and White has a small edge, Saint-Amand – Robinson, Bermuda 1995.

D)

3...d6 4 f4 c6 5 ♗e3 *(D)*

This move is theoretically looked down on in comparison to 5 ♘f3 but in practice White has been successful with it.

5...♕b6

Or:

a) 5...♘f6 6 ♘f3 0-0 transposes to a line of the Pirc Defence (Chapter 8, Part 2, Line A) from the move-order 1 e4 d6 2 d4 ♘f6 3 ♘c3 g6 4 f4 ♗g7 5 ♘f3 0-0 6 ♗e3 c6. It is likely that if Black plays 5...b5 or 5...♘d7 and then 6...b5 he will at some stage play ...♘g8-f6 and transpose back to that type of system.

b) 5...d5?! 6 e5 and White is a tempo ahead in a Gurgenidze (compare to 1 e4 g6 2 d4 ♗g7 3 ♘c3 c6 4 f4 d5 5 e5) and while Black is still solid, the extra tempo should ensure White the advantage.

c) 5...e5 6 ♘f3 ♗g4?! (6...♕b6 7 ♖b1 transposes back to the main line) 7 dxe5 ♗xf3 (7...dxe5 8 ♕xd8+ ♔xd8 9 ♘xe5 ♗xe5 10 fxe5 ♘d7 11 h3 ♗e6 12 0-0-0 ♔c7 13 ♗d4! and Black will find it hard to recover his pawn and even if he manages it, he will be left with dark-squared weaknesses and facing the bishop-pair) 8 ♕xf3 dxe5 9 ♗c4 ♕c7 (9...♘d7 10 f5! is unpleasant to face; 9...exf4 10 ♗xf4 and despite the isolated pawn White is better due to the bishop-pair, lead in development and potential pressure down the f-file) 10 0-0 ♘d7? 11 ♗xf7+ ♔xf7 12 fxe5+ ♔e8 13 ♕f7+ ♔d8 14 ♕xg7 ♕xe5 15 ♖f8+ 1-0 Kais-Denk, Schwäbisch Gmünd 1996.

6 ♖b1 e5 *(D)*

Others:

a) 6...f5!? 7 ♕d2 ♘f6 8 e5! ♘g4 (8...♘e4!? 9 ♘xe4 fxe4 10 ♘e2 d5 11 ♘c3 0-0 12 ♗e2 and White has a reasonable position, e.g. 12...♘a6 13 0-0 ♗e6 14 b4!) 9 ♘f3 ♘xe3 10 ♕xe3 0-0 11 ♗c4+ and despite the bishop-pair White is positionally better.

b) 6...♘f6 7 ♘f3 0-0 8 ♕d2 d5 (8...♕c7 gives Black a similar set-up to the line in the Pirc previously mentioned a tempo down though it would remain to be seen how useful the white rook is on b1) 9 e5 ♘g4 (9...♘e4!? 10 ♘xe4 dxe4 11 ♘g5 ♗f5 12 ♖g1! h6 {12...h5 13 ♗c4! followed by h3 and g4 is good for White} 13 g4 ♗xg4 {13...hxg5 14 gxf5 gxf4 15 ♗xf4 and Black must be very careful} 14 ♘xe4 ♗f3 15 ♗d3 and White is doing fine) 10 ♗g1 f6 11 h3 ♘h6 12 g4 and White has an edge, Zinn-Minić, Berlin Lasker mem 1968, for example 12...f5 13 g5 ♘f7 14 h4 and White has a bind and a ready-made kingside attack, e.g. 14...h5 (14...♗e6 15 h5 ♘d7 16 ♕h2!) 15 gxh6 ♘xh6 16 h5.

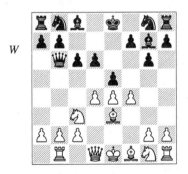

W

7 ♘f3 ♘d7

7...♗g4 8 fxe5 dxe5 9 ♗c4! with the idea of ♗xf7+ is good for White, for example 9...exd4 10 ♗xf7+ ♔f8 11 ♗f2 ♕c7 12 ♗xg8 dxc3 13 ♗b3 cxb2 14 0-0 and the exposed position of Black's king causes him continuing difficulties.

8 ♕d2 ♕c7 9 ♗c4 ♘gf6 10 0-0 0-0 11 ♗b3 ♘g4 12 fxe5 dxe5 13 d5! ♘xe3 14 ♕xe3

Despite the bishop-pair Black has problems especially from the evil intentions of White's bishop 'lurking' on b3.

14...h6

14...♘b6 15 ♕c5! ♘d7 16 ♕f2 and White has gained a useful tempo; 14...c5?! 15 ♘b5 ♕b6 16 ♘a3!.

15 ♖bd1 ♘b6 16 d6 ♕d7

As we know, the queen is not a good blockader.

16...♕d8 17 ♘xe5!! ♗xe5 18 ♕xh6 ♕e8 (18...♗g7 19 ♕xg6 ♕e8 20 ♕g5! ♗e6 21 ♖f3 and White has very good play for the piece) 19 ♕xg6+ ♔h8 20 ♗xf7 wins.

17 ♘h4! ♔h7 18 ♕g3 ♕e8 19 ♖xf7! ♖xf7 20 ♕xg6+ ♔g8 21 ♖f1 ♘d5 22 ♘xd5 ♖xf1+ 23 ♔xf1 ♕xg6 24 ♘f6+

1-0 Van der Plassche-Westerman, corr. 1990.

E)

3...d6 4 f4 ♘c6 5 ♗e3 (D)

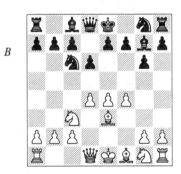

B

Now if Black plays 5...♘f6 (the most common move here) we transpose with 6 ♘f3 0-0 to the Pirc (Line C of Part 2 of Chapter 8). Therefore this section will only deal with alternatives for Black:

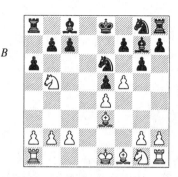

B

E1)

5...d5?! 6 ♘xd5 e6 7 ♘c3 ♘xd4

7...♗xd4 8 ♗xd4 ♘xd4 (8...♕xd4 9 ♕xd4 ♘xd4 10 0-0-0 c5 11 ♘a4 b6 12 b4! e5 13 bxc5 ♗g4 14 ♖d2 bxc5 15 ♘xc5 ♖c8 16 ♘d3 and White is well on top as 16...exf4? loses material to 17 ♘e5) 9 ♘f3 ♘xf3+ (9...c5 10 ♗b5+ ♘xb5 11 ♕xd8+ ♔xd8 12 ♘xb5 and White is better) 10 ♕xf3 and White has a positional edge due to Black's lack of space and weakness on the dark squares.

8 ♘f3 ♘c6 9 ♕xd8+ ♔xd8 10 0-0-0+ ♗d7

White has an advantage, Escobar-Fulgenzi, Buenos Aires 1990.

E2)

5...e5?! 6 dxe5 dxe5 7 ♕xd8+ ♘xd8 8 ♘b5! ♘e6 9 f5 a6 *(D)*

9...gxf5 10 exf5 a6 11 fxe6 axb5 12 ♗xb5+ c6 13 exf7+ ♔xf7 14 ♗c4+ ♗e6 15 ♗xe6+ ♔xe6 is very similar to the game except White has in effect exchanged his e-pawn for Black's g-pawn. As Black's e-pawn does not appear to be too useful and White has the potential outside passed pawn this doesn't seem to be much in the way of an improvement.

10 fxe6 axb5 11 ♗xb5+ c6 12 exf7+ ♔xf7 13 ♗c4+ ♗e6 14 ♗xe6+ ♔xe6 15 ♘f3

White eventually converted his advantage in Shirov-Vial, Oviedo rpd 1992.

E3)

5...e6 6 ♕d2 ♘ge7 7 0-0-0 d5 8 e5 a6 9 g4 b6 10 h4

Instead of 10 ♘ge2, as in Bangiev-Morozov, USSR corr. 1989.

10...h5 11 gxh5 gxh5

11...♖xh5 12 ♗e2 ♖h8 13 h5 ♘f5 14 ♗f2 ♘ce7 15 ♘f3! ♖xh5 (15...gxh5 16 ♖h2 ♘g6 17 ♗d3 ♗h6 18 ♘e2 ♘g7 19 ♗xg6 fxg6 20 ♖g1 is better for White) 16 ♖xh5 gxh5 17 ♖h1 and Black has yet to equalize.

12 ♘f3

White has an edge since he can make better use of the open g-file and his outpost on g5 is stronger than Black's on f5.

E4)

5...♘h6 6 ♗e2 d5?!

Black is going to reach a Gurgenidze set-up a tempo down and where his knight on c6 will be misplaced.

7 e5 ♘f5 8 ♗f2 h5 9 ♘f3 e6 10 ♕d2 ♗f8!? 11 g3 ♗e7 12 0-0-0 ♘a5 13 h3

Black can no longer prevent g4 coming with advantage, e.g. 13...h4 14 g4 ♘g3 15 ♗xg3 hxg3 16 h4! and Black has problems, Sznapik-Kempys, Polish Ch 1991.

10 Alekhine Defence

1 e4 ♘f6

The Alekhine is unique. Rather than take his fair share of the centre by occupying it with pawns or by attacking White's centre in the medium- or long-term by some hypermodern means, Black immediately attacks White's e4-pawn with a minor piece. One idea of this is to lure White's central pawns to advance too far forward and then hit them by active piece-play, stepping in when the cracks start to appear. The system I advocate for White cuts across this plan by calmly playing 2 ♘c3, asking Black to make a choice. He can play 2...d6 transposing to a Pirc Defence, which is covered in full elsewhere in this book. He can also play 2...e5 transposing into a Vienna or Four Knights depending on how White reacts but again in my experience this is unlikely. Most Alekhine players seem to prefer 2...d5, trying to 'punish' White for his audacity in not playing 2 e5, and this chapter will focus on that move.

2 ♘c3 d5 3 e5 (D)

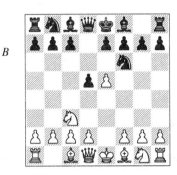

This, then, is our basic position.

At this point it is time for Black to make a choice on how to deal with his threatened knight. If he plays **3...♘fd7** then White can force a transposition into the variation I recommend against the French with 4 d4, meeting 4...e6 with 5 ♘f3 or 4...c5 5 dxc5, when Black has nothing better than 5...e6

when 6 ♘f3 once again transposes. Therefore this chapter will deal with the independent lines and split into two parts depending on whether Black plays **3...d4** (Part 1) or **3...♘e4!?** (Part 2).

Part 1

1 e4 ♘f6 2 ♘c3 d5 3 e5 d4 (D)

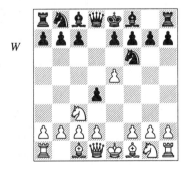

Rather than move his knight out of danger Black counterattacks White's knight on c3. Though once a popular choice, it has now been shown that White can keep a nice edge and leave Black in a position with few prospects. With a series of forcing moves White can steer the game into a queenless middlegame where Black must battle for equality.

4 exf6 dxc3 5 fxg7 cxd2+

After 5...♗xg7? 6 bxc3 Black has little to show for being a pawn down.

6 ♕xd2

6 ♗xd2 is more speculative, and less convincing.

6...♕xd2+ 7 ♗xd2 ♗xg7 8 0-0-0 *(D)*

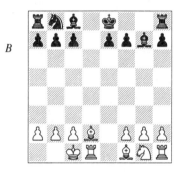

Now Black has a choice:

A: 8...♗g4? 201
B: 8...0-0?! 201
C: 8...♗e6 201
D: 8...♗f5 202
E: 8...♘c6 202

A)

8...♗g4?

After the simple 9 f3 ♗e6 White has gained a useful tempo over Line C in that he wants to develop his knight via e2 to f4 anyway and so playing 9 f3 has in no way disrupted his development or weakened his structure.

B)

8...0-0?! 9 ♗d3

Now:

a) 9...♘c6 10 ♘f3 ♗g4 11 ♗e4! followed by 12 ♖he1. Despite having his pieces on reasonable squares Black has problems. White is threatening ♗xc6 followed by ♖xe7 and White also has ♗f4 looming, putting pressure on c7. Meanwhile Black is without a useful plan.

b) 9...♗e6 10 ♘f3 and after this natural developing move it appears Black has nothing better than 10...h6 to stop ♘g5. Having to play a move like this shows the sorry state of his position.

c) 9...♗g4 (aiming to stop ♘f3-g5 when Black retreats his bishop to the natural e6-square) 10 f3 ♗e6 11 ♘h3! ♗xh3 12 gxh3 ♘c6 13 ♖hg1 and with the two bishops and the open g-file to work on, White's position is preferable.

d) 9...c5 10 ♗e3! (simply attacking the c-pawn gives Black problems) 10...♗d4 (10...♘d7 11 ♗b5!) 11 ♗xd4 cxd4 12 ♘f3 ♗g4 13 ♗e4! and White wins a pawn while maintaining an initiative.

C)

8...♗e6 9 ♘e2

Now:

a) 9...♗c4?! 10 ♘f4 ♗xf1 11 ♖hxf1 ♘c6 12 ♗e3! and Black has problems completing his development.

b) 9...♘d7 10 ♘f4 ♘c5 11 ♗e3 ♗h6 12 ♘xe6! ♗xe3+ 13 fxe3 ♘xe6 14 ♗c4 ♘c5 15 ♖hf1 e6 16 ♖d4! gives White a good position, with ideas of doubling rooks on the f-file or d-file followed by b4 and infiltrating with his rook to the seventh.

c) 9...♘c6 10 ♗c3! (exchanging off the dark-squared bishops leaves Black with a long-term inferior pawn-structure) 10...0-0 11 ♗xg7 ♔xg7 12 ♘f4 ♗f5 13 ♗d3! ♗xd3 14 ♖xd3 ♖fd8 15 ♖hd1 ♖xd3 16 ♖xd3 and with control of the d-file (16...♖d8? 17 ♖xd8 ♘xd8 18 ♘d5 winning a pawn), a more active knight and a better pawn-structure, White is well placed.

D)

8...♗f5 9 ♘e2

With these possibilities:

a) 9...h5!? 10 ♗c3 ♗xc3 11 ♘xc3 c6 12 ♗d3 ♗xd3 13 ♖xd3 ♘d7 14 ♖e1 ♘f6 15 ♘e4 ♘xe4 16 ♖xe4 ♖g8 and now, rather than 17 ♖g3?!, which led to equality in Kaplan-Day, Jerusalem jr Wch 1967, 17 g3! leaves White much better placed for the ending.

b) 9...♘c6 10 ♗c3 ♖g8 11 ♗xg7 ♖xg7 12 ♘g3 ♗d7 and now 13 ♗b5? is inaccurate, and led to equality in Shaw-Ljubojević, Buenos Aires OL 1978. Instead by 13 ♗c4 0-0-0 14 ♖he1 White maintains a pleasant edge.

c) 9...♘d7 10 ♗c3 ♗xc3 (10...♖g8 11 ♗xg7 ♖xg7 12 ♘d4! is better for White) 11 ♘xc3 c6 12 ♗d3 ♗g6 13 ♖he1 and White is well placed, e.g. 13...♘c5 14 ♗c4 b5 15 ♗e2 b4 16 ♗f3!, when Black's structural weaknesses give him problems.

E)

8...♘c6 9 ♗b5! ♗d7 10 ♘f3 0-0-0 11 ♖he1 ♖de8

11...e6 12 ♘g5 ♖df8 13 ♗f4! a6 14 ♗c4 is uncomfortable for Black.

12 ♘g5! h6 13 ♘e4
White has a small but durable edge.

Part 2

1 e4 ♘f6 2 ♘c3 d5 3 e5 ♘e4!? *(D)*

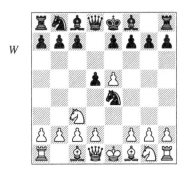

Black aims to maintain the tension especially because 4 ♘xe4?! promises White nothing, e.g. 4...dxe4 5 d4 exd3 6 ♗xd3 ♘c6 7 ♘f3 ♗g4 8 h3 ♗xf3 9 ♕xf3 ♕d4! 10 0-0 ♕xe5 11 ♗f4 ♕f6 is equal, Rõtov-Karpov, USSR 1969.

In the position after 3...♘e4 White has tried no fewer than fourteen different moves though most are harmless.

4 ♘ce2!

This is without doubt the most promising. The idea is to hit the knight with d3, dislodging it from its outpost on e4 without giving Black the opportunity to exchange it off for another minor piece. Black must in turn plan how he intends to deal with this, the main three alternatives being:

A: **4...♘c5**   203
B: **4...d4**   203
C: **4...f6!?**   204

Other moves have been tried but are just inferior, e.g. 4...♗f5? 5 d4! (better than hitting the knight with an immediate 5 d3, as the threat of f3 winning a piece causes Black all sorts of problems) 5...e6 6 f3 ♕h4+ 7 g3 ♘xg3 8 ♘xg3 and Black has little to show for being a piece down, Shtanchaev-Sheshukov, Russia Cup 1997.

A)

4...♘c5 5 d4 ♘e6

5...♘cd7? has been tried but just leads to a bad version of the French, viz. 6 ♘f4 e6 7 ♗d3 ♘b6 8 ♘f3 c5 9 c3 ♘c6 10 0-0 and White has a comfortable edge especially as the 'normal' ideas of ...f6 or a later ...0-0 are just asking for trouble with White's active piece placement, Gendre-Touze, French Cht 1991.

6 f4

Black must now decide between:

A1: **6...c5**   203
A2: **6...g6**   203

A1)

6...c5 7 c3 g6

7...♘c6 8 ♘f3 cxd4 9 f5! ♘c5 10 ♘exd4 and Black has an unenviable position.

8 ♘f3 ♘c6 9 ♗e3 cxd4 10 cxd4 ♘g7 11 ♘c3!

White is better due to the amount of time Black has wasted with his knight, i.e. ...♘g8-f6-e4-c5-e6-g7, from where at some point it presumably wishes to go to the f5-square. Compare this position to one from the Modern Defence arising from the moves 1 e4 g6 2 d4 ♗g7 3 ♘c3 c6 4 f4 d5 5 e5 h5 6 ♗e3 ♘h6 7 ♘f3 ♗g4 8 ♗e2 e6 *(D)*:

Although I am not recommending this variation for White, his moves

have been sensible and we can see he has a similar structure to Line A1 above. However, look how far Black is away from achieving the same set-up as the diagram and we can appreciate the kind of difficulties he is in.

A2)

6...g6 7 ♗e3!

Better than 7 ♘f3 as it slows down Black's counter in the centre of ...c5.

7...♘g7 8 ♕d2 b6 9 h3 e6 10 ♘f3 c5 11 g4 ♘c6 12 ♗g2 ♗d7 13 c3

White has the advantage due to her better development and extra space, Gaprindashvili-Alexandria, Pitsunda wom Wch (7) 1975.

B)

4...d4

Black aims both to gain space in the centre and to cut across White's natural plans of d2-d3 hitting the black knight or d2-d4 forming a strong centre. In turn White should now play...

5 ♘f3 *(D)*

This not only develops a piece but more importantly puts pressure on d4.

5...♘c6

5...♗g4 6 c3 ♘c6 transposes to the main line, while 5...c5? 6 c3! is very

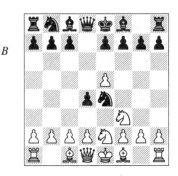

strong for White because 6...dxc3? 7 ♕a4+ wins a piece, as does 6...♘c6? 7 d3.

6 c3 ♗g4 7 ♘exd4! ♘xe5

7...♘xd4 8 ♕a4+! regains the piece with advantage.

8 ♕e2 ♕d5 9 ♘b5!

This idea is credited to Jürgen Graf.

9...0-0-0

After 9...♖c8!? 10 c4 ♕e6 11 ♕xe4 ♗xf3 12 ♕e3! ♗g4 13 f3 ♗f5 14 ♘xa7 ♖d8 15 ♘b5 ♖d7 16 b3 c6 17 ♗b2 ♘xf3+ 18 gxf3 cxb5 19 ♕xe6 ♗xe6 20 c5! Black is in trouble.

10 c4!

This is the rather unusual idea behind 9 ♘b5!.

10...♕e6

10...♘d3+? 11 ♕xd3 ♕xd3 12 ♗xd3 ♖xd3 13 ♘e5 wins material.

11 d4 ♘d3+

11...♗xf3!? 12 gxf3 ♘d3+ 13 ♕xd3 ♘g3+ 14 ♕e3! ♘xh1 15 ♕xe6+ fxe6 16 ♗e3! and White will pick up the knight on h1 at his leisure.

12 ♕xd3 ♘g3+

12...♗xf3 13 d5 ♕e5 14 ♕e3! ♗h5 15 f3 a6 16 ♘c3 wins.

13 ♗e2 ♘xh1 14 ♘xa7+ ♔b8 15 ♘b5

Black is busted.

C)

4...f6!? *(D)*

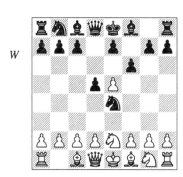

This move is well motivated, and not as strange as it first looks. Not only does it attack White's unsupported central pawn on e5 but also gives the knight the possibility of redeveloping once it leaves e4 to the f7-square via g5.

5 d3

Black can choose between two continuations:

C1:	**5...♘c5?!**	204
C2:	**5...♘g5**	205

C1)

5...♘c5?! 6 d4! ♘e4

After 6...♘e6?! 7 f4 White is doing well, e.g. 7...f5 8 g4! or 7...c5? 8 f5! ♘xd4 9 ♘xd4 cxd4 10 e6! was good for White in Tolnai-Karolyi, Kecskemet 1990. Black probably needs to try 7...fxe5!? or 7...g6!? but neither is that inspiring.

7 f3 ♘g5 8 ♗xg5 fxg5 9 ♕d3!

White has the better of it since he intends to castle queenside and then open up the kingside to his advantage. Meanwhile Black is undeveloped and his king is stuck in the centre.

C2)

5...②g5 6 ②xg5 fxg5 7 h4! *(D)*

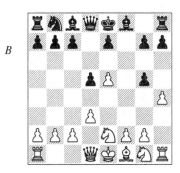

A logical move to remove Black's pawn from g5 so as to be able to occupy f4 with a knight and at last enabling White to untangle his minor pieces for development. After this Black must decide between capturing on h4 or pushing his pawn to g4:

C21: 7...gxh4?! 205
C22: 7...g4 205

Hitting back at White's pawn on e5 with 7...②c6? works out badly due to 8 d4 ②f5 9 ②g3 ②g6 10 ②d3! ②f7 11 hxg5 ②xd4 12 g6! ②e6 13 ③xh7 ③g8 14 c3 ②c6 15 f4 ②d7 16 ②f3 e6 17 ②h5 1-0 Vajda-Appleberry, Budapest 1996.

C21)

7...gxh4?! 8 ②f4 g6 9 ③xh4 ②g7 10 d4 c5 11 ②d3 ♛a5+ 12 ♔f1 cxd4 13 ③xh7! ③xh7 14 ②xg6+ ♔d8 15 ②xh7 ②xe5 16 ♛f3

White's position is more comfortable, for example 16...②c6 17 ②xd5 ②e6 18 ♛f8+ ♔d7 19 ♛xa8 ♛b5+ 20 ②d3 ♛xb2 21 ②b6+ ♛xb6 22 ②f3, Vorotnikov-Kengis, Riga 1983, or

16...②xf4 17 ♛xf4 ②c6 18 ②f3 ♛c7 19 ♛f8+ ♔d7 20 ③e1, Polovodin-Palatnik, USSR Spartakiad 1979.

C22)

7...g4

Normally the player with the two bishops would prefer to open up the position, but this is an exception. Black wisely wants to keep the h-file closed and, while giving up the f4-square for White's knight on e2, takes away f3 and h3 for the knight as yet undeveloped on g1.

8 d4!

Better than 8 ②f4 d4!, when Black is comfortable.

8...c5!?

A bold attempt to gain the initiative as 8...②f5? 9 ②g3 ②g6 10 h5! is very powerful and other tries on move eight for Black just seem a little too passive.

9 dxc5 ②c6!

9...e6?! 10 ②d4 ②xc5 11 ♛xg4 ②xd4!? (after 11...0-0?! 12 ②gf3 White is a pawn ahead with everything under control) 12 ♛xd4 ②c6 13 ♛g4 0-0 14 ②f3 ♛b6 15 0-0-0 ♛xf2 16 ②d3 and White's attacking chances give him the advantage, J.Sørensen-Burgess, Århus 1991.

10 ②f4 g6 11 ♛xd5 ♛a5+

After 11...②f5 12 ②c4! ♛xd5 13 ②xd5 ②g7 14 0-0-0 ②xe5 15 ②ge2 Black has insufficient play for the pawn.

12 c3 ②h6

Thus far we have been following the game Baker-Burgess, Bristol 1991.

13 ②ge2! ②f5

13...③f8 14 g3 ②f5 15 ②d4 ②xd4 (15...②xf4 16 ②xc6!) 16 ♛xd4 ③d8

17 ♕e3! and despite his activity Black still has to prove adequate compensation for the material invested.

14 b4 ♕a3 15 ♕b3 ♕xb3 16 axb3 ♘xe5 17 ♖d1 ♗c2

17...0-0!? calmly seeks play against the queenside pawns and is less committal than the text-move.

18 ♖d5 ♘d7

18...♖d8 19 ♖xd8+ ♔xd8 20 ♘e6+ ♔d7 21 ♘2d4 and White is better.

19 ♘d4 ♗e4!

19...♗xb3?! 20 ♘xb3 ♗xf4 21 ♗b5 ♖d8 22 ♘a5 and Black is in trouble.

20 ♗b5! ♗xd5

20...♖d8!? leads to great complications, for example 21 ♘de6! ♗xf4 22 ♖d4 ♗xg2 23 ♘xd8 ♗xh1 24 ♗xd7+ ♔xd8 25 ♗xg4+ ♔c7 26 ♖xf4 and White is a good pawn ahead.

After 20...0-0-0!?, 21 c6! is White's best try for advantage.

21 ♘xd5

This is difficult for Black to meet.

11 Scandinavian Defence

1 e4 d5

The idea of the move is quite straightforward in that it immediately both occupies and challenges the centre.

2 exd5

This is White's only real attempt for an advantage. Black now has the choice between the positional 2...♕xd5 (Part 1) and the more tactically based 2...♘f6 (Part 2), a move which is quite often played with a gambit in mind. This chapter will now split into two parts depending on which Black opts for.

Part 1

1 e4 d5 2 exd5 ♕xd5

This was the original idea behind 1...d5. Black hopes that despite the fact he will have to lose time with his queen after 3 ♘c3 in the long term he will have the freedom to develop his minor pieces to decent squares and that White will have 'nothing special' in terms of central pawn occupation. Recently 2...♕xd5 has undergone a revival based on some new ideas for Black and due to the casualness with which White tends to approach the move. White's main chance of an opening advantage is in my opinion to use this temporary lead in development to build up momentum for an initiative based on early active minor-piece play.

3 ♘c3 *(D)*

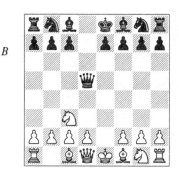

B

Black now has the choice between:

A: 3...♕d6!? 207
B: 3...♕d8 208
C: 3...♕a5 209

A)

3...♕d6!?

A rather odd-looking square for the queen. White should develop normally and look at exploiting his lead in development and the position of Black's queen when the opportunity arises.

4 d4 ♘f6 5 ♘f3 a6!

Black needs to 'invest' a move to stop either a white bishop or knight coming to b5 at an inopportune moment. After 5...♗g4?! 6 h3 ♗h5 7 g4! ♗g6 8 ♘e5 c6 9 ♗f4 ♘d5 10 ♕d2 ♘xf4 11 ♕xf4 ♘d7 12 0-0-0 ♘xe5 13 dxe5 ♕c7 14 ♗d3 ♗xd3 15 ♖xd3 g6 16 ♘e4 White has a massive lead in development, Psakhis-Sygulski, Jurmala 1987.

6 ♗e2 e6

6...♘c6 7 0-0 ♗g4 8 ♗e3 e6 9 ♕d2 ♗e7 10 ♖ad1 ♗xf3?! 11 ♗xf3 0-0-0 12 ♕c1 ♘b4 13 a3 ♘bd5 14 ♘xd5 exd5 15 c4! dxc4 16 ♗f4 ♕b6 17 ♕xc4 ♖d7 18 ♗e5 ♚b8 19 ♖d3 ♕b5 20 ♕c2 ♘d5 1-0 L.Schneider-D.Gurevich, Eksjö 1992. 21 ♖b3 ♕a5 22 ♕c6 wins.

7 0-0 ♘bd7

7...♗e7!? may be a better try for equality although after 8 ♘e5! ♘c6 9 ♘xc6 ♕xc6 10 ♗f3 ♕d6, 11 ♘e2! is an improvement on 11 g3, Rozentalis-Bronstein, Reykjavik 1996, and should offer White a slight advantage.

8 ♗g5 c5 9 ♗h4 cxd4 10 ♘xd4 ♗e7 11 ♗g3 ♕b6 12 ♘b3 0-0 13 a4 *(D)*

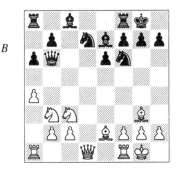

White has the advantage as although the pawn-structure is identical to the variation in the French Tarrasch 1 e4 e6 2 d4 d5 3 ♘d2 c5 4 exd5 ♕xd5 5 ♘gf3 cxd4 6 ♗c4 ♕d6 7 0-0 ♘f6 8 ♘b3 ♘c6 9 ♘bxd4, etc. The important difference is that the White's bishop controls the important diagonal h2-b8.

B)

3...♕d8

A passive-looking retreat, the main idea of which was originally to fianchetto Black's dark-squared bishop but in view of what happens to him in Line B1 Black now tries to follow up with development along more classical lines.

4 d4

Now Black can choose between:

B1: 4...g6?! 208
B2: 4...♗f5?! 209
B3: 4...♘f6 209

Others such as 4...c6 or 4...e6 tend to transpose to 4...♘f6 lines but offer less flexibility.

B1)

4...g6?!

Not a popular choice since Fischer gave Robatsch a mauling in the 1962 Olympiad.

5 ♗f4! ♗g7 6 ♕d2 ♘f6

Black will suffer badly if he captures on d4, as Fischer analysed: 6...♗xd4? 7 0-0-0 ♘c6 8 ♗b5 ♗d7 9 ♘d5! e5 10 ♘f3 or 6...♕xd4 7 ♕xd4 ♗xd4 8 ♘b5 ♗b6 9 ♘xc7+ ♗xc7 10 ♗xc7 and Black has no compensation for White's bishop-pair.

7 0-0-0 c6 8 ♗h6 0-0 9 h4! ♕a5 10 h5 gxh5 11 ♗d3 ♘bd7 12 ♘ge2 ♖d8 13 g4! ♘f8

After 13...♘xg4?! 14 ♖dg1! Black will find it hard to meet the threats, while 13...hxg4? loses to 14 ♗xg7 ♚xg7 15 ♕h6+ ♚h8 16 ♗xh7.

14 gxh5 ♘e6 15 ♖dg1 ♚h8 16 ♗xg7+ ♘xg7 17 ♕h6 ♖g8 18 ♖g5 ♕d8 19 ♖hg1 ♘f5 20 ♗xf5

1-0 Fischer-Robatsch, Varna OL 1962.

B2)

4...♗f5?!

It is logical enough in itself to develop the light-squared bishop outside the pawn-chain. However, in conjunction with 3...♕d8, it offers little chance of equality for Black due to his lack of development, e.g.:

5 ♘f3 e6 6 ♗c4 ♗b4 7 0-0 ♗xc3?! 8 bxc3 h6 9 ♘e5 ♘f6 10 ♗a3

White already has a strong edge on account of the bishop-pair and dark-square control particularly on the a3-f8 diagonal, Steinitz-Long, Dublin 1865.

B3)

4...♘f6 5 ♘f3 c6 6 h3! *(D)*

White can afford to use some of the time he has gained to play this move and stop Black developing his light-squared bishop to its most natural square, g4.

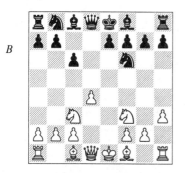

6...e6?!

6...♗f5!? would appear a more logical approach than 'shutting the bishop in'.

7 ♗e2 ♗e7 8 0-0 ♘bd7 9 ♗g5 ♘b6 10 ♕d2 ♘bd5 11 ♘xd5 cxd5 12 ♗d3 ♗d7 13 ♖fe1 ♗c6 14 ♘e5 0-0

15 ♕e2 ♕e8 16 c3 ♘d7 17 ♗f4 ♘xe5 18 ♗xe5 f6 19 ♗g3 ♗d7

Now 20 ♗f5! is very strong (and an improvement on Radocaj-N.Zecević, Croatian Cht (Opatija) 1995).

C)

3...♕a5

The usual choice.

4 d4 *(D)*

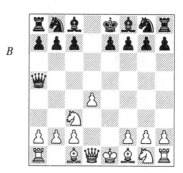

Now Black can choose from:

As Line C5, 4...♘f6, is regarded as the main line, in which Black can play the moves ...♘f6, ...♗f5 and ...c6 in virtually any order, Lines C3 and C4 will only deal with independent plans for Black.

C1)

4...g6?!

An unusual move in this type of position which has little practical experience.

5 ♘f3 ♗g7 6 ♗c4 c5?!

Now instead of 7 0-0?!, as in Mu-jagić-Nemety, Budapest 1989, 7 ♘e5! seems to get White a nice position because after 7...e6 he can play 8 ♗b5+! meeting a black king move with ♕f3. Instead 7...♗xe5 is hardly inspiring.

C2)
4...e5

Black attempts to obtain equality by exchanging off all of the central pawns. While this is a logical idea in itself, with accurate play White can obtain a good lead in development and a promising initiative.

5 ♘f3

White doesn't fear Black exchanging immediately on d4 as this will give him a well-centralized knight that will not only cause Black problems due to its location but will also restrict Black's development and be difficult to shift, e.g. 5...exd4 6 ♘xd4 ♘f6 7 ♗e2 c6 8 0-0 ♗e7 9 ♗f4 0-0 10 ♘b3 ♕f5 11 ♗g3 ♕g6 12 a3 ♖d8 13 ♗d3 ♗f5 14 ♖e1 ♖e8 15 ♗xf5 ♕xf5 16 ♖e5 ♕c8 17 ♕e2 and without having done anything special White's advantage is obvious on account of his lead in development and control of the e-file, Hardicsay-Laszlo, Hungarian Cht 1992.

5...e4? allows 6 ♕e2! ♘f6 7 ♗d2 ♕f5 8 ♘g5, when Black will lose a pawn for nothing.

Therefore Black should chose between:

C21)
5...♗b4?! 6 ♗d2 exd4

6...♗g4?! 7 a3! ♗d6 8 h3 exd4? 9 hxg4! dxc3 10 ♗xc3 ♕b6 11 ♗xg7 winning, Ralls-Senter, IECC 1996.

7 ♕e2+ ♘e7 8 ♘xd4 0-0 9 a3

Now:

a) 9...♘bc6!? is an interesting try when White must be careful to unravel his pieces before enjoying his material advantage, i.e. 10 ♘b3 ♕f5 11 axb4 ♕xc2 12 ♘c1! ♘f5 (12...♕xb2 13 ♖b1 ♕a3 14 ♘b5 wins; 12...♗e6 13 ♘d3 is good for White) 13 ♕e4 and White has consolidated.

b) 9...♗d6 10 ♘db5 ♕b6 11 0-0-0 ♗e6 12 ♗g5! ♘g6 13 ♘xd6 cxd6 14 h4 ♘c6 15 ♗e3 ♕a5 16 h5 ♘ge5 17 ♖h4! d5 18 h6 g6 19 f4 ♘c4 20 f5! ♘xe3 21 ♕xe3 ♗xf5 22 ♘xd5 ♖ad8 23 b4! ♕a4 24 ♕c3 ♘e5 25 ♘e7+ ♔h8 26 ♕xe5+ f6 27 ♕xf6+! 1-0 Tal-Skuja, Latvian Ch 1958. Tal knew how to handle these type of positions!

C22)
5...♗g4 6 h3!

This move immediately puts Black under pressure by forcing him to commit himself.

6...♗xf3

6...exd4?! 7 ♕xd4 ♗xf3 8 ♕e3+ ♗e7 9 ♕xf3 c6 10 ♗c4 ♘f6 11 0-0 0-0 12 ♖e1 ♗d6 13 ♗d2 ♕c7 and White has the edge due to his bishop-pair and lead in development, Schumi-Babar, Dortmund 1992. In particular Black will notice the weakness on his light squares around the centre and his kingside.

7 ♕xf3 ♘d7

7...♗b4?! 8 ♕xb7 ♗xc3+ 9 ♔d1! ♗xd4 10 ♕xa8 ♕b6 11 f4 and Black has insufficient counterplay in return for the exchange, Cornell-C.Smith, corr. 1995.

8 ♗d2 ♗b4 9 0-0-0 ♘gf6 10 dxe5 ♘xe5 11 ♗b5+! ♕xb5

11...c6 12 ♖he1 ♘fd7 13 ♗f4 ♗xc3 14 ♕xc3 ♕xc3 15 bxc3 f6 16 ♗d3 favours White in view of his bishop-pair.

12 ♘xb5 ♗xd2+ 13 ♖xd2 ♘xf3 14 ♘xc7+ ♔f8 15 gxf3 ♖c8 16 ♖e1

White is in complete command, Blazkova-Stankova, Czech wom Ch 1996.

C3)

4...♗f5 5 ♘f3 c6 6 ♘e5! ♘d7?!

6...f6?! 7 ♘c4 ♕d8 8 ♗f4 e6 9 ♘e3 ♗g6 10 ♗c4 ♗f7 11 0-0 is obviously better for White, Showalter-Hanham, New York 1893.

7 ♘c4!

This is much better than 7 ♕f3 e6!, when White has no advantage.

7...♕c7 8 ♕f3 ♗xc2 9 ♗f4

Black is struggling.

C4)

4...c6 5 ♘f3

Now Black can try:

5...h6? has been tried but is not a move I understand in that it doesn't assist in development and appears to create a further weakness on Black's kingside. After the thematic 6 ♘e5 Black seems to be just a tempo behind other variations.

5...♗f5 6 ♘e5 ♘d7 transposes to Line C3.

C41)

5...♗g4 6 h3 *(D)*

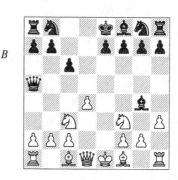

6...♗h5

6...♗xf3 7 ♕xf3 ♘f6 8 ♗c4 e6 9 ♗d2 ♕d8 10 0-0-0 ♗e7 (10...♕xd4 11 ♗b3 ♗e7 12 ♗e3 ♕h4 13 ♘b5! ♘a6 14 ♖d4 ♕h5 15 ♘d6+ ♗xd6 16 ♕xh5 ♘xh5 17 ♖xd6 and with the bishop-pair and control of the d-file, White has adequate compensation for the pawn) 11 ♗f4 gives White an edge due to his bishop-pair, extra space and lead in development, Torres-Arnold, Thessaloniki OL 1984.

7 g4 ♗g6 8 ♘e5 e6 9 ♗g2 ♘f6 10 h4 ♗e4 11 ♗xe4 ♘xe4 12 ♕f3 ♘d6 13 ♗f4! f6

13...♘a6? is a blunder due to 14 ♘xc6!, Gufeld-Korolev, Russia 1985.

13...♘b5!? leads to interesting play after 14 ♘xf7!? ♘xd4 15 ♕e4 ♘xc2+ 16 ♕xc2 ♔xf7 17 0-0-0, when White has good play for the pawn.

14 ♘d3 ♘b5?!

14...♘d7 15 0-0-0 0-0-0 16 ♖he1 ♖e8 and White is slightly better.

15 0-0! ♘xd4?!

15...♘xc3 16 bxc3 ♕xc3 17 ♕e4 ♕c4 18 ♖ab1 is uncomfortable for Black.

16 ♕e4 ♕d8

16...e5? loses to 17 ♘xe5! fxe5 18 ♗xe5 ♘e6 19 ♗xb8.

17 ♖ad1 ♕d7 18 ♗e3! c5 19 ♘xc5! ♗xc5 20 ♗xd4 ♗xd4 21 ♖xd4 ♕c6 22 ♖fd1!

Despite the simplifications Black has failed to equalize, Popović-I.Rogers, Vršac 1987.

C42)
5...♘f6 6 ♘e5 *(D)*

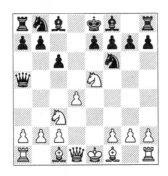

Now 6...♗f5 has traditionally been the main line, when 7 ♗c4 transposes to Line C5. Here we deal with alternatives.

6...♗e6

6...♘bd7 is a tough nut to crack, though surprisingly rare in practice. 7 ♘c4 ♕d8 (7...♕c7 8 ♕f3 ♘b6 9 ♗g5!? ♗g4 10 ♕g3 ♕xg3 11 hxg3 ♖d8 12 ♘e3 ♗e6 13 ♗xf6 exf6 14 0-0-0 gives White a useful queenside majority, Suetin-Kasüschke, Bad Wörishofen seniors Wch 1992) 8 ♗e2 e6 9 0-0 ♗e7 has been generally claimed as a little better for White on the basis of Black's cramped queenside, but with no real guidance as to how White should maintain his edge. 10 f4 (a little ugly, but nailing down e5) 10...0-0 11 ♗f3 c5 12 ♗e3 cxd4 13 ♗xd4 ♕c7 and now, rather than 14 ♘e5 ♗c5, which left Black with few problems in Kostić-Puc, Yugoslav Ch (Zagreb) 1946, 14 ♕d3 should keep some pressure, e.g. 14...♘c5 15 ♕e3, 14...♗c5 15 ♘b5 or 14...a6 15 ♖ad1 ♖d8.

7 ♘c4

This move will take many opponents by surprise; it has scored well, but is quite rare – for instance it is not mentioned in John Emms's book on the Scandinavian.

7...♗xc4

Or:

a) 7...♕d8 8 ♗e2 g6 9 0-0 ♗g7 10 a4 a5 11 ♗f4 0-0 12 ♕d2 ♘a6 13 ♖ad1 gave White a stable advantage in Reyes-Dončević, San Fernando 1991. After 13...♘b4 14 ♖fe1 ♘bd5 15 ♘xd5 cxd5 16 ♘a3 ♘e4 17 ♕e3 ♘d6 18 c3 b6 19 ♘b5 ♘xb5 20 ♗xb5 White's positional pluses were evident.

b) 7...♕c7!? 8 a4 (it is not clear that this is necessary; is Black really intending a quick ...b5 here? 8 ♗e2 and especially 8 ♗g5!? come into consideration) 8...g6 9 ♗e2 ♗g7 10 ♗g5 ♘bd7 11 ♕d2 ♖d8 12 ♗f4 (since this arrives one move too late to cause real inconvenience, perhaps White should have prepared it sooner) 12...♕c8 13 0-0 and White retained just a slight spatial plus in Kuczynski-Gomez Baillo, Novi Sad OL 1990.

8 ♗xc4

Now that White has the advantage of the bishop-pair, he can expect a pull in many types of simplified position.

8...e6

Here are two examples of play from this point:

a) 9 0-0 ♗e7 10 ♕d3 ♘bd7 11 ♘e4 ♖d8 12 ♗f4 0-0 13 c3 ♘h5!? (13...e5 14 b4 ♕c7 15 ♗g3) 14 ♗d6 ♗xd6 15 ♘xd6 ♕g5!? (15...♕c7 invites 16 ♘xf7 ♖xf7 {16...♔xf7 17 ♕f5+ ♘df6 18 ♕xe6+ ♔g6 19 g4} 17 ♗xe6, when White will have rook and two pawns versus two knights) 16 ♕f3 (16 ♘xb7 ♘e5 17 f4! ♘xf4 18 ♕e4 ♘xc4 19 ♘xd8 ♘h3+ 20 ♔h1 ♘d2! 21 ♕xe6! is unclear) 16...♘b6 17 ♘e4 ♕f5 18 ♗e2 ♘f4 19 ♖fe1 ♘xe2+ 20 ♕xe2 and Black has almost equalized, Rabiega-Beliavsky, Austrian League 1996/7.

b) 9 ♕e2 ♘bd7 10 ♗d2 ♗b4 11 0-0 0-0 12 a3 ♗xc3 13 ♗xc3 ♕c7 14 g3 b5 15 ♗d3 ♘b6 16 b3 a5 17 ♕e5 ♘bd5 18 ♗d2 ♕xe5 19 dxe5 ♘d7 20 ♖fe1 and White was able to exploit his extra space and bishop-pair in the game Mainka-Mathonia, Bundesliga 1995/6.

C5)
4...♘f6 5 ♘f3 ♗f5 6 ♘e5 c6 7 ♗c4 e6 8 g4 *(D)*

The critical position. Now Black can choose between:
C51: 8...♗e4?!   213
C52: 8...♗g6   213

C51)
8...♗e4?! 9 0-0 ♗d5 10 ♗d3 ♗d6

After 10...♘bd7 11 f4 h6 12 ♗e3 h5 13 g5 ♘g4 14 ♘xg4 hxg4 15 ♕xg4 g6 16 a3 and White has the better position as well as being a pawn ahead, Søbjerg-Sinkbæk, Denmark 1994.

10...c5?! 11 ♘xd5 ♘xd5 12 c4 ♘f6 13 d5! is also strong for White.

11 f4 c5 12 g5! cxd4 13 ♘b5 ♗c5

13...♘e4? 14 ♖e1 ♗b4 15 ♖xe4 ♗xe4 16 ♘c4 ♕xb5 17 ♘d6+ ♗xd6 18 ♗xb5+ wins.

14 f5! ♘c6 15 ♗f4! ♘xe5 16 ♗xe5 0-0-0 17 fxe6 ♗c6

17...fxe6?! 18 gxf6 gxf6 19 ♖xf6 ♖hg8+ 20 ♗g3 and White is a clear piece ahead.

18 exf7 ♖d5 19 gxf6 g6

19...♖xe5 20 ♕g4+ ♗d7 21 fxg7! wins.

20 ♕e1?!

Up to now we have been following Aseev-Koenig, Munich 1990 but instead of 20 ♕e1?!, even better would have been 20 ♕g4+! ♗d7 21 ♕e4 ♗c6 22 ♗g3, winning outright.

C52)
8...♗g6 9 ♗d2 ♕b6

After 9...♘bd7, 10 ♕e2 with the idea of castling queenside is strong, for example 10...♘xe5 11 dxe5 ♘d7 12 f4 ♗b4 13 a3 0-0-0 14 0-0-0 ♗xc3 15 ♗xc3 ♕c7 16 ♖df1 ♘b6 17 f5 exf5 18 gxf5 ♗h5 19 ♕xh5 ♘xc4 20 f6 ♖d7 21 fxg7 ♖g8 22 e6 fxe6 23 ♖f8+

♖d8 24 ♖xg8 ♖xg8 25 ♖f1 1-0 German-Garcia, Buenos Aires 1995.

10 ♕e2!? ♘bd7

10...♕xb2? 11 ♖b1 ♕xc2 (11...♕a3 12 ♖xb7 with the idea of ♘xg6 followed by ♖xf7 is winning) 12 ♖xb7 ♗e7 13 ♘xf7! ♗xf7 (13...♔xf7? 14 ♕xe6+ ♔f8 15 ♕xe7#) 14 ♗d3 wins the queen.

10...♕xd4 11 0-0-0 ♘bd7 12 ♘xg6 hxg6 13 ♗xe6! fxe6 14 ♕xe6+ ♗e7 (14...♖d8?? 15 ♗g5 wins outright) 15 ♖he1 0-0-0 16 ♕xe7 and White has the advantage.

11 f4 0-0-0

11...♕xd4? 12 ♘f3 ♕b6 13 f5 wins a piece.

12 0-0-0 ♘xe5

12...♗b4 13 h4 is better for White.

13 dxe5 ♘d5 14 ♖hf1 h6 15 f5 ♗h7 16 ♖f3 ♗e7

After 16...♘xc3 17 ♗xc3 ♖xd1+ 18 ♕xd1 exf5 19 gxf5 ♕c7 20 e6 White's advantage is obvious.

17 ♘xd5 cxd5 18 ♖b3! ♕d4

18...♕c7? 19 ♗a6! wins, as does 18...♕c6? 19 ♗b5.

19 ♗a6! ♖d7

19...bxa6? 20 ♕xa6+ ♔d7 21 ♕b5+ ♔c7 22 ♕b7#.

20 ♗xb7+

1-0 Trindade-Soppe, São Paulo Z 1993. 20...♖xb7 21 ♕a6 ♕b6 22 ♖xb6 axb6 23 ♕a8+ ♖b8 24 ♕c6+ ♔d8 25 ♗e3 ♗g5 26 ♗xg5+ hxg5 27 ♕d6+ ♔c8 28 ♖d3.

Part 2

1 e4 d5 2 exd5 ♘f6

Already it is time for White to make a choice. He can try to hang on to the extra pawn with 3 c4 and prepare to meet the gambits Black can play with 3...c6!? or 3...e6!?. This is quite reasonable, especially if after 3...c6!? White wishes to transpose to the Panov Attack with 4 d4. On the other hand he can play calmly for a small positional edge by playing 3 d4 to meet 3...♘xd5 with 4 c4, although Black may also cross this plan by playing 3...♗g4!?. However, neither of these options is likely to 'startle' your opponent and for this reason I am opting for 3 ♗b5+!?, a move which immediately unbalances the position and requires careful play by both players.

3 ♗b5+!? *(D)*

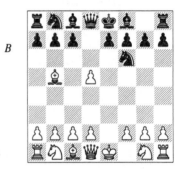

Now Black must decide between:

A: 3...♗d7   214
B: 3...♘bd7   216
C: 3...c6!?   217

A)

3...♗d7

A very natural response, especially as 4 ♗xd7+ ♕xd7 5 c4 c6! offers White no advantage. Because of this White should avoid the exchange of bishops and instead retreat by playing either the solid 4 ♗e2 hoping to make Black's extra move of ...♗c8-d7 a liability rather than an asset or, as I recommend, 4 ♗c4, which puts the onus on Black to show he has enough compensation for the pawn.

4 ♗c4

Black can now choose between:

A1: 4...g6?! 215
A2: 4...c6?! 215
A3: 4...b5 215
A4: 4...♗g4 216

A1)

4...g6?!

Black hopes to show by normal development that he can gain enough positional compensation for the pawn but in reality this is not the case. After 5 ♘c3 ♗g7 6 ♘f3 0-0 7 0-0 ♗g4 8 h3! ♗xf3 9 ♕xf3 ♘bd7 10 ♖e1 ♘b6 11 d3 a6 12 a4 ♘xc4 13 dxc4 ♖e8 14 ♗f4 ♕d7 15 ♗e5! White has a good position and is a pawn ahead, Narciso-Hidalgo, Catalan Ch 1995.

A2)

4...c6?! 5 ♘c3! ♗g4

5...cxd5 6 ♘xd5 ♘xd5 7 ♗xd5 ♘c6 8 ♘f3 is good for White because Black has no real compensation for the pawn, especially as 8...♗g4?? allows 9 ♗xf7+ ♔xf7 10 ♘g5+.

6 f3 cxd5 7 ♘xd5 ♘xd5 8 fxg4 e6 9 ♘f3 ♗c5 10 d4

10 c3! may be even better as 10...0-0 (10...♘f4? 11 d4 ♘xg2+ 12 ♔f2 wins) 11 d4 ♗d6 12 0-0 is fine for White.

10...♗b6

10...♗b4+?! 11 c3 ♘xc3 12 bxc3 ♗xc3+ 13 ♗d2 ♗xa1 14 ♕xa1 is better for White.

11 0-0 ♘c6 12 c3 0-0

White is well placed, Kun-Visloczki, Hungary 1994.

A3)

4...b5 5 ♗b3

Black has now tried:

A31: 5...a5 215
A32: 5...♗g4 216

A31)

5...a5 6 a3

With the following possibilities:

a) 6...c5?! 7 dxc6 ♘xc6 8 ♘f3 e6 9 ♕e2! and White's long-term prospects are good.

b) 6...♘a6 7 d4 ♗g4 8 ♕d3! a4 9 ♗a2 ♕d7 10 c4 b4!? 11 ♘d2 e6 12 dxe6 ♗xe6 13 ♘gf3 ♗d6 14 0-0 0-0 15 ♗b1 and White is already better, for example 15...g6 16 ♘h4 ♕e7 17 ♘df3, Brychta-Stulik, Czechoslovakian Ch 1991.

c) 6...♗g4 7 f3 ♗c8 (7...♗f5? 8 ♘c3 a4 9 ♗a2 ♕d7 10 d4 e6 11 dxe6 fxe6 12 ♕e2! c6 13 g4 ♗g6 14 ♗xe6 ♕xd4 15 ♘xb5! 1-0 Langschmidt-Weteschnik, Dortmund 1993) 8 ♘c3 ♗a6 9 ♘ge2 g6 (9...♘bd7 10 ♘d4 ♘c5 11 ♘c6 ♕d7 12 ♘xa5 ♗c8 13 d4! ♘a4 14 ♗xa4 ♖xa4 15 ♗b3 b4 16 ♘e4 ♘xd5 17 ♘c5 and Black is struggling) 10 a4! b4 11 ♘b5 ♗xb5 12 axb5 ♘xd5 13 c4 ♘f6 14 d4 ♗g7 15 ♗e3 0-0 16 0-0 ♘bd7 17 c5 and White has a nice positional advantage due to his bishop-pair and control of the light squares as long as he controls Black's ...e5 break, e.g. 17...e6 18 ♗f2 ♕e7 19 ♖e1 ♖fd8 20 ♕c2 ♘f8 21 ♖a4 ♘d5 22 ♖ea1 e5 23 ♕e4! ♘f6 24 ♕xe5 Kneževic-Ippolito, France 1997.

A32)
5...♗g4 6 f3 ♗c8!

Having taken the square f3 at least temporarily away from White's knight and hopefully created a weakness, Black retreats his bishop to fight another day. It is far better for Black to fall back to c8 than to play ...♗h5, where it would be a target for either a white pawn thrust or a knight going to f4.

7 ♕e2

After this move Black has tried the following:

a) 7...♗a6 8 ♕e5! (the start of a subtle queen manoeuvre; despite taking three moves to reach its destination Black seems unable to exploit the loss of time) 8...♘bd7 9 ♕d4 ♘b6 10 ♕c5! ♕d7 11 ♘c3 e6!? 12 dxe6 ♗xc5 13 exd7+ ♔xd7 14 ♘ge2 ♖ae8 15 d3! (with the idea of ♘e4) 15...♗b4 16 0-0 and White has excellent chances of finishing his development and making the extra pawn tell.

b) 7...♗a6 8 a4 b4 9 c4! bxc3 10 ♘xc3 ♗b7 11 ♕c4 ♕d6 12 ♘e4! ♘xe4 13 fxe4 ♘d7 14 ♘f3 0-0-0 15 0-0 e6 16 dxe6 ♘b6 (Odler-Groch, Slovakian League 1994) 17 e5! ♕e7 18 ♕g4 seems strong for White.

A4)
4...♗g4 5 ♘f3 ♘xd5

5...♘bd7?! 6 d4 a6 (6...♘b6 ♗b5+! ♗d7 8 ♕e2 ♘bxd5 9 ♗xd7+ ♕xd7 10 ♘e5 ♕a4 11 c4 ♕a5+ 12 ♘d2 ♘b4 13 0-0 is good for White) 7 ♗b3! b5 8 h3 ♗h5 9 a4 ♘b6 10 axb5 axb5 11 ♖xa8 ♕xa8 12 ♕d3! and Black has failed to find equality.

6 h3! ♗h5 7 d4 e6 8 0-0 ♗e7 9 ♘bd2 0-0 10 c3 c5!

It's necessary for Black to aim for a central break to avoid becoming too passive.

11 dxc5 ♗xc5 12 ♘e4 ♗e7 13 ♘g3 ♘b6

13...♗g6 14 ♘e5 ♘c6 15 ♘xg6 hxg6 16 ♕e2 and White has a small but lasting edge.

14 ♗e2 ♗g6 15 ♘e5 ♕xd1 16 ♗xd1!

16 ♖xd1?! ♗c2! 17 ♖d2 ♗a4 18 b3 ♗f6! is unclear.

16...♖d8 17 ♗f3

Black has problems, Moizhess-Truus, Moscow 1996.

B)
3...♘bd7

Black intends to gain time by following this up with ...a6 forcing White to make a decision between ♗a4 and conceding the bishop-pair.

4 c4 a6 5 ♗xd7+ ♗xd7 6 d4 e6

6...b5!? 7 b3 e6 8 dxe6 ♗xe6 9 d5 ♗g4 10 f3 ♗f5 11 ♘e2 ♗c5 12 ♗b2 ♕e7 13 ♗d4! ♗xd4 14 ♕xd4 0-0 15 ♔f2 ♖ad8 16 ♘bc3 b4 17 ♘g3! ♕d7 18 ♘ce2 c6 19 dxc6! ♕xc6?? 20 ♘xf5 ♕e6 21 ♕f4 1-0 Anand-Galego, Oviedo rpd 1993.

7 dxe6 ♗xe6

7...♕e7!?.

8 d5 ♗g4 9 ♘f3 ♗b4+ 10 ♗d2 ♕e7+ 11 ♕e2 ♘e4 12 ♗xb4 ♕xb4+ 13 ♘c3 0-0 14 a3 *(D)*

The critical position.

14...♕b6!

14...♘xc3!? 15 axb4 ♘xe2 16 ♔xe2 ♖ae8+ 17 ♔d3 ♗f5+ 18 ♔c3 ♖e2 19 ♖hf1 ♖c2+ 20 ♔b3 ♗d3 21 ♖fd1! ♗f5 22 ♖d2 ♖xd2 23 ♘xd2 ♖e8 24 ♘f3 ♖e2 25 ♖e1! and White

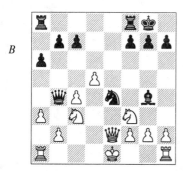

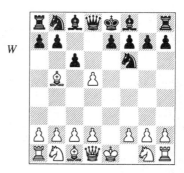

has good chances of winning the end-game.

14...♗xf3!? 15 axb4 ♗xe2 16 ♘xe2 ♖fe8 17 f3 ♘d6 18 ♖c1 a5 19 b5 ♖e3 20 ♔d2 ♖ae8 21 ♘d4 and White is better.

15 ♘xe4 ♖ae8 16 0-0 f5 17 ♕e3 ♕xe3 18 fxe3 ♖xe4 19 ♘g5! ♖xe3

19...♖xc4?! 20 ♘e6 ♖f7 21 ♖fc1 and White has the advantage.

20 ♖ae1 f4 21 ♖xe3 fxe3 22 ♖xf8+ ♔xf8 23 ♘xh7+ ♔e7 24 ♘g5 ♔f6 25 ♘f3!

White should win the ending with careful play.

C)

3...c6!? *(D)*

Black immediately reveals his intentions by sacrificing a pawn hoping to gain enough compensation in the form of a lead in development and extra space.

4 dxc6 bxc6

4...♘xc6?! 5 d4 ♕b6 6 ♗a4 ♗f5 7 ♘f3 0-0-0 8 c3 e5 9 ♗xc6 ♕xc6 10 0-0 ♗g4?? 11 ♘xe5 ♕e6 12 ♘xg4 ♘xg4 13 h3 h5 14 ♗f4 ♗d6 15 ♕f3 f6 16 ♘d2 g5 17 ♖fe1 1-0 Lang-Loef, Reinland-Pfalz U-17 1991.

5 ♗e2

This position resembles a Two Knights Defence (1 e4 e5 2 ♘f3 ♘c6 3 ♗c4 ♘f6 4 ♘g5 d5 5 exd5 ♘a5 6 ♗b5+ c6 7 dxc6 bxc6 8 ♗e2) where although Black hasn't got the awkwardly placed knight on a5 he hasn't got as much lead in development in compensation for the pawn either.

5...e5 6 d3 ♗e7

6...♗c5 7 ♘c3 ♗f5 8 ♗f3! 0-0 9 ♘ge2 ♕c7 10 ♘g3 ♗g6 11 0-0 ♘bd7 12 ♘ge4 and White is fine.

7 ♘c3 0-0 8 ♘e4 ♘bd7 9 ♘f3 ♕b6?! 10 0-0 ♖d8 11 ♘xf6+ ♗xf6 12 ♘d2

Black has little to show for the pawn.

12 Nimzowitsch Defence

1 e4 ♘c6

Black develops a piece and waits to see how White continues. It isn't clear how White can prove an edge with 2 d4 so we are going to look at...

2 ♘f3 *(D)*

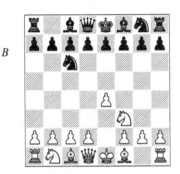

B

If Black now plays 2...e5 we can transpose to the chapter on the Max Lange by playing 3 ♗c4 so in this chapter will concentrate on Black's other options, some of which are bizarre to say the least:

A: **2...f5?!**   218
B: **2...♘f6?!**   219
C: **2...g6**   220
D: **2...e6**   221
E: **2...d5**   223
F: **2...d6**   224

A)

2...f5?!

The main use of this is surprise and the hope that White will go into some long and technically good 'refutation'

line where Black is well up on the latest wrinkles thus receiving good practical chances.

3 exf5 d5 4 ♗b5!

This is the way to play for a nice calm edge.

4...♗xf5

4...♕d6 5 d4 ♗xf5 will just transpose to the main line.

5 ♘e5 ♕d6

5...♗d7 6 ♗xc6 ♗xc6 7 0-0 ♘f6 8 ♕e2 g6 9 d4 ♕d6 10 ♘c3 (White already has a positional edge due to Black's backward e-pawn and weak square on e6; sure enough Black has the bishop-pair but why should White want to give up his lovely knight on e5 for Black's light-squared bishop unless there is an ulterior motive?) 10...a6 11 ♗f4 ♘h5 12 ♗g5 h6 13 ♗h4 (all Black has managed to do is put his knight on the edge of the board and create further weaknesses) 13...♖h7 14 ♕g4 ♖g7 15 ♖fe1 ♘f6 16 ♗xf6 ♕xf6 17 ♘xd5! ♕d6 18 ♘f4, Pirrot-Gross, German Cup 1991, and White is well on top especially as 18...♕xd4? 19 ♖ad1 wins, e.g. 19...h5 20 ♖xd4 hxg4 21 ♘e6 mates.

6 d4 ♘f6 7 ♘c3 0-0-0?

7...♘d7 8 0-0! e6! (8...♘dxe5 9 dxe5 ♕xe5 10 ♖e1 ♕d6 11 ♘xd5 0-0-0 12 c4 a6 13 ♗a4 e6 14 ♗f4 e5 15 ♗g5 and White has a lovely position; 8...♘cxe5 9 dxe5 ♕xe5 10 ♖e1 ♕d6 11 ♕xd5 ♕xd5 12 ♘xd5 0-0-0 13

♘xe7+ ♗xe7 14 ♖xe7 ♖he8 15 ♗xd7+ ♗xd7 16 ♖xe8 ♖xe8 17 ♗e3 with a technical task ahead but the pleasure is all White's) 9 f4 with an edge to White as 9...♘cxe5 10 fxe5 ♕b6 11 ♗xd7+ ♔xd7 12 ♘xd5 exd5 13 ♖xf5 is obviously good for White.

8 ♗xc6! bxc6 9 ♕e2

Black's queenside starts to look a bit sick.

9...♕e6 10 ♘e4!!

This seems to finish things off nicely, for example 10...♗xe4 11 ♕a6+ ♔b8 12 ♘xc6+ ♕xc6 13 ♕xc6 ♖d6 14 ♕c3 ♗xg2 15 ♖g1 and Black's compensation for the queen is totally inadequate; or 10...c5 11 ♘xc5 ♕b6 12 ♘f7.

B)

2...♘f6?! 3 e5 *(D)*

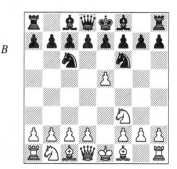

3...♘d5

Or:

a) 3...♘g8?! 4 d4 d6 5 ♗b5 a6 6 ♗a4 b5 7 ♗b3 d5 8 c3! and White is more comfortable, for example 8...♗f5 9 ♘h4! ♗e4 10 ♘d2 e6 11 ♘xe4 ♕xh4 (11...dxe4 12 ♕g4 and the c4-pawn falls) 12 ♘g5 and White has the advantage in space, development and the bishop-pair while Black's queen on h4 looks a little offside.

b) 3...♘g4!? 4 d4 d6 5 h3 ♘h6 6 ♘c3! dxe5 7 d5 e4 (7...♘d4 8 ♘xe5 ♘hf5 9 ♘b5! ♘xb5 {9...c5 10 c3!} 10 ♗xb5+ c6 11 ♘xc6 bxc6 12 ♗xc6+ ♗d7 13 ♗xa8 ♕xa8 14 0-0 with an edge for White) 8 ♘xe4 ♘b4 (8...♗f5 9 ♕d3! ♘b8 10 ♕b5+ ♘d7 11 ♗d3 and White has a comfortable position) 9 ♗xh6 gxh6 10 ♗b5+ ♗d7 (10...c6 11 dxc6 ♕xd1+ 12 ♖xd1 bxc6 13 ♗a4 and White is better, e.g. 13...♗f5 14 ♖d4 ♖b8 15 a3 ♗xe4 16 ♖xe4, etc.) 11 ♕e2 ♗g7 (11...♘xd5 12 ♘e5! wins, e.g. 12...c6 {12...♘f4 13 ♘xd7 ♘xe2 14 ♘df6#} 13 ♘d6+ exd6 14 ♘xc6+) 12 ♗xd7+ ♕xd7 13 ♘c5 ♕xd5 14 ♕b5+ ♘c6 15 ♖d1 ♕xa2 16 ♕xb7 0-0 17 ♕xc6 and White is winning, Holmsgaard-Weith, Denmark 1997.

4 d4 d6 5 c4 ♘b6

By a strange coincidence we have transposed to a variation of the Alekhine which has a dubious reputation. It is normally reached via the move-order 1 e4 ♘f6 2 e5 ♘d5 3 d4 d6 4 ♘f3 ♘c6?! 5 c4 ♘b6.

6 e6 fxe6

6...♗xe6? loses a piece to 7 d5.

7 ♗e3! *(D)*

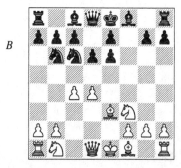

There are not too many games from this position but results have definitely favoured White. Indeed, the realization that 7 ♗e3 is strong has been a major reason for Black largely avoiding this whole variation in recent years.

7...e5

A thematic move in this line, but with d4 securely guarded, it makes little impact here. Others:

a) 7...♘d7 8 ♘c3 ♘f6 9 ♗d3 g6 10 h4 ♗g7 11 ♘g5 e5 (11...0-0? 12 h5) 12 d5 ♘d4 13 h5 gxh5!? (13...♗g4 14 f3; 13...♘xh5? 14 ♖xh5) 14 ♗xd4 exd4 (Vogt-Cibulka, Trenčianske Teplice 1974) and now Plachetka gives 15 ♘ce4!? ♗g4 16 ♕c2 as good for White, and this assessment seems correct.

b) 7...g6?! works out badly when White plays a quick h2-h4-h5, viz. 8 h4 ♗g7 9 h5 and now:

b1) 9...♘d7 10 ♘g5 ♘f8 11 ♕f3 ♗f6 12 hxg6 ♘xg6 13 ♘xh7 ♗xd4 14 ♗xd4 ♘xd4 15 ♕g4 ♘c2+ 16 ♔d2 ♘xa1 17 ♕xg6+ ♔d7 18 ♘f6+! with a substantial advantage for White, Gallagher-Landenbergue, Geneva 1987.

b2) 9...e5 10 d5! (best) 10...e4 11 ♘g5! ♗xb2 12 ♘d2 ♗xa1 13 ♕xa1 ♘e5 14 ♘dxe4 ♖g8 15 hxg6 hxg6 (Lau-Fleck, Bundesliga 1985/6) and now 16 f4! leaves Black in desperate trouble: 16...♘exc4 17 ♗xb6 ♘a3 18 ♕c3 axb6 19 ♖h8 ♖xh8 20 ♕xh8+ ♔d7 21 ♕g7; 16...♘g4 17 ♖h8 ♔d7 18 ♘e6 ♖xh8 19 ♘xd8 ♖xd8 20 ♕g7; or 16...♘bxc4 17 ♗d4! (Lau and Kavalek) 17...b5 18 fxe5 dxe5 19 ♗xc4 bxc4 20 ♗c5! – in all cases it is hard to imagine Black surviving.

8 d5 ♘d4

8...♘b4? is feeble, with one game continuing 9 ♘c3 ♗f5 10 ♖c1 e6 11 dxe6 ♗xe6 12 ♘g5 ♗xc4 13 ♗xc4 ♘xc4 14 ♕a4+ c6 15 ♕xb4 ♘xe3 16 fxe3 ♕xg5 17 ♕xb7 ♕xe3+ 18 ♘e2 ♖d8 19 ♕xc6+ ♔e7 20 ♖f1 ♕b6 21 ♕d5 ♔d7 22 ♘d4 ♗e7 23 ♕e6+ ♔e8 24 ♖f7 ♕b7 25 ♘c6 ♖d7 26 ♖c4 ♖f8 27 ♖xe7+ 1-0.

8...e4 9 ♘g5 ♘e5 10 ♘xe4 ♕d7 11 ♘bd2 e6 12 f4 is clearly better for White, Popov-Peshina, Riga 1968.

9 ♘xd4! exd4 10 ♗xd4 e5 11 dxe6 ♗xe6 12 ♗d3 ♕d7 13 0-0

White has a secure edge, for example 13...c5 (or 13...♘xc4 14 ♗xc4 ♗xc4 15 ♖e1+ ♔d8 16 ♕f3) 14 ♖e1 0-0-0 15 ♕c2 ♔b8 (15...cxd4 16 ♖xe6!) 16 ♗e3 ♗e7 17 ♘d2 is a little better for White, Rabar-Rellstab, Sarajevo 1958.

C)

2...g6 3 d4 ♗g7 4 d5

Or by 4 ♘c3 you are very likely to transpose into positions discussed in Line F21.

4...♘e5

After 4...♘b8?! 5 c4 d6 6 ♘c3 ♘d7 7 ♗e2 e5 Black is really just two tempi down on a normal King's Indian position, Saravanan-Mitra Swapan, 1994.

5 ♘xe5 ♗xe5 6 ♗e2 d6 7 0-0

Practical examples are scarce but strongly favour White, e.g.

a) 7...♗g7 8 c4 ♘f6 9 ♘c3 0-0 and now instead of 10 ♗e3 (Brunner-Høi, Budapest 1989), 10 ♗g5! seems stronger, when Black will find it hard to equalize as eventually he will want to break with ...c6, ...c5, ...e6 or ...e5, all of which are likely to lead to King's Indian-type positions where Black is tempi down.

b) 7...c5 8 ♘d2 ♗g7 9 a4 ♘f6 10 f3 0-0 11 ♘c4 b6 12 c3 gives White an ideal Benoni-type set-up where he can build up pressure in his own good time.

D)

2...e6 3 d4 d5 4 ♘bd2 (D)

We have now reached a French Defence position where Black's knight on c6 blocks Black's natural advance ...c5. Although this system is played occasionally it tends to leave Black a little cramped.

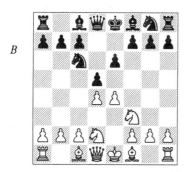

B

4...♘f6

Others are less good:

a) 4...dxe4 has not been played at all at higher levels mainly because after 5 ♘xe4 the knight on c6 is inconsistent with any lines in which Black exchanges early on e4.

b) 4...♘ge7?! 5 c3 ♘g6 6 ♗d3 a6 7 0-0 ♘f4 8 ♗c2 e5 (Black had to do something quick otherwise the knight was going to feel awfully lonely on f4!) 9 ♖e1 reaches a key position in which nothing quite works for Black:

b1) 9...exd4 10 exd5+ ♘e7 11 ♘e4 ♘fxd5 12 ♘xd4 and White's pieces are extremely active while Black still has to think about some kind of real development.

b2) 9...dxe4 10 ♗xe4! is very awkward for Black to meet.

b3) 9...♗g4 10 exd5 ♕xd5 11 ♗b3 ♕d7 12 ♘xe5! and White is on top.

b4) 9...♗h3?! 10 gxh3 ♕d7 (after 10...♘xh3+ 11 ♔f1 Black has no real attack) 11 ♔h1 ♕xh3 12 ♖g1 dxe4 13 ♗xe4 exd4 14 ♗xc6+ bxc6 15 ♕e1+ ♗e7 16 ♖g3 and Black's attack has crumbled, Laschet-Schaffer, Feldbach 1996.

c) 4...e5?! 5 ♗b5 exd4 (5...dxe4 6 ♘xe5 is just good for White, e.g. 6...♕g5 7 ♔f1! and Black will drop a pawn) 6 ♘xd4 and now:

c1) 6...♘ge7 7 0-0 gives White an edge, e.g. 7...♗d7 8 ♘4b3 dxe4 9 ♘xe4 ♘e5 (9...a6 10 ♘bc5!! axb5 11 ♘xb7 ♕b8 12 ♘ed6+ cxd6 13 ♘xd6+ ♔d8 14 ♘xf7+ ♔c8 15 ♘xh8 and Black's position is totally disrupted) 10 ♕e2 a6 11 ♗xd7+ ♕xd7 12 ♘ec5 winning a pawn.

c2) 6...♗d7 7 ♘xc6 bxc6 8 ♗d3 gives White the advantage on account of Black's static central pawn weakness, for example 8...♗c5 9 0-0 ♘f6 10 e5 ♘g4 11 ♘f3 h5 12 h3 ♘h6 13 ♕e2 ♘f5 14 e6! ♘g3 15 exd7+ ♔f8 16 ♕e8+ ♕xe8 17 dxe8♕+ ♖xe8 18 ♖e1 ♖xe1+ 19 ♘xe1 1-0 Fiorito-Feige, Argentina 1997.

d) 4...f5!? (Black's main problem with this move is that although it appears to give him a strong outpost on e4 White will soon undermine it by playing c2-c4) 5 exf5 exf5 6 ♗d3 ♗d6

7 0-0 ♘ge7 8 c4! ♘b4 9 ♗e2 0-0 (an attempt to keep a pawn on d5 doesn't help, for example 9...c6 10 a3 ♘a6 11 c5 ♗c7 12 b4 0-0 13 ♖e1 f4 14 ♘e5, and White has a pleasant position) 10 a3 ♘bc6 11 cxd5 ♘xd5 12 ♗c4 ♘ce7 13 ♘e5 ♗xe5 14 dxe5 ♔h8 15 ♘f3 and though Black is solid, White's bishop-pair, control of the dark squares and passed e-pawn give him the advantage, Canfell-Ozols, Adelaide 1990.

e) 4...g6?! 5 ♗b5 ♗d7 6 ♕e2 ♘ge7 7 0-0 a6 8 ♗a4 ♗g7 9 c3 0-0 10 ♗c2 leaves Black solid but his light-squared bishop is not a happy piece and he has potentially weak dark squares around the kingside, Leko-Bischoff, Dortmund 1992.

5 e5 ♘d7 *(D)*

5...♘e4 6 c3 ♘xd2 7 ♗xd2 and now:

a) 7...b6 8 ♗d3 ♗b7 9 ♕e2 ♕d7 10 a4 ♘a5? 11 b4 ♘b3 12 ♖b1 ♘xd2 13 ♔xd2! (despite the bishop-pair you only have to look at the position to appreciate White's advantage in space and development) 13...♗e7 14 h4 ♖c8 15 ♖b2 c5?! 16 bxc5 bxc5 17 ♖hb1 ♗c6 18 ♗a6 ♖d8 19 ♖b7! ♗xb7 20 ♖xb7 c4? 21 ♗b5 1-0 Tredinnick-Ferris, Adelaide 1990.

b) 7...♗e7 8 ♗d3 a5 9 a4 b6 (an attempt by Black to swap off his poor light-squared bishop) 10 ♕e2 ♘b8 11 b4! c5 12 b5 ♘d7 13 h4 h6 (Black decides not to castle 'into it', e.g. 13...0-0 14 ♗xh7+ ♔xh7 15 ♘g5+ and White has a standard winning attack) 14 h5 ♗b7 15 ♕e3 ♕c7 16 ♕f4 (Black still doesn't want to castle kingside and face ♖h3-g3) 16...f5? (an attempt to block the centre and kingside before considering castling queenside) 17 exf6 ♕xf4

18 ♗g6+! 1-0 (White wins a piece) Minzer-Bosco, Buenos Aires 1993.

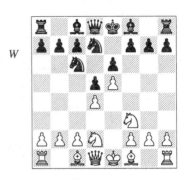

6 ♗e2 f6

6...♗e7 7 ♘f1! (anticipating that Black will eventually play ...f6 and that after the exchange of pawns, a knight on e3 will prevent Black from easily getting in ...e6-e5) 7...0-0 8 ♘e3 f6 9 exf6 ♘xf6 10 0-0 ♗d6 11 c4! b6 12 a3 ♔h8 13 b4 dxc4 (Black needed to exchange now to stop White rolling through on the queenside) 14 ♗xc4 e5 15 ♗b2 with an edge to White, for example 15...exd4 16 ♘xd4 ♘xd4 17 ♕xd4 and White has the better attacking chances, Wolff-Gallagher, Hastings Challengers 1989/90.

7 exf6 *(D)*

Now:

D1: 7...♘xf6 222
D2: 7...♕xf6 223

D1)

7...♘xf6 8 0-0 ♗d6 9 c4! b6?

9...0-0 10 c5 ♗e7 (or 10...♗f4 11 ♗b5 ♗d7 12 ♘b3 ♗xc1 13 ♖xc1, with advantage to White, Reinderman-I.Rogers, Wijk aan Zee 1996) 11 ♗b5 with an edge to White as he can restrict Black from playing ...e5.

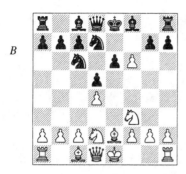

B

10 cxd5 exd5 11 ♗b5 ♗d7 12 ♖e1+ ♘e7 13 ♗xd7+ ♛xd7 14 ♘e5

White is a little better. Khalifman-Timman, Reykjavik World Cup 1991 continued 14...♛f5 15 ♛a4+ ♔f8 16 ♘f1 ♗xe5 17 dxe5 ♘g4 18 ♗f4 c5 19 ♘g3 ♛e6 20 ♗g5 ♘h6 21 f4! (now whichever knight goes to f5 White captures the other one with advantage) 21...♘ef5 22 ♗xh6 gxh6 23 ♘xf5 ♛xf5 24 ♛c6 ♔g7 25 ♛xd5 ♛xf4 26 ♖e4 (Black is in deep trouble) 26...♛f5 27 ♛b7+ ♔g6 28 ♖f1 1-0.

D2)
7...♛xf6 8 ♘f1!

As stated before the idea of this manoeuvre is to redevelop the knight to e3 restricting Black from a future ...e5 advance.

8...♗d6
8...e5?! 9 ♘e3! exd4 (after 9...e4, 10 ♘xd5!? ♛d6 11 c4 exf3 12 gxf3 is interesting while 10 ♘e5 offers White an edge; 9...♘xd4?! 10 ♘xd4 exd4 11 ♘xd5 ♛e5 12 c4! dxc3 13 ♗f4 c2 14 ♗xe5 cxd1♛+ 15 ♔xd1 is good for White) 10 ♘xd5 ♛d6 11 ♗c4 ♘de5 12 ♘xe5 ♛xe5+ (12...♘xe5 13 ♗f4 and Black has big problems) 13 ♔f1 ♗d7 14 ♗f4 ♛f5 15 g4! ♛g6 16

♘xc7+ ♔d8 17 ♘xa8 ♗xg4 18 ♛d3 ♛h5 19 ♔g2 1-0 (Black quite rightly had had enough) Garcia Carbo-Andres Gonzalez, Torrevieja 1997.

8...b6?! 9 ♘e3 ♗b7 10 0-0 ♗e7 11 c3 with an edge to White, Epishin-Vaganian, Reggio Emilia 1991.

9 ♘e3 0-0 10 0-0
White has done well in practice, as the following examples show:

a) 10...♔h8?! (a typical 'French' move but unnecessary here) 11 b3 h6 12 c4 dxc4 13 bxc4 ♘e7 14 ♗b2 b6 15 ♖b1! ♗b7 16 c5 ♗f4 17 d5 e5 18 c6 and White wins a piece, Roberts-Spice, Pula Echt 1997.

b) 10...♛f7 11 c4 ♘f6 12 g3 b6 13 ♘g5 ♛g6 14 ♗d3! ♛e8 (14...♛xg5?? 15 ♘xd5 wins the queen because 15...♛h5 16 ♘xf6+ follows) 15 cxd5 exd5 16 ♘f5 ♗xf5 17 ♗xf5 ♘e7 18 ♗h3 ♛g6 19 ♘e6 ♖fe8 20 ♘f4 ♗xf4 21 ♗xf4 and White has a long-term edge due to the bishop-pair, for example 21...c6 22 ♖c1 ♘e4 23 ♖e1 ♛f6 24 f3! and White is doing very well, Kapengut-Landenbergue, Reggio Emilia 1991/2.

c) 10...♛g6 11 c4 ♘f6 12 c5 ♗f4 13 ♖e1 ♗d7 14 ♘f1 ♘g4 (14...♗xc1 15 ♖xc1 ♘e4 16 ♗d3 ♖f4 17 ♘g3 ♖af8 and White has an edge, Kindermann-Hug, Beersheba 1985) 15 ♗d3 ♛f6 16 h3 ♗xc1 17 ♖xc1 ♘h6 18 ♗b5 and White has a very pleasant position, Malaniuk-Short, Lvov 1984.

E)
2...d5 3 exd5 ♛xd5 4 ♘c3 ♛a5

4...♛h5 5 ♘b5! gives White an edge, as Black must defend the c-pawn with his king.

We have now reached a position akin to the Scandinavian, in which the c6-knight blocks Black's usual system of playing ...c6. This move is normally important to provide an avenue for retreating his queen as well as covering the vital b5- and d5-squares.

5 ♗b5 *(D)*

5...♗d7

Other tries for Black are less successful:

a) 5...♗g4?! 6 h3 ♗h5? 7 g4 ♗g6 8 ♘e5 ♗e4 9 f3 (9 ♘c4 ♕b4 10 a3 ♕c5 11 d4 0-0-0! is not so clear) 9...a6 10 ♘c4 ♕b4 11 a3 ♕c5 12 d4 ♕a7 13 fxe4 axb5 14 ♘xb5 ♕b8 15 ♗f4 e5 16 ♘xe5 ♗d6 17 ♘xd6+ cxd6 18 ♘c4 ♘f6 19 ♘xd6+ ♔d7 20 g5 1-0 Bednarski-Allegro, Sion 1990.

b) 5...a6?! 6 ♗xc6+ bxc6 7 ♕e2 ♘f6 8 ♘e5 e6 9 0-0 (White doesn't want to lose time by taking Black's shattered pawn – Karpov knows how to handle this type of position) 9...♗d6 10 d4 (Black's queen looks totally out of the game) 10...0-0 11 ♖d1 c5 12 ♘c4 ♕b4 13 a3 ♕b8 14 ♗g5 and White's pieces are in full flow, Karpov-Hort, Oslo 1984.

6 a3!? e6!

6...a6?! 7 b4 ♘xb4 (7...♕b6? 8 ♘d5 ♕a7 9 ♘xc7+ ♔d8 10 ♗xc6 and White is well on top) 8 ♗xd7+ ♔xd7 9 axb4! ♕xa1 10 ♘d4 (Black's queen is doomed) 10...a5 11 ♘b3 axb4 12 ♘xa1 ♖xa1 13 ♘e4 e6 14 0-0 ♗e7 15 ♕g4 g5 16 ♘xg5 1-0 S.Schmidt-Porth, 2nd Bundesliga 1994/5.

6...0-0-0 7 ♖b1! is strong, for example 7...♘f6 8 b4 ♕b6 9 ♗c4 and Black has problems.

7 ♖b1 a6 8 b4 ♕b6 9 ♗c4 ♘d4

9...0-0-0 10 d4 gives White a strong queenside initiative, e.g. 10...♘ce7 11 b5 a5 (11...♕a5 12 ♗d2 is strong for White; 11...axb5 12 ♘xb5 ♗xb5 13 ♖xb5 ♕c6 14 ♕d3 ♘f6 15 0-0 and with the bishop-pair and the open b-file White has the edge) 12 ♗f4 ♘d5 13 ♘a4 ♕a7 14 ♗xd5 exd5 15 ♘e5 and Black has problems.

10 ♘e5 ♘f6

10...♘c6 11 0-0 ♗d6 12 ♖e1 ♘f6 13 d3 0-0 14 ♗b2 and White has an edge.

11 0-0 ♗d6 12 ♘xd7 ♔xd7 13 d3

In my view White is already better, e.g. 13...h5!? 14 ♘a4 ♗xh2+ (consistent with 13...h5) 15 ♔xh2 ♘g4+ 16 ♔g1 ♕d6 17 f4 ♘f5 18 ♘c5+ ♔e7 19 c3 ♘fe3 20 ♗xe3 ♘xe3 21 ♕f3 ♘xf1 22 ♖xf1 g6 23 ♘xb7 ♕b6+ and White is doing well, Zollbrecht-Schubert, Munich 1985.

F)

2...d6 3 d4 *(D)*

Now Black can play:

After 3...g6 4 ♗e2 ♗g7 5 d5 ♘e5 6 ♘xe5, 6...♗xe5 transposes to Line C,

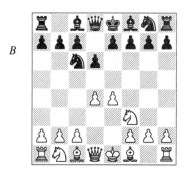

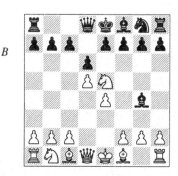

while 6...dxe5?! 7 c4 allows White too much scope for queenside play.

F1)

3...♗g4 4 d5 ♘e5

4...♘b8!? 5 c4 e5 6 dxe6 fxe6 7 ♘c3 ♘c6 8 ♗e2 ♘f6 9 h3 ♗h5 10 ♗e3 ♗e7 11 0-0 ♕d7 12 ♘d4 ♗g6 (12...♗xe2 13 ♘dxe2 0-0 14 ♕d2 gives White a small but lasting edge) 13 ♘xc6 bxc6 (13...♕xc6 14 c5! a6 15 cxd6 cxd6 {15...♗xd6 16 ♗f3! ♗e5 17 ♖c1 ♖d8 18 ♕b3 and White is doing well} 16 ♗f3 ♘xe4 {16...♗xe4 17 ♘xe4 ♘xe4 18 ♖c1 ♕d5 19 ♕a4+ wins} 17 ♖c1! wins) 14 e5 dxe5 15 ♕a4 0-0 (15...c5?! 16 ♕a5 ♕c6 17 ♘b5 is good for White) 16 ♖ad1 ♕e8 17 ♕a5 and White has a definite edge, Fischer-Emma, Mar del Plata 1959.

5 ♘xe5!!? (D)

5...♗xd1 6 ♗b5+ c6 7 dxc6 ♕a5+ 7...♗e2!? 8 ♔xe2 ♕a5 9 ♘c3 0-0-0 (after 9...dxe5 10 cxb7+ ♕xb5+ 11 ♘xb5 ♖b8 12 ♘xa7 White is going to be two pawns up for nothing) 10 ♘c4 ♕b4 (10...♕c7 11 ♘d5 ♕b8 12 c7 ♕a8 13 ♗d2 and Black can only sit and wait) 11 ♗e3 bxc6 12 ♗a6+! ♔c7 (12...♔d7 13 ♗xa7 ♖a8 14 ♘b6+ ♔e8 15 ♘xa8 ♕a5 16 ♘b5 cxb5 17 c4

♔d7 18 cxb5 gives White masses of compensation for the queen) 13 ♗xa7 ♖a8 14 a3 ♕xc3 15 ♗b6+ ♔d7 16 bxc3 ♖xa6 and after all that, White has a clear extra pawn!

8 ♘c3 0-0-0

8...a6 9 b4 axb5 (9...♕xb5 10 ♘xb5 axb5 11 cxb7 ♖b8 12 ♘c6 ♖xb7 13 ♔xd1 and White is a good pawn up) 10 bxa5 bxc6 (10...♗xc2 11 cxb7 ♖b8 12 a6 wins) 11 ♘xc6 ♗xc2 12 a6 ♗d3 (12...♖xa6? loses to 13 ♘b4) 13 ♘d5 ♗xe4 14 ♘c7+ ♔d7 15 ♘xa8 ♔xc6 16 f3 ♗d5 17 ♗e3 and White has a substantial advantage.

9 ♘c4 ♕c7

Or:

a) 9...♕xc3+!? 10 bxc3 ♗xc2 11 ♘a5! leaves Black worse, for example 11...♗xe4 12 ♘xb7 ♖e8 13 f3! ♗g6 14 c7 ♘f6 15 ♗xe8 ♘xe8 16 ♘a5 ♘xc7 17 ♗e3 a6 and White is the exchange for a pawn up.

b) 9...♕b4 10 a3 ♕c5 11 ♗e3 ♕h5 (11...♗xc2 12 ♗xc5 dxc5 13 ♖c1 and White is doing very well) 12 ♖xd1 gives White a good deal of play for the queen, e.g. 12...bxc6 13 ♗xc6 ♔c7 14 ♖d5 e5 15 ♖a5! ♔xc6 16 g4! ♕h3 17 ♖xa7 and Black is at last lost.

10 ♘d5 ♗xc2

10...♕xc6 11 ♗xc6 bxc6 12 ♔xd1 cxd5 13 exd5 and White is a pawn to the good.

11 ♘xc7 ♔xc7 12 cxb7 ♗xe4 13 ♗e3 ♔xb7

Or 13...♗xg2!? 14 ♖g1 ♗xb7 15 ♗xa7 ♖a8 16 ♗b6+ ♔b8 17 a4 with an unclear ending.

14 f3

The position is unbalanced since Black's extra pawn is countered by his open king and lack of development, Palkövi-Brandics, Hungarian Cht 1992.

F2)

3...♘f6 4 ♘c3 *(D)*

Now it is time for Black to choose again:

F21: 4...g6   226
F22: 4...♗g4   226

F21)

4...g6 5 d5 ♘b8

5...♘e5?! 6 ♘xe5 dxe5 7 ♗e2 ♗g7 8 0-0 0-0 9 ♗e3 a6 10 ♕d2 ♕d6 11 ♖fd1 ♖d8 12 h3 ♗d7 13 a4 transposes to the game Vogt-Ftačnik, East Germany-Czechoslovakia match 1978, with a dismal position for Black.

6 ♗e2 ♗g7 7 0-0 0-0 *(D)*

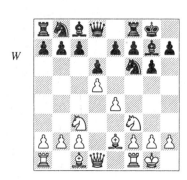

By transposition we have arrived at a line from the Pirc via the move-order 1 e4 d6 2 d4 ♘f6 3 ♘c3 g6 4 ♘f3 ♗g7 5 ♗e2 0-0 6 0-0 ♘c6 7 d5 ♘b8, which is regarded as slightly inferior for Black.

8 ♖e1 e5

8...♗g4 9 h3 ♗xf3 10 ♗xf3 c6 11 g3 ♘bd7 12 ♗g2 ♖c8 13 a4 ♘e5 14 ♘e2 cxd5 15 exd5 ♕a5 16 ♗d2 ♕c5 17 ♗c3 similar to a g3 anti-Dragon system where White's pressure against the backward e-pawn gives him a slight advantage.

9 dxe6 ♗xe6 10 ♗f4 ♘c6

Not 10...h6?! 11 ♘d4 ♗d7 12 ♕d2 ♔h7 13 e5! dxe5 14 ♗xe5 ♘e4? 15 ♘xe4 ♗xe5 16 ♘f3 ♗g7 17 ♖ad1 ♕c8 18 ♗c4 ♗e8 19 ♘eg5+! hxg5 20 ♘xg5+ ♔g8 21 ♕f4 ♘d7 22 ♖xd7 ♗xd7 23 ♗xf7+! 1-0 Tal-Petrosian, USSR 1974.

11 ♕d2

White has a slight advantage.

F22)

4...♗g4 5 ♗b5 a6

5...♘d7?! 6 d5 and now:

a) 6...♘ce5? 7 ♘xe5! ♗xd1 8 ♗xd7+ ♕xd7 9 ♘xd7 leaves White a piece up.

b) 6...♗xf3?! and either recapture offers White an initiative.

c) 6...♘cb8 7 h3 ♗xf3 (7...♗h5 8 ♗e3 and White has an edge) 8 ♕xf3 c6 9 dxc6 bxc6 10 ♗c4 ♘e5 11 ♕e2 ♘xc4 12 ♕xc4 gives White a positional advantage, Kaula-Kiedrowicz, Polish Ch (Bielsko-Biala) 1991.

6 ♗xc6+ bxc6 7 h3 ♗h5 8 ♕e2 e6 9 g4 ♗g6 10 ♘h4 *(D)*

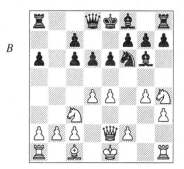

10...♗e7

10...d5 11 ♘xg6 hxg6 12 ♗g5 and then:

a) 12...♕b8 13 0-0-0 ♘xe4 14 ♘xe4 dxe4 15 c4 ♕b4 (15...f5 16 f3! is good for White as he can blast open the centre while Black's king is still there) 16 ♗d2 ♕a4 17 ♔b1 ♖b8 18 ♗c1 ♗e7 19 b3 ♗a3 20 ♗b2 ♕b4 21 ♕xe4 and White has a nice edge, Palac-Tomičić, Croatia 1994.

b) 12...♗e7 13 ♗xf6 gxf6 14 0-0-0 and White has a pleasant position due to his safer king, better minor piece and superior pawn-structure, Hulak-Miles, Indonesia 1982.

11 ♘xg6 hxg6 12 ♗e3 ♕b8 13 0-0-0 ♕b4 14 a3 ♕b7 15 f3 ♖b8 16 b3 d5

Although it appears that Black may work up some queenside attacking chances in reality they can be prevented quite easily, leaving White with all the long-term weaknesses.

17 ♔b2 ♘d7 18 ♔a2 ♘b6 19 ♖b1 0-0 20 h4! *(D)*

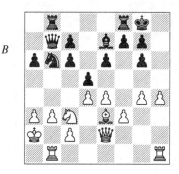

Now it is White's turn to have some fun.

20...a5 21 ♗g5 f6 22 exd5! e5 23 h5 gxh5

Not 23...fxg5? 24 hxg6, when White mates by ♖h8+.

24 ♖xh5 ♔f7

24...fxg5? 25 ♕xe5 gives White an excellent attack, e.g. 25...♗f6 (25...♔f7 26 ♖xg5! ♔e8 27 ♖xg7 ♘c8 28 ♖e1 ♖f7 29 ♖g8+ ♖f8 30 ♕h5+ ♔d7 31 ♖xf8 and Black can give up) 26 ♕e6+ ♖f7 27 ♖h8+! ♔xh8 28 ♕xf7 mating.

25 ♗e3 cxd5 26 dxe5

White is well on top, Tolnai-Pytel, Zurich 1993.

13 Odds and Ends

This is the best way to describe a chapter that covers some of the more exotic and unusual openings for Black. Some of these variations are played for shock value, some out of habit for something that was once in vogue and then out again and some as a trend or fad. However, I draw the line at analysing the North Sea Oil (also called the Norwegian Defence), 1 e4 g6 2 d4 ♘f6 3 e5 ♘h5 4 ♗e2 ♘g7 which Andrew Dyce played on occasion before he realized he was a good player, or the Reversed Grob (1 e4 g5?!), whose only real advocate was one of England's greatest free-thinkers Michael Basman. Let us look at what is left to make this opening repertoire book complete. The chapter divides into four parts:

Part 1 deals with **1 e4 e5 2 ♘f3 d5**, the so-called Elephant Gambit.

Part 2 considers **1 e4 a6 2 d4 b5**, the St George – popular for a while after Miles's famous victory over Karpov.

Part 3 features **1 e4 b6**, Owen's Defence (named after the Reverend Owen), which came back into popularity for a short while around the same time as 1 c4 b6.

Part 4 discusses two ideas after **1 e4 d6 2 d4**, viz. **2...e5** and **2...♘f6 3 ♘c3 e5**. I'm not sure what to call these but both have recently become fairly popular as a way of trying to equalize (but nothing more) as Black out of the opening.

I believe that against these systems it is best not to try to blast them off the board (that may be what your opponent wants you to try to do!) but to play something that gives you a pleasant position, even if it is not 'the theoretical best'. Nevertheless, the lines recommended, I believe, give Black quite a challenge.

Part 1: The Elephant Gambit

1 e4 e5 2 ♘f3 d5

Already White has to make a decision! He must take action in the centre, but should it be 3 ♘xe5, 3 exd5 or 3 d4? In fact all three have been played and it depends more on style which may suit you best. I know when I first met this over the board it came as a complete surprise and my opponent was no less a player than Mark Hebden! Not wishing to be caught out unawares I played 3 ♘xe5 dxe4 4 d4 ♗d6 5 ♗c4?! Although this offers White almost nothing in terms of advantage after 5...♗xe5 6 dxe5 ♕xd1+ 7 ♔xd1, at least I had the bishop-pair and wasn't going to fall for any 'cheap' traps! In fact I remember the look of disgust on his face when I played 5 ♗c4?! and after the game (which we drew) telling me how I couldn't expect to win games with this. Sorry Mark, but in this case I was more interested in not losing!

3 exd5

This is my recommendation as a good way to test the soundness of the gambit. Black can reply:

A: 3...♗d6   229
B: 3...e4   230

A)

3...♗d6

It is on this move that the modest upsurge in popularity for this gambit is based.

4 d4

White decides to take his fair share of the centre.

4...e4

To justify his gambit Black gains time and space. He has no intention of trying to regain the pawn – even if he could, the number of moves it would take would leave him sadly behind in development. White, though, more than being a pawn ahead is using the pawn on d5 to restrict Black's movement and queenside development.

5 ♘e5 ♘f6 6 ♘c3 *(D)*

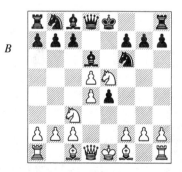

A lot of players may have been tempted to play 6 ♗b5+ or 6 c4. In fact both are probably quite playable but also rather provocative. With the text, as played by Motwani, White is quite happy just to develop and make sure Black cannot comfortably regain his pawn by exchanging on e5 and then taking on d5. We want to play things calmly but not give away all of our opening advantage. Unlike my philosophy against Hebden, White would like genuine winning chances as well as keeping things tight.

6...0-0

After 6...♘bd7!? 7 ♘xd7 ♗xd7 8 ♗g5 h6 9 ♗xf6 ♕xf6 10 ♘xe4 ♕e7 11 ♕e2 0-0-0 12 0-0-0 Black still has to prove what he has for the pawn, e.g. 12...♗f4+ 13 ♔b1 ♖he8 (13...♗f5 14 ♘g3 ♕xe2 15 ♗xe2! ♗xg3 16 hxg3 ♖xd5 17 ♗f3 and White is a good pawn up) 14 ♘c3, when he has a certain amount of activity but is it enough for the material invested?

7 ♗c4 ♘bd7

7...♖e8 8 0-0 ♗xe5 9 dxe5 ♖xe5 10 ♗f4 regains the pawn but leaves White with the two bishops and complete development. It is true that Black is solid but his position is hardly inspiring. The text-move is an attempt to play for an advantage through active piece-play.

8 ♘xd7 ♗xd7 9 ♗g5

Black needs to react quickly – otherwise White will castle and look forward to the middlegame a good pawn up.

9...h6 10 ♗h4 g5!? 11 ♗g3

Black has gained a little time and space but at the cost of weakening his kingside.

11...♗xg3?!

Black can now aim to set his f-pawn in motion, but this exchange looks to me as if it may lead to a long-term weakness for Black on the kingside.

12 hxg3 ♘g4 13 ♗e2!

Now Black cannot get in ...e3 and the knight looks vulnerable on g4. White doesn't mind exchanging some pieces to reduce Black's activity and at the right time perhaps give back the extra pawn and start playing on some of Black's weaknesses.

13...f5 14 ♗xg4 fxg4 15 ♕e2!

This move guarantees White an advantage and leaves Black with all the weaknesses still to cope with.

Instead 15 ♘xe4 ♕e7 16 ♕e2 ♗b5! is too messy, while I'm sure 15 ♖xh6!? ♖xf2! 16 ♔xf2 ♕f8+ 17 ♔g1 ♕xh6 18 ♘xe4 ♖e8 19 ♘c5 ♗c8 should be good for White but is unnecessary when there is a calm safe move available.

15...♕f6 16 0-0-0! ♖ae8

16...♕xf2? 17 ♕xf2 ♖xf2 18 ♘xe4 ♖f5 19 ♖xh6 ♔g7 20 ♖dh1 and White is not only material up but has much the better position as well.

17 ♘xe4 ♕g6 18 ♖de1 ♗f5 19 f3 gxf3 20 gxf3 g4

Black is still trying to play for every bit of activity he can, knowing that otherwise his prospects are bleak.

21 ♕d2!

Unpinning and looking at that pawn on h6.

21...♔g7 22 ♘f2!

Giving back one pawn but stopping any nonsense.

22...gxf3 23 ♖e5

To a player of Motwani's standard the rest is almost just a matter of technique. Motwani-J.Rogers, British Ch (Plymouth) 1989 concluded 23...♖d8 24 g4! (this pawn is immune due as the

pawn on h6 would be hanging at the end) 24...♗c8 25 ♖e7+ ♖f7 26 ♖xf7+ ♔xf7 27 ♖xh6 ♕g7 28 ♕f4+ ♔g8 29 ♘e4 ♖f8 30 ♘f6+ ♖xf6 31 ♕xf6 f2 32 ♕d8+ ♔f7 33 ♕xc7+ 1-0.

B)

3...e4 4 ♕e2 *(D)*

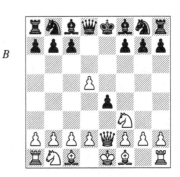

B

Now Black can try:

B1)

4...f5?! 5 d3

Now:

a) 5...♘f6 6 dxe4 and here:

a1) 6...♘xe4 7 ♘c3 ♕e7 (7...♗b4? 8 ♕b5+) 8 ♘xe4 fxe4 (8...♕xe4 9 ♕xe4+ fxe4 10 ♘g5 ♗f5 11 ♘e6! and Black has problems) 9 ♘g5 and Black has nothing left to play for.

a2) 6...fxe4 7 ♘c3 ♗b4 8 ♕b5+! c6 9 ♕xb4 exf3 10 ♗g5 cxd5 (10...fxg2 11 ♗xg2 ♘xd5 12 ♘xd5! ♕xg5 13 ♘c7+ is winning for White) 11 0-0-0 ♘c6 12 ♕a3, Tal-Lutikov, USSR Cht 1964. True, White is no longer material ahead but who cares – he has the safer king, better development, open lines, files and diagonals and the bishop-pair. A man like Tal needs little else!

b) 5...♕xd5 6 ♘fd2 ♘c6 7 ♘c3 ♕e6 8 dxe4 ♗b4 9 ♘d5! and White is better, e.g. 9...♗a5 10 exf5 ♕xe2+ 11 ♗xe2 ♗xf5 12 ♘e3 ♘d4?! 13 c3, when Black really has little to show for the pawn.

c) 5...♗b4+ 6 c3 ♗e7 7 dxe4 and then:

c1) 7...♘f6 8 ♘g5! and Black has very little, e.g. 8...fxe4 9 ♘e6 ♗xe6 10 dxe6 0-0 11 ♕c4 ♘g4 12 f3! exf3! (12...♘e5?! 13 ♕xe4, etc.) 13 ♕xg4 ♗h4+ 14 g3 f2+ 15 ♔e2 ♕d5 16 gxh4 ♕xh1 17 ♗e3 ♘c6 18 ♕g2 ♕xg2 19 ♗xg2 and Black's position is going downhill.

c2) 7...fxe4 8 ♕xe4 ♘f6 9 ♗b5+ ♗d7 10 ♕e2 ♘xd5 11 ♘e5! (better even than 11 ♗c4, Morphy-Paulsen, New York mutual blindfold simul 1857), e.g. 11...♘f6 12 0-0 and it seems to me that White has the better position as well as being a pawn up.

B2)

4...♘f6 5 ♘c3 ♗e7

5...♗c5?! 6 ♘xe4 0-0? 7 ♘xc5 ♖e8 8 ♘e5 and it is difficult to see what Black has for the material.

6 ♘xe4 *(D)*

6...0-0

6...♘xd5 is met by 7 ♕d1!, a subtle move since it gets the queen off the e-file and lets out White's light-squared bishop. While it loses a little time, White is a pawn up so Black still has something to prove. There is no practical experience with this move, so I will give a few sample lines: 7...0-0 (7...♗f5 8 ♘g3 ♗g6 9 ♗c4 and Black

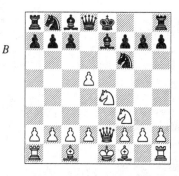

appears to have nothing special) 8 ♗c4 ♖e8 (8...♘b6 9 ♗e2 c5 10 d4 and I don't see that Black has anything much) 9 0-0 ♘c6 10 d4 ♘b6 11 ♗e2 and Black seems to have little for the pawn.

7 ♘c3 ♖e8 8 ♕d1 ♗b4+ 9 ♗e2 ♕e7! 10 a3 ♗xc3 11 dxc3 ♘xd5! 12 ♗g5 ♕e6

12...♕e4 13 ♕d3 ♘f4 14 ♕xe4 ♖xe4 (14...♘xg2+? 15 ♔f1 ♖xe4 16 ♗d3 ♖g4 17 h3 wins for White) 15 ♗xf4 ♖xf4 16 0-0-0 ♗d7 17 ♖he1 and although it is still technically difficult, White is a pawn up with the better development and so all the fun is his.

13 ♕d3! ♘d7

13...b6 14 0-0-0! ♗a6 15 ♕xd5 ♕xd5 16 ♖xd5 ♗xe2 17 ♖e1! ♘c6 18 ♘d4 and White emerges on top.

14 0-0-0!

White is doing fine as 14...♕xe2? loses to 15 ♖he1.

Part 2: The St George

1 e4 a6 2 d4 b5

The St George is so-called in honour of the English Dragon slayer Tony Miles for his famous victory over Karpov. There are various set-ups that have been tried from both sides of the board but the best option for White is to develop pieces naturally and see what develops!

3 ♘f3 ♗b7

If Black plays 3...e6 White should continue with the set-up below and the game is likely to transpose.

4 ♗d3 *(D)*

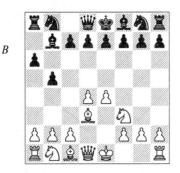

B

4...♘f6

4...e6 is one of the main digressions, with the following possibilities after 5 0-0:

a) 5...♗e7 6 a4 c5 7 c3 c4?! (I don't like this move as it takes away some of the tension in the centre, which means it is then White's kingside play vs Black's queenside activity; I don't know about you but I like attacking kings!) 8 ♗c2 ♘f6 9 ♕e2 d5 10 e5 ♘fd7 11 ♘e1! (making way for the advance) 11...♘c6 12 f4 g6 13 g4 b4 (13...h5?! 14 f5! just speeds things up for White) 14 f5 b3 15 ♗d1 (this means long-term White's a-pawn is weak but you can't have everything!) 15...♗g5 16 ♘d2 gxf5 17 gxf5 h5?. It must be me but they seem to be both attacking on the same side of the board and I know whose chances I fancy! Now instead

of 18 ♕f3, as in Milicević-Bidal, Canada 1996, 18 fxe6! fxe6 19 ♘xc4 wins: 19...dxc4 20 ♕xh5+ ♖xh5 21 ♗xh5+ ♔e7 22 ♗xg5+ ♘f6 23 ♗xf6+ ♔d7 24 ♗xd8. Black can call it a day.

b) 5...♘f6 6 e5 ♘d5 7 ♘g5! (preparing for kingside action!) 7...d6?! 8 ♗xh7 dxe5 (8...♗e7 9 ♕g4 dxe5 10 dxe5 ♘d7 11 ♘xe6 fxe6 12 ♗g6+ ♔f8 13 ♕xe6 ♘xe5 14 ♕xe5 ♗d6 15 ♕f5+ ♕f6 16 h3 and although Black is active he is two pawns down) 9 dxe5 ♘d7 10 ♘xf7! and now:

b1) 10...♔xf7 11 ♕h5+ ♔e7 12 ♖d1! (12 ♗g5+ doesn't lead anywhere) 12...♘7f6 (12...♖xh7 13 ♗g5+ ♘7f6 14 ♕xh7 and White has a crushing position) 13 ♗g5 ♕e8 14 ♕xe8+ ♖xe8 15 ♗g6 ♖d8 16 ♘a3 and White can pick his moment to take on f6 to end up a sound pawn ahead.

10...♕h4 11 ♘xh8 ♕xh7 12 ♕g4 ♕xh8 13 ♕xe6+ leaves White with ♖+3♙ vs ♗+♘, which is plenty as long as he is careful, Levačić-T.Pedersen, Burgas 1991.

c) 5...c5 (the most common) 6 c3 and now:

c1) 6...cxd4 7 cxd4 ♘f6 8 ♕e2 ♗e7 9 ♗g5 0-0 10 ♘bd2 ♘c6 11 ♖ac1 ♘h5 12 ♗e3 and White has a comfortable position, Kauschmann-Brustkern, Berlin 1987.

c2) 6...♗e7 7 e5 c4 8 ♗c2 f5 9 b3 ♗d5 10 a4! and here:

c21) 10...cxb3 11 ♗xb3 ♗xb3 12 ♕xb3 ♕a5 13 ♗a3! ♘c6 14 axb5 ♕xb5 (14...axb5 15 ♗b2 ♕d8 16 ♖xa8 ♕xa8 17 ♕xb5 is good for White) 15 ♘bd2 and White has an edge.

c22) 10...♘c6 11 ♘a3 ♘a5 (or 11...cxb3 12 ♗xb3 ♗xb3 13 ♕xb3

♘a5 14 ♕d1 b4 15 cxb4 ♗xb4 16 ♖b1 ♖b8 17 d5! and White is better) 12 ♘d2 ♖b8 13 axb5 axb5 14 ♖b1 ♘h6 15 bxc4 bxc4 and White has an edge as the pawn on c4 is weak, Macieja-Kania, Poland 1994.

c3) 6...♕c7 7 ♖e1 ♘f6 8 ♘e5 h5 (8...d6 9 ♘g4 ♗e7 10 ♗g5 leaves White more comfortable) 9 ♗g5 ♘g4!? 10 ♘xg4 hxg4 11 e5 cxd4 12 cxd4 ♗b4 13 ♗d2! ♕a5 14 a3 ♗xd2 15 ♘xd2 and White is doing well due to the weak pawn on g4.

c4) 6...♘f6 7 ♘bd2 and then:

c41) 7...d5 8 e5 ♘fd7 9 ♖e1 ♘c6 10 ♘f1! (a typical regrouping) 10...♗e7 11 ♘g3 h5 12 ♘e2! (and again!) 12...♘b6 13 a3 ♖c8 14 ♘d2 ♗a8 15 f4 g6 16 ♘f3 with a hard game ahead but one in which I prefer White's chances.

c42) 7...♘c6 8 ♕e2 cxd4 (8...d5 leads to positions similar to the last note) 9 cxd4 ♗e7 10 e5 ♘d5 11 ♘e4 with a tense position.

5 ♕e2 e6 6 a4

A standard kind of thrust at Black's queenside, trying to provoke a weakness. It would be a mistake for Black to take as this would concede space and leave Black's a-pawn miserable.

6...c5 7 dxc5 ♗xc5 8 ♘bd2 *(D)*

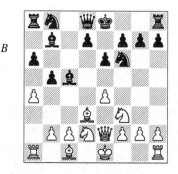

White gets on with natural development, and renews the threat to b5.

8...b4

8...♕b6!? 9 ♘b3 ♗e7 (9...0-0 10 ♘xc5 ♕xc5 11 0-0 and the bishop-pair will leave White with an edge) 10 e5 ♘d5 (10...♘g4 11 h3 bxa4 12 ♘bd2! ♘h6 13 ♘c4 and White has a pleasant position) 11 axb5 ♘b4 12 ♗e4 ♗xe4 13 ♕xe4 and now:

a) 13...d5?! 14 exd6 ♕xd6 15 ♕xa8 ♘xc2+ 16 ♔e2 ♘xa1 17 ♘xa1 is strong for White.

b) 13...♕xb5 14 ♕xa8 ♘xc2+ 15 ♔d1 ♘xa1 16 ♘xa1 leaves White a piece up but he still has some work to do, e.g. 16...♗c5 17 ♕e4 ♗xf2 18 ♕e2 ♕a4+ (Black needs to keep the queens on) 19 b3 ♕xa1 20 ♕xf2 and as long as White is careful he should score the full point.

9 e5 ♘d5

9...♘g4?! 10 0-0 d5 11 ♘b3 ♗a7 12 h3 h5?! 13 ♗g5 ♕c7 14 hxg4 hxg4 15 ♘fd4 and Black is a piece down for not much, Hennigan-Accardo, Rome 1990.

10 ♘e4 ♗e7 11 ♗g5! *(D)*

This is the improvement on the Karpov-Miles game, where White played the natural 11 0-0 and went on to lose.

White at long last develops his dark-squared bishop with a vengeance, keeping an eye on the d6-square for his knight as well.

11...0-0

Alternatives:

a) 11...♗xg5 12 ♘d6+ ♔f8 13 ♘xb7 ♕e7 (13...♕c7?! 14 ♘xg5 ♕xb7 15 ♘xh7+ ♔g8 16 ♘g5 ♘f4 17 ♗e4!) 14 ♗e4! ♘c6 15 ♕c4 and White has a lovely position.

b) 11...f6 12 exf6 and now:

b1) 12...gxf6 13 ♘e5!! 0-0 (13...fxe5 14 ♕h5+ ♔f8 15 ♗h6+ ♔g8 16 ♘d6!! ♗xd6 17 ♕g4+ mating) 14 ♕h5 with a violent attack.

b2) 12...♘xf6 13 0-0 0-0 14 ♖fe1 ♘xe4 15 ♗xe4 ♗xe4 16 ♕xe4 ♘c6 17 ♗xe7 ♕xe7 18 ♖ad1 and White has a positional advantage.

12 ♘d6 ♗c6

12...♗xg3 13 ♕e4 f5 14 exf6 g6 (14...♘xf6? 15 ♕xb7 wins material) 15 ♘xg5 ♕xf6 (15...♗c6 16 ♗xh7! is very strong for White) 16 ♕h4! and White will come out on top.

12...♕c7? 13 ♘xb7 ♕xb7 14 ♕e4 is very powerful for White.

13 h4!? f6 14 exf6 gxf6?!

Alternative captures are better:

a) 14...♘xf6 15 ♘c4! with an edge to White.

b) 14...♗xf6! 15 ♘e5! ♕c7 16 ♕e4 g6 17 ♘xg6! ♕xd6 18 ♘xf8 ♔xf8 19 ♗h6+ ♔e8 20 ♕xh7 with an unclear position.

15 ♘e5! fxg5?!

Again not the best capture, for example:

a) 15...♗xd6!? 16 ♗xh7+ and then:

a1) 16...♔xh7 17 ♕h5+ ♔g8 18 ♕g6+ ♔h8 19 ♗h6 ♕e7 20 ♗xf8

♕xf8 21 ♘f7+ ♕xf7 22 ♕xf7 and White should be doing well in this position with a bizarre material imbalance.

a2) 16...♔g7! 17 ♘xc6 ♘xc6 18 ♕h5! with a strong attack.

b) 15...fxe5 16 ♗xh7+ ♔xh7 (after 16...♔g7 17 ♕h5 ♗xg5 18 ♕g6+ ♔h8 19 hxg5 Black gets mated) 17 ♕h5+ ♔g8 18 ♕g6+ ♔h8 19 ♗h6 ♗f6 20 ♗xf8 ♕xf8 21 ♘f7+ ♕xf7 22 ♕xf7 with a position similar to line 'a1'.

16 ♕h5 ♖f5

16...♘f6 17 ♕xg5+ ♔h8 18 ♘ef7+ ♖xf7 19 ♘xf7#.

17 ♗xf5 exf5 18 ♕f7+ ♔h8 19 ♘g6+

1-0 Volovik-Kozlov, USSR 1987. A fascinating struggle!

Part 3: Owen's Defence

1 e4 b6

Here I recommend a set-up that is quite new.

2 d4 ♗b7 3 ♘c3 e6 4 ♗d3 *(D)*

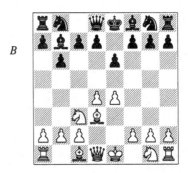

The plan that I am advocating here is based on 5 ♘ge2!?, anticipating that the knight will for various reasons be more useful on this square than on f3.

4...♞f6

Or:

a) 4...♝b4 5 ♞e2 and now:

a1) 5...♞f6 6 0-0 and Black's bishop looks misplaced on b4, e.g. 6...c5 7 e5 cxd4 8 ♞xd4 ♝xc3 9 bxc3 ♞d5 10 ♛g4 and White has a nice position.

a2) 5...d5 6 0-0 ♞f6 7 exd5 and here:

a21) 7...exd5 leads to a position akin to the Exchange French, where Black's bishop on b7 looks a little out of place, e.g. 8 a3 ♝e7 9 ♞f4 0-0 10 ♛f3 c5?! 11 dxc5 bxc5 12 ♝c4! and White is better.

a22) 7...♞xd5! 8 ♞xd5 ♛xd5 9 ♞f4 ♛g5 10 d5! 0-0 (10...♛xd5 11 c4 ♝b7 12 ♞d5 and White wins material) 11 c4 with a good position for White.

b) 4...g6 5 ♞ge2 ♝g7 6 h4!? ♞c6 7 ♝g5 ♞ge7 8 h5! ♞xd4!? (8...h6 9 ♝e3 g5 leaves White slightly better) 9 hxg6 hxg6?! (9...fxg6 10 ♞xd4 ♝xd4 11 ♛d2 with an unclear position) 10 ♜xh8+ ♝xh8 11 ♞xd4 ♝xd4 12 ♛f3 ♝g7 13 0-0-0 (planning ♜h1-h7) 13...♚f8! 14 ♜h1 ♛e8 15 ♝f6 ♞g8 (15...♝xf6 16 ♛xf6 ♞g8 17 ♜h8 ♛d8 18 e5! is strong for White) 16 ♝xg7+ ♚xg7 (I.Rogers-Spassky, Reggio Emilia 1983/4) and now Rogers gave 17 ♛h3! ♛e7 18 f4 ♛f6 19 g3! as better for White, as he plans to play e5.

5 ♞ge2 c5!?

5...d5?! 6 e5 ♞fd7 (6...♞e4 7 0-0 ♞xc3 8 bxc3 c5 9 ♞f4 and I like White's position) 7 ♞f4 c5 8 ♞xe6! ♛e7 (8...fxe6? 9 ♛h5+ wins outright) 9 ♞xd5 (and Black did the honourable thing as he is going to be two pawns down for nothing after 9...♝xd5 10

♞c7+ ♚d8 11 ♞xd5) 1-0 Bhend-Schneiders, San Bernardino 1985.

6 e5

Now:

a) 6...♞g4!? 7 ♞f4 cxd4 (7...♛h4?! 8 g3 ♛d8 9 0-0 has done nothing to help Black's cause) 8 ♛xg4 dxc3 9 ♞h5! f5 (9...g6 10 ♞f6+ ♚e7 11 ♛b4+ d6 12 ♝g5! wins) 10 ♞xg7+ ♚f7 11 ♞xf5! and White is doing well as Black cannot afford to take the piece.

b) 6...♞d5 7 ♞xd5 ♝xd5 8 ♞f4 ♝b7 9 ♛g4 cxd4 10 ♞h5! and here:

b1) 10...♝b4+ 11 c3! and White is well on top.

b2) 10...d6 11 ♞xg7+ ♚d7 12 ♝g5 ♝e7 (12...♛c7 13 ♝f6 gives Black big problems) 13 ♝xe7 ♛xe7 14 ♛xd4 ♝xg2 15 ♜g1 ♝d5 16 ♞f5! leaves White well placed, e.g. 16...dxe5 17 ♝b5+ ♚d8 (17...♞c6? 18 ♝xc6+ wins) 18 ♞xe7 exd4 19 ♞xd5 exd5 20 ♜g5 and White is doing well.

Part 4: 1 e4 d6 2 d4 with 2...e5 or 2...♞f6 3 ♞c3 e5

This section divides naturally into:

A)

1 e4 d6 2 d4 ♞f6 3 ♞c3 e5

At this point White could play 4 ♞f3, when Black would have little better than to transpose back to a mainline Philidor with 4...♞bd7. However, seeing as this is not the way I have recommended White should meet the Philidor we will look at the other main option available to White, viz:

4 dxe5 dxe5 5 ♕xd8+ ♔xd8

Black is very solid in almost a symmetrical position and the fact that his king is on d8 is not too relevant now that the queens have been exchanged.

6 ♗g5 *(D)*

This is the safe way of playing for a small advantage. Currently White has not been getting any remarkable results with 6 ♗c4 ♗e6! 7 ♗xe6 fxe6. Although Black has doubled isolated e-pawns they are not particularly vulnerable and they control some key central squares.

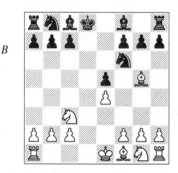

Now Black has tried three moves, of which the last is the most common:

A1: 6...♘d7?! 236
A2: 6...c6 236
A3: 6...♗e6 237

A1)

6...♘d7?!

The main problem with this move is that Black will have to waste another move with his king while White makes a natural developing move.

7 ♗c4 ♔e8 8 ♘b5 ♗d6 9 f3

White is in no rush to take on d6 and would prefer Black to use a move such as ...a6 first.

9...♘b6 10 ♗b3 ♗e6 11 0-0-0

White feels no obligation to exchange on e6.

11...♗xb3 12 axb3 ♔d7?! 13 ♗xf6 gxf6

Now we can start to see how White has developed positional advantages.

14 ♘e2 ♖ad8 15 ♘g3 ♘c8 16 ♘f5

Black is unable to challenge White's knight on f5 with 16...♘e7? because White could win a pawn on d6.

16...a6 17 ♘bxd6 ♘xd6

17...cxd6? 18 ♖d3 ♖hg8 19 g3 and with the weakness on the d-file and doubled f-pawns Black is distinctly worse.

18 ♖d3 ♔c8 19 ♘e7+ ♔b8

19...♔d7?! 20 ♘d5 f5 21 exf5 ♘xf5 22 ♖e1 is awkward for Black to handle.

20 ♖hd1 ♖de8 21 ♘d5 f5 22 ♘xc7! ♔xc7 23 ♖xd6 fxe4 24 ♖d7+ ♔b6 25 fxe4

White has an extra pawn, dominates the d-file and has a rook on the seventh, and can look forward to a pleasant time, Estrin-Hennings, Leipzig 1976.

A2)

6...c6 7 0-0-0+ *(D)*

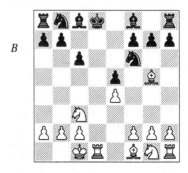

7...♔c7

7...♔e8!? 8 ♘f3 ♘bd7 9 ♗h4 ♗b4 10 ♗d3 and then:

a) 10...♗xc3 11 bxc3 ♘h5 12 ♗g5! (now it is more important to redevelop the bishop along the g1-a7 diagonal) 12...f6 13 ♗e3 ♔e7 14 g3 ♖d8 15 ♘h4 g6 16 f4 ♘g7 17 ♖d2 and White is slightly better due to his bishop-pair and better development.

b) 10...♗a5!? 11 ♖d2 ♗c7 (11...♘h5 12 ♖hd1 ♘f4 13 ♗g3! ♘xg2 14 ♗f1 ♘f4 15 ♖xd7! ♗xd7 16 ♘xe5 ♗e6 17 ♗xf4 ♗xc3 18 bxc3 leaves White better, e.g. 18...♗xa2 19 c4 f6 20 ♘f3 b5 21 cxb5 and White has two pieces for a rook) 12 ♖hd1 ♘c5 13 h3 ♗e6 14 ♗g3 ♘fd7 with a balanced position.

8 ♘f3 ♗d6 9 ♗c4 ♗e6 10 ♗xe6 fxe6

The disadvantage over this line and the one where White plays 6 ♗c4 ♗e6 7 ♗xe6 fxe6 is that now Black has played ...c6 and so the central dark squares are weaker. Not only that but Black's king is less well placed on the queenside than on a central square.

11 ♗h4 ♘bd7 12 ♖d2

Now White intends to get superior control of the d-file. Salakhova-Titorenko, Russian wom Ch 1994 continued: 12...♗b4 13 ♖hd1 ♘c5 14 ♗g3 ♗xc3 15 bxc3 ♘cxe4 16 ♗xe5+ ♔b6 (now although it is White who has the doubled pawns they are not particularly weak and she has a good bishop together with Black's weak e-pawn to work on) 17 ♖e2 ♘c5 18 ♗d4! (this leads to an incredibly nasty pin on the knight) 18...♖he8 19 ♘e5 ♖ad8 20 ♖ed2 ♖c8 21 ♘c4+ 1-0.

A3)

6...♗e6 7 g3!? *(D)*

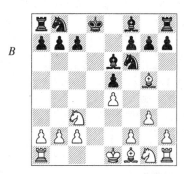

With the following possibilities:

a) 7...h6 8 0-0-0+ ♔c8 9 ♗xf6 gxf6 10 f4 c6 (10...exf4 11 gxf4 f5 12 ♗h3 ♗d6 13 ♘ge2 ♖e8 14 ♗xf5 ♗xf5 15 exf5 and White should have an edge in the endgame) 11 fxe5 fxe5 12 ♗h3 ♗xh3 13 ♘xh3 ♗e7 14 ♖hf1 f6 15 ♘g1! ♘d7 16 ♘f3 ♔c7 17 ♘h4 ♗b4 18 ♘b1! ♖hg8 19 c3 ♗f8 20 ♘d2 gives White an edge due to his control of the f5-square and Black's bishop not being a happy piece, Kengis-Leutke, Biel 1990.

b) 7...♘bd7 8 f4 h6 9 ♗xf6+ ♘xf6 10 0-0-0+ and now:

b1) 10...♔c8 11 f5 ♗d7 12 ♘f3 ♘g4 13 ♗c4! f6 (13...♘f2 14 ♖xd7 is strong for White) 14 ♖he1 ♗c5 15 ♗e6 ♗xe6 16 fxe6 with a very difficult position to judge.

b2) 10...♔e8 11 ♗h3 ♗xh3 (or 11...♗d6 12 ♗xe6 fxe6 13 ♘f3 ♘g4 14 ♘b5 exf4 15 ♘xd6+ cxd6 16 ♖xd6 ♔e7 17 ♖hd1 with an unclear position) 12 ♘xh3 ♗d6 13 ♖he1 ♘g4 14 ♘b5 ♔e7 15 ♖e2 with a level position.

c) 7...♔c8 8 ♗h3 ♗b4 9 ♗xe6+ fxe6 10 f3 ♘c6 (10...♗xc3+ 11 bxc3

♖d8 12 ♘e2 and White may be a little better on the grounds that Black's kingside pawns are more of a liability than White's queenside structure) 11 0-0-0 ♘d4 12 ♘ce2 with a pleasant edge to White.

In conclusion I think it is very hard for White to prove a substantial advantage with 6 ♗g5 but unless he can come up with something better in the 6 ♗c4 ♗e6 7 ♗xe6 fxe6 lines this may be his best chance. Otherwise White will have to consider going into the main line of the Philidor.

B)

1 e4 d6 2 d4 e5

White now has more choice. He can go directly into the Philidor with 3 ♘f3 using the lines I have suggested in Chapter 3 or he can direct the game towards variations of Line A of this section. His third choice is to play...

3 dxe5 dxe5 4 ♕xd8+ ♔xd8

...and then not to play an early ♘c3 but to keep his options open. Obviously

if White hasn't played ♘c3 then Black may refrain from playing ...♘f6.

5 ♗c4 f6

5...♗e6 6 ♗xe6 fxe6 7 ♗e3 ♘f6 8 f3 ♗d6 9 ♘e2 ♔e7 10 ♘d2 ♘bd7 11 0-0-0 and although Black is solid he does have some long-term weaknesses without any real targets of his own.

6 ♗e3 ♘d7 7 ♘c3 ♗c5

7...c6 8 0-0-0 ♔c7 9 g3 g5?! 10 f3 ♘e7 11 h4! gxh4 12 ♖xh4 ♘g6 13 ♖h5 ♗e7 14 ♘ge2 ♘df8 15 ♖dh1 ♗d7 16 ♗f7 ♗e8 17 ♗xe8 ♖xe8 and White has an edge but it will not be easy to convert, Caselli-Mordiglia, Corsica 1996.

8 ♗xc5 ♘xc5 9 0-0-0+ ♘d7 10 ♘ge2 c6 11 ♖d2 ♔c7 12 ♖hd1 ♘b6 13 ♗b3 ♘e7

The position is level, Hald-T.Sørensen, Køge 1997.

Again I am not convinced White can prove a real edge and I would definitely be tempted to play 3 ♘f3 to go back into a Philidor line. To a degree though that is a matter of taste.

Index of Variations

Numbers refer to pages.

F)

1...g6 2 d4 ♗g7 3 ♘c3 *186* **d6**
3...c5 4 dxc5 *186*
3...c6 4 ♗c4 *190*
4 f4 ♘c6
4...a6 5 ♘f3 *196*
4...c6 5 ♗e3 *197*
5 ♗e3 *198*

G)

1...♘f6 2 ♘c3 d5
2...d6 3 d4 *176*
3 e5 *200* **♘e4**
3...d4 4 exf6 dxc3 5 fxg7 cxd2+ 6 ♕xd2 ♕xd2+ 7 ♗xd2 ♗xg7 8 0-0-0 *201*
3...♘fd7 4 d4 *200*
4 ♘ce2 *202*
4...d4 *203*; 4...f6 *204*

H)

1...d5 2 exd5 *207* **♘f6**
2...♕xd5 3 ♘c3 *207*
3 ♗b5+ *214*

I)

1...♘c6 2 ♘f3 *218* **d6**
2...e5 3 ♗c4 *7*
2...f5 3 exf5 *218*
2...♘f6 3 e5 *219*
2...g6 3 d4 ♗g7 4 d5 *220*
2...e6 3 d4 *221*
2...d5 3 exd5 ♕xd5 4 ♘c3 *223*
3 d4 *224*

J)

1...a6 2 d4 b5 3 ♘f3 *232*
1...b6 2 d4 ♗b7 3 ♘c3 e6 4 ♗d3 *234*